The evolving ethernet

Data Communications and Networks Series

Consulting Editor: Dr C. Smythe, University of Sheffield

Selected titles

Other related Addison Wesley Longman titles

The evolving ethernet

Alexis Ferrero

translated by Stephen S. Wilson

Addison-Wesley

*Harlow, England • Reading, Massachusetts • Menlo Park, California • New York
Don Mills, Ontario • Amsterdam • Bonn • Sydney • Singapore • Tokyo • Madrid
San Juan • Milan • Mexico City • Seoul • Taipei*

© Addison Wesley Longman 1996

Addison Wesley Longman Limited
Edinburgh Gate
Harlow
Essex
CM20 2JE
England

and Associated Companies throughout the world.

Published in the United States of America by Addison Wesley Longman Inc.,
New York.

The programs in this book have been included for their instructional value. They have been
tested with care but are not guaranteed for any particular purpose. The publisher does not
offer any warranties or representations nor does it accept any liabilities with respect to the
programs.

Many of the designations used by manufacturers and sellers to distinguish their products
are claimed as trademarks. Addison Wesley Longman has made every attempt to supply
trademark information about manufacturers and their products mentioned in this book.
A list of the trademark designations and their owners appears on page viii.

Translated and typeset by Stephen S. Wilson
Cover designed by odB Design & Communication
and printed by The Riverside Printing Co. (Reading) Ltd
Printed and bound by The University Press, Cambridge

First printed 1996

ISBN 0-201-87726 -0

British Library Cataloguing-in-Publication Data
A catalogue record for this book is available from the British Library.

Library of Congress Cataloging-in-Publication Data is available

Contents

Introduction

Introduction

- How to read this book

- The requirement

- The main characteristics of Ethernet

- The components

- Operation

- Commercial position

- Evolution

How to read this book

This book is divided into three parts, each with a different aim.

- Part I is an introduction to the technical framework with which we shall be concerned throughout the book. It contains an explanation of the basic notions of telecommunications and networks, which will be useful to an understanding of the following chapters.

- Part II provides a detailed technical description of the Ethernet standard and the characteristics of the hardware components of a network.

- Finally, Part III describes specific methods and tools to be used at different stages in the design, development and maintenance of an Ethernet local area network.

Thus, this book is addressed towards anyone faced with the management of one or more networks at any stage; he or she will find theoretical data, information and practical advice here.

Parts II and III may be read separately from each other, however, Part III requires some knowledge of the technical environment of Ethernet. After reading the whole book, the engineer who wishes to know even more will be able to get to grips with the relevant standards and norms more easily.

A list of contents is given at the beginning of each of the three parts. The book ends with a fairly complete glossary of technical terms, whose brief explanations provide readers with an introduction to connected areas.

The requirement

The technology of Ethernet local area networks was developed at the beginning of the 1980s by a grouping of computer-industry companies who perceived a need for high-speed (at least for the period) data communications between relatively close computers.

The aim of these manufacturers was to define a communications standard which was capable of guaranteeing the interconnectability of machines at the level of a building or an industrial site (Figure I.1).

They wanted their product to permit rapid data transfer, and to be easy to install, evolve and maintain. They were ready to conform to a layered architecture such as that recommended by the standardization bodies. Moreover, they intended to publish the definition and the characteristics of the elements of this network. Thus, up until the differences in proprietary solutions, they were able to open the market for hardware adapted to Ethernet networks to all manufacturers.

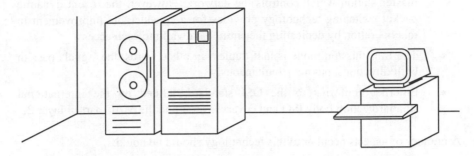

Figure I.1   Elementary aim: to enable two machines to intercommunicate.

Today, Ethernet is the most common local area network standard. It still provides an adequate performance for the large majority of applications and its cost, given its popularity, continues to decrease. The equipment which constitutes the network (that which effectively carries out the data transfer) is constantly improving and increasing in capacity and security.

The main characteristics of Ethernet

The fundamental technical characteristics of Ethernet can be summarized using a number of phrases which follow. All these specific points will be discussed in detail elsewhere in the book.

- Ethernet has become a 'universal' network, in the sense that interfaces have been developed for all types of machine (from the smallest portable to the mainframe).

- The maximum distance between two stations connected to the same network is 4 km.

- Up to 1024 machines can be connected to an Ethernet network.

- It is possible to connect or disconnect a machine from the network without disturbing the operation of the whole network.

- The global speed is 10 Mbps in serial mode (or approximately 10^6 characters per second) on the network as a whole, where this capacity is shared between all the stations. With the latest developments, this speed can be multiplied by 10 (namely 100 Mbps).

- It permits short waiting-time delays prior to emission, in normal situations.

- Ethernet uses a distributed access method for all the machines connected. All stations are equal as far as the network is concerned, and there is no master station which controls the network. However, the recent dynamic packet switching technology provides for a considerable improvement in this operation by dedicating the entire bandwidth to each access.

- The transmission mode is half duplex, in other words, the signals pass in both directions, but not simultaneously.

- Ethernet conforms to the OSI standard defined by the international standardization body ISO and covers layer 1 and the MAC part of layer 2.

A number of aspects peculiar to this technology should be noted:

- The absence of levels of priority for transmission.

- The difficulty of implementing a system with privacy protection (since the data circulating in the network is accessible to all stations) and a relative vulnerability to malicious acts.

- The recovery of packets when numerous successive errors have occurred is left to the communication system.

The components

In a simplified view, an Ethernet network consists of stations interconnected as shown in Figure I.2.

The following components are indispensable to the operation of an Ethernet network:

- The medium or physical carrier of the signals, which may be coaxial or twisted pair cable for electrical signals, or fiber optic cable for optical signals.

- The transceiver, a unit responsible for emitting and receiving signals on the medium.

- The repeater, a device capable of interconnecting several cable segments.

- The Ethernet controller, usually in the form of a slot-in card for the machine to be attached. This implements the link between the computer backplane and the transceiver.

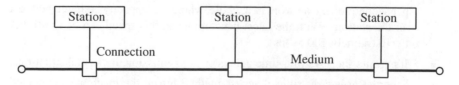

Figure I.2 Schematic view of an Ethernet network with three stations.

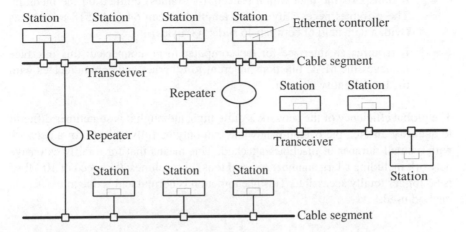

Figure I.3   Schematic diagram of an Ethernet network consisting of three interconnected cable segments.

- A cable segment may be several hundred meters long (up to 500 meters for coaxial cable and 100 meters for twisted pair).

- The transceiver is located on the medium; it is the point at which the machine is connected to the network.

- The repeaters shown in Figure I.3 have two ports, which is the most general case.

- The link between the Ethernet controller and the transceiver is often implemented by quite a short cable (several meters).

Finally, one should not forget the human component which constitutes a resource that is all too often hidden. Clearly, a network of several tens of machines inevitably requires management tasks to manage the communication facilities as a whole (network equipment, software, resource sharing). A procedure to plan and organize the resources, both material and human, should be provided for in conjunction with any important installation.

Operation

The logical operation of an Ethernet network may, in turn, be summarized as follows:

- It is based on a fair distributed access method, in which each item of equipment is always capable of deciding on its own whether it can occupy the medium with its emission.

- It transports the data within packets (or frames) emitted on the medium. These frames necessarily have a length between 64 and 1518 8-bit bytes (with a data field of between 46 and 1500 bytes).

- It requires an interface for the computer to be connected; this interface manages the MAC functions inherent to Ethernet and communicates with the level 2 entity above it.

The global efficiency of the network is quite high, although it is sometimes difficult to quantify. In fact, the overall bandwidth can only be fully utilized for a network with a small number of machines attached. This means that for a fairly extensive network including a large number (several tens) of machines, the speed of 10 Mbps is no longer totally accessible. This phenomenon is normal and is due to the access method used.

Commercial position

Ethernet is a type of network dating from some ten years ago and is thus well tried and tested. It represents the technology most frequently used in business-related local area networks, followed by its competitor network, Token Ring.

The current cost of an Ethernet network has become relatively low, thanks to the large amount of hardware already installed. Moreover, since Ethernet is the most common technology in terms of the different types of machine that may be attached, it is equally applicable to PC, PS/2 and Apple Macintosh microcomputers and workstations of all kinds, and to supercomputers (using their front-end interface).

The division of market shares analyzed by *Data Communications* provides evidence of the dominance of Ethernet among local area network architectures (Figure I.4).

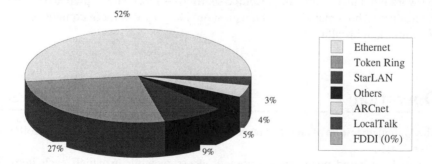

Figure I.4   Market shares of local area network architectures in Europe (*Data Communications*, January 1992).

Evolution

Finally, the recent evolutions of Ethernet give a new impetus to this technology as we reach the last years of the millenium. Thus, it is now possible to double the bandwidth with a full duplex operation, to work at 100 Mbps instead of 10 Mbps based on the same infrastructures with the extension of the standard, 100baseT, or to dedicate the entire bandwidth to each network connection, at the same time eliminating the limitations of the access method, with dynamic packet switching. A doorway to the area of voice and video communications is also on its way with IsoEthernet, which associates a supplementary synchronous channel with the data exchange channel.

PART I

The world of telecommunications

Chapter 1

The standardization bodies

- Aims
- The main bodies
- The stages of standard documents

Several standardization bodies are involved in the area of telecommunications and local area networks, and the documents they produce (standards) have an important impact on the industrial world and on the choices available to users.

Warning

As in the remainder of the book, we are principally interested here in digital data communications.

1.1 Aims

Historically, manufacturers of computer equipment have developed proprietary communication systems permitting the exchange of data between their machines. This service was a response to needs voiced by users who had an important set of machines, some of which were distant from others. The first solutions that were implemented resolved the problem for a few specific machines, but they were only rarely suitable for several types of configuration.

Moreover, in the best case, these hardware and software solutions were still adapted solely to the equipment of a single constructor. This meant that a specific gateway was needed to permit intercommunication between heterogeneous computer equipment.

With the enormous growth of computer hardware, the cost and complexity of developing these specific interconnection elements soon became prohibitive. This led to the definition, for certain types of hardware intended for general use, of detailed technical characteristics which were strongly recommended to developers and manufacturers. These specifications were then circulated widely, published or distributed free of charge (in electronic form, over networks). When they are laid down by the relevant competent bodies, these technical documents become standards or working standard documents. When they come from a manufacturer or private company, but have not been officially standardized, they are called *de facto standards*.

More generally, the role of these bodies is to provide a well-defined specification of all the characteristics and values, which can be used to develop hardware that will function in an identical manner or that will be mutually compatible.

1.2 The main bodies

- The International Organization for Standardization (ISO), as its name indicates, operates at an international level and is responsible for standardization in almost all areas.

The ISO dates from 1947 and now has a membership of almost a 100 standardization bodies. It is organized into technical committees, subcommittees and working groups. This is a body that cannot be ignored and its standards (denoted IS, for International Standard) are the result of a great deal of development work. ISO is not only involved in telecommunications; some of its standardization work in other areas covers the sensitivity of photographic films, programming languages, units of physical measurement, and so on.

- The Comité Consultatif International Télégraphique et Téléphonique (CCITT) is a body which brings together the network providers (PTTs of various countries) and which has a fundamental role in the standardization of telecommunications (principally in relation to technical operation-related aspects and to the fixing of price scales). The CCITT is a permanent member of the International Telecommunication Union (ITU) and publishes its recommendations or advice every four years (1984, 1988, 1992) in several volumes.

- The American National Standard Institute (ANSI) plays a similar role to that of the ISO but at the national level in the United States.

- The French equivalent of ANSI is the Association Française de Normalisation (AFNOR). Similarly, Germany has the Deutsches Institut für Normung (DIN) and Britain has the British Standards Institution (BSI).

- The Institute of Electrical and Electronics Engineers (IEEE, pronounced 'i triple e') is an American body which manages various research projects; it has international authority.

  The IEEE played a very active part in the standardization of the Ethernet and Token Ring local area network types, by evolving the manufacturers' standards (Xerox–Digital–Intel and IBM) into an ISO standard. The results of its standardization work in the area of local area networks are known by the number of the committee responsible for them (committee 802, since it was created in February 1980); thus, they are of type 802.X where X is the number that identifies the project more specifically. For example, IEEE 802.3 corresponds to the standardization of Ethernet, IEEE 802.5 to that of Token Ring and IEEE 802.6 to that of DQDB.

  For information, we note that the IEEE standardized the HP-IB bus (frequently used to communicate with measuring instruments) in IEEE 488.

1.3 The stages of standard documents

In the standardization process the document produced by the standardizing body passes through several stages.

For example, for ISO, new subjects are first catalogued as NWI, for *New Work Item*. Then, the document produced may be accepted as a Committee Draft (CD, formerly Draft Proposal (DP)). It then becomes a Draft International Standard (DIS) and finally, an International Standard (IS).

Supplementary paragraphs may be added via Addenda, which may also pass through the stages of Proposed Draft Addendum (PDAD) and subsequently Draft Addendum (DAD). Similarly, corrections to a published standard may be issued in the form of Amendments (AM) which may pass through the stages of Proposed Draft Amendment (PDAM) and Draft Amendment (DAM).

We shall see later that certain specifications take several years to pass through all the stages that lead to effective standardization. In their impatience to market their solutions as quickly as possible, equipment manufacturers and software developers refer to draft versions of the future document. In this way, they try to place themselves as close as possible to the future standard, but do not respect the simple fact that drafts are clearly made to be commented on and should not be used to claim conformance to.

Moreover, these drafts evolve regularly, which implies that only the last one can be identical with the standard, being voted to be so, while the previous drafts differ from the final version in at least one respect, and possibly in several.

Conclusion

It should be borne in mind that the standardization bodies, be they national or international, have become increasingly useful to users by virtue of the strict rules which they lay down in each of the areas in which they operate.

Moreover, manufacturers should ultimately also benefit from this increasing tendency towards homogeneity.

Chapter 2

The OSI model

- Introduction to the model

- The lower layers

- The higher layers

- Other models

One of the most important ISO standards in the areas of data transmission and networks consists of a segmentation of the functions which a telecommunications system must perform (hardware and software).

This segmentation involves a breakdown into layers and is used to divide the work as a whole into modules, each having its own well-defined task. The interfaces between the layers are clearly standardized, and the signals passing through these are called services or indications, depending on their direction (the lower layer provides services to the higher layer which, in return, transmits indications).

2.1 Introduction to the model

ISO was led to define a standard partitioning of the functions of a telecommunications system, going from the physical transmission medium to the applied software for use on the system. This partitioning gave rise to the Open Systems Interconnection (OSI) model, known as ISO standard IS 7498 (15 November 1984) (Figure 2.1).

The first document defining the OSI model dates back to 1984, but the definition work in ISO began as early as 1977. The proposed standard was accepted in 1978, but amendments have also been made since then.

It should be understood that, as in the case of programming languages, for which only the functionality is standardized (and not the compilation or interpretation procedures), the standards relating to telecommunication technologies forming part of open systems define the exchanges with the outside world, but not the internal operation.

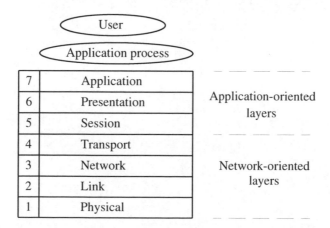

Figure 2.1   The seven layers of the ISO OSI reference model.

A terminology was chosen to denote messages passing from one layer to another. Accordingly, if layer N transmits a request to the layer below, the latter replies with a confirmation. On the contrary, if layer N emits towards the layer above, this is an indication, and the latter will return a response. In all cases, these messages pass through the service access points (SAPs) of each layer. The multilayer reference model had its origins in a desire to create standards that were more homogeneous and easier to apply. The subdivision of the functions of an arbitrary telecommunications system into layers with well-defined tasks results in an overall description which is necessarily more structured and better organized.

Thus, the OSI model constitutes a point of reference with which one should seek to make the system to be developed coincide. This makes it possible to determine the specifications of each layer of the technology in question, and to make each layer compatible with existing higher and lower layers from the design stage on.

Encapsulation

When a data packet passes from a layer N to the layer below, $(N - 1)$, it is supplemented by the addition of extra fields to its beginning and/or end. In the first case, the extra field is referred to as a header; in the second case it is a trailer (postfix or suffix). This added information supplements the frame at the level of the layer at which it was emitted (N here). Thus, when received by the layer of the same level (N) of the destination station, these fields are used in the processing which the latter must carry out. These fields may include the source and destination addresses (of level N), a parity check, the packet length, priority bits, identification of the protocol in the layer above ($N + 1$) for decoding purposes, acknowledgment numbers, and so on.

This process of gradual enrichment of the message is called encapsulation, since the data arriving from the higher layer is incorporated in a more complete structure (Figure 2.2).

As an inverse to encapsulation, which takes place when data passes downwards through the communications model of the emitting machine, the receiving station applies a decapsulation (upwards movement).

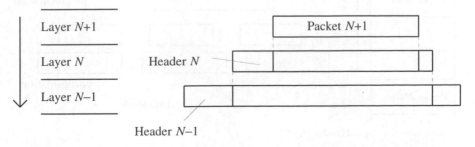

Figure 2.2   Process of encapsulation with passage through successive layers.

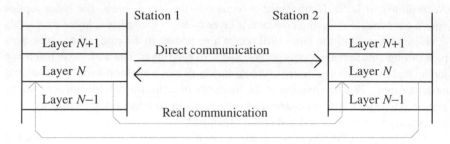

Figure 2.3   Virtual communication between equivalent layers.

It will have become apparent that the layers of the same level of each machine intercommunicate in some way (Figure 2.3). The information contained in the level N header is only of significance to level N of the target machine. This is made possible by the contribution of all the lower layers used.

Segmentation

The packets reaching the layer of level N may have a length greater than that which may be handled by layer $N - 1$; layer N must then split up the original packet. This operation, called segmentation, must be performed in such a way that layer N of the receiving station is advised that it must reconstitute the original packet before transmitting it to layer $N + 1$ of the receiver, and so that it is able to perform this reassembly without difficulty (Figure 2.4).

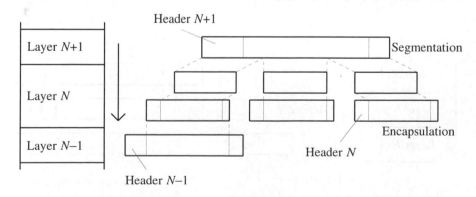

Figure 2.4   Segmentation, followed by the encapsulation of each resulting packet.

Generalizations of this model have sought to ensure that:

- each layer could be developed separately and inserted to replace a layer of the same level in an existing unit (this provides for a progressive evolution of a complex system and facilitates its maintenance);

- architectures from different manufacturers would eventually conform to this model and would, by the same token, become compatible and inter-operable (this is intended to make the system user friendly for end users and reduce the need for interconnection gateways).

2.2 The lower layers

In this study of Ethernet local area networks, the layers with which we are concerned are the lowest ones, namely layers 1 and 2. In fact, Ethernet covers level 1 and only part of level 2.

The functionality of Ethernet ends at the interface between the Medium Access Control (MAC) and Logical Link Control (LLC) layers, as is the case for other local area networks such as Token Ring or the FDDI.

The physical layer

It falls to the lowest layer of a telecommunications system to emit and receive the data in the form of physical signals on the transmission medium. This requires the definition of the mechanical, electrical or optical characteristics of the medium, the type of coding and the signal shape and levels in the standard for this layer. At this level, one thus finds a description of the medium, including the type of coaxial cable, the characteristics of optical fibers, the attenuation of twisted pairs as a function of frequency, and so on. Each medium is associated with a particular type of connection, the structural details of which must also be known in full. In addition, associated with each of these physical media, there will also be a description of the element responsible for emission and receipt, its effect on the medium (for example, possible perturbation of the characteristic impedance), the levels it should generate, its detection thresholds, its internal operational delays and the effect it may have on the network through its links.

Finally, there are restrictions (length of cable segments, number of connections, strength of background interference) which vary as a function of the medium and are inherent to each network technology.

The MAC layer

The MAC layer represents the lower half of layer 2, the other half being constituted by the LLC layer (Figure 2.5).

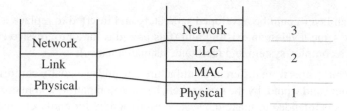

Figure 2.5 Subdivision of level 2.

The role of layer 2 is to permit the transfer of data between the connected systems and to detect transmission errors. Thus, it is responsible for formatting the data into frames, establishing the physical communications, and releasing them, using the access procedures.

The MAC layer itself controls the sharing of the medium using an access method. The choice of this sublayer is associated with that of the topology (the physical architecture), since the same method cannot be implemented on arbitrary topologies. In addition, the MAC layer determines a number of qualities of the network such as the reliability, the effect of inserting a machine or the behavior under heavy loads.

The LLC layer

As previously stated, the functionality of Ethernet does not cover this level; however, since this is the layer with which it interfaces in the OSI model, we must describe it. The IEEE 802.2 subcommittee standardized a layer of the LLC level possessing several types of operation, each of which provides services of a different quality. The document was standardized by the IEEE in 1985, and subsequently by ISO in 1989 in ISO standard IS 8802-2.

The first type of operation is a minimum connectionless service (no physical link) without acknowledgments (no information on the progress of the forwarding process is returned). Type 1 permits point-to-point (one emitter, one receiver) or broadcast (one emitter, several receivers) communications.

In a type 2 operation, LLC is a connection-oriented service (logical link between SAPs) with acknowledgment, verification of the packet order, error detection and correction, detection of duplicates and flow control. The identifier corresponding to the Source Service Access Point/Destination Service Access Point (SSAP/DSAP) is unique. This type of operation only permits point-to-point communications (Figure 2.6).

Finally, a type 3 operation is an acknowledged datagram service (connectionless) without retransmission (no error correction), providing performance of an intermediate quality, which is both simple and effective. A fourth type of LLC (XTP) is also being studied by IEEE 802.2.

Figure 2.6   Logical links established between two LLC layers.

In all cases, the data of the LLC level is presented in the form of an LLC Protocol Data Unit (LPDU), as illustrated in Figure 2.7.

Thus, the LSAP values (LLC access points, SAP source and destination) are held in a byte and are relative to the protocol of the level above. For information only, Table 2.1 shows the numbers which are currently assigned (as for IEEE 802 addresses, the first bit of the DSAP indicates whether the address is an individual or a group address).

As explained above, an LLC packet is encapsulated in the lower-level frame (MAC), which means that the PDU illustrated in Figure 2.7 corresponds to the data field of that frame. The SNAP (value AA) means the the LLC is extended by two complementary fields: Organizationally Unique Identifier (OUI) and EtherType.

DSAP address	SSAP address	Control	Information
8 bits	8 bits	8 or 16 bits	N.8 bits

Figure 2.7   Fields of an LLC protocol data unit (PDU).

2.3 The higher layers

In the context of Ethernet networks, the higher layers are those above and including the network layer.

The network layer

The network layer is responsible for processing the switching and routing information associated with a packet, establishing the logical link to the remote machine and providing connection indications. However, different, more or less complete, services may be offered. For example, the network layer may implement

Table 2.1 Current assignment of LSAP values.

Value	Assignment
00	Null LSAP
02	LLC administrative function (IEEE)
03	LLC group administrative function (IEEE)
04	SNA Path Control SAP Individual
05	SNA Path Control Group SAP
06	TCP/IP (DoD)
08	SNA Path Control SAP Individual
0C	SNA Path Control SAP Individual
0E	Administration PROWAY 2B
10	NetWare
42	Bridge protocol (STU BPDU)
4E	EIA RS-511 message service
5E	ISI IP
7E	ISO 8202 (X.25)
80	XNS (3Com)
8E	PROWAY network
AA	SNAP (Subnetwork Access Protocol)
BC	VINES IP (VIP)
D4	LAN Station Manager
E0	NetWare
F0	NetBIOS
F4	LAN Network Manager (LM functions at LLC Level)
F5	LAN Network Manager Group
F8	default for IMPL (Initial Micro-Program Load)
FA	Ungermann-Bass
FC	Discovery
FD	RPL
FE	CLNS IS 8473. ISO connectionless network protocol
FF	LSAP destination global

an error check or a monitoring of the flow associated with actions in the event of failure. This layer may also be responsible for multiplexing, if that takes place. We shall also see that protocols specific to routing equipment (for exchanges between routers) are found at this level.

Three types of service are defined to quantify the quality of the network layer:

- Type A. Reliable service: an acceptable (low) rate of notified errors, an acceptable rate of unnotified errors.

- Type B. An unacceptable (high) rate of notified errors, an acceptable rate of unnotified errors (requires a restart procedure on errors notified at the transport level).

- Type C. An unacceptable rate of notified and unnotified errors (requires detection procedures and procedures for restarting on errors, sequencing correction procedures and procedures to eliminate duplicates).

According to the properties of level 3, layer 4 may or may not be released from certain control tasks.

The following are to be found at this level (or the equivalent for other models): the ISO 8473 network layer; CLNP; the DoD protocols IP and ICMP; Digital Equipment Corporation's (DEC) DRP protocol, and certain routing protocols such as RIP, OSPF, IS–IS and ES–IS (ISO 9542).

Outside the area of local area networks, one may find, for example, the X.25 layer 3 (IS 8208) and the network protocol of ISDN channel D (CCITT I.451).

Each of these protocols belongs to a particular structure, the OSI model being the only one which respects the standard completely. However, the blocks which constitute it appeared after the non-conforming protocols, which were already proven. Thus, there exist certain similarities. For example, the qualities of ISO's Connectionless Network Protocol (CLNP), Internet Protocol (IP) and the DoD's Internet Protocol are fairly similar. The ISO/CLNS header, which is illustrated in Figure 2.8, could be compared with that of the DoD's Internet Protocol, described a little later in the section on TCP/IP.

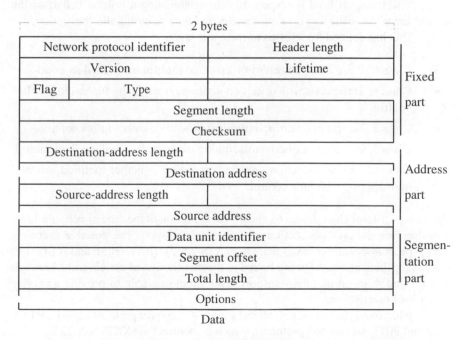

Figure 2.8   Header for ISO's connectionless network layer (CLNS).

The information of this layer 3 includes items which are useful for the routing of datagrams, such as logical source and destination addresses and the maximum number of jumps (via routers) that may be taken to reach the target station. If the message from the layer above has been segmented, data which can be used to reconstitute it from the fragments emitted by the network layer of the correspondent will be found. This data comprises the data unit identifier, which actually corresponds to a sequence number, the offset (or displacement) of the segment in the complete packet and the total length of the packet before fragmentation.

Globally, layer 3 enables two transport-layer modules to exchange data. Finally, it should be stressed that the network level addresses are defined by the user, that they incorporate the logical sub-network or domain concept and can be used to denote a station with the group to which it belongs, and that they are not defined by the manufacturer.

The transport layer

This layer controls the transparent transfer of data between end systems over the network. It checks the inherent properties of the network and may have to re-order (sequence) packets reaching it, to control the flow (for example, by informing the remote machine that it should slow down its emissions) if the selected layer below does not implement this service. Similarly, the transport layer may have to detect errors, losses, and duplicates and recover the correct information when these events occur, to provide, if necessary, a reliable service to the layer above.

The transport level is responsible for establishing a link on behalf of the session layer (5), managing the data transfer and then releasing the connection.

ISO has defined five classes of transport layer:

- Class 0. Basic class, no restart on error, no multiplexing, no flow control.

- Class 1. Basic class with restart on notified errors, no multiplexing, no flow control.

- Class 2. No restart on error, multiplexing with or without flow control.

- Class 3. Restart on notified errors, multiplexing with or without flow control.

- Class 4. Error detection, restart on errors whether notified or not, multiplexing with flow control.

The transport-level class should be chosen as a function of the type of network layer available (see the previous section on the Network layer). The possible (network layer type, transport layer class) pairs are (A,0), (A,2), (B,1), (B,3), and (C,4). The reasons for these associations are linked to the distribution of certain tasks between levels 3 and 4, given that the transport layer should be able to provide a service which is of practical use.

Moreover, ISO has standardized a class 4 transport protocol called TP4 (IS 8072 and 8073, service and protocol), which is identical to CCITT's X.224.

The upper layers

The application-oriented layers begin with level 5. Thus, these protocols are more concerned with the formatting of the information exchanged between the application layers than with the connection and communication processes on networks (which are the responsibility of layers 1 to 4).

Thus, there exist standard notations such as ASN.1, which defines the format of all data types, whether numerical (integers, long integers, floating point) or alphanumeric.

At the very top of the model are those protocols which have a function of an applied level that is directly linked to the network capabilities such as virtual (remote) terminal emulation, messaging, file transfer, the sharing of peripherals, access to shared databases, and the use of distributed applications.

For example, one easily comprehensible level 7 application is *electronic mail* (or *e-mail*). This is used to send messages or transmit files to one or more users quickly and, with the generalization of network interconnections, almost anywhere in the world. Intermediate equipment interprets the name of the addressee and routes the packet to the target station to deposit it in the appropriate mailbox. A true two-way communication, with real-time questions and answers, can only be envisaged if the transmission delays are acceptable (for example, on a local area network). These messaging applications may be associated with directory management protocols.

In the ISO world, electronic mail is implemented by the MHS X.400 layer (message handling service), standardized by CCITT, while in the DARPA world, we have the Simple Mail Transfer Protocol, (SMTP, RFC 821) over TCP/IP. Note that the directory system relies on the X.500 standard in the ISO world and DNS in the DARPA world.

The protocol stacks of certain manufacturers conform approximately with OSI and may be represented in parallel with the seven layers. For example, Xerox has defined Xerox Network System (XNS), Apple has developed AppleTalk and Digital Equipment has developed DECnet. Each system is modular and includes functionalities which can also be found in the seven layers standardized by IS 7498.

XNS

XNS is used in Xerox's architecture and also in the protocol stack Net/One defined by Ungermann Bass, in that of 3Com and, with slight modifications, in Novell's IPX. In Xerox's case, XNS includes the modules shown in Figure 2.9.

The logical addresses of XNS consist of a physical network number (in 32 bits, represented in decimal) and the number of the machine (in 48 bits, represented in hexadecimal, usually taken from the MAC address).

AppleTalk

Similarly, AppleTalk has the following layers:

- Level 7: Application (utility- and application-oriented network).
  AppleShare, file and print servers

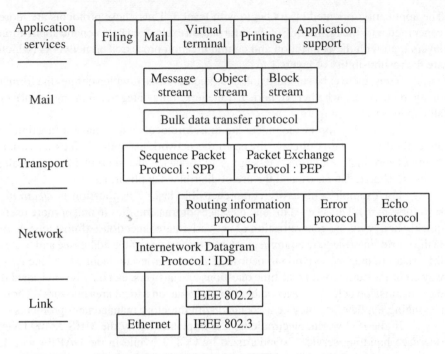

Figure 2.9 Protocols of the XNS layer structure.

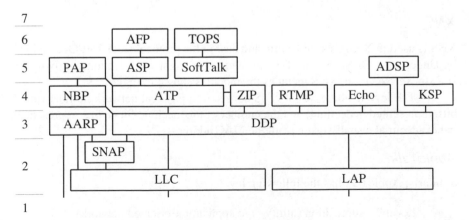

Figure 2.10 AppleTalk protocol family.

- Level 6: Presentation (representation, format conversion).
  Apple Filing Protocol (AFP), PostScript

- Level 5: Session (synchronization of dialogue).
  AppleTalk Data Stream Protocol (ADSP), Printer Access Protocol (PAP)
  AppleTalk Session Protocol (ASP), Zone Information Protocol (ZIP)

- Level 4: Transport (transport, splitting of messages into packets).
  AppleTalk Transaction Protocol (ATP), Name Binding Protocol (NBP)
  Routing Table Maintenance Protocol (RTMP)
  AppleTalk Echo Protocol (AEP), TCP, UDP

- Level 3: Network (routing of packets).
  Datagram Delivery Protocol (DDP), Internet Protocol (IP)

- Level 2: Link (data transfer, error detection).
  AppleTalk Link Access Protocol (ALAP):
  LocalTalk (LLAP), EtherTalk (ELAP), TokenTalk (TLAP)

- Level 1: Physical (transmission medium, electrical interface).
  LocalTalk, Ethernet, Token Ring

AppleTalk's logical addresses have 24 bits, comprising a network number in 16 bits and a node number in 8 bits (hence the limitation on the number of machines per network inherent in this technology). This address is usually represented by two decimal digits separated by a full stop. We note that value 0 in one of these fields corresponds to the notion of unspecified (this applies to all networks or nodes).

The AppleTalk routing protocols (Figure 2.10) such as DDP are simple but not very reliable. By propagating erroneous data they can cause a large network to crash. They have evolved with the introduction of the AppleTalk, Update-based Routing Protocol (AURP), which also reduces the bandwidth consumption in its routing exchanges by sending only the modified data. The AppleTalk Phase 2 routers are therefore less talkative than in Phase 1.

DECnet

DECnet is the architecture used in all Digital's machines with the VMS or Ultrix operating system. Like its competitors, it permits exchanges between applications, file management, resource sharing, remote virtual terminals, and network management. DECnet cohabits with TCP/IP in certain Unix stations.

Since Digital was one of the creators of the initial Ethernet technology, with Xerox and Intel, as far as its hardware is concerned, Ethernet may be considered as the *de facto* local area network. On Ethernet, the physical addresses of machines implementing DECnet consist of the manufacturer's prefix AA-00-04 and two bytes of the level 3 logical address. This is a special case for Ethernet, where the physical address cannot generally be parametrized. The logical address comprises the area number in 6 bits, followed by the node number in 10 bits.

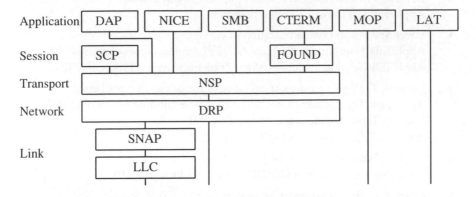

DAP: Data Access Protocol
MOP: Maintenance Operation Protocol
LAT: Local Area Transport
SCP: Session Control Protocol
NSP: Network Services Protocol

Figure 2.11 DECnet protocol stack.

One of the main innovations in DECnet Phase V is the replacement of the architecture by the OSI model (Figure 2.11). Thus, the management protocol becomes CMIP/CMIS and other proprietary modules are replaced by blocks conforming to ISO: HDLC replaces DDCMP for exchanges over wide area networks, and X.400 is chosen as the messaging system. Similarly, the IS–IS and ES–IS routing protocols are supported. The addresses are of the NSAP (network service access point) type with a (variable-length) prefix, an area number (in 2 bytes, but which must lie between 0 and 63), a station identifier (in 6 bytes, beginning with AA-00-04), and a selector field (in one byte).

The MOP protocol is used for maintenance operations and may be used for the remote loading of a remote machine or to test a station by exchanging a packet.

The LAT protocol, which is used to manage terminal server exchanges, does not have a network layer and thus cannot be routed. Moreover, any perceptible delay in the routing of packets may lead to their elimination. Thus, one might envisage reserving a special priority for traffic of this type.

ISO

Finally, returning to the layers of the OSI model, we shall describe a number of modules already standardized by the ISO (Figure 2.12). There exists a terminology for information structures at every level. This is not necessarily always used properly, or even respected, even in this book. Thus, the data passing through the layers is referred to as shown in Table 2.2.

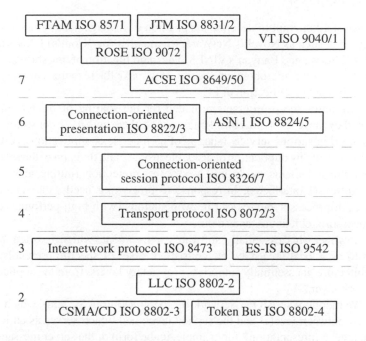

FTAM: File Transfer Access and Management
JTM: Job Transfer and Manipulation
VT: Virtual Terminal
ROSE: Remote Operation Service Element
ACSE: Association Control Service Element
ASN.1: Abstract Syntax Notation 1
ES–IS: End System to Intermediate System

Figure 2.12   Examples of protocols standardized by ISO at each level.

In addition, well-defined abbreviations are used to identify the level from which a communication unit (or PDU, Protocol Data Unit) comes. For example, a frame may be denoted LPDU (for Link Protocol Data Unit), a message from the transport level by TPDU (for Transport Protocol Data Unit), and so on.

Table 2.2   Terminology for information structures at every level.

Physical level	1	Bit sequence
Link level	2	Frame
Network level	3	Packet
Transport level	4	Message
Session level	5	Transaction

Network managers

Finally, we shall attempt to describe the position of management systems for local area networks, such as Novell's NetWare, Microsoft's (or 3Com's) LAN Manager, IBM's LAN Server and Banyan's VINES. The main function of this software, which was developed in the microcomputer world, is to make the resources of one or more servers available to a collection of PCs.

Originally, these programs provided for the sharing of printers or disks; however, they have evolved considerably since then and now constitute proper systems offering various services (sharing of peripherals or applications, distributed databases, security by duplication of disks, electronic mail, division of the set of users into hierarchical domains, password-based access protection, routing, and gateways between different interfaces). In response to processing needs, the servers have become multiprocessor micros or true workstations (with high-perfomance CPU, multiprocessor architecture, and so on).

However, this essentially software environment, which is often wrongly referred to as a local area network, consists of a set of specific protocols. In the OSI architecture, it essentially comprises proprietary layers, from the application to the network layer.

We mention NetBIOS (Network Basic Input Output System), which may be positioned between level 3 and the session level, and which serves as an interface between level 6 (presentation); for example, in the form of the server message block protocol and the MS-DOS software at the application level on the one hand, and the LLC or the controller card (direct interface) on the other (Figure 2.13). NetBIOS was originally produced by IBM, but this interface has become a fundamental building block in the systems of other manufacturers.

These network managers are intrinsically related to the technologies of local area networks, since they exploit the facility for establishing communication between several workstations (principally of the PC type) within a building, which usually corresponds to the area covered by local area networks. However, they are

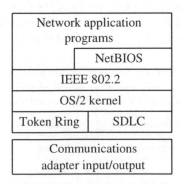

Figure 2.13   Position of NetBIOS in the OS/2 Communications Manager.

fundamentally powerful software packages, which give added value to a collection of microcomputers by improving the global context (common resources, centralized updating) and not simply by describing communication layers. Thus, they have to be properly positioned in relation to the local area network technologies which they use.

These management systems are referred to as NOS (for Network Operating System). The distribution of market shares in the United States shows a proportion of 59% of client–server environments is attributed to NetWare, ahead of LAN Server (~17%), LAN Manager (~7%) and Unix with NFS (~4%).

2.4 Other models

In parallel with the model developed by ISO, other models have been implemented in global network solutions offered by the major manufacturers. We mention the most important of these.

SNA

IBM has defined a layer model associated with its communications architecture SNA (System Network Architecture) which can be used to link all IBM hardware, from large systems to PCs.

SNA has evolved since 1974 to offer increasingly rich functions, permitting more global hardware configurations and providing more extensive software capabilities.

Since IBM is the most important computer manufacturer on the world scale, the number of machines connected by SNA links is considerable and communications in SNA format represent the majority of data transfers.

Similarly, other manufacturers such as Bull and DEC, have their own architecture models (Distributed System Architecture (DSA) and Digital Network Architecture (DNA), respectively). However, we note that the recent evolution of Digital's DNA system has made it similar to that of ISO.

TCP/IP

TCP/IP is an example of an architecture produced by a government body (the American Department of Defense (DoD)), rather than a manufacturer.

Research in DARPA (Defense Advanced Research Project Agency) began in the 1970s, and by the end of that decade the protocol architecture had acquired its current form. The physical carriers were primarily based on packet-switching circuits, before the appearance of Ethernet. In 1983, having standardized the main modules, DARPA required all machines connected to the ARPANET network to use TCP/IP. The spread of this protocol family was also ensured by its integration into the Unix world, which is primarily directed towards universities, with the provision of a low cost implementation. The protocol stack has been enriched and improved by the contribution of users, and its evolution takes place under the aegis of the Internet Activities Board (IAB) and through standardization documents, Requests for Comments (RFC). Today, the TCP/IP protocol family remains a reliable and well-known model which offers all the useful services at the applied level, and which is continually enriched as the requirements evolve. Thus, a new generation of the IP protocol (IPng or IPv6) is to replace the current IPv4, which will reach its limits in several years time, in terms of the number of addresses managed, functionality, and performance. We note that the system employed in TCP/IP standardization, involving RFCs and their distribution by electronic mail, is much more subtle than an effective standardization and permits rapid modifications.

Thus, the TCP/IP stack is implemented on all Unix systems and, to some extent, on other types of operating system such as VMS (DEC) or, more simply, for DOS or Windows (Microsoft). It is often the default protocol and certainly the great rival to OSI, which, it is assumed, will replace it in years to come, even though certain layers standardized by ISO are extensively inspired by TCP/IP.

The main modules of TCP/IP are described in brief in what follows, and we note, in passing, that the name comes from the connection-oriented protocol of the transport layer and that of the Internet level. Since this nomenclature is not generic and is imperfect, it may be replaced in the future.

The OSI model is only placed in parallel in Figure 2.14 to indicate that the TCP/IP protocol family covers the same area; however, it is relatively difficult to establish exact correspondences between the layers of each architecture.

- IP stands for Internet Protocol; it is in some way the network layer of the structure with the following characteristics: connectionless, unreliable packet delivery service. IPv4 is standardized under MIL-STD-1777 (August 1983) by DARPA and by RFC 791, and its extensions are standardized by RFC 919, 922 and 950.

- ARP (Address Resolution Protocol) describes the procedure for obtaining the Ethernet address from the IP address. It is standardized by RFC 826.

- ICMP (Internet Control Message Protocol) is the protocol for managing control messages (error, loss, no response, overload, and so on). It is standardized by RFC 792.

- TCP (Transmission Control Protocol) is the transport protocol which provides a reliable connection-oriented transport service and flow of bytes. TCP is standardized under MIL-STD-18-782 (May 1983) by DARPA and by RFC 793.

- UDP (User Datagram Protocol) provides an unacknowledged (unreliable) transaction-oriented service at the transport level. It is standardized by RFC 768.

- FTP (File Transfer Protocol) is based on TCP/IP and is therefore reliable (unlike TFTP). FTP is standardized under MIL-STD-1780 (May 1984) by DARPA and by RFC 959.

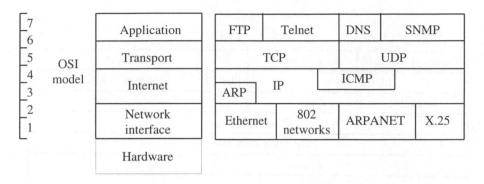

Figure 2.14   TCP/IP stack structure.

- Telnet permits the connection of remote terminals for interactive access on the host machine, with various possible parametrizations. Telnet is standardized under MIL-STD-1778 (August 1983) by DARPA and by RFC 854 and 855.

- DNS (Domain Name System) manages the correspondence between symbolic machine names and their IP-level addresses, and provides a directory service. It is standardized by RFC 1034 and 1035.

- SNMP (Simple Network Management Protocol) is the most common management system in the TCP/IP world and in the rest of the local area network world. It is described in more detail in Chapter 4. The protocol itself is standardized by RFC 1157 and the structure of the information is standardized in RFC 1155 and 1213.

For TCP/IP, the underlying local area network was originally Ethernet, which means that the field type is actually used and that certain protocols such as ARP had to be adapted to IEEE 802.3 networks (we shall see that the standardized version differs slightly from Ethernet).

There is also a specific terminology for this model, according to which the data consists of frames, datagrams, packets and, finally, messages (from the bottom up).

The Internet layer includes the routing information for packet routing together with the logical IP-level source and destination addresses, the maximum number of passes through intermediate routers and various options such as the choice between delay and speed. The IP addresses are encoded on four bytes and are represented as a sequence of four decimal numbers separated by full stops (for example, 128.38.53.247). These addresses decompose into a field identifying the IP network to which the machine belongs: the Internet part of 1, 2 or 3 bytes depending on the classes, followed by a machine number on this network: the local

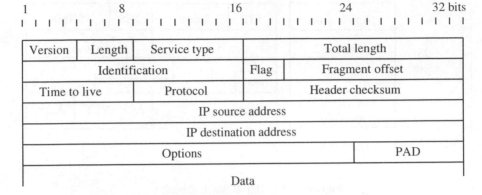

Figure 2.15   Fields of the IP protocol header.

part. There is a subnetwork concept, which involves a subdivision of the local part into a subnetwork number and a machine number. The IP header includes other fields such as the number of the protocol above (transport level), the number of the segment in the datagram, a segmentation flag, and a header parity check (Figure 2.15).

We recall that the DoD's TCP/IP architecture continues to evolve and be enriched in a realistic process in which the protocols are effectively field tested and modified periodically, as required. Today, the program for migration of the current protocol stacks which use IPv4 to support IPv6 is well defined, and a progressive transition is scheduled to take place under optimal conditions, so as not to give concern to the set of users and not to destabilize the international networks which rely on these protocols.

This represents a non-trivial advantage in comparison with the much more theoretical development of the building blocks of the ISO model. Finally, we also note that the major computer manufacturers have all opted for an implementation of TCP/IP on their machines, in parallel to the choice of Unix and despite the announced intention to move towards OSI.

Conclusion

The OSI model is omnipresent in the technical environment with which we are concerned here, even though its implementation has been long and at times laborious.

Although older, rival models, which have had a long life, have not yet disappeared, and criticisms are already being leveled against the effectiveness of the OSI model. While this model is not really in question at present, tests have been carried out using a 'reduced' protocol stack (omitting certain levels) with a view to obtaining higher performance.

Chapter 3

Data communication networks

- Machine bus

- LAN

- MAN

- HSLAN

- WAN

For a long time, the main objective of telecommunications was voice transport (using the telephone). However, now, image transport (by video) and digital data transfer represent a considerable part of the exchanges.

Voice and video have the analog nature of their signals in common and do not generally form part of the area of digital communications; thus, we shall often leave them aside in the remainder of this book.

In the closing years of this century, the arrival of information technology has generated a real need for communication between computers. As machines dedicated to digital data processing became increasingly numerous and grew to be indispensable in almost all areas, it often appeared advantageous to make them 'talk' to each other. For them to work in a cooperative manner, sharing the same files (applications or data) or the same peripherals (storage units, printers, terminals), it is of course preferable to provide rapid and efficient communications. Solutions have been found and implemented for all requirements, whether between two buildings, two towns or two continents. However, these solutions must also evolve as machines progress in terms of speed and processing capability.

There are several main categories of network, classified according to the distances they cover. From the largest down, these are machine buses, LANs, MANs and WANs (Figure 3.1).

Remark   The network technologies to be discussed here are located at levels 1 and 2 of the OSI model and are therefore comparable.

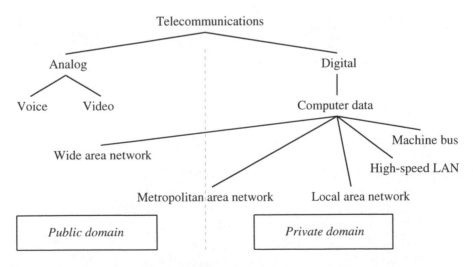

Figure 3.1   Hierarchical organization of the different technologies.

3.1 Machine bus

The machine bus, or backplane, is presented here more as an example than as a true network.

This is an old technology, since it dates from the modular design of electronic systems. The machine bus comprises all the wires and connectors which are generally found behind the computer and which enable the various cards (CPU, FPU, graphics processor, input/output, disk manager) to intercommunicate. This set often consists of passive elements (conductors) and has a bus, or sometimes a chain topology. The binary data circulates in parallel on the 8, 16, 32 or 64 wires, depending on the capability of the microprocessor. The speed on the backplane is a performance criterion for the machine.

Despite its apparent simplicity, this network needs rules concerning the right to emit, which, at the end of the day, simply comprise the protocol associated with the physical carrier.

For information, we mention the best known buses: Industry Standard Architecture (ISA), Extended ISA (EISA), Micro Channel Architecture (MCA,) and the more recent Vesa and Peripheral Component Interconnect (PCI) in the microcomputer world; Small Computer Systems Interface (SCSI) and Versa Module Eurocard (VME) in the world of minicomputers; and IEEE 488 in the measurement area.

3.2 LAN

LAN stands for local area network. Local area networks first appeared at the beginning of the 1980s and thus correspond to the multiplication of 'small' computers – workstations and microcomputers.

To be precise, we note that there are two classes of local area network: enterprise local area networks and industrial local area networks. The first category brings together the technology and hardware which may be found in an enterprise, while the second category corresponds to local area networks which are able to support industrial environments (more severe robustness and reliability constraints, resistance to electromagnetic interference). We must immediately point out that enterprise (or establishment) local area networks are far more numerous and that their standardization is more complete. The introduction of industrial networks is generally linked to the manufacturer who produces and therefore promotes them. In fact Ethernet, the local area network which we shall study here, is an enterprise local area network, as are Token Ring, LocalTalk and ARCnet.

In practise, local area networks are always controlled by the user; thus, they are part of the private domain of telecommunications. As their name indicates, their extent is limited to a few kilometers (from 1 to 10 km), their speed ranges from several hundred kilobits per second (kbps) to several megabits per second (Mbps) (say, 250 kbps to 20 Mbps, or, very recently, 100 Mbps).

Local area networks are often easy to install and implement, particularly for small configurations. They are also fairly reliable and certainly very economical.

However, the niche originally occupied by local area networks, which was limited to departmental needs, has tended to expand towards an organized structure relevant to the whole enterprise.

Networks installed in production structures sometimes use enterprise network technologies such as Ethernet. However, standards also exist for industrial networks, for example MAP (Manufacturing Automation Protocol) from General Motors (which is based on the IEEE 802.4 Token Bus standard, IEEE 802.2, and other protocol modules standardized by ISO). Since these networks have to connect automata, robots, sensors, calculating machines, and workstations (to collect and process the measurements), the constraints on industrial LANs are quite different from those on enterprise LANs. A high speed is not indispensable (some industrial LANs rely on RS 232 links), however, the network technology should be oriented towards real-time operation with an access method that guarantees, if possible, a maximum delay for access to the medium and transmission. Since the exchanges are sometimes rudimentary (sequence of digital data) the seven OSI layers are not always indispensable. Moreover, the exchanges are predefined (return of measurements, programming of automata) and the set of elements in communication changes little.

The category of industrial LANs includes, for example, FACTOR, MODBUS (from Gould), BITBUS (from Intel), and the field bus FIP (Factory Instrumentation Protocol).

3.3 MAN

MAN stands for Metropolitan Area Network. This is a category which has appeared in the last ten years with the advent of products which were difficult to classify in any other way, since they were clearly superior to conventional LANs.

The MAN is characterized by connection capabilities over greater distances than the LAN, namely of the order of several kilometers. However, by virtue of their recent appearance, these technologies also have higher speeds than those of LANs, of the order of 100 Mbps. The best known representatives of this category are FDDI and DQDB.

FDDI

Fiber Distributed Data Interface (FDDI) was developed by former members of the Sperry Corporation in 1982. It was put forward to the ANSI X3T9.5 committee and then standardized by ISO in IS 9314 (except for a number of parts, including SMT management, which are still pending). In this sense, FDDI, as a local area network, has, exceptionally, always been manufacturer independent (Ethernet was a product of Xerox–DEC–Intel, Token Ring was a product of IBM). ANSI's X3T9 committee, which is responsible for interfaces and input/output, among other things, has dealt with the SCSI bus (X3T9.2) and the Fiber Channel (X3T9.3).

FDDI is currently firmly entrenched in the market place; its capabilities are regularly enhanced and its price continues to decrease. Possible media include single-mode and multimode optical fibers and (shielded and unshielded) twisted pairs, together with media which are not yet standardized, such as coaxial cable and laser links. Controller cards are available for a full range of machines, down to the PC, even though, in the latter case an FDDI card is not justified in terms of proportional cost and potential performance.

A derivative of FDDI, capable of transporting synchronous traffic, has been defined, FDDI-II. However, this technology, which is more general as it is able to transport voice and data, has an uncertain future, given that it is overshadowed by the relative success of the MAN from which it stems and that FDDI-II hardware is essentially non-existent. Moreover, if it were to take off, it might compromise the development of FDDI by offering purchasers a choice between two partially incompatible technologies of the same family.

DQDB

Queued Packet and Synchronous Exchange (QPSX) originated in Australia and was taken up by IEEE 802.6 as Distributed Queue Dual Bus (DQDB). This network uses a (possibly looped) double unidirectional bus and, in addition to data signals, also supports voice or video by virtue of its synchronous capabilities.

The speed is a function of the physical layer chosen and may, for example, be 45 Mbps (ANSI DS3) or 139 Mbps (CCITT G.703). The access method is based on relatively complex distributed queue management, whose fairness it has been difficult to obtain.

The use of cells compatible with those of Asynchronous Transfer Mode (ATM) potentially provides for an easy integration of DQDB metropolitan area networks into the ATM architectures of service providers in the near future.

Except for FDDI, very few products are currently available; however, there appears to be a tendency towards the belief that the days of DQDB should not be long in coming.

3.4 HSLAN

High Speed Local Area Network (HSLAN) is a fairly recent technology which aims to offer an even greater bandwidth, in response to the requirements of heavy applications such as graphical transfers (real-time synthesized moving images, saving of whole disk units, and so on).

Existing solutions on the market are directed solely towards these demanding gaps, and are often proprietary products (since there is no need for standardization).

We mention HyperChannel from Network Systems Corporation (NSC), which is a network based on 75 Ohm CATV coaxial cable, offering a speed of

50 Mbps per channel and using a CSMA/CD access method. Four channels may be grouped together to form 200 Mbps links between at most 16 machines.

More recently, the UltraNet product from Ultra (purchased by CNT) has appeared. This has a star topology and offers a speed of 1 Gbps (gigabit per second) on optical fiber or coaxial cable. It can be used to link the most important machines of a computing center over quite short distances (several tens of meters).

We also mention the High Performance Parallel Interface (HIPPI) developed by the Los Alamos National Laboratory, which is being studied by ANSI working group X3T9.3. This defines a network operating at 100 or 200 Mbytes/s (32- or 64-bit bus) based on wound copper twisted pairs, over distances up to 25 m and, later, on optical fiber (up to 10 km) or coaxial cable (36 m), when the signal is transmitted in serial mode.

Other products offering a speed in gigabits per second over greater distances, such as IBM's Rainbow-1 and Hitachi's SuperLAN Sigma, are being studied.

A simple calculation of the bandwidth needed to display a moving image with high resolution in real time gives an idea of the enormous requirements in this area: 24 images per second with a definition of 1024×1024 points and 24 color planes (16 million possible shades) ~ 600 Mbps. It becomes clear that a rate in gigabits per second is justified for this type of application.

Finally, for information, we note that the propagation delay for a packet on a link in a network is independent of the speed, and that it depends solely on the speed of the physical signal on the medium. This factor should be taken into account when one increases the speed offered by virtue of the new technologies, for example, by providing for adapted acknowledgment methods or longer messages.

3.5 WAN

Wide Area Network (WAN) is a vast category of networks which covers almost all capabilities for transmission of digital data over large distances. These distances may amount to several kilometers or several tens of thousands of kilometers.

Wide area networks are distinguished from the networks described previously by the fact that they are provided by national service providers and generally represent a public service. In fact, the great majority of local area networks, metropolitan area networks and machine buses are located within an enterprise and are therefore private (even if they borrow public lines for some of their sections).

The physical carriers that may be used for WANs include twisted pairs, coaxial cables, fiber optic cables, radio links, and satellite links. The transmission modes are also quite varied and may include:

- dedicated leased lines with speeds from 9600 bps to 2 Mbps, or 34 Mbps in the near future;
- X.25 packet-switching circuits with speeds from 9.6 to 512 kbps and above;
- Integrated Services Digital Networks (ISDN) with speeds of 64 kbps for basic access (BRI) and 2 Mbps for primary access (PRI).

We note that broadband ISDN services will probably be offered on top of the ATM technology which some carriers have selected for their infrastructure.

Conclusion

We have seen that all potential niches in data communications are occupied by technologies of various ages, associated with hardware which is evolving at different rates.

On the one hand public wide area networks are old, but increasing in performance, while on the other hand private local area networks are more recent and are evolving more rapidly; at the same time, other categories have come to respond to needs lying between the limits of LANs and WANs.

Standardization is undoubtedly proceeding in all areas, and in time will provide homogeneity and a long-awaited greater interoperability. Finally, to summarize the relative positions of each class, Figure 3.2 shows the hierarchy of class types.

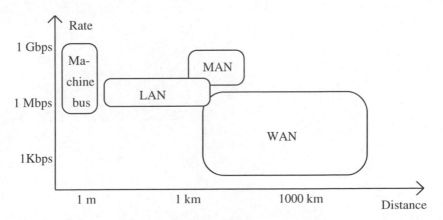

Figure 3.2   Relative positions of networks.

Chapter 4

Local area networks

- Definition of local area networks

- The physical media

- The topologies

- Multiplexing

- Access methods

- Encoding and transmission

- Local area network rivals to Ethernet

- The place of local area networks in telecommunications

4.1 Definition of local area networks

As we have seen above, local area networks form part of the world of telecommunications and, to be precise, concern the requirements for the exchange of data communications within an enterprise.

Thus, they permit the transfer of digital data between computers and allow users of computer applications to copy files or share certain resources via the network.

4.2 The physical media

The communication bearer is part of the first layer of the model. Thus, it should be described in the document which standardizes the type of technology used for the lower layers.

Coaxial and twisted pair cables transport electrical signals, optical fiber transports optical signals, the air transports electromagnetic waves.

We note that the attenuation induced by the medium is measured in dB (decibel, tenth of the unit called a Bel) which is a relative (rather than absolute) unit corresponding to $10 \times \log_{10}$(signal power/reference power). Thus, the dBm corresponds to a measurement with respect to a reference signal of 1 mW and 1 mW = 0 dBm.

Coaxial cable

Coaxial cable is a cylindrical cable consisting of two concentric electrical conductors (which are different and said to be asymmetric). The first, solid cable constitutes the core, while the second external conductor, which is cylindrical and hollow, is placed around the first, but insulated from it (Figure 4.1).

Electrical signals are emitted using the external conductor (often braided) for a reference potential. The two conductors are separated by an insulating dielectric and, in addition, the external conductor is surrounded by a layer providing mechanical and electrical protection.

To obtain a minimal attenuation, calculations show that the optimal ratio between the diameters of the two conductors is 3.6.

The advantages of coaxial cable are:

- Its good transmission properties (high propagation speed, low attenuation, wide bandwidth, limited RF emission).
- Its high immunity to electromagnetic interference.
- The ease with which it can be manipulated (connector crimping, laying in cable run) and its general robustness.

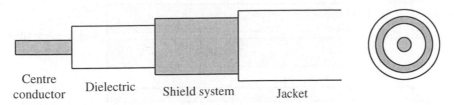

Centre
conductor   Dielectric   Shield system   Jacket

Figure 4.1   Sideways and face on views of a bare coaxial cable.

Its disadvantages are:

- Its relatively high cost, since it is a quality component.
- Its bulk, due to its large diameter for a single physical link (in comparison with other media) and its rigidity.

Optical fiber

Optical fiber is a conductor of optical signals, which is made from silica (pure and doped) or from plastic.

Plastic Optical Fibers (POF) are more recent, and although they are currently evolving rapidly, they do not have the performance of silica fibers. Their attenuation remains very high and, even though their robustness and low price are very attractive, they are, for the present, restricted to a number of atypical applications.

Thus, we shall concentrate on silica optical fibers, which may be of different types according to the diameter of the fiber core and the curve of variation of the (refractive) index as a function of the distance from the center of the fiber. If the core has a very small diameter, of the order of ten microns or less, the fiber only permits a single rectilinear optical path without reflection from the walls of the silica cylinder and the transmission performance is then of a high level (very large bandwidth, very low dispersion, low attenuation).

Optical fiber of this type is called single mode (or unimode) and, given its capabilities, it is primarily used for high speeds and large distances, and, in particular, for international connections. Of course, the disadvantages of this type of fiber are the cost (due to the quality requirements on its production) and assembly difficulties (laying of connectors, cable splicing). Thus, single-mode optical fibers are rare in local area networks since the distances and the speeds are not sufficiently restrictive.

If the fiber core has a diameter of several tens of microns, there are several optical paths between the two ends and the fiber is called multimode. There are two categories of multimode fiber: stepped-index fibers and graded-index fibers.

These categories are distinguished by the curve of the index of the core as a function of the distance from the center (Figure 4.2). In the former case, the

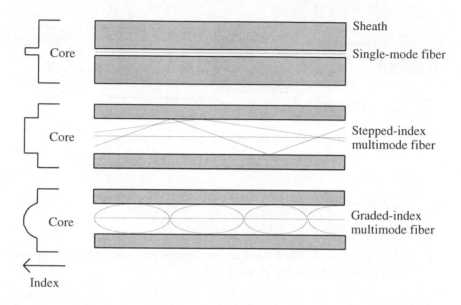

Figure 4.2   Cross sections of three types of optical fiber and trajectories of the light rays.

index jumps abruptly from the value for the core to the value for the sheath (we note that single-mode fiber is also stepped index), while in the latter case, the index changes gradually from the maximum value (at the center) to the value for the sheath on the outside.

Stepped-index fiber thus has several possible paths for the light rays, since these are reflected from the walls when the index changes. Graded-index fiber deflects rays moving away from the core by its variation of the index, which brings them back towards the center.

Stepped-index fiber performs less well than graded-index fiber, which is explained, with some simplification, by the fact that the total difference in length between the shortest path and the longest path is greater, so the dispersion is greater for light rays in broken lines. Thus, graded-index fiber is often preferred, and is the fiber type most commonly used in computer networks.

In each category, the diameters of the core and the sheath may take several standard values. For example, for local area networks, the 62.5/125 μm graded-index fiber has become the most common optical fiber. However there are also other fibers, which are described in Table 4.1.

The IEC has listed certain optical fibers together with their properties, such as the 50/125 μm fiber as described in Table 4.2 which carries the number IEC 793-2 type A1a; similarly, the 62.5/125 μm fiber corresponds to IEC 793-2 type A1b, the 85/125 μm fiber to IEC 793-2 type A1c and the 100/140 μm fiber to IEC 793-2 type A1d.

Table 4.1   The characteristics of different optical fibers.

Conductor material	Type	Diameters core/sheath	Attenuation dB/km	Bandwidth MHz.km	Numerical aperture
Silica	Single mode	9/125	0.4 at 1300 nm		
	Multimode graded index	50/125	3 at 850 nm	400–2000	0.2–0.3
		62.5/125	3.5 at 850 nm	150–1000	0.275
		85/125	3.2 at 850 nm	200–1000	0.26
		100/140	3.8 at 850 nm	150–600	0.29
	Multimode stepped index	200/380	6 at 850 nm	25	0.27
Plastic	Multimode stepped index	750/1000	230–650 nm	20	0.5

Table 4.2   Table of loss on the signal passing between two different types of fiber.

Receiving fiber	Emitting fiber					
	Diameters, μm	50/125	50/125	62.5/125	85/125	100/140
Diameters, μm	NA	0.2	0.22	0.275	0.26	0.29
50/125	0.2	0 dB	0.4 dB	2.2 dB	3.8 dB	5.7 dB
50/125	0.22	0 dB	0 dB	1.6 dB	3.2 dB	4.9 dB
62.5/125	0.275	0 dB	0 dB	0 dB	1 dB	2.3 dB
85/125	0.26	0 dB	0 dB	0.1 dB	0 dB	0.8 dB
100/140	0.29	0 dB	0 dB	0 dB	0 dB	0 dB

Silica is a material with an attenuation which is a function of the signal frequency. Developers have always sought to work with the least attenuated frequencies, such as the most common frequency at 1.17 MHz (850 nm). However, over time, improvements in the manufacturing process for silica fibers have reduced the attenuation at the frequencies used, but other wavelengths offering a greater performance, such as 1300 nm, then 1550 nm, have appeared (Figure 4.3).

These wavelengths require fibers of higher quality, but provide a clearly superior performance. For example, at 1300 nm, the 62.5/125 μm fiber has an attenuation of less than 0.8 dB/km, while at 1550 nm the single-mode fiber has an attenuation of less than 0.2 dB/km.

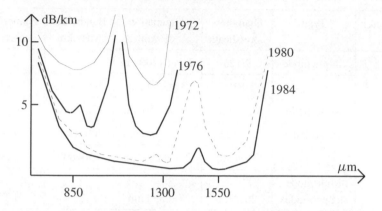

Figure 4.3   Improvement in the attenuation of silica fibers as a function of the wavelength.

One additional factor is the Numerical Aperture (NA) of the fiber. The NA corresponds to the maximum angle at which a ray may be incident on the fiber core on entry and be guided by it. The wider the numerical aperture is, the greater the fraction of light from the optical energy source which finds a path across the fiber will be. The numerical aperture is directly associated with the idea of the cone of acceptance, which is the angular delimitation between the rays reaching the fiber which will be led to the interior of it by refraction and those which will not enter the fiber (by reflection) or will leave it immediately.

The aperture is a fundamental parameter in the evaluation of the amount of light produced by the emitter which will effectively enter the fiber. Since electronic components emit within a well-defined angle, the larger the angle is, the greater the signal strength at point zero will be and the greater the distance traveled before reaching the minimum detection threshold of the receiver will be.

Connection of two fibers of different types results in an additional loss over and above the losses incurred due to the connectors themselves. In fact, changes in the diameter and numerical aperture are generally responsible for substantial attenuation. Thus, the FDDI PMD standard gives a table of the additional attenuations (apart from connectors) due to the connection of two different types of fiber.

We note that if the diameter and the numerical aperture (corresponding to the cone of acceptance) of the receiving fiber are larger than those of the emitting fiber, the loss is zero, since no light rays are lost.

Optical connection is an area rich in diverse solutions. The criteria for quality are a low attenuation, high reproducibility of this attenuation (on successive connections), robustness to numerous manipulations, and a mechanical resistance relatively independent of the movements of the fiber. There is a great variety of connector types (ST, SMA, MFO, PFO, FC, SC) with characteristics generally linked to the cost. In fact, these are expensive and fragile elements whose criticality is inversely proportional to the diameter of the fiber. For example, the typical insertion losses of these connectors on the 62.5/125 μm fiber are 0.5 dB for ST, 1.5 dB for SMA and 0.35 dB for MFO and PFO. The locking resistance varies from 100 to 250 N.

In practise, an optical cable contains several fibers (from two to more than ten) which are all arranged in a protective tube or in grooves. Through its structure, the cable guarantees the necessary mechanical protection by limiting the torsion, elongation, and flattening of the whole.

It should not be forgotten that the implementation of the corresponding emitters has also become more complex with these developments. The delivery of sufficient power for an increasing cable-segment length inevitably leads to the use of lasers instead of Light-Emitting Diodes (LED). When single-mode fiber with a very thin core is used, lasers become mandatory because of the emitted power. Moreover, LEDs have a relatively broad spectrum of emission in comparison with lasers, which have a narrow spectrum consisting of a few rays only. However, one should also bear in mind that LEDs are now reliable and inexpensive, while lasers are more complex and have a greater variation with temperature.

In all cases, these emitters are getting old and their characteristics may change. Thus, an acceptable range of variation between the initial operation of a component and the end of its life may be defined in a standard (it is 1 dB in 10baseF).

Optical receivers may be PIN photodiodes, avalanche photodiodes or integrated detector/amplifiers, the first type being the most common. These receivers each have a range of operational frequencies (usually from ~500 to ~1000 nm for silicon photodiodes) depending on their sensitivity. However, generally, they can be dazzled by excessively powerful light signals. Thus, care should be taken to insert at least a minimum length of optical fiber or jumper cable between an emitter and a receiver (from 1 to 5 meters). This is also sufficient to ensure that rays passing through the sheath are definitely lost.

The twisted pair

The medium based on the twisted pair consists of two conductor wires wound around each other. In the majority of cases, several pairs are grouped together inside the same cable. This is an inexpensive medium, but one which also has a limited capacity.

There are different types of twisted pair, which vary according to the diameter of the conductors, the number of twists per meter, the periodic variation of the twist length, the shielding (per pair, per group of pairs, per cable) or the absence of shielding (Figure 4.4). The electrical performance depends upon these construction parameters.

Figure 4.4   A twisted pair of electrical conductors (unshielded).

Table 4.3   Standard characteristics of twisted pair cables.

	UTP 100 and 120 Ohm	STP 150 Ohm
Conductor diameter	0.4–0.65 mm	0.6–0.66 mm
Diameter over insulated conductor	$\leq$ 1.4 mm	$\leq$ 2.6 mm
Shield around cable unit	No	Yes
Outer diameter of cable	$\leq$ 20 mm	$\leq$ 11 mm
Minimum bending radius for pulling during installation	8 times outer cable diameter	7.5 cm
Minimum bending radius installed	4 times outer cable diameter	
One-time bend radius		20 mm
Pulling strength	$\geq$ 50 N/mm$^2 \times$ Cu$_{min}$	

Electrical signals are emitted in a symmetrical manner, in other words, by applying a voltage $V(t)$ to one conductor and $-V(t)$ to the other.

The main computer manufacturers each have their own range, which they originated themselves. This enables them to base all the physical interconnection facilities of their equipment on a given type of medium and to propose homogeneous solutions. For example, IBM has a complete range of media and connectors adapted to its needs, namely the ICS (IBM Cabling System).

The ICS defines several cable types (types 1 to 9) each with particular characteristics and adapted to a given use. The most common cable is that of type 1, which consists of two twisted pairs shielded individually and globally (the screening consists of an aluminum ribbon). The copper conductors have diameters of 0.64 mm (22 AWG). The colors are red and green for one pair and orange and black for the other. The screening consists of aluminized polyester ribbons. The braiding consists of electroplated copper wires and the external sheath is made of supple PVC (generally black). ICS type 1 cable has a characteristic impedance of 150 ± 15 Ohm, from 3 to 20 MHz (and 270 Ohm at 9.6 kHz). The signal speed is of the order of 0.75 c. The DC resistance is 57.5 Ohm/km (115 Ohm/km in loop). Finally, the attenuation is less than 11 dB/km at 1 MHz, 36 dB/km at 10 MHz and 45 dB/km at 16 MHz. IBM refers to this cable type as 'data grade media' and associates it with a general hermaphrodite connector type (wall socket and patching). It pushes this for its Token Ring installations at both 4 and 16 Mbps.

Similarly, AT&T has its Systimax Premise Distribution System (PDS) which consists of a cable with four unshielded twisted pairs, where each conductor has a diameter of 24 AWG (0.5 mm). The cable has a characteristic impedance of 100 Ohm and an attenuation of 7.5 dB at 10 MHz and 10 dB at 16 MHz over 100 meters.

Table 4.4   Standard electrical characteristics of different twisted pair.

	100 Ohm			120 Ohm			150 Ohm
Category	3	4	5	3	4	5	
Characteristic impedance	100 ± 15 Ohm (> 1 MHz) 125 ± 25 (64 kHz)			120 ± 15 Ohm (> 1 MHz) 125 ± 45 (64 kHz)			150 ± 15 (> 1 MHz)
Maximum DC loop resistance	19.2 Ohm/100 m						12 Ohm/100 m
Minimum phase velocity of propagation (1–100 MHz)	0.4.c	0.6.c		0.4.c	0.6.c		0.6.c
Minimum DC insulation resistance	150 MOhm.km						1 GOhm.km
Attenuation (dB/100 m)							
at 64 kHz	0.9	0.8			0.8		
at 256 kHz	1.3	1.1			1.1		
at 512 kHz	1.8	1.5			1.5		
at 772 kHz	2.2	1.9	1.8		1.5	1.7	
at 1 MHz	2.6	2.1			2	1.8	
at 4 MHz	5.6	4.3			4	3.6	2.2
at 10 MHz	9.8	7.2	6.6		6.7	5.2	3.6
at 16 MHz	13.1	8.9	8.2		8.1	6.2	4.4
at 20 MHz	NA	10.2	9.2	NA	9.2	7	4.9
at 31.25 MHz	NA	NA	11.8	NA	NA	8.8	6.9
at 62.5 MHz	NA	NA	17.1	NA	NA	12.5	9.8
at 100 MHz	NA	NA	22	NA	NA	17	12.3

Finally, in France, Bull offers a cable called Bull A 2 and a patching system (modules and patch panel arrangement) which constitute the Bull Cabling System (BCS). The Bull A 2 cable is available in the form of 4 to 112 twisted pairs encased in a global shielding and a synthetic layer for mechanical protection. This cable is said to be screened. The copper conductors have a diameter of 0.6 mm, the insulation is heavy colored polyethylene. The order of the four pairs (wires 1 to 8) is as follows: white–gray, blue–colorless, yellow–orange, brown–violet. The screening is an aluminized ribbon. The exterior sheath consists of fireproof PVC (generally yellow). Bull A 2 has a characteristic impedance of 100 ± 15 Ohm at 1 MHz. The in loop DC resistance is bounded above by 130 Ohm/km. Finally, the attenuation is less than 1.4 dB/km at 1 kHz, 25 dB/km at 1 MHz, and 72 dB/km at 10 MHz. Within the BCS, this cable is associated with RJ45 connectors in the form of wall sockets and plugs and modules for patching purposes.

Carriers similar to the twisted pair may also be developed based on four twisted wires (quads); CNET's L120 (France Télécom) is an example of this. This is available in the form of 8, 16, 24, 64 or 256 wires, the whole being screened. The conductors of annealed copper have a diameter of 0.6 mm, and the insulator is a double layer of polyethylene. The screening is a ribbon of aluminized polyester with a thickness of 0.04 mm and the sheath consists of a thermoplastic halogen-free material (with an ivory color). The minimum bend radius supported without deformation is five times the external diameter of the cable. The L120 has a characteristic impedance of 120 ± 10 Ohm from 1 to 16 MHz (or 100 MHz) and 110 ± 10 Ohm at 100 kHz. The in loop resistance is less than 133 Ohm/km. The propagation speed is greater than or equal to 0.75 c. Finally, the attenuation is less than 5.5 dB/km at 100 kHz, 18 dB/km at 1 MHz, 52 dB/km at 10 MHz, 60 dB/km at 16 MHz, and 150 dB/km at 100 MHz. The cable with two quads (or four pairs) of 6 mm wires is designated by L120 4 6.

This last medium, with characteristic impedance and performance between those of ICS type 1 cables and unshielded cables or those which are only screened, could be standardized at the European level and would be useful in an international homogenization of installations.

Other manufacturers also have their own, more or less original, cabling ranges, some of which (for example, that of DECnet) include a modular connection system (borrowed from AMP) with easily interchangeable sockets, which can be used to adapt a fixed cable to various uses, incorporating baluns if necessary (small connection elements placed between two cables which can adapt the impedances from one to the other).

Finally, we note that the first solution implementing FDDI on shielded twisted pairs (150 Ohm characteristic impedance) requires an attenuation less than 12 dB over 100 meters at a frequency of 62.5 MHz. This solution, called CDDI, has made way for the future TP-PMD standard, which operates at 31.25 MHz on shielded and unshielded twisted pairs (category 5).

The air

The atmosphere, in other words, the ambient air over short distances, can be used as a transmission medium for electromagnetic waves.

The frequency of these waves causes variations in their transmission quality, in terms of the distance covered, the permeability of buildings, reflection by certain materials, and so on.

Of course, all these radio links pass through the Earth's atmosphere, like satellite links which use this medium on part of their path.

However, as far as local area networks are concerned, the constraints are different and the applications more recent. Emitters should not be dangerous for people working in associated buildings, and the length of the links should preferably be limited to several hundred meters. The radio waves of the communication system should not interfere with electronic and computer equipment in the vicinity and should not suffer interference from these. Transmission should support a speed of the order of megabits per second at least.

Wireless local area networks are very easy to install as far as the integration of a machine into the network is concerned, since it is sufficient to direct the antenna for connection purposes. They are also financially advantageous, since, even though they may sometimes be more expensive initially, they prove to be very economical when machines are moved frequently.

Other technologies, such as microwave transmission, transmission by laser beam over 1 km and infrared transmission, have been applied to local area networks, as we shall see in the next chapter.

4.3 The topologies

The topology of a network defines the structure of its logical layout; in other words, how the elements of the network are interconnected.

Like the medium, the topology forms part of the physical layer of the model. Thus, the rules for installation and connection are given in the standard associated with this level. We shall see later that there is a difference between the logical topology and the physical layout.

There are two main categories of elementary topologies:

- topologies based on point-to-point links (the star, the ring, the chain, the mesh);

- topologies which allow more than two physical accesses to the carrier (the bus).

Other, more complex topologies, such as tree structures, may be obtained by combining the elementary topologies (these will be described later).

The mesh

If all the machines of the network are linked together in pairs they form a fully meshed topology. If only some of these connections exist the topology is meshed, but not fully (Figure 4.5).

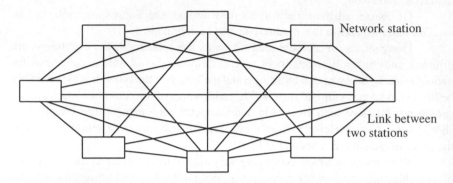

Figure 4.5 Example of a meshed topology (not fully meshed).

Historically, this was the first topology implemented, which is easily understandable, since it stems from the evolution of a set of machines with point-to-point links.

The main advantage of such a topology follows from the fact that there is a direct link between two machines which it is desired to bring into communication with each other and thus the whole bandwidth is accessible. However, the meshed topology has the disadvantage that its evolution is fraught with difficulty as the number of attached machines increases. Moreover, the cost of such a technology is strongly linked to the number of machines and rapidly becomes prohibitive. For N machines, the number of links needed for a fully meshed topology is $N(N-1)/2$, which is of the order of $N^2/2$.

The star

If all the machines in the network are attached to a single element, which is then the heart of the network, the topology is that of the star (Figure 4.6).

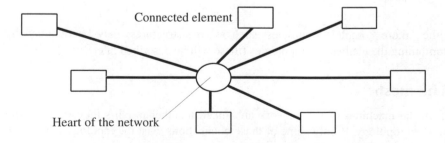

Figure 4.6 Star configuration.

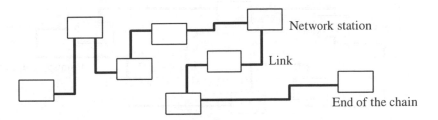

Figure 4.7   Network of several machines in a chain.

One of the main advantages of this topology is that each medium segment is used as a point-to-point link, so it is possible to operate it at its maximum speed. However, this network as a whole is very vulnerable, since it depends entirely upon the operational state of the central node. We also note that at the physical level, the central element does not have the same characteristics as the peripheral elements.

The chain

The chain consists of a set of machines which are interconnected in pairs. Although it resembles the bus, the chain differs in the fact that the network communication bearer is not just a single medium segment but also includes the intermediate elements which propagate the signal (Figure 4.7).

The connection points are thus not totally passive; even when they are not involved in a communication, they serve as repeaters. When a machine wishes to withdraw from the network, it has to replace its attachment by a direct connection (a bypass), which may be done using a relay. This constraint is identical in the case of a ring topology, and care should also be taken not to exceed the maximum permissible distance between two active connections.

The chain can be installed with a very short medium length and, together with the bus, it is the most economical topology in this respect. However, high reliability of the network cannot be guaranteed, since the communication between two stations may be interfered with by malfunctioning of any one of the elements between these.

We note that LocalTalk uses a topology of this type, a daisy chain on a twisted pair.

The ring

The concept of the ring arises when one thinks of a loop in which each machine is only connected to each of its two nearest neighbors (Figure 4.8).

The ring is the only topology which does not require a bidirectional link between the connection points. In fact, if the ring has a direction in which the information circulates, the unidirectional link does not prevent any exchanges, but the path followed is not always the shortest.

We note that the ring can be constructed using a unidirectional chain topology looped back on itself.

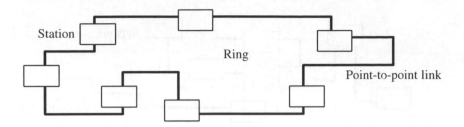

Figure 4.8   Simple ring linking seven stations.

The advantages of the ring topology are:

- The provision of an efficient access method capable of supporting heavy loads without degradation of performance;

- The possibility of exceeding 100% efficiency (with respect to the speed provided by the physical layer) by causing several messages between different pairs of correspondents to circulate simultaneously on the ring;

- A high level of security due to the fact that it is easy to list all the machines present (each has ready knowledge of its nearest neighbor(s)).

The disadvantages of the ring are:

- A complex and elaborate, thus expensive, management of the right to emit;

- A vulnerability to machines suffering chronic failures (repetitive and short duration) which cause reinitialization of the ring whenever the problem occurs;

- A physical topology which is in general very different from a ring, because of the structure of the prewiring.

The bus

If the elements are connected alongside each other (in parallel) on the same medium, the topology used is called the bus (Figure 4.9).

In general, the data propagates along the medium from the point of connection of the emitting station in both directions. When an emission takes place the receiving stations have no influence over the signal and their presence or absence is therefore transparent.

The advantages of this topology are:

- A transparency to the presence or absence of machines not implicated in the exchange (this is also linked to the fact that the machines all have the same status – no machine is indispensable to the operation of the network as a whole);

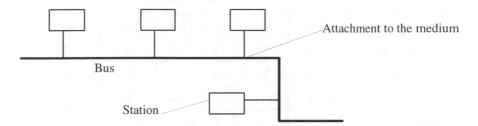

Figure 4.9   Bus configuration.

- A relatively short length of medium is needed to connect all the elements;
- The bus topology may be associated with a simple, distributed access method.

The disadvantages of the bus topology are:

- The management of the right to emit is vulnerable to the network load;
- The network is relatively insecure, due to the shared medium.

Examples of existing topologies which use this topology include Ethernet, MAP and LocalTalk in certain configurations.

Finally, we note that all the technologies which use the air as a physical bearer of electromagnetic waves shared between several emitters are equivalent to buses (except for techniques based on narrow directed beams).

The tree

The previous topologies are, in some way, basic topologies from which more complex configurations can be developed. Thus, it is possible to construct a tree-like

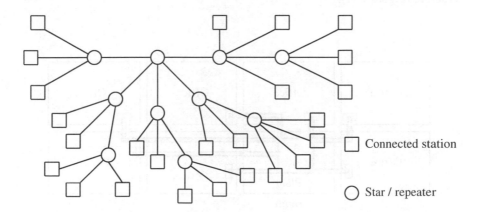

Figure 4.10   Tree-like structure based on cascaded stars.

Table 4.5 Characteristics of the various topologies.

	Star	Ring	Bus	Chain	Tree	Mesh
Symmetry	No	Yes	Yes	No	No	Yes
Order	No	Yes	No	Yes	No	No
Directional	No	*A priori*	No	No	No	No
Number of segments	$N-1$	N	1	$N-1$	$N-1$	$N(N-1)/2$
Privacy	Yes	No	No	No	Possible	Yes

topology from buses or stars (Figure 4.10).

In fact, these examples are closer to reality than the basic topologies, since by virtue of their numerous evolutions, local area networks have adopted different topologies which can be found gathered together in certain heterogeneous configurations. Ethernet on coaxial cable uses a bus-based tree-like structure, as described in Chapter 1.

Table 4.5 summarizes a number of the major characteristics of each topology.

The physical topology

Once the logical topology has been chosen, it remains to install the network in the building. At this stage, a certain number of practical questions arise (see Chapter 15 for more details), which almost inevitably lead to media segments being laid in a star structure. The heart of the star is the plant room which contains the patch cabinet serving an office at each end. Thus, the chain, ring or logical bus is reconstructed by jumper connections at the level of the patch panel, based on the physical star structure (Figure 4.11).

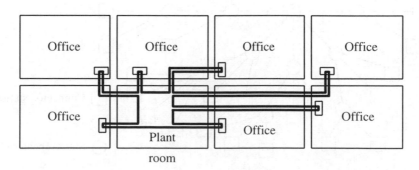

Figure 4.11 Star-cabled ring.

We end by recalling that the bus topology is the only one in which the presence or absence of other attached machines is transparent to all stations. This characteristic may be viewed as a desirable quality if one has to manage a network in a very dynamic way. On the other hand, the ring (which may be viewed as a looped chain) requires the cooperation of all the connected elements in order to pass messages. This has the advantageous result that it is easy to monitor the state of each machine. Finally, the evolution to tree-like topologies is inevitable, with the use of interconnection hardware interlinking different networks.

4.4 Multiplexing

Readers will have realized that for most of the topologies described up to this point (except the fully meshed topology), the medium, or the physical bearer of the network, is shared between all the connected machines. Thus, there is a need to determine how the machines will behave when several of them wish to emit data at the same time. This leads to the choice of a type of multiplexing: in time or in frequency.

Time-Division Multiplexing (TDM) involves letting the machines have full use of the medium, but sequentially. Frequency-Division Multiplexing (FDM) corresponds to a simultaneous sharing of the medium with the assignment of distinct and separate frequency ranges.

Time-division multiplexing

Time-division multiplexing is simpler to implement at the physical level, since all the machines emit in a similar way and only the method governing the contention for and assignment of the right to emit must follow a logical procedure (Figure 4.12). Thus, the data items emitted by each station follow consecutively on the same transmission medium and have similar characteristics (physical size, encoding, structure). There are several methods for managing and allocating the right to emit, which will be described in the following section.

This form of multiplexing has the advantage of a certain homogeneity, but remains generally limited as far as the use of the bandwidth is concerned. In fact, to increase the total speed (and thus the frequency of the signals), one needs to be able to manage the packet scheduling even more rapidly.

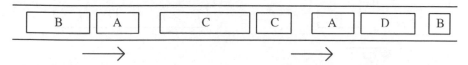

Figure 4.12   Packets from different sources sharing the same transmission channel.

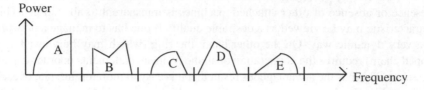

Figure 4.13 Five dedicated frequency channels sharing the spectrum.

Frequency-division multiplexing

Frequency-division multiplexing involves dedicating a specific frequency channel to each type of exchange (Figure 4.13). To establish diverse or multiple communication, several windows have to be individually managed by the connected stations. Frequency-division multiplexing is complicated to implement on a network of machines which must all be able to intercommunicate. In fact, the number of frequency bands available is always limited and the distribution of the links to be established is not necessarily self-evident.

An important application of frequency-division multiplexing is found in the world of voice transport. Telecommunications providers concatenate several thousand telephone communications on a single broadband link by frequency-division multiplexing. However, frequency-division multiplexing also exists for local area networks.

The global efficiency of frequency-division multiplexing is not always optimal, since the logical channels are each reserved for a single communication (at least while that is taking place).

Finally, the assembly of several physical communication links between two entities for a single transmission requirement may be referred to as space-division multiplexing (Figure 4.14). In this case, it must be physically possible to share

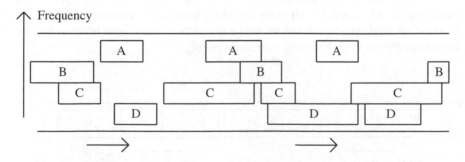

Figure 4.14 Packets from different sources sharing the same transmission channel.

the traffic between the different channels available; it is not the case that each line is dedicated to a particular use. Otherwise, one link might remain unused while another was overloaded.

4.5 Access methods

The access method is the method used to manage the right of access to the medium. It is a layer 2 attribute and, more precisely, an attribute of the MAC sublayer when that is separated from the LLC.

   The access method corresponds to the protocol for managing the emissions, which is indispensable to the proper operation of the whole and is responsible for the merits and shortcomings of the network technology. Thus, the behavior of Ethernet or Token Ring as a function of the number of active machines, their respective positions and the traffic they seek to transmit, is determined by the choice of access method.

Master–slave

This is the easiest method conceivable. A single element is the master, which is responsible for successively interrogating all the machines which it believes are likely to wish to emit in order to grant them the right to occupy the media in response.

   This technique, also called polling, implies that one machine is responsible for ensuring the operation of the whole network. Thus, it is a relatively easy method to implement and is reliable as far as the distribution of emission times is concerned, since the element which takes the decision knows all the connected machines, is aware of all the previous exchanges and may recall the priorities of each. On the other hand, this technique depends entirely upon the availability and trouble-free operation of the master, which makes it vulnerable to faults and bugs.

   Finally, we note that the topology most naturally associated with this access method is the star, although other topologies may also be used.

Slot

The slot method is easy to understand. This method, which should preferably be implemented on a ring, but may be implemented on a double bus (unidirectional), uses an entity responsible for generating and continuously transmitting empty cells of a fixed size (slot) consecutively on the medium (Figure 4.15).

   These cells have a bit which indicates whether or not they are occupied by data. When a station wishing to transmit sees a free slot pass it, it places data there and sets the bit to the value corresponding to 'occupied'. Then, in the case of a ring topology, a station is responsible for releasing the cell by deactivating the occupation bit; this will be either the emitting station or the destination station. In the case of a bus, the cells are lost at the ends of the bus; moreover, they have to be reserved using a relatively complex procedure.

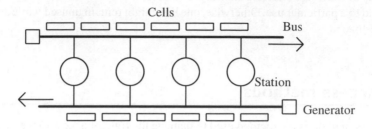

Figure 4.15   Example of a double unidirectional bus with slots.

Aloha

Aloha is the expression of greeting in the Hawaiian language. It is also a multiple access technique in stars (where the center is a satellite) proposed in 1969 by the American University of Hawaii.

This access method can be used to share a single radio channel (possibly high speed) between several unsynchronized emitters and receivers. Each is authorized to emit when it has a message to communicate and its addressee, the central node, operating on the same channel, will be able to capture these emissions. If all goes well, the stations transmit their messages one after the other and the central station stores these to pass them to protocols which are capable of decoding them. On the other hand, if two or more stations decide to emit almost simultaneously, the signals emitted are superposed and become jumbled (producing a collision) and all the messages transmitted at the same time are lost. In this case, the upper layers have to salvage the process and try to retransmit the lost packet.

One clear advantage of this method is its simplicity, together with the fact that it is perfectly distributed. Its most restrictive shortcoming is the rapid degradation in its performance under heavy load. In fact, if a large number of machines seek to communicate on the channel, the losses due to collisions are more numerous and the system tends to a state of complete blockage, since each lost frame requires a retransmission attempt (and thus additional traffic).

A version exists in which all the machines are synchronized (this is not always easy to implement) and only attempt to emit at well-defined time intervals; this is slotted Aloha. These periodic gaps, corresponding to possible transmissions of packets, reduce the probability of contention.

CSMA/CD

The Carrier Sense Multiple Access (CSMA) method is an improved derivative of the Aloha method. The progress comes from the fact that, before emitting, a station senses the medium to detect whether it is occupied.

If a packet is already circulating, the emission is deferred, which considerably reduces the proportion of collisions of signals. However, since the transmission speed on the medium is finite (and even less than c, the speed of light in the vacuum) it is possible that a station may have failed to detect signals on the channel even though an emission had just begun a little further away. In this case, there will again be a collision.

Ethernet has the advantage over CSMA of being able to detect these collisions (Collision Detection – CD) and then attempting to retransmit in cases of loss. This considerably increases the reliability of layers 1 and 2. The detection of collisions during transmission involves a comparison of the message seen on the medium with that which it wishes to emit.

There are several different CSMA/CD methods, whose differences relate to the way in which the transmission is managed after the wait for the channel to become free. If a retransmission attempt is not made at the end of the packet but only after a random delay, the method is said to be non-persistent. If the attempt is always triggered immediately after the packet has passed (as soon as the channel is free), the method is said to be persistent or 1-persistent. On the other hand, if the attempt is only initiated with a probability P (less than 1), the method is said to be P-persistent. If the machine waits (complementary probability $1 - P$) it reloops on the same procedure of sensing the channel, waiting for it to become free and then transmitting (immediate, with probability P).

We note that CSMA/CD is very effective for low loads, although this method cannot guarantee a speed proportional to the load and is not adapted to the management of levels of priority.

Token

In the token method, the station possessing the token has the right to emit. The token is unique and must then circulate among all the machine controllers to ensure that each has the possibility of transmitting the messages confided to it.

The token-passing method thus requires the existence of an order among all the machines; the token must circulate in a precise direction. Thus, each item of equipment must at least know its predecessor in the chain, and sometimes its successor. Therefore, it seems that there must be an initial discussion stage in which the machines get to know each other and position themselves in the virtual loop. Thus, the efficiency of the system is not optimal for low loads.

This access method has the advantage of being efficient, since, as we have just seen, each machine is guaranteed a regular right to emit (in a deterministic manner, once for each passage of the token around the loop). However, it has the disadvantage of complexity. In fact, whenever a machine is added or withdrawn, or whenever the token is lost, a certain time is inevitably lost while the loop is reinitialized by an agreement of all the elements. Moreover, the delay in accessing the medium does not tend to zero, but remains bounded when the load is very low.

Conclusion The access methods described above have all the merits and shortcomings, which make them more-or-less well adapted to the constraints of each network. CSMA/CD is particularly suitable for networks subject to continual evolution, on which the load does not approach the maximum bandwidth too frequently (since the performance is then considerably degraded). Token passing has a higher performance and can guarantee a bounded delay in the access to the medium, but is more complex and more sensitive to connections and disconnections; it is also more limited as far as the number of machines is concerned.

Finally, in summary, we present the interdependences of these methods in the form of a diagram (Figure 4.16).

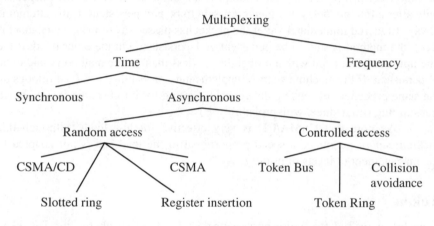

Figure 4.16   Hierarchical organization of access-control techniques.

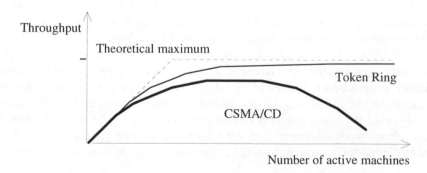

Figure 4.17   Graphs showing the relative efficiency of two access methods, in terms of actual speed.

Some of the asynchronous access methods (that is, those which are not based on a set of synchronized elements and cannot guarantee a minimum speed and a given minimum transmission delay under all conditions), such as token passing or register insertion, may be adapted to synchronous communications without too much difficulty. Others, such as CSMA/CD, are not readily suitable for transporting signals requiring synchronous multiplexing (essentially voice and video).

A comparison of the behavior of Token Ring and CSMA/CD shows that the performance may degrade quite rapidly as the load increases when a random access technique is used (Figure 4.17).

4.6 Encoding and transmission

Encoding and transmission form part of level 1 and are thus defined in the standardization documents for that layer.

The transmission may be carried out with amplitude, frequency or phase modulation, which is still found in analog domains. In the digital domain, we essentially speak of encoding, although these methods of processing signals before their emission on the medium are sometimes similar. The aim is the same: to facilitate transmissions by improving the signal quality after it has passed. Various encoding methods exist, each with qualities of simplicity or immunity to certain degradations (noise, attenuation, distortion) which make them appropriate for a given technology. One major constraint still remains, namely the suitability for the binary world; for example, a very high-performance encoding method adapted to the transport of data with 3, 5, 6 or 7 bits will not be easy to use.

The NRZ code

Non-Return to Zero (NRZ) code is one of the simplest, since it consists of a sequence of two possible electrical levels, V and $-V$, where V corresponds to the binary value 1 and $-V$ to 0. This code tends to minimize the continuous component of the transmitted signal. Thus, if 1s and 0s are present in approximately equal numbers and well distributed, the average level of the electrical signal is close to zero. However, the spectrum of the NRZ code has a large part of its power around the frequency 0, which is sometimes a hindrance.

The NRZI code

In Non-Return to Zero Inverted (NRZI) code, the number 1 is encoded by a change of state (rising or descending edge) after the clock pulse, 0 is encoded by an absence of a change in state. Thus, this code does not have a polarity.

A comparison of signals encoded using the NRZ and NRZI codes is shown in Figure 4.18.

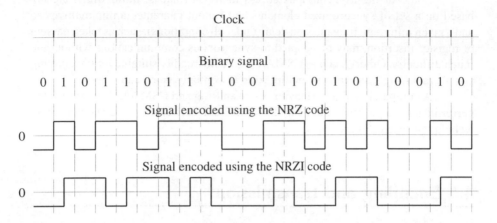

Figure 4.18   Comparison of signals encoded using the NRZ and NRZI codes.

The Manchester code

This is a code in which 1 is represented by a rising edge and 0 by a descending edge. Thus, it cannot be read correctly by inverting the direction. The Manchester code guarantees one transition (rising or descending edge) per clock pulse, which is equivalent to transporting a synchronization signal. The continuous component is always constant and may therefore be chosen to be zero. The signal spectrum is bunched between $1/2T$ and $1/T$ with zero power at frequency zero, but it has a total width twice that of the NRZ. The code has an efficiency of 50% since two levels are used to encode one bit of data.

This is the code used for Ethernet local area networks, Finally, we note that this code may be viewed as a code in phase $(-\pi/2, \pi/2)$ of the signals to be transmitted, which also explains why it is called a biphase code.

The differential Manchester code

The differential Manchester or biphase differential code consists of two signals with a binary significance and two non-data symbols. A 0 is encoded by a change in level (rising or descending edge) at the start and in the middle of an interval, while a 1 is encoded by a simple change of level in the middle of an interval. If no edge is present between two clock pulses, the signal is neither 0 nor 1 and therefore does not constitute data; however, despite this it can be used as a flag. Two non-data symbols are defined, one with a change of level on the clock pulse and the other without a change of level (called K and J). These may be used to identify certain MAC level fields within the frame and to delimit the data field.

Readers will have noted that the encoding is only defined in terms of changes of level and is thus independent of the polarity. Moreover, it does not have a continuous component and thus capacitance or inductance coupling is easy. Finally, the regular transition in the middle of a clock pulse transports inherent synchronization information. This code, which, like the Manchester code, has an efficiency of 50%, is used in the Token Ring technology.

A comparison of signals encoded with the Manchester and differential Manchester codes is shown in Figure 4.19.

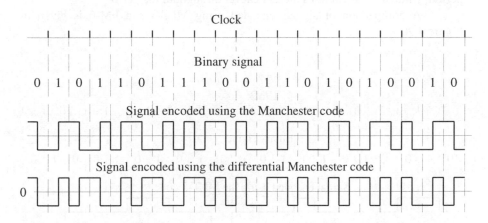

Figure 4.19 Comparison of signals encoded using the Manchester and differential Manchester codes.

The 4B/5B code

The 4B/5B code is a code which uses 5 bits to encode 16 possible values (whence the equivalent of 4 bits) by adding a built-in check. This coding is used for the FDDI technology in conjunction with an NRZI coding for the 5 bits produced. Of the 32 possible states, 2^4 are used for significant numerical values, eight are used for start- and end-of-frame indications, and eight are code violations. This code has the advantage over the previous two codes of having an intrinsic efficiency of 80%, since 16 numbers are effectively encoded with 5 bits.

The MLT-3 code

MLT-3 stands for Three Levels MultiLine Transmission, and is a code which permits a reduction in the emitted frequency spectrum by using more than two states. This code is very similar to NRZI; it has three possible levels -1, 0, and 1. The transmission of a bit at 0 does not require a change of level, while the transmission of a bit at 1 does require a change of level. The levels follow the four-state period: 0, 1, 0, -1.

At the present time, a proposed standard which adapts FDDI technology to the Shielded or Unshielded Twisted Pair (UTP category 5), referred to as Twisted Pair – Physical Media Dependent (TP-PMD), uses this type of encoding. Similarly, the 100baseTX Ethernet Addendum to IEEE 802.3 covers this mode of emission.

The FM-0 code

FM-0 (also referred to as biphase space) is the code used by LocalTalk. This code is fairly similar to the Manchester codes in the sense that the clock frequency is transported explicitly by the signal: there is one transition for each bit transmitted, but at the beginning and the end of the period (instead of in the middle, as in the Manchester codes). A bit at 0 requires an additional transition in the middle of the period, while a bit at 1 retains the same level throughout the period.

A comparison of signals encoded using MLT-3 and FM-0 is given in Figure 4.20.

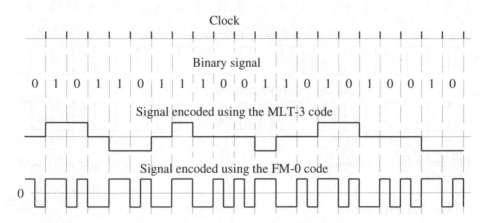

Figure 4.20   Comparison of signals encoded using MLT-3 and FM-0.

4.7 Local area network rivals to Ethernet

Setting aside Ethernet, we have seen that other enterprise local area networks are commercially available, each with its own merits and shortcomings. In what follows, we review their main characteristics, leaving readers to judge them for themselves.

Token Ring

This local area network was developed by IBM and, like Ethernet, was ultimately standardized by the IEEE (in IEEE 802.5), then by ISO in 1992 in IS 8802.5.

It is based on a logical ring topology (with a physical implementation based on a star and a capacity for redundancy on inter-concentrator links). It uses a token-passing access method and has a speed of 1 Mbps (historically) or, more generally, 4 or 16 Mbps. The medium used comprises two individually shielded or

Table 4.6 Number of different elements in a Token Ring network.

	Type of MAU	STP IBM type 1		UTP categ. 4 or 5		UTP IBM type 3	
Speed (Mbps)	MAU	4	16	4	16	4	16
Number of	Passive	250	250	144	250	144	72
machines	Active	144	180	72			

unshielded twisted pairs (such as ICS type 1) and optical fiber for certain extensions. Communication is carried out in synchronous serial mode (at the physical level) with a baseband signal. Differential Manchester coding is used with a binary big-endian order of emission (highest-order bit of the byte sent first). The original connector technology was of an hermaphrodite type (but more commonly RJ45) on the network elements (MAU, for example) and of type DB9 on the NIC connector interfaces. The data is emitted in the form of frames (with a structure similar to that of Ethernet) whose minimum length is 21 bytes and whose maximum length is dependent on the capabilities of the set of attached machines, but may extend to 4450 bytes (at 4 Mbps) or 17 800 bytes (at 16 Mbps).

The restrictions are a maximum of 260 connections per ring (250 according to ISO) and a recommended length of 100 meters or less for lobes between the station and the MAU (750 meters being theoretically acceptable on STP with two repeaters).

Following the early release of the 16 Mbps Token Ring, more recent developments have made it possible to exceed the capabilities of the technology, whether by increasing the speed using 100VG-AnyLAN at 100 Mbps (which will be discussed later), or by using dynamic packet switching which makes it possible to dedicate the whole bandwidth to each pair of ports when a packet is exchanged. This switching may also be associated with a full duplex operation which would then offer 32 Mbps for each access, this mode being called Dedicated Token Ring (DTR).

We note that Token Ring was, in the first instance, essentially a manufacturer's proprietary product, which explains why it has interfaces for all IBM machines, although this is not necessarily true for the market as a whole.

LocalTalk

LocalTalk is a local area network developed by Apple for its Macintosh range, although it has never been standardized.

It is a technology with modest capabilities, which is practical and very easy to implement. The access method is CSMA/CA (CA for collision avoidance, which corresponds to a phase of exchange of indications before the emission of the packet), the speed is 230.4 kbps, the original topology is the chain and the medium is a twisted pair with characteristic impedance 120 Ohm (the diameter of the conductors may range from 0.4 to 0.6 mm). Originally, at most 32 nodes could be linked on a single segment over a total distance of less than 300 meters, but the evolution of compatible and rival products has led to support for two other topologies (bus and star, with passive or active hardware) and the raising of the maximum distance to 1.5 km in certain configurations. The maximum number of machines per network is 254. Connectors are of the RJ11 or 3-pin mini-DIN type.

We note that all Macintoshs and all Apple printers have a native LocalTalk interface.

Finally, we must distinguish between AppleTalk and LocalTalk: the former brings together the whole area of Apple network communication, and thus covers the seven layers, with different possible network technologies (EtherTalk, TokenTalk), while the latter defines a specific LAN technology (lower layers).

ARCnet

ARCnet was developed by Datapoint Corporation, but has only recently been considered by one of the standardization bodies (ANSI 878.1 standard, for its latest extension). However, its capabilities are interesting and its market is not negligible. It is an inexpensive technology, focused on the world of microcomputers.

The speed on offer is 2.5 Mbps and 20 Mbps (multiplication by a factor of 8) with the recent version of ARCnet plus, which is upwards compatible. The topology used is the star, the access method is based on token passing and the media are RG62 (93 Ohm) coaxial cable, fiber optic cable or twisted pair. The network can accommodate 255 machines and the frames contain up to 507 bytes of data.

FDDI

Although FDDI is not a LAN, it undeniably constitutes an alternative to Ethernet networks. FDDI was introduced as a replacement for top-of-the-range Ethernet since it provides a generally superior performance (in terms of length, speed, number of machines). We note that it is still considerably more expensive than Ethernet. However, FDDI may also be viewed as a network for interconnecting several Ethernet networks, that is, as a backbone of the architecture. It is then no longer a direct competitor, but a complementary element in the construction of a global solution. We shall now describe some of the main technical characteristics of FDDI.

The network uses a token-passing method with early release, on a (basic) topology comprising a contra-rotating double ring. In case of failure of a link or a machine, the secondary ring is used to ensure the continuity of the ring by looping (or wrapping) back to the primary ring. FDDI offers a speed of 100 Mbps and uses mainly fiber optic cable. Its restrictions include a maximum of 500 stations (doubly attached) per network and a circumference of 100 km. The distance between two stations may extend to 2 km (62.5/125 μm fiber recommended) for multimode fibers and 35 to 58 km for single-mode fibers (according to the category of the emitters and receivers). The FDDI frames have a structure similar to those of Token Ring

Table 4.7   Characteristics of the most common local area networks.

Technology	**Ethernet**	**Token Ring**	**LocalTalk**	**FDDI**
Standard	ISO 8802-3	ISO 8802-5	–	ANSI X3T9.5
1st topology	Bus	Ring	Chain	Double ring
Complemen. topology	Tree Star	Star	Bus Star	Tree
Maximum speed	10 Mbps 1 Mb 1base5 100 Mb 100baseT	4 Mbps and 16 Mbps	230.4 kbps	100 Mbps
Encoding	Manchester	Differential Manchester	FM-0	4B/5B NRZI
Code efficiency	50%	50%	50%	80%
Basic medium	Coaxial	STP	UTP	Multimode
Complemen. medium	Optical UTP	UTP Optical	STP Multimode	Single mode Twisted pair Coaxial
Access method	CSMA/CD	Token passing and early release (16 Mb)	CSMA/CA	Token passing and early release
Max. frame	1518 bytes	4450/17800 bytes (4/16 Mbps)	605 bytes	4500 bytes
Machines per network	1024	260 (ISO: 250)	254	500 DAS
Network size	2.8 km 4 km 10baseF	Variable	300 m (1.5 km)	100 km
Segment length	500 m coaxial 2 km optical	750 m STP 3 km optical	300 m (1.5 km)	2 km multimode 40 km single mode

and may contain up to 4500 bytes of data. The encoding is of the 4B/5B type and requires only 125 Mbaud. The connector technology comprises a pair of connectors: ST duplex.

The concentrator is an important element which can be used to create branches of a tree-like topology, while retaining the redundancy of the links by dual homing. Simple attachments in a master–slave configuration are also available, but at the logical level the overall network topology remains a single ring.

Finally, since FDDI was developed according to the OSI model, the highest layer is naturally the LLC IS 8802-2.

Conclusion   In an attempt to provide impartial advice, we now give a rapid comparative review of the local area networks discussed above.

Ethernet has the advantage of being a standardized, manufacturer-independent network, which is very common, easy to modify, broadly extensible, and relatively inexpensive (medium and active elements). Its disadvantage is that it does not cope well with increases in the global load.

Token Ring is a fairly common standardized network, which has a high performance and retains it capabilities under all loads. Its disadvantage is that it is more expensive (active elements) and sometimes not available for certain computers (workstations, mainframes). It retains a strong link with its original manufacturer (IBM).

LocalTalk is a network which focuses on the interconnection of Apple microcomputers. It is very practical, very user-friendly and simple to implement. However, it is limited in terms of speed and the total number of machines supported.

ARCnet is a network which was standardized belatedly. Its capabilities are often sufficient, it is easy to use and very user-friendly but has an uneven distribution.

FDDI is not a true local area network, but has been perceived as a top-of-the-range challenger. It is a standardized, manufacturer-independent, high-performance network whose principal disadvantage is still its price (medium and active materials).

The main characteristics of the most common local area networks are summarized in Table 4.7.

4.8 The place of local area networks in telecommunications

Local area networks are relatively recent in the world of telecommunications. They have a high performance in terms of speed and transmission quality and have led users to consume large bandwidths, which partly explains why the providers are now offering higher speeds. For example, after 256 and 512 kbps, X.25 is now moving towards T1/E1 (1.544/2 Mbps) and leased lines at E3/T3 (34/45 Mbps), then 140 or 155 Mbps in response to the requirements for exchanges between research centers.

Thus, in summary, local area networks provide communication facilities on the scale of a building or a site which are now almost always owned by the enterprise; they are of a high quality without always being expensive and provide support for the evolution of long-distance digital telecommunications.

Chapter 5

Current trends

User requirements are evolving with the increase in consumer-based telecommunications-related information technology, and there is an incontestable demand for higher speeds, both at the local level (between the supercomputers in a computing center or simply between the servers) and at a distance (between remote sites), and on a unitary scale (in terms of access) or a global scale (for the infrastructure). The United States still retains a slight lead in the WAN area, which, for example, explains why what ISDN has to offer in terms of basic access is of less interest in the US.

The bandwidth has become the main criterion, given that the transmission quality has improved to a sufficient extent that the protocols of certain layers are capable of reducing the quality controls they implement.

Thus, a certain number of new technologies will respond to these demands in the short or long term. These principally include ATM, Frame Relay, SMDS, and possibly DQDB. Some will be stages leading to a more homogeneous architecture. Several providers have thus embarked on important research and development work relating to ATM technology which provides a fast cell-switching technique (a packet may have a variable length, while a cell has a fixed size). A rapid review of these new arrivals is given in Figure 5.1.

Frame Relay is a technique for relaying frames at level 2, which is beginning to spread in the USA, as a higher-performance substitute for conventional packet switching (X.25). This standard provides an interface between private network switches and the services of service providers, and allows one to keep the architectures in place. The current speeds are now generally of the order of T1/E1 (T1/E1 denotes the throughput in USA/Europe: 1.5/2 Mbps) and the price/performance ratio is less than that for existing technologies. In fact, the simplification of the protocol considerably reduces the checks on exchanges and thus avoids all the time lost in waiting for confirmation of receipt, which is particularly appropriate for irregular traffic (for example, in bursts).

Switched Multimegabit Data Services (SMDS) is a connectionless service provided for the interconnection of local area networks. Defined by Bellcore, it is based on the cell formatting of the IEEE 802.6 standard and was designed as a WAN. Unlike DQDB, it has no isochronous capabilities and thus does not offer voice or

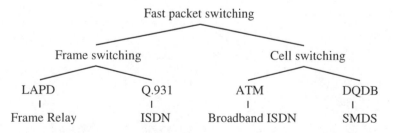

Figure 5.1   The four levels of the broadband world: concept, technologies, standards and services.

video transport. It currently operates at T1/E1 or T3/E3. Using a cell format similar to that of ATM, SMDS could become a common service for access to trunk networks.

As we have already seen, DQDB is a MAN which now has a very small market share (which is normal, since the products are not common). However, it could eventually be successful, as it uses a data format based on cells of a size compatible with that of ATM. As previously mentioned, ATM is perceived to be the technology of the future for all long distance data transmission supported by the service providers. From this point of view, DQDB could be the privileged enterprise network for interfacing with the public domain.

Those technologies using broadband are now tending to abandon time-division or frequency-division multiplexing in favor of fast cell switching, as is the case for ATM. The gain attributable to this service, which should soon be offered by telecommunication providers over large distances, will be even more perceptible for irregular traffic (such as that of local area networks) which, with ATM, will have access to a complete bandwidth when necessary (generally 2 Mbps and above) without the corresponding cost of leased lines or circuit switching. Moreover, this technology should be capable of handling all types of traffic, including digital data, voice, and video. Thus, use of ATM to link PABXs amongst themselves and to the public network may be envisaged. The ATM cell circulating on the virtual channels is short (53 bytes) and will result, if necessary, in the subdivision of frames. The speed may range from 51.8 Mbps to 155 Mbps, 622 Mbps, 2.4 Gbps, and above. Finally, ATM will form the main basic element of broadband ISDN associated with a whole range of service qualities. In the provider's network the physical layer supporting ATM is likely to be Synchronous Digital Hierarchy (SDH), and SONET in the USA. FDDI circuitry has also been proposed as a physical carrier for ATM (TAXI). Equipment in the form of patch panels, switches, brouters, and NIC cards is already commercially available.

Thus, it is foreseeable that users will install private ATM switches on their sites to interconnect the different communication-related units. ATM would then have to find its place as a technology for the site backbone network, which, in addition to integrating the existing local area networks (by consistent connection of existing concentrators and interconnection devices to one or more ATM switches), would also permit direct connection of computers requiring various speeds and provide the privileged means of attachment to a WAN. Ultimately, ATM could become the sole technology applicable at all levels, from PC connection to high-speed inter-site connection. However, even though ATM has a number of advantages, in terms of isochrony, quality of service, speed, congestion management and management, the existing base of LAN equipment could not be suddenly called into question, and the migration would have to be quite gradual.

Today's hubs are multiport, modular, multi LAN-technology repeaters (also referred to as multimedia) and multibus and multiring repeaters, to which additional functions have been added. We shall see later that active hubs or stars may already accommodate several technologies (Ethernet, Token Ring, LocalTalk, FDDI, serial links) in the same chassis. Consequently, the simple function of a repeater has been extended by dynamic switching, bridging and routing, and terminal server and gateway capabilities, with the subsequent implementation of management facilities (hardware management and traffic monitoring by a standard protocol). These chassis have thus accumulated more and more resources, bringing together the equivalent of many boxes and combining various processing faculties. These hubs continue to improve incessantly, in terms of performance, modules implementing new technologies, higher internal speeds, and the sensitivity of observation or parametrization of each port. Thus, they have become vital nodes of the network, and henceforth will take on the position of a server to the network management system (such as NetWare or LAN Manager). This is an odd event, in the sense that the server function is not located in the telecommunications area proper, but in the applications area. Under this trend, all the main elements comprising the communications infrastructure will be combined in a single device.

Another process, with its origin in a completely different field, involves the integration of these network level functions (above all, the repeater, bridge, and router stages) into tomorrow's PABX. Some major manufacturers thus see their PABXs becoming the center of global telecommunications installations. With the ability to process and transport voice, images and data in large quantities and with sufficient speed, these machines will offer multiple services which will enable them to advantageously replace the multmedia hubs and multiprotocol routers of today. Do not forget that, at the end of the day, these aspirations are consistent with the wish to circulate data on ATM circuits over large distances.

As far as protocols are concerned, high-speed networks sometimes prefer to omit certain layers of the OSI model in order to gain in performance. Thus, we are in a situation where, although the OSI reference model has finally gained in popularity among users, and is spreading among manufacturers, the constraints it imposes appear sufficiently restrictive to encourage moves towards a simplified or modified (and thus, partially non-standard) suite of protocols. The long-awaited 'all ISO' solution thus seems to be slightly compromised.

After looking at recent developments, one might detect a tendency towards an increased stratification in the telecommunications world, comparable with that which is already in place in the world of electronics and information technology. Just like the complex software systems which are now being developed in a hierarchy of modules (beginning with the operating system and moving towards the application), or the memory of an electronic system which is divided into ever smaller and faster units (tape back-up, hard disk unit, disk cache, central memory, CPU cache memory, internal registers), communication systems will be constructed from the set of all commercially available technologies by placing these one above each other (see Figure 5.2).

Thus, we foresee that tomorrow, the computing center will have an HSLAN for its supercomputers, which will be interconnected with one or more backbone MANs to meet the connection needs of servers and powerful graphics stations, these networks being in turn connected to a multitude of small LANs, feeding all the offices. Of course, ATM may act as a backbone technology before taking up a position similar to an HSLAN and ultimately becoming a commonplace LAN attachment.

LAN hardware is, therefore, becoming ever richer with concomitant overall performance benefits for all elements (repeaters, hubs and stars, switches, bridges, routers, gateways).

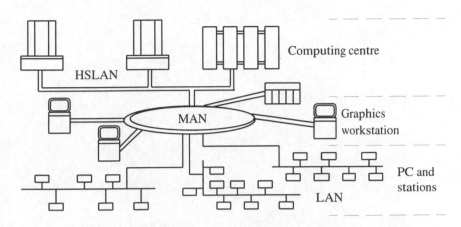

Figure 5.2 Composition of a data communication system with three layers.

PART II

Ethernet

Chapter 6

History and evolution of the standard

- Ethernet

- The IEEE 802.3 standard

- The ISO 8802-3 standard

To provide the reader with a sound introduction to the current Ethernet specifications, we shall rapidly review the stages leading from the preliminary documents to the IEEE 802.3 standard, and then to the IS 8802-3 standard.

6.1 Ethernet

In the early 1970s, Xerox was working on open office automation systems and embryos of local area networks. It developed an experimental version of Ethernet operating at 3 Mbps on 75 Ohm coaxial cable which could cover up to one kilometer, but the technologies were still evolving.

In collaboration with the Digital Equipment Corporation (DEC) and Intel, Xerox published the blue book *The Ethernet* in September 1980. This was version 1.0. The name stood for network of the ether (the passive cable, in this case). The main features of Ethernet, including the method, the topology, the physical medium and the main constraints, were already present, and the modifications which followed later only amounted to improvements of the hardware components (Figure 6.1).

In November 1982, the developers published version 2.0 (AA-K759B-TK), which was fairly complete but partially incompatible with the previous version (for example, at the transceiver level). This document covered aspects of the MAC and

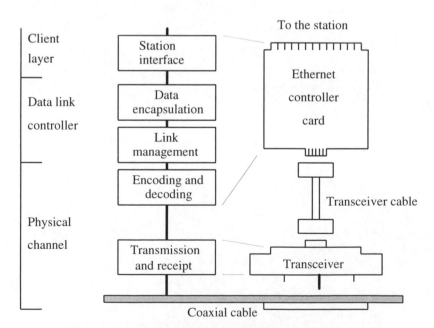

Figure 6.1   Ethernet architecture and typical implementation.

physical layers and, unlike the IEEE and ISO standards, gave a relatively clear explanation of the operation of a whole network. The document contains few acronyms and its style and structure make it very readable. The MAC layer functionality (the access method, in fact) was written in Pascal. The conceivable media at that time were coaxial cable with 50 Ohm characteristic impedance and optical fiber (which was only intended for point-to-point links between two half repeaters). The largest network could have an extent of up to 2.8 km with, at most, two repeaters on a path between two stations (the repeater between the coaxial cable and the optical fiber was considered to be a half repeater), which corresponds to three 500 m cable segments, a 1 km optical link and six 50 m drop cables ($3 \times 500 + 1000 + 6 \times 50 = 2800$ m). These specifications included the description of a means of testing equipment at the level of the lower layers, the loopback mode, which used the type field value of 9000, which has disappeared in the standard documents.

As far as the available hardware was concerned, very few manufacturers were present, but DEC and Xerox already offered satisfactory solutions. The devices were cumbersome, the performance of the controller cards was even more modest, and only the basic elements of the construction kit for networks as we know them today (such as transceivers for monoport coaxial cable and biport repeaters) were available. There was little or no hardware for test, analysis or observation, and so at that time, any form of operation, without further detailed qualification, was acceptable.

6.2 The IEEE 802.3 standard

The IEEE took over the specifications for Ethernet and reformulated them in 1985 in a standard publication, ANSI/IEEE 802.3 (ISO/DIS 8802-3). Although this document was unprepossessing, and thus initially difficult, it was complete and left no ambiguity. The parallelism with the OSI model was established, and layer 2 was split in two to insert Ethernet in the MAC and physical layers (Figure 6.2).

A certain number of modifications were introduced, but the main features were retained and equipment conforming to IEEE 802.3 was to be interoperable with that conforming to Ethernet V 2.0. The drop cable was increased from 9 to 15 wires, the entire connector technology was redefined, and, in particular, the times were recalculated and the type field replaced.

Remark   Since IEEE 802.3 is less meaningful than Ethernet, current networks – which almost all conform to the standard – have retained the original name. Similarly, in the rest of this book, we shall use IEEE 802.3 or Ethernet interchangeably when referring to current hardware, and specify Ethernet V 2.0 explicitly when referring to that particular standard.

In 1988, the IEEE published a collection of supplements to the IEEE 802.3 standard, which correspond to extensions, choices of other media, or other available speeds and technologies. As we shall see below, these complementary specifications were to become more or less important with time.

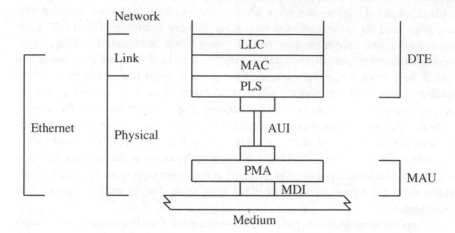

DTE: Data Terminal Equipment
LLC: Logical Link Control
MAC: Medium Access Control
PLS: Physical Layer Signaling
AUI: Attachment Unit Interface
MAU: Medium Attachment Unit
PMA: Physical Medium Attachment
MDI: Medium Dependent Interface

Figure 6.2   Decomposition of Ethernet into sublayers and relative positions in the OSI model.

Finally, ISO standardized the IEEE document in February 1989, incorporating thin coaxial cable (10base2 or IEEE 802.3a) as the medium. Thus, Ethernet reached the end of its evolution, at least as far as the basic technical specifications with the standard media are concerned, despite the progress which had taken place since its conception which might have permitted regular improvements to the performance of such a network. This clearly illustrates the advantages and disadvantages of standardization, which ensures compatibility for the medium term, albeit based on a technology which is already aging.

The differences between Ethernet V 2.0 and IEEE 802.3

The transition from Ethernet to IEEE 802.3 required a number of modifications, which should be recorded, even though they were minor and do not hinder compatibility.

The main difference lies in the fact that the third MAC field of the frame, the type field, changed its meaning and became a length field. The addresses have a second special Individual/Universal bit following the Unicast/Multicast bit.

Moreover, the addresses may theoretically have 16 or 48 bits, rather than just 48. The pin diagram for the drop cable is supplemented by an additional pair: Control Out (very rarely used) and by an individual screening per pair.

The maximum propagation time for a network was slightly increased, to be on the safe side and in order to impose weaker constraints on the hardware, and rose from a round-trip delay (RTD) of 46.38 μs to 49.9 μs. A test signal for the collision pair of the AUI cable was added, namely the SQE test which passes from the transceiver to the interface card. The transceiver is no longer necessarily connected to the cable by branching and may now be connected using type N screw connectors.

The supplements to IEEE 802.3

The IEEE 802 standards introduced a particular notation, whereby a technology is denoted by the maximum speed, the modulation type and the segment length. For example, Ethernet as we have described it above is denoted by 10base5, signifying that it operates at 10 Mbps in baseband with segments of a maximum length of 500 m (5 × 100). Similarly, Ethernet on thin cable is denoted by 10base2, signifying that the cable segments are limited to a length of 185 meters (~2 × 100).

Several supplements to IEEE 802.3 have been issued or are in hand (a, b, c, d, and so on). They are intended to supplement the basic document with implementations on other media or with special information. They are designed for insertion in the standard, to which they add certain paragraphs or replace certain chapters with new ones. The numbers of the sections (which correspond to chapters) are thus consistent with the IEEE 802.3 and IS 8802-3 documents. We shall review the main features of these supplements in order. We include technical details which readers may return to after reading the paragraphs describing the operation of each element.

Supplement IEEE 802.3a   Also called 10base2, Thinnet, Thin Ethernet or Cheapernet. This adaptation was originally introduced by the InterLAN company.

The supplement describes the use of thin coaxial cable of the RG58 type with BNC connectors. The length of a thin cable is limited to 185 meters, and with these less cumbersome connectors the transceivers can be more easily incorporated in the connector interfaces. On its own, the 10base2 type of medium retains all the main features of Ethernet 10base5 (topology, number of segments, electrical levels, frame structures, and so on). However, the number of connections per segment decreases to 30 and the distance between these connections must be greater than 50 cm.

This technique is used widely, since it is very practical and reasonably priced, therefore, in what follows, the main constraints on Ethernet (10base5) will also be given for 10base2. Finally, we note that supplement IEEE 802.3a has been incorporated in the IS 8802-3 standard (section 10).

Supplement IEEE 802.3b   Also called 10broad36, that is, 10 Mbps in broadband, with maximal distances of 3.6 km per segment.

The medium is CATV-type coaxial cable with 75 Ohm characteristic impedance. The code is Differential Phase-Shift Keying (DPSK). The topology uses single or double accesses to the cable (Figure 6.3). In the first case, a frequency converter is placed at the end, which requires emission and reception at different carrier frequencies at the point of access. In the second case, the cable is looped at one end and access is via the two segments with the same carrier frequency for a single MAU. In the first case, the carrier frequencies range from 43 MHz to 73 MHz with a spacing of 6 MHz and from 43 MHz to 265 MHz in the second case.

It is apparent that this is a (rare) implementation of Ethernet which can be used to mix several data communication channels with serial links or video on a single cable, using frequency-division multiplexing.

Supplements IEEE 802.3c and d These supplements give a more detailed specification of the characteristics of the repeater in a network of type 10base5 or 10base2 and of the characteristics of FOIRL-type optical links (fiber optic inter-repeater link).

The repeater interconnects the cable segments by regenerating the signals, extending the fragments (frame fragments of less than 96 bits may result from a collision), completing the preamble to 56 bits and propagating collisions by emitting Jam. It can also interrupt an excessively long emission or deactivate a port judged to be a regular source of faults. The repeater is called a repeater set when it incorporates the transceivers (of type 10base5, 10base2 or FOIRL). A full description of how it operates is given in Section 10.6.

The FOIRL link is a point-to-point optical link, preferably reserved for the interconnection of two repeaters. The recommended fiber is graded-index multimode silica fiber with a 62.5 ± 3 μm core and a 125 ± 3 μm sheath. The numerical aperture should be 0.275 ± 0.015 (corresponding to IEC 793-2 type A1b). The recommended connector technology is of the FSMA type (IEC 874-2) with an attenuation of at

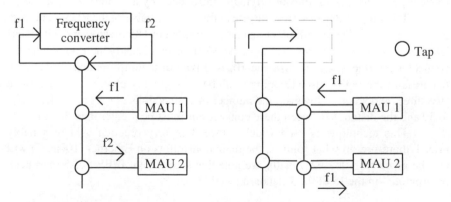

Figure 6.3 Example of emission on a system with broadband coaxial cable (single and double access).

most 2.5 dB per connector pair. Other fiber types are also provided for, including the 50/125 μm, the 85/125 μm and the 100/140 μm. The wavelength at which these transceivers (called fiber optic media access units – FOMAU) operate is 850 nm (actually, between 790 nm and 860 nm). At this frequency, the attenuation of the fiber should be limited to 4 dB/km and to 8 dB over the whole link, where the bandwidth should be greater than 150 MHz per km. An optical power of 9 dB for a complete link is budgeted for, together with a maximum time of 500 ns (the longest link which can be implemented is less than or equal to 1 km). The optical transceiver has a crossing delay of 3.5 bit times in each direction for a valid signal and 3.5 bit times for collision detection. An idle signal (inactivity) is defined for the FOMAU, consisting of periodic pulses (short signals of one or two oscillations) with a frequency of 1 MHz (+25%, −15%), which is emitted when there is no traffic.

Supplement IEEE 802.3e   Also called 1base5, or StarLAN, this is a point-to-point method offering a speed of 1 Mbps on twisted pair. It currently uses a star topology (in which the multiport repeater is at the center; it is called the hub and incorporates built-in transceivers).

The unshielded twisted pair is of the telephone-pair type, comprising conductors with a diameter from 0.4 mm to 0.6 mm. It has a characteristic impedance of 100 ±15 Ohm and a maximum attenuation of 6.5 dB at 1 MHz. The physical copper link between the transceiver and hub (or multiport repeater) may extend to 250 meters (the 5 of 10base5 is not very explicit here, because one has to consider the distance between two network attachment points, that is, two transceivers: $500 = 5 \times 100$ m), and the optical links may extend to 4 km. Five storeys of hubs may be installed in a cascade. The electrical levels lie between 2 and 3.65 V. There is an *idle* signal which occupies the line continuously during silences and alerts the hub to the presence of the transceiver. Manchester code violation signals (no change in level after the clock pulse) are used to transmit a notification of the presence of a collision or the idle signal. The connector technology is of the RJ45 type (ISO 8877) and only pins 1, 2, 3, and 6 are used (or two pairs) in unidirectional transmission (Figure 6.4).

This version of Ethernet, which was originally developed by AT&T, has now been abandoned in favor of 10baseT. Since the rate in 1base5 is a factor of ten less than that of Ethernet, there is no direct compatibility, but we shall see that there are (MAC level) bridges which can be used to link a 1base5 network and a 10base5 or 10base2 network. The frame structure remains identical in all cases.

Supplement IEEE 802.3g   This supplement provides a description of the methodology and implementation of conformance tests of the drop cables. This supplement, which dates from 1991, defines an abstract method for testing the conformance of different types of AUI cable.

Supplement IEEE 802.3h   Supplement IEEE 802.3h, Layer Management, dates from 1991 and defines certain possibilities for monitoring or controlling the physical, MAC and LLC layers of a CSMA/CD network by adjoining a Layer Management Entity (LME) to each of these three functional blocks.

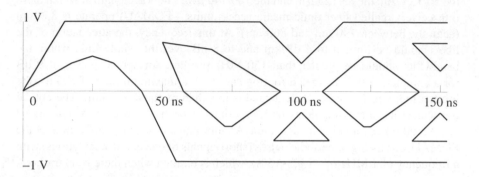

Figure 6.4 Approximate template of a Manchester signal on twisted pair.

These entities correspond with the System Management Application Entity (SMAE) via Layer Management Interfaces (LMI). As far as the MAC level is concerned, signals such as the emission control (inhibition of all transmission), the change of MAC address, the acceptance of frames destined for another machine, the deactivation of the MAC layer, the management of recognized (and accepted), group addresses and the rejection (non reading) of multicast frames are defined there. This supplement replaces a part of Chapter 5 left empty in the IS 8802-3 standard.

Supplement IEEE 802.3i   This fairly recent supplement defines the 10baseT (T for twisted pair) part, that is, the possibility of constructing an Ethernet-type network on an unshielded twisted-pair medium.

Since the physical carrier is the same as that of 1base5, 10baseT is also commonly referred to as StarLAN 10 Mbps. Because the topology is a star, the accesses to the hub are made from point to point, and the links can be viewed as IRL. Thus, it is possible to cascade two levels of hubs. The cable segments have a maximum recommended length of 100 meters, a characteristic impedance of 85 to 111 Ohm between 5 and 10 MHz, a maximum delay of 1 μs and an attenuation of less than 11.5 dB from 5 to 10 MHz. The conductors may have a diameter from 0.4 to 0.6 mm (26 AWG to 22 AWG). The connector technology is still of type RJ45 (IS 8877 standardized by ISO) with the two pairs connected to the contacts: 1 and 2 for the transmission and 3 and 6 for receipt. Since the cabling is straight, crossover takes place inside the hub. The electrical data signals are between ±0.7 and 1 V. An idle signal is used to validate the receiving pair on each port of the hub and on each transceiver. This is called LinkIntegrityTest and consists of periodic pulses formed from a single oscillation. Supplement i adds Chapters 13 and 14 to IS 8802-3 (which originally only had 12 chapters).

We note that the limitation of the segment length to 100 meters is a recommendation, but is not in itself a criterion, since it has to be determined from a consideration of the time budget and the attenuation of the link. Some manufacturers offer solutions capable of covering 250 m or more.

Supplement IEEE 802.3j   Better known as 10baseF (F for fiber optic), this has been an IEEE 802.3 standard since 1993. This section is very detailed and readers are advised to return to it after reading about certain more recent aspects of Ethernet, described later.

10baseF covers three subjects: passive asynchronous optical networks (or 10baseFP, where P denotes passive star, Section 16); active synchronous optical networks (10baseFB, B for backbone, Section 17), and the redefinition of FOIRL with more interesting capabilities (10baseFL, Section 18). These three types of optical network define different, incompatible technologies, to meet different requirements. Given the range of aspects covered by this supplement to IEEE 802.3, the document includes the redefinition of several points relating to the operation of a network. Thus, it constitutes an important extension for Ethernet. The new Section 15 covers the elements common to the three applications of type 10baseF, including the specification of the wavelength at which emitters operate at 850 nm (between 800 and 910 nm), the spectral width (less than 75 nm) and the templates of the optical signals for the synchronous and asynchronous cases. The recommended type of optical fiber is still the 62.5 μm, with a numerical aperture of 0.275. The attenuation is less than 3.75 dB/km (a value of 3.5 dB/km is still under discussion) and the bandwidth is at least 160 MHz per km. The connector technology is now of the ST type (IEC 86B, from AT&T) with a maximum insertion loss of 1 dB.

Fibers other than the 62.5/125 μm are authorized and the 10baseF standard includes a table of the supplementary attenuations due to the use of these with the end machines specified for the 62.5/125 μm cable.

10baseFP defines an optical network technology based on a star topology, with passive stars. We shall see later that the passive star consists solely of optical fibers fused together. For preference, the star consists of 62.5 μm fiber, but 50/125 μm fiber is also an alternative. It is connected to segments with transceivers at their ends. The cable segments from the transceivers to the star should not be longer than 500 m. The star may have up to 33 ports (each port includes a connector on input and a connector on output) or 17 ports for 50/125 μm. The attenuation due to a star between an input port and an output port should be between 16 dB and 20 dB.

Table 6.1   Additional loss of optical power for different types of fiber.

Diameters μm Core/Sheath	Numerical aperture	Loss on emission dB	Loss on receipt dB	Total loss dB
50/125	0.2	5.7	0	5.7
50/125	0.21	5.2	0	5.2
50/125	0.22	4.8	0	4.8
85/125	0.26	1.6	2.6	5.2
100/140	0.29	0.5	4.5	5

The attenuation on a link, from transceiver to transceiver, including the passive star, should be less than 26 dB, measured with a signal with a wavelength of 850 nm and a spectral width of 75 nm. The loss of power suffered by a signal on reflection on a connector should be greater than 25 dB. The crossing delays for a transceiver are 3.5 bit times for emission and 2.5 bit times for reception. The delay in detecting a collision is 3.5 bit times. Since the star has no electronic components (the signal is not processed there, only split), its crossing delay is essentially zero. Like the other supplements, 10baseFP tends to standardize a technology which is already in the market place and, even, relatively old. The passive optical implementations have not always been very convincing to date, since they do not ensure exhaustive collision detection (provided for in CSMA/CD); the tendency has been to reserve them for situations in which only they are suitable, for example, in a very disturbed electromagnetic environment, or when the star set-up has no electrical power.

10baseFB (B for backbone), called 10baseFA in earlier drafts, defines a new technology for Ethernet, namely synchronous communications. It is notable that this supplement goes beyond the usual framework, in that the transmission mode is no longer a simple adaptation of the original one specified for coaxial cable segments on point-to-point links.

Taking advantage of the point-to-point topology, the IEEE decided to choose a transmission mode which would ensure that no bits were lost at the start of reception. In asynchronous mode the receiver has no knowledge of the emitter's clock and has to begin by synchronizing itself on the received signal, which inevitably leads to the loss of a number of the leading bits; however, in synchronous mode the receiver is always synchronized with the only possible emitter, situated opposite it. This means that there is no longer any need for a clock signal preceding the frame (thus, the preamble loses its main function) and the receiver can read the message immediately with no bits lost. This gain gets around the constraint of the maximum number of repeaters on a path and the size of the network is no longer limited by the round-trip delay, which is unchanged. The transceiver then becomes the entry (or exit) point separating the asynchronous world (from the drop cable) and the synchronous world (the star or the group of synchronous stars).

More specifically, the medium is always occupied either by a signal denoting the state (wait, jabber, incorrect receipt) or by data (frames). Code violations of the Manchester code (code rule violation: CRV) are used to form the non-data signals. For example, the synchronous idle is a signal in the 2.5 MHz frequency slot and the remote fault (RF) has a frequency of 1.667 MHz. The remote fault signal covers the following three problems: jabber received, insufficient optical power, and invalid data. A link has a maximum length of 2 km and must have an end-to-end attenuation less than 12.5 dB. The maximum crossing delay for the transceiver is 2 bit times for emission and receipt; collision detection (presence of signals being emitted and received simultaneously) should be less than 3.5 bit times. However, the advantage of the synchronous mode accrues principally from the gains achieved at the level of the repetition stage. When the latter includes synchronous built-in transceivers, it is limited to 2 bit times plus the delay of 1 bit time on receipt and on emission in the transceivers.

Some drafts showed a desire to give the synchronous active star at least two ports compatible with the asynchronous FOIRL links. This should then avoid any communication in the case of improper connection of FOIRL transceivers on synchronous ports.

10baseFL, called 10baseFF in earlier drafts, is a new FOIRL with enhanced performance, which still uses active, asynchronous point-to-point links, but is upwards compatible. Like FOIRL, 10baseFL can be used to enable two transceivers opposite each other to intercommunicate (see Figure 6.5) or to construct a star topology around a multiport repeater, incorporating several optical transceivers. The optical power budget rises from 9 dB to 12.5 dB and the maximum length of a link increases to 2 km. On the other hand, the crossing delay for an optical transceiver is 5 bit times (still identical in both directions), while the collision detection delay remains 3.5 bit times.

Supplement IEEE 802.3k   Dating from 1992, this deals with baseband repeaters and corresponds to section 19 of the standard.

Supplement IEEE 802.3l   Supplement IEEE 802.3l, standardized in 1992, describes the conformance testing methods (Protocol Implementation Conformance Statement: PICS Proforma) for 10baseT transceivers.

Supplements IEEE 802.3p and q   Supplements IEEE 802.3p and q, defined in 1993, defined Guidelines for the Development of Managed Objects (GDMO), the format of managed objects, and the management layer for 10 Mbps transceivers, which corresponds to Sections 5 and 20 of the standard. These objects, or variables, belong to specific MIB, under the branches 'csmalayermgt' and 'mauMgt' defined for CMIP. These elements are also associated with the available types of action: Get and/or Set.

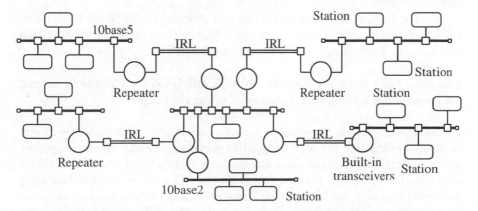

Figure 6.5   Example of an extensive Ethernet network incorporating coaxial cables and FOIRL links.

Supplements IEEE 802.3u   Better known as 100baseT or Fast Ethernet, this is a standard which describes a version of Ethernet on twisted pair and optical fiber operating at 100 Mbps. This technology is described in greater depth in Chapter 14. It covers Sections 21 to 30, which correspond to the following topics:

- Section 21: introduction to 100 Mbps networks.
- Section 22: reconciliation sublayer and MII.
- Section 23: 100baseT4, which is based on four UTPs of category 3, 4 or 5.
- Section 24: 100baseX, which uses the physical level of FDDI.
- Section 25: 100baseTX which is based on two STPs or UTPs of category 5.
- Section 26: 100baseFX which is based on two multimode optical fibers.
- Section 27: 100 Mbps repeater, specifications and functions.
- Section 28: Auto-negotiation at 10 and 100 Mbps.
- Section 29: 100 Mbps networks and characteristics.
- Section 30: Management at 10 and 100 Mbps.

The IEEE 802.1D standard

The IEEE 802.1D standard is not solely concerned with Ethernet networks, otherwise it would have been handled by the IEEE 802.3 working group, but also deals with the interconnection of local area networks of the IEEE 802 type by MAC level bridges.

As for the other standards, the hardware was already in existence before this document; this hardware was generally proprietary, but functioned without problems in a heterogeneous environment. The effect of the standard was to fix certain values and formats which had been freely implemented up to then. From then on, bridges conforming to IEEE 802.1D would work in cooperation and the automatic management of the set of all bridges interlinking the networks would be more consistent.

The IEEE 802.1D standard, which was taken up by the ISO in IS 10038 in 1993, therefore incorporates the description of Source-Routing-type bridging, which is inherent to Token Ring and, to a lesser extent, to FDDI.

Remark   For a better understanding of IEEE 802.1D, readers should try to read this paragraph in parallel with that on MAC bridges in Chapter 11.

The standard defines the content of the packets circulating between the bridge chosen as the root bridge and the other bridges (the packets are configuration or topology change BridgePDUs), and includes specifications relating to the behavior of bridges respecting the Spanning Tree Protocol (STP). The STP is the protocol that manages the global topology resulting from the interconnection of the networks, including loop detection and the choice of the fastest paths. This IEEE standard includes the lifetime of the entries in the learning table (300 seconds), the group address of the bridges (01-80-C2-00-00-00), the STP LSAP (01000010: 42 in hexadecimal), and the maximum diameter in terms of bridges (maximum number of bridges between two stations: 7). It also includes the maximum delay in crossing a bridge (one second, with subsequent deletion of the frame), the maximum delay in the transmission of a BPDU (one second after detection of the requirement) and an overestimate of the increment in the maximum age of the message. In particular, as far as the operation of the STP is concerned, the standard includes the hello time (2 seconds), the maximum age attainable by a BPDU from its emission (20 seconds), the time in retransmission mode (15 seconds), and the minimum time a BPDU is retained. The priority of the bridge should be set between 0 and 65535, with 32768 as the default value; that of a bridge should be between 0 and 255 (default 128) and the cost of a path to the root should lie between 1 and 65535. We note that most numerical values have recommended or default values, accompanied by an indication of the absolute maximum acceptable value, which is often very much greater. The procedures for this standard are written in C (ANSI X3.159).

The 802.1 committee is also working on a draft concerning remote bridges, which should become the standard IEEE 802.1G. This includes the definition of certain values of the Organizationally Unique Identifier (OUI) and Protocol Identification (PID) fields of the SNAP. Thus, the OUI and the PID, in hexadecimal, corresponding to different types of network can be seen in Table 6.2.

Table 6.2   Description of the LAN type by the SNAP fields.

Type of network	OUI	PID
IEEE 802.3 (CSMA/CD)	00-80-C2	00-01
IEEE 802.4 (Token Bus)	00-80-C2	00-02
IEEE 802.5 (Token Ring)	00-80-C2	00-03
ANSI X3T9.5 (FDDI)	00-80-C2	00-04
IEEE 802.6 (DQDB)	00-80-C2	00-05
IEEE 802.9	00-80-C2	00-06

6.3 The ISO 8802-3 standard

The standardization dates from February 1989, which is some time after the appearance of Ethernet V 2.0, and which shows that an effective standardization may be belated and thus late in reaching an already very advanced market place. A new edition of IS 8802-3 was published in 1993 which integrates the IEEE 802.3 Supplements a, b, c, d, e, h and i.

Furthermore, the original ISO document did not incorporate all the existing supplements at that time, since only 10base2 occupies the relevant section (number

10), while other chapters remain open for study, untouched or incomplete. This is the case for Section 5 (network management), Section 9 (repeater and FOIRL), Section 11 (specification of broadband media), Section 12 (specification of 1base5 type), and many others subsequently.

Chapter 7

Access method

- The CSMA/CD principle

- Operation of the MAC

The access method is the main procedure for which the MAC layer is responsible. Ethernet is based on CSMA/CD, which is described in Pascal in the standard and, as we shall see, is relatively simple.

7.1 The CSMA/CD principle

The CSMA/CD method is a particular version of the Aloha type method, in which every emitter is free to manage its emissions as a function of its needs and the availability of the medium.

When there is no traffic to transmit, the station remains silent and listens in to (or receives) the packets circulating on the cable. On a cable, this information may circulate in either direction and a machine has no way of determining this direction; however, that is not important.

When the machine needs to talk (that is, to emit one or more packets), it will act independently of the others because it knows nothing about them, except that when it senses a frame then one of them must be emitting. Since each machine has the possibility of beginning a transmission autonomously at any time, the access method is distributed and is said to be a Multiple Access (MA) method. Thus, the machine observes the medium in an attempt to detect a carrier (carrier sense, CS). If no frames are in transit it does not find the carrier. It then deduces that the medium is free and that it can therefore start to talk without interrupting anything. Thus, it sends it packets on the physical carrier, but continues to listen for the result of its emission for some time, in order to check that no other machine has behaved in the same way as itself at the same time.

In fact, two different stations may start to talk simultaneously, after each has checked immediately beforehand that no-one is talking. In this case, the signals interfere and are lost to everyone. For an access method with collision detection, a machine is able to detect a contention problem at the time it emits and to stop with the intention of resending its packet later when it again has the right to talk. To minimize the risk of encountering a second collision with the same machine, each waits for a random delay period before attempting to emit again. This reduces the probability of successive collisions between a pair of stations. However, so as not to saturate a network which is already heavily loaded, the machine will not attempt indefinitely to retransmit a packet if, on every attempt, it finds itself in collision with another. After a certain number of fruitless attempts, the packet is deleted, which means that it does not cause the network to collapse (by not overloading it further); this action tells the higher layers that there is a problem, since the exchange was perturbed by the loss of a message.

Readers will have noticed that this method has a weakness when the traffic is too heavy. The number of collisions increases with the load, and the effective bandwidth is correspondingly reduced further. Eventually, if the number of packets to be transmitted is actually too large, a state of complete blockage of the network, with a drastic fall in performance, might be reached.

7.2 Operation of the MAC

The function of the MAC layer is to manage the CSMA/CD and to communicate with the layer above to proffer its services. Thus, the MAC must be able to format the data packets into frames, recognize its address in the destination field and check the validity of frames received.

MAC encapsulates the information from the level above in a frame, by placing the packet that it is asked to transmit in the frame's data field. It fills the other MAC fields (which we shall discuss in detail later) using information accompanying the data. Thus, it supplements the physical address of the destination station with the layer 3 information, including the source address relative to the physical address of its own connector, the type (with an identification of the layer for which it is working) or the length (counting the number of bytes which are entrusted to it). Finally, it calculates the elaborate parity control field for the Cyclic Redundancy Check (CRC) and ends the frame.

Figure 7.1, which is taken from the standard, shows the main stages in the emission of a frame (but not how it is constituted). For a more complete description of all the states, readers should refer to Section 9.3 which explains the collision phenomenon in detail. Note that because the response to a test shown in an oval (for example, Deferred?) is binary (yes or no), sometimes only one option is shown, since the other can be deduced logically.

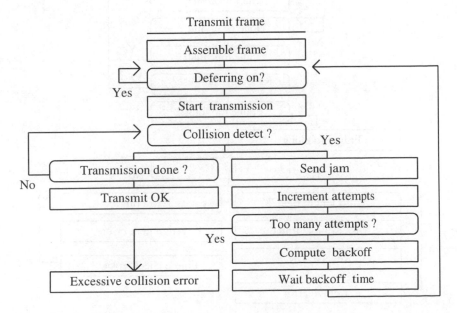

Figure 7.1 Block diagram of the emission of a frame.

On receipt a check is made to verify that the bit sequence can form a correct frame. Several criteria are used for this. The total number of bits should not be too small, otherwise it would be impossible to reconstitute all the fields of a complete frame. The destination address should be the physical address of the station, or should relate to a group of which the station is a member. The frame should not be too long, otherwise it would infringe a basic rule of Ethernet and could not be valid. The calculation of the parity control for the fields received should give a result identical to the value transported by the frame, otherwise there is a bit error (wrongly transmitted or wrongly received). The total number of bits received should be divisible by eight, so as to give an integral number of bytes, otherwise the reconstituted frame is invalid, since at least one of its fields has one or more bits too many (too few).

We shall see later that IEEE 802.3 introduced a length field into the frame by replacing the type field. This explains the presence of the additional test shown in Figure 7.2. In fact, this field provides additional information about the consistency of the frame received.

We note that the CSMA/CD method, despite its procedures for retrial on collision and its tendency to slow down all the emissions on a heavily loaded

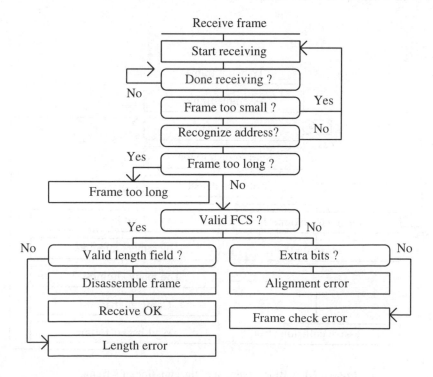

Figure 7.2 Block diagram of the receipt of a frame.

network, does not guarantee a minimum waiting time for the emission of a frame. In fact, the transmission of a frame may be delayed because the medium is busy at the time the MAC layer tries to send it, or because a collision occurred at the time of emission and a fresh attempt is needed. Thus, the more the traffic on the network increases, the more the average waiting time before the correct transmission of a frame increases (and this exponentially). The delay in emission may become unacceptable when the network is about to collapse. Other methods derived from CSMA, such as CSMA/DCR (deterministic collision resolution) can guarantee a limit on the delay prior to emission. In the case of CSMA/DCR, this is made possible by a deterministic, rather than probabilistic, conflict resolution procedure. The fact that the medium access time is not bounded for Ethernet may turn out to be very restrictive for real-time applications.

Chapter 8

Physical layer

The physical layer defines all the electrical and mechanical parameters relating to the communication medium. It also describes the elements responsible for the transmission, receipt, and regeneration of signals on the medium (transceivers and repeaters). For each type of element, a specification of its action, its effect, its encoding, and the procedures it uses is given.

For example, transceivers on coaxial cables should be able to read and write on a single pair of electrical conductors and detect the superposition of signals on the bus, while at the same time disturbing the impedance of the medium to which they are attached as little as possible. Other types of transceiver operating on point-to-point links are not subject to the same constraints, since the collision then corresponds to a situation of simultaneous emission and reception (easier to detect) and an imperfect adaptation does not necessarily harm the communication.

The code used by baseband Ethernet is always of the Manchester type, whether on coaxial cable, twisted pair, fiber optic cable or the AUI cable. However, the electrical levels are different. In the first case, the continuous component is non-zero and the signal varies between 0 and -2 V, in the second case the signal is symmetric and varies between ± 1 V.

As we have already seen, the Manchester code carries a polarity (the 1 and the 0 are distinguished by the direction of the edge), which implies that care must be taken not to invert the two conductors. This is easy when working on a coaxial cable (where the pair is naturally asymmetric), but is less straightforward for symmetric twisted pairs.

The characteristics of the electrical signals are defined later, together with the characteristics of transceivers, and the elements responsible for emission and receipt of the physical signals.

Generally, the power spectrum of Ethernet signals has its main frequency peaks between 5 and 10 MHz (with harmonics on each side). The figures for the attenuation on the media are therefore given for the frequency range from 5 to 10 MHz.

On optical fiber, the signals are encoded using the Manchester code, but in the case of 10baseFP (passive) and 10baseFB (active synchronous), code violations are used to transmit certain fields. Thus, in passive technology, correct receipt of the start of a frame is unambiguously detected using a single clock time, without transition. In synchronous optical technology, waiting-state (idle, free) and remote-fault indications are communicated by periodic sequences of code violations over four or six clock periods.

Figure 8.1 shows the template of the optical signals. Note that the template for 10baseFP signals is stricter, its margins being reduced by approximately one half.

A basic unit of time is often used in the Ethernet standards, namely the bit time, which represents the delay equivalent to the emission of a bit, or $0.1 \, \mu s = 100$ ns (at 10 Mbps). Another time unit is the slot time, which is the minimum duration of a valid frame (512 bits). This is also used to measure other delays and timers (see the backoff algorithm in Section 9.3).

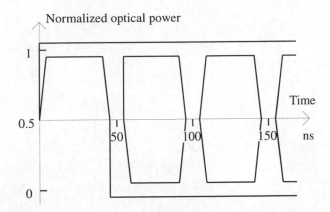

Figure 8.1   Template of optical signals for 10baseFB and 10baseFL.

Chapter 9

Packet formatting and errors

- The frame

- Defective frames

- Collision

- The idle signal

The data circulating on an Ethernet network is encapsulated in an entity called a frame. When various problems arise on the network (such as collisions), the resulting packet fragments may no longer possess the characteristics of a valid signal; these are errors.

9.1 The frame

The frame is the elementary structure used to circulate data on the network. It is defined at the MAC level and follows a number of rules. For example, the fields constituting it identify the emitting station, the destination station, and the type of data transported (indicated by the level 3 protocol) (Figure 9.1). It also has an elaborate parity control which is located in the last four bytes of the frame.

Finally, the minimum and maximum lengths are regulated, firstly by the need to always be able to detect collisions, and secondly, by the desire not to transfer power to a single machine for too long a period.

The transmission is in serial mode on the medium and the useful data, which is usually represented in the form of 8-bit bytes, has to be arranged in a bit sequence. The bytes are transmitted in order, that is, respecting the ordering used by the layer above. The bits of each byte are transmitted beginning with the least-significant bit (0 or 1) and ending with the most-significant bit (factor of $128 = 2^7$).

The preamble

In reality, the preamble precedes the frame and allows the receiver's clock to synchronize itself with that of the emitter (do not forget that the transmission mode is asynchronous). It is sent to stabilize the decoding circuits and, therefore, it is envisaged that part of the preamble may be lost. Thus, it is considered normal for the first bits (up to 18 bits) not to reach the layer above (MAC layer).

The preamble may be considered to be at the physical level, while the other fields of the frame emanate from the MAC layer. The preamble consists of a sequence of successive 1s and 0s, and thus it does not contain any specific information. It can be decomposed into two subfields: a first of 56 bits in length, comprising alternating 1s and 0s, followed by a subfield called the Starting Frame Delimiter (SFD), which is eight bits long and continues the preceding sequence, except that the very last bit is set to 1. This double 1 tells the receiver that the actual frame is about to start and

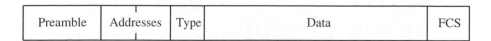

Figure 9.1   The different fields of the Ethernet frame.

that the subsequent bits therefore comprise significant fields.

We note one further detail: if a collision is detected during the emission of the preamble, the emitting station should, nevertheless, continue to transmit the complete preamble.

In conclusion, a representation of the complete preamble, transmitted from left to right, is shown below:

10101010	10101010	10101010	10101010	10101010	10101010	10101010	10101011 SFD

MAC addresses

The frame includes two addresses: that of the addressee and the emitter. The destination address is transmitted first, followed by the source address (Figure 9.2). The Ethernet addresses are represented conventionally in hexadecimal, with a hyphen separating each of the six bytes.

The reason for the existence of these addresses is, of course, to enable the machine targeted by the message to recognize itself as the addressee and to identify the machine which generated the frame circulating on the network. The two addresses have similar structures. They are six bytes long with, for IEEE 802.3, a possibility of using a two byte reduced format (which is very rare). The first three bytes identify the manufacturer of the connector card (and thus often of the machine) in a one-to-one fashion. The entries for these bytes are allocated to the manufacturers by a unique worldwide organization (in this case, the IEEE), which ensures the consistency of the system. The following three bytes give this manufacturer's number for the connector card ($256^3 = 16.78$ million possibilities). Thus, the whole forms a unique number for each interface card and, by the same token, for each machine with an Ethernet card.

In fact, what we have just seen is not really applicable when a frame has to be sent to a single machine, since Ethernet also allows one to reach several targets simultaneously, by what is known as diffusion. There is a choice of emitting to everyone (general diffusion or *broadcast*) or to a group of stations (*multicast*). The broadcast destination address is FF-FF-FF-FF-FF-FF in hexadecimal (which corresponds to a sequence of 1s in binary). The group address has the property that the first bit transmitted is set to 1 (or the first byte is odd), while the other bits of the

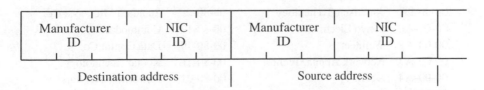

Figure 9.2   Position and partitioning of the two MAC addresses.

Table 9.1 List of prefixes for different manufacturers.

00-00-0C	Cisco	00-00-A7	Network Comput. Dev.
00-00-0E	Fujitsu	00-00-A9	Network Systems
00-00-0F	NeXT	00-00-AA	Xerox
00-00-10	Sytek	00-00-B0	RAD Network Devices
00-00-15	Datapoint Co.	00-00-B3	CLIMLinc
00-00-1B	Novell	00-00-B5	Datability
00-00-1D	Cabletron	00-00-B7	Dove
00-00-20	Data Industrier AB	00-00-BB	TRI Data
00-00-22	Visual Technology	00-00-BC	Allen-Bradley
00-00-2A	TRW	00-00-C0	Western Digital/SMC
00-00-32	GPT Limited (GEC)	00-00-C5	Farallon
00-00-44	Castelle	00-00-C6	HP I.N.O/Eon Systems
00-00-46	ISC-Bunker Ramo	00-00-C8	Altos
00-00-4F	Logicraft	00-00-C9	Emulex
00-00-5A	S & Koch	00-00-D7	Dartmouth College
00-00-5D	RCE	00-00-D8	Novell (~1987)
00-00-5E	US DoD (IANA)	00-00-DB	British Telecom
00-00-62	Honeywell	00-00-DD	Gould
00-00-65	Network General	00-00-DE	Unigraph
00-00-69	Concord Communicat.	00-00-E2	Acer Counterpoint
00-00-6B	MIPS	00-00-E5	Sigmex
00-00-6E	Artisoft	00-00-E8	Accton Technology Cor
00-00-6F	Madge	00-00-EF	Atlantec
00-00-77	Interphase	00-00-F0	Samsung
00-00-7A	Ardent	00-00-F3	Gandalf Data Limited
00-00-7B	Research Machines	00-00-F4	Allied Telesis Inc
00-00-80	Dataco	00-00-FD	High Level Hardware
00-00-81	Synoptics	00-01-02	BBN
00-00-84	ADI System Inc.	00-01-63	National Datacom Corp
00-00-86	Megahertz Co.	00-01-68	Wandel & Goltermann
00-00-89	Cayman Syst Gatorbox	00-17-00	Kabel
00-00-93	Proteon	00-20-AF	3Com
00-00-94	Asante	00-40-0D	LANNET
00-00-95	Sony/Tektronix	00-40-C8	Milan Technology Corp
00-00-98	CrossComm	00-60-8C	3Com
00-00-9F	Ameristar Technology	00-80-0F	Standard Microsyst Cor
00-00-A0	Sanyo Electronics	00-80-10	Commodore
00-00-A2	Wellfleet	00-80-19	Data Comm Co.
00-00-A3	Network Applic. Techn.	00-80-1B	Kodiak Technology
00-00-A4	Acorn	00-80-21	Newbridge Networks C
00-00-A5	Compatible Syst. Corp.	00-80-29	Microdyne Corporation
00-00-A6	Network General	00-80-2B	IMAC

Table 9.1   (cont.)

00-80-2D	Xylogics		08-00-20	Sun
00-80-2E	Plexcom Inc		08-00-22	NBI
00-80-34	SMT-Goupil		08-00-23	Matsushita Denso
00-80-51	ADC Fibermux		08-00-25	Control Data Corp.
00-80-5C	Agilis		08-00-26	Norsk Data
00-80-64	Wyse Tech/Link Tech		08-00-27	PCS Computer Systems
00-80-7C	FiberCom		08-00-28	Texas Instruments
00-80-87	Okidata		08-00-2B	Digital Equipment
00-80-8C	Frontier Software Devel		08-00-2E	Metaphor
00-80-A1	Microtest		08-00-2F	Prime
00-80-B2	Network Equipm. Tech.		08-00-36	Intergraph
00-80-C2	IEEE 802.1		08-00-37	Fujitsu-Xerox
00-80-C7	Xircom		08-00-38	Bull
00-80-C8	D-Link/Solectek		08-00-39	Spider Systems
00-80-D3	Shiva Corporation		08-00-3E	Motorola
00-80-D8	Network Peripherals		08-00-41	Digital Com. Associates
00-AA-00	Intel		08-00-44	DAVID Systems Inc.
00-DD-00	Ungermann-Bass		08-00-45	Xylogics
00-DD-01	Ungermann Bass		08-00-46	Sony
02-04-06	BBN		08-00-47	Sequent
02-07-01	Interlan/Micom		08-00-49	Univation
02-60-86	Satelcom Megapac		08-00-4C	Encore
02-60-8C	3Com		08-00-4E	Isolan/BICC
02-CF-1F	CMC		08-00-51	Experdata
08-00-01	Computer Vision		08-00-56	Stanford University
08-00-02	Bridge Inc. (3Com)		08-00-58	DECsystem-20
08-00-03	Advanced Comput Com		08-00-5A	IBM
08-00-05	Symbolics		08-00-60	Industrial Networking
08-00-07	Apple		08-00-67	Comdesign
08-00-08	BBN		08-00-68	Ridge/Bull Univation
08-00-09	Hewlett-Packard		08-00-69	Silicon Graphics
08-00-0A	Nestar Systems		08-00-6A	AT&T
08-00-0B	Unisys		08-00-6E	Excelan
08-00-0D	ICL		08-00-70	Mitsubishi
08-00-0E	NCR		08-00-74	Casio
08-00-11	Tektronix		08-00-75	Dansk Data Elektronik
08-00-14	Excelan		08-00-7C	Vitalink
08-00-17	NSC		08-00-80	XIOS
08-00-1A	Data General		08-00-81	Crosfield Electronics
08-00-1B	Data General		08-00-83	Seiko Denshi
08-00-1E	Apollo		08-00-86	Imagen/QMS
08-00-1F	Sharp		08-00-87	Xyplex

Table 9.1   (cont.)

08-00-89	Kinetics	48-44-53	HDS
08-00-8B	Pyramid	80-00-10	AT&T
08-00-8D	XyVision	80-AD-00	CNET Technology Inc.
08-00-8E	Tandem	AA-00-00	DEC obsolete
08-00-90	Retix	AA-00-01	DEC obsolete
09-00-09	Hewlett-Packard Multicast	AA-00-02	DEC obsolete
40-52-43	American Research Corp.	AA-00-03	DEC Global physical
44-46-49	DFI	AA-00-04	DECnet Local logical

first three bytes are able to retain the number of the manufacturer whose machines are targeted. Thus, a group may consist of machines from the same manufacturer.

We note that a source address corresponding to the exact address of the emitting connector card cannot logically have a group bit set to 1; thus, its first byte is necessarily even.

Table 9.1 contains a list of the first three bytes allocated to manufacturers.

Table 9.2 contains the list of prefixes used by certain multicast (group destination) traffic, the first byte of which is necessarily odd. Note, however, that the type field generally provides complementary information.

In the IEEE 802 structure, the first bit of an address (long or short) is termed the Individual/Group (I/G) bit (Figure 9.3). However, for long addresses, the second bit transmitted also has a special meaning and indicates whether the address is of a universal type (as described above) or whether it is administered locally. In the latter case, the following 46 bits are chosen by the user and are not necessarily the manufacturer and connector Card IDs. This second bit is called the Universally/Locally (U/L) administered bit. These address formats are also found in other IEEE standards such as Token Ring and in ANSI's FDDI.

Table 9.2   List of prefixes for diffusion.

01-00-5E	Multicast Internet	09-00-56	Stanford V Kernel
01-80-C2	Spanning Tree	09-00-77	Retix Spanning Tree
09-00-02	Vitalink	09-00-7C	Vitalink
09-00-09	HP probe	0D-1E-15	Hewlett Packard
09-00-1E	Apollo Domain	AB-00-0X	DECnet Multicast
09-00-2B	DEC	CF-00-00	Ethernet Test Loopback
09-00-4E	Novell IPX		

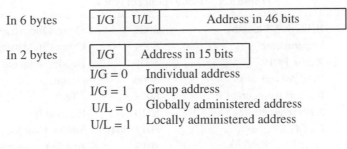

Figure 9.3   IEEE 802 address format.

The type/length field

This two-byte field was defined in the Ethernet standard to indicate the type of level 3 protocol used to transport the message. This information could thus be used to switch the frame towards the software (driver) adapted for its decoding.

However, the meaning of this field changed with standardization (IEEE 802.3, then IS 8802-3), and it now carries length information about the data field (the following field), according to the standard. This length is not indispensable to the operation of the receiver, since the start and end of the frame can be deduced from the end of the preamble (two consecutive bits set to 1) and the fall in the carrier in the last bit; moreover, the lengths of other fixed fields (addresses, type, FCS) are known. This information is also of interest both when the data field is not entirely full (a case in which it is desired to transmit only a few bytes using a short frame) and to verify the consistency between the total length of the frame received and the number of bytes as given by this field.

In all cases, the important question is to know how Ethernet frames can be distinguished from IEEE 802.3 frames on the network. The two may coexist perfectly well, which is often the case in reality. We know that the data field has a length of between 46 bytes (with insertion of a PAD, if necessary) and 1500 bytes, which makes 2E (or less, if there is a PAD) or 5DC in hexadecimal. Thus, if the content of the field following the two addresses is greater than 5DC, it is determined to be a type field and hence an Ethernet frame; otherwise, it must be a length field and an IEEE 802.3 frame.

Table 9.3 lists the most common protocol types, which may help readers to identify the traffic to which the frames circulating on their network belong.

We note that certain protocol types with numbers less than 5DC (prior to the IEEE 802.3 standard) have been reproduced further in the list.

Table 9.3   List of protocol types.

0000–05DC	IEEE 802.3 lengths	8003	Cronus Industries VLN
[0101–01FF	Experimental	8004	Cronus Industries Direct
[0200	Xerox_PUP	8005	Hewlett-Packard Probe
[0201	PUP_Addr_Trans	8006	Nestar
[0400	Nixdorf Computer	8008	AT&T
0600	XNS Internet	8010	Excelan Inc
0660–0661	DLOG	8013–8016	Silicon Graphics
0800	DoD IP	8019	Apollo Computers (HP)
0801	X.75 Internet	802E	Tymshare
0802	NBS Internet	802F	Tigan Inc.
0803	ECMA Internet	8035	Stanford Univers RARP
0804	CHAOSnet, Symbolics	8036	Aeonic Systems
0805	X.25 level 3	8038	DEC_BRIDGE STP
0806	Ethernet ARP	8039–803A	DEC unassigned
0807	XNS_Compatibility	803B	VAXELN software
081C	Symbolics_Priv	803C	DNA Naming Service
0888–088A	Xyplex	803D	CSMA/CD Encryption
0900	U.B Network Debugger	803E	DEC unassigned
0A00	Xerox_PUP	803F	DEC_LTM
0A01	PUP_Addr_Trans	8040	NetBios emulator PCSG
0BAD	Banyan System	8041–8042	DEC Reserved
1000	Berkeley Trailer	8044	Planning Research Corp
1001–100F	Berkeley IP Trailer	8046–8047	AT&T
1600	Valid Systems	8049	Experdata
4242	PCS BasicBlockProtocol	805B–805C	Stanford University
5208	Bolt Beranek–Newman	805D	Evans & Sutherland
6000	DEC unassigned	8060	Little Machines
6001	DEC_MOPDL (MOP)	8062	Counterpoint Computers
6002	DEC_MOPRC (MOP)	8065–8066	University of Massach.
6003	DECnet Ph IV Routing	8067	Veeco Integrated Auto.
6004	DEC_LAT	8068	General Dynamics Corp
6005	DEC_DIAG	8069	AT&T Computers
6006	DEC_C_USE	806A	Autophon
6007	DEC_LAVC (SCA)	806C	ComDesign
6008–6009	DEC unassigned	806D	Computgraphic (Bayer)
6010–6014	3 Com Corp.	806E–8077	Landmark Graphics
7000	Ungerm-Bass download	807A	Matra
7001–7002	Ungermann-Bass (NIU)	807B	Dansk Data Elektronik
7003	Interlan	807C	Univ. Michigan/Merit
7020–7029	LRT	807D–807F	Vitalink Communicat.
7030	Proteon	8080	Vitalink Bridge Manag.
7034	Cabletron	8081-8083	Counterpoint Computer

Table 9.3 (cont.)

809B	AppleTalk	815C–815E	Computer Protocol Pty
809C–809E	Datability	8164–8166	Charles River Data Syst.
809F	Spider Systems	817D–818C	Protocol Engines
80A3	Nixdorf Computer	818D	Motorola Computer
80A4–80B3	Siemens Gammasonics	819A–81A3	Qualcomm
80C0–80C3	Digital Com. Associates	81A4	ARAI Bunkichi
80C4–80C5	Banyan Systems	81A5–81AE	RAD Network Devices
80C6	Pacer Software	81B7–81B9	Xyplex
80C7	Applitek Corp.	81CC–81D5	Apricot Computers
80C8–80CC	Intergraph Corp.	81D6–81DD	Artisoft
80CD–80CE	Harris Corp.	81E6–81EF	Polygon
80CF–80D2	Taylor Instruments	81F0–81F2	Comsat Labs
80D3–80D4	Rosemont Corp.	81F3–81F5	SAIC
80D5	IBM SNA service Eth.	81F6–81F8	VG Analytical
80DD	Varian Associates	8203–8205	Quantum Software
80DE–80DF	Integr. Sol. Transp. RFS	8221-8222	Ascom Banking System
80E0–80E3	Allen Bradley Co.	823E–8240	Advanced Encryption S
80E4–80F0	Datability	8263–826A	Charles River Data Syst.
80F2	Retix	827F–8282	Athena Programming
80F3	Kinetics AppleTalkARP	829A–829B	Inst Ind Info Tech
80F4–80F5	Kinetics	829C–82AB	Taurus Controls
80F7	Apollo Computer (H.P.)	82AC–8693	Walker Richer & Quinn
80FF–8103	Wellfleet Communica.	8694–869D	Idea Courier
8107–8109	Symbolics	869E–86A1	Computer Network Tec
8130	Waterloo Manufactur.	86A3–86AC	Gateway Communicat.
8131	VG Laboratory Systems	86DB	SECTRA
8132–8136	Bridge Communicat.	86DE	Delta Controls
8137–8138	Novell Inc	86DF	ATOMIC
8139–813D	KTI	86E0–86EF	Landis & Gyr Powers
8148	Logicraft	8700–8710	Motorola
8149	Network Comput. Dev.	8A96–8A97	Invisible Software
814A	Alpha Micro	9000	CTP_Loopback
814C	SNMP	9001	Bridge (Bridge Managt)
814D–814E	BIIN	9002	Bridge (Term. Server)
814F	Technical. Elite Concept	9003	Bridge Inc/3Com
8150	Rational Corp	AFAF	Logicraft
8151–8153	Qualcomm	FF00	Bolt Beranek–Newman

The data

The data field contains the LLC-level or the level-3 packet, thus it has no intrinsic meaning as far as Ethernet is concerned (at the MAC level). The field is viewed as a sequence of 46 to 1500 bytes, incorporated in the frame, and no attempt will be made to interpret it. The only processing applied to the data will be the calculation of the CRC.

Within an ISO architecture, the IEEE 802.3 frame will encapsulate an IEEE 802.2 LLC packet.

Finally, if less than 46 bytes are provided by the layer above, the data field is filled out by the PAD.

The PAD

The PAD or stuffing sequence is only used to fill the data field to obtain at least 46 bytes. It is therefore indispensable in completing the generation of a short frame from a message consisting of only a few bytes. It consists of a sequence of meaningless bits placed after the data itself.

In the case of Ethernet, the MAC level of the frame did not transport any information about the number of data bytes. The differentiation between the useful bytes and the stuffing therefore had to be provided by the upper layers. In IEEE 802.3, the length field indicates whether the data field contains a PAD and gives its length (obtained by subtraction).

The FCS

Frame Check Sequence (FCS) is a four-byte field placed at the end of frames which is used to check the validity of the frame after receipt, up to a one bit. It uses a Cyclic Redundancy Check (CRC) calculated using a generator polynomial of degree 32. It covers the two address fields, the type/length field and the data (including PAD), and is thus used by the receiving station to decide whether the frame is perfectly correct and can be transmitted to the layer above (LLC or level 3).

On the subject of FCS transmission, we note that it is the only field of the frame to be transmitted beginning with the most significant bit (coefficient of X^{31} first, coefficient of X^0 last).

The interframe gap

We saw with the description of the method that all machines can take their turn on a single network in which regular exchanges between other equipment take place, with a relatively small delay. This is due in part to the fact that a machine cannot transmit all the frames it has to transmit one after the other. There is an obligatory 9.6 μs interval between the fall of the signal occupying the medium and the start of the frame emitted; this is known as the interframe gap, or spacing. This silence allows the electronic circuits to recover the rest state of the medium (absence of signal), and it may enable other stations wishing to transmit to take over at that time.

We note that this delay would correspond to the time taken to emit 96 bits, or 8 bytes, which is quite substantial. We shall see later that after the crossing of the repeaters this interframe gap may be reduced to less than 9.6 μs.

Summary To review the important elements of the composition of a frame, Figure 9.4 gives a representation of the typical frame with its various fields together with the order of emission of the bits of each byte. The frame thus consists of bytes which are emitted on the cable in serial mode. Therefore, an order of transmission for the bits of each byte must be chosen. For Ethernet networks, the first bit emitted is the least-significant bit and the last is the most-significant (eighth) bit (MSB). This order, also referred to as little endian, is respected for all the fields of the frame, with the exception, as we have seen, of the FCS. Readers should be aware that not all IEEE local area networks necessarily use this order.

To conclude, we note that sometimes a special (and partially inexact) terminology is used in the literature, whereby the term 'packet' is used to denote the succession of the eight fields discussed here (preamble, SFD, destination address, source address, type/length, data, PAD, FCS) and the term 'frame' refers to a packet without a preamble or SFD (this corresponds to the significant data).

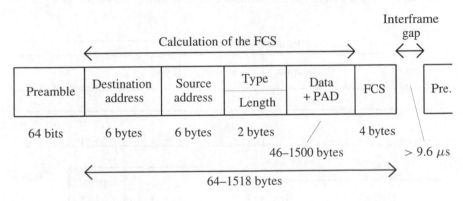

Figure 9.4   Schematic view of the structure of a complete frame.

9.2 Defective frames

The frame as described above is the entity intended for emission to exchange data between the stations of the network. However, problems may hinder its emission or propagation.

Packets which do not respect a consistent frame structure, or do so only imperfectly, may be found on the media. These may be the result of events such as a collision, abrupt disconnection of a machine, loss of the terminator or malfunctioning of one or more machines in the network. In all cases, at least one of the fields of the message infringes one of the rules for the constitution of a frame. Thus, a precise terminology may be used to denote each defective packet. As you will see, this vocabulary is, of course, largely of American origin.

One should also be aware that, although all these dubious frames may cross the repeaters and be transmitted to the connector cards by the transceivers, they go no further. In fact, the MAC layer of each station deletes the incorrect frames immediately and retains no trace of any field of the defective packet (except for certain internal software for monitoring and statistical purposes).

The runt

This term is used to denote a frame which is too short, that is, less than 64 bytes (Figure 9.5). In most cases, this is a frame which has been truncated for some reason (often because of a collision), and what remains of the original frame no longer has any meaning. In fact, the receiver does not necessarily know whether it has received the complete data field and whether the last four bytes are those of the CRC. Since this frame might actually be the result of a collision, its presence on a healthy network is perfectly acceptable. However, in this case the runt frame will usually be misaligned (non-integral number of bytes) with a bad FCS.

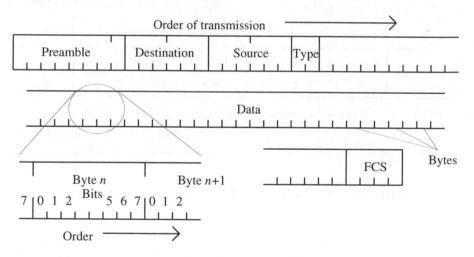

Figure 9.5   Details of a short frame and order of transmission of the bits and bytes.

The jabber

The jabber is a frame which is too long, that is, with a length greater than 1518 bytes. Theoretically, this type of fault should never occur in a healthy network. However, the original causes of instances in which the frame contains between 1500 and 3000 bytes or several tens of thousands of bytes vary.

In the first case, we shall suppose that it is a superposition of two long frames involved in an undetected collision. The fact that a collision has not been detected reveals an important problem. In fact, we have seen that the Ethernet technology is based on a CSMA/CD method; now, if the CD (collision detection) is no longer guaranteed, the Ethernet layers 1 and 2 can no longer guarantee the same quality of service. Of course, a frame may be lost entirely, when it enters the MAC layer (if its emission is subject to 16 successive collisions), but that should not happen too regularly, otherwise this lack of Ethernet reliability will result in numerous retransmissions which, in turn, will disturb all the traffic and degrade the global performance.

In the second case, the packet probably does not have a frame structure and must be produced by a defective component which has remained in emission mode for far too long. *A priori*, there will be a tendency to accuse low-level elements (transceivers, repeaters, connector cards) rather than the software driver or the application used. This is because the problem appears rudimentary and directly linked to the production of the physical signals, and because, as we shall see later, there exist watchdogs upstream of the driver.

This fault should be located and repaired quickly since it may be very injurious for the network. It is clear that an element which takes over to emit for several milliseconds blocks the network totally and unnecessarily for this period.

The misaligned frame

A misaligned frame is one in which the number of bits is not divisible by eight and which, therefore, cannot be reconstituted in the format of a sequence of complete bytes. This is one proof that the frame is unusable, for the receiver has no way of knowing whether it has counted too many or too few bits at the start of the frame, in the middle or at the end. Thus, all the bytes are potentially incorrect.

In practise, the misaligned frame may have an arbitrary length (from 64 to 1518 bytes, plus or minus several bits), but it almost always has a bad CRC. In fact, it is clear that a reading of the bytes of the frame which is shifted by several bits cannot produce a CRC value consistent with the last four bytes.

The bad FCS

The frame with a bad FCS is a frame for which the CRC calculated by the receiving (or reading) machine does not correspond to the last four bytes of the frame received. This may occur when one or more bits of the frame is incorrect (because of poor transmission, interference, and so on), in which case the calculation of the redundancy checksum finds its justification. However, it is also possible to obtain a frame with a bad FCS when the frame is truncated and thus the last four bytes which are compared with the calculated CRC are not those of the CRC for the whole frame (in this case, the frame is often misaligned and runt, since, first, there is little chance of the truncation occurring at the end of a byte and, second, the collision must have occurred before 64 bytes). We recall that in this instance a truncated frame normally results from a collision.

In conclusion, the frame with a bad FCS is either a complete frame, in which at least one bit was not received as it was emitted, or the residue of a collision.

9.3 Collision

The collision is the phenomenon resulting from the superposition of two signals (*a priori* two frames) on the medium. Of course, the collision occurs if the two emitters started up simultaneously (or at a sufficiently short interval apart) (Figure 9.6).

This event is normally linked to and resolved by the access method. However, its occurrence should not exceed certain alarm thresholds (for example, one collision per 1000 frames) otherwise the traffic flow will be harmed. We shall now discuss the conditions under which the collision occurs.

Let us suppose that two machines wish to transmit a frame at the same time. They will sense the medium and, assuming that it is free at that time, will both decide that they can act and move simultaneously to transmit mode. What happens? Their signals are superimposed and the two frames become invisible, even for the two addressees.

In fact, it is not necessary for the machines to set off the process at exactly the same time; it is sufficient for the time separating the two decisions to be less than the transmission time between their two points of attachment to the network. If this is the case, it was quite possible for the two machines to find the medium empty at the time they sensed the carrier before emission. However, a conflict will arise after a delay of less than the transit time separating them.

This event is acceptable if the emitters are informed of it. Thus, they should be able to detect this event which prevents correct reading of the signal at any point on the medium. For this, it is decided to extend the collision sufficiently. In fact, the aim is to ensure that the collision does not go undetected, when the network would be incapable of detecting the problem which has arisen and would fail to recover the frame or pass the information on to the layer above.

Figure 9.7 illustrates the occurrence of an undetected collision. Note that the collision is not visible at any point on the medium and that the emitters see the two packets pass one after the other.

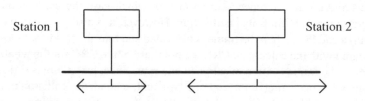

Figure 9.6   Two quasi-simultaneous emissions on a segment.

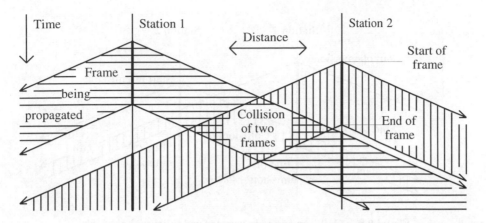

Figure 9.7   Illustration of an undetected collision.

There is a way of avoiding this type of event, which is difficult to manage. For this, one must ensure that the time taken to transmit a frame is always greater than twice the transit time between the two points of emission. Since the size of an Ethernet network is bounded (the number of segments, transceivers and repeaters is limited, as is the maximum length of each segment), the round-trip delay for an Ethernet network should not exceed a fixed value (499 bit times), and the corresponding minimum frame should consist of at least 512 bits (or 64 bytes, excluding preamble and SFD).

With this constraint, all collisions last long enough to ensure that they are propagated to the emitters concerned, wherever these are located, which, when informed that the last frame was lost, may then attempt to retransmit from their buffer, according to an algorithm which we shall describe later.

In practise, when a collision occurs, the MAC layer of the station is alerted by the transceiver which emits on the Signal Quality Error (SQE) pair of the drop cable. This indicates that the transceiver considers that the quality of the signal being emitted is unacceptable (Figure 9.8). The coaxial transceiver (10base5 or 10base2) detects the collision either because it cannot read the bits it is emitting correctly or because the continuous component of the signal on the cable is greater than that for a signal emission (−1 V). Other types of transceiver operate on point-to-point links (10baseT, FOIRL, 10baseFB and 10baseFL) with a channel in each direction; there can be no superposition and the collision simply involves the detection of a reception during a transmission. The collision on a 10baseFP network is a special case, which is handled in Section 10.6.

We shall see later that, although 100baseT operates on point-to-point links, collision detection is implemented differently for UTP cables of category 3 and 4.

Up to now, we have seen that the collision was an inevitable, but not grave,

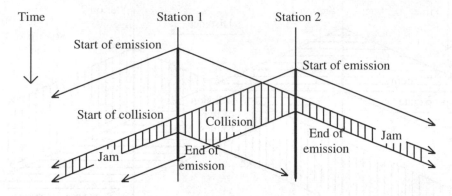

Figure 9.8   Collision correctly detected and followed by the jam.

event. However, if one or more elements of the network are operating incorrectly all of the traffic may be affected. We stress that the collision rate per frame and per second is generally a good indicator of the health of a network. If this increases abnormally, users may experience a loss of quality in their exchanges. Thus, it is useful to be able to judge a collision rate in order to quantify the state of a network.

The probability of a collision is difficult to calculate rigorously, but it is known to be linked to (and increase with) the following parameters:

- The total traffic on the network at a given time (measured in frames per second).
- The number of active stations on the network (sharing the global load).
- The separation of the machines (in terms of distance and number of repeaters).

There exist simulation programs which provide indicative results based on these parameters as input. Unfortunately, it is generally difficult to know the parameters to be provided with accuracy, since that corresponds to modeling a real network with all its intrinsic irregularity.

Remark   An elementary way of provoking collisions involves removing the impedance adaptation plug or terminator at the cable end. Then any frame emitted in the circuit is reflected on the open circuit and collides with itself.

This exemplifies the attention which must be paid to the cabling and to its protection, since an untimely disconnection of this 50 Ohm plug may block a network completely.

The backoff algorithm

The access method used for Ethernet is of the persistent CSMA/CD type. Moreover, it is capable of returning to its transmission process after collisions have occurred. As we shall see, the Ethernet access method manages transmission attempts after the incident using a random distribution on an increasing time interval.

More precisely, Ethernet uses the backoff algorithm (Figure 9.9) to handle collision during attempts to transmit a frame. When the emission of a frame is perturbed by a collision, the machine produces a jam, then ceases all emission until the medium becomes free again. After an interval, randomly determined so as not to restart simultaneously with its 'rival', it again tries to send its message and loops on the same emission procedure as before. If a serious problem prevents all transmission, the Ethernet MAC level ensures that the station stops its series of attempts to emit by simply deleting the frame to be emitted from its buffers after 16 unsuccessful attempts.

It is here that one notes the unreliability of the network, since, in certain cases, it authorizes the loss of a packet without informing the layers above.

Moreover, if the collisions are due to the network load, the more the stations try to re-emit their data rapidly, the more they load the network, resulting in an

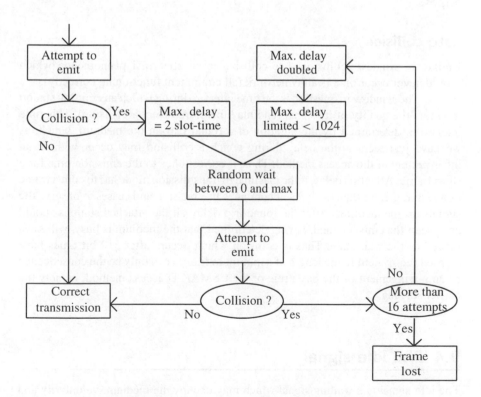

Figure 9.9 Block diagram summarizing the backoff algorithm.

avalanche effect which tends towards a complete network blockage. To counter this eventuality, Ethernet uses a waiting time randomly chosen in an increasing window of possible delays. Thus, after the first collision, there are two possible choices for the window (0 or 1 slot times), which increases by a factor of two with every new attempt. Finally, after the tenth attempt, this window is bounded by 1023 slot times, which is already a relatively high value ($1024 \times 512 \times 0.1 \ \mu s = 52.4$ ms). The attempts then continue, if necessary, up to the sixteenth time, with this same delay window.

The jam

The jam is a signal with no intrinsic meaning; it assures elements that have detected a collision on their emissions that the rest of the network is aware of this collision. This is simply implemented by making the collision last at least 32 bit times, by emitting a sequence of arbitrary bits from the time the emitter detects a collision.

We note that, to avoid confusion, the value of these 32 bits should be different from the CRC, which would correspond to the start of the frame already transmitted. In reality, the sequence transmitted is always the same.

This signal is also called 'collision enforcement', which is evocative of its purpose.

Late collision

Unlike 'in-window' collision, late collision is an abnormal phenomenon which should never occur on a healthy network (all equipment functioning correctly).

The window in question is the time interval during which an emitting station monitors the quality of its signal (and may therefore detect a collision). This time interval is determined by the duration of a round trip on the medium, which, as we have just seen, is the delay during which a collision may occur without an infringement of the access method. Thus, it corresponds to the emission time for a short frame. After this delay, if the machine in transmission mode has to emit a frame of a length greater than 64 bytes, it continues its emission and ceases to observe the signals on the medium. After the round-trip delay all the attached stations should have seen the emission and, having determined that the medium is busy, will have moved to the wait state. Thus, a collision which occurs after 512 bit times have elapsed (equivalent to the length of a minimum frame) can only be the consequence of an infringement of the basic rule of the CSMA/CD access method, namely the carrier sensing.

9.4 The idle signal

The idle signal is a waiting signal which may occupy the medium, voluntarily and regularly, during periods of inactivity. This signal is only used on point-to-point links (twisted pair and optical fiber) and provides information about the presence of an active element at the other end. It is a safeguard, designed to protect the network against a breakdown on a link. For example, a machine which is unaware that its transceiver's reception pair is defective might emit without respecting the CSMA and cause numerous collisions.

In the case of Ethernet on twisted pair, the transceiver (external or built into the hub), whenever it is switched on and there is no traffic, emits a peak with a frequency of approximately 5 MHz every 16 milliseconds. The hub or receiver opposite is thus informed that the transceiver connected to this port is active and that the pair in its direction (reception) is in good condition. The idle signal is known as the Link Test Pulse (in the 10baseT Addendum). We note that this description applies in one direction only and that the quality of the hub's emission pair to the transceiver has to be determined from an exchange.

The hub, knowing the state of the transceiver for each port, may adapt its behavior to isolate the port completely (transmission and reception) after an excessively long period of silence.

More precisely, the idle signal consists of a unique oscillation, whose first part is positive and has a duration of between 250 and 600 ns. In the absence of useful traffic, the emission of these peaks is periodic, with silences of 16 ± 8 ms separating the pulses. If the 10baseT port does not receive a valid signal or pulse from its correspondent during a maximum delay interval (from 50 to 150 ms), it decides that it has lost communication with the port which has become silent, and partitions it. After receiving 2 to 10 pulses, the port should recover its normal operational state. Two pulses are deemed to be consecutive if they are not too far apart (between 25 and 150 ms).

In reality, the sequence of pulses in a period of inactivity begins with a TP_IDL (Twisted Pair Idle) signal whose template is similar to that of the Link Test Pulse (see Figure 9.10), where the homothety depends upon the time axis. The TP_IDL emitted after the last frame has a global duration twice that of a Link

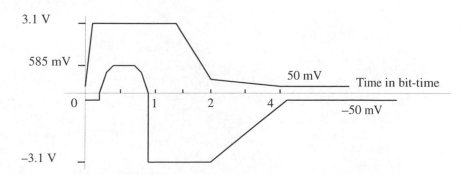

Figure 9.10   Template of an idle signal pulse in 10baseT.

Test Pulse, whence half the corresponding frequency (approximately 2 MHz). When a transceiver decides it has lost communication with its peer it begins to emit a sequence of pulses, beginning with a TP_IDL to the silent transceiver.

Finally, we note that the idle signal provides an indication in one direction only (unidirectional). If only one of these two directions of communication of a link is cut or perturbed, one end will detect the absence of correct pulses, but will still generate its idle signal in return, since it cannot inform the other end that it thinks the link is inoperable. Some manufacturers have improved the idle signal by varying the level and/or frequency within the standard template, to transport information similar to the 'remote fault' of 10baseFB. The idle then becomes a more complete, bidirectional means of communication.

Chapter 10

Elements of the network

- The medium

- Transceivers

- The AUI cable

- The MII interface

- The interface card

- Repeaters

- Test equipment

The network consists of the passive medium and the active components (Figure 10.1). The medium is the base to which the devices that will use it for their communications are attached. The transceiver (sometimes abbreviated to Xver) is the medium attachment unit, which is attached to the connector card by the drop cable. The connector card is the interface which interprets the packets from the network for the station or, conversely, which adapts the data from the applications to send them on the cable.

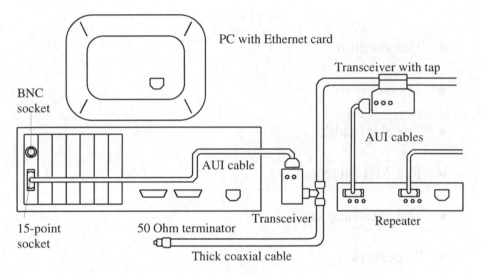

Figure 10.1 Schematic view of the main components of the network.

10.1 The medium

The physical carrier for Ethernet consists of segments of coaxial cable, possibly interconnected by fiber optic links. Other media were subsequently added to these possibilities, such as the twisted pair or, more recently, the air.

50 Ohm coaxial cables

Originally, Ethernet was defined for operation with a coaxial cable (relatively bulky) as the bus. Later, a much more practical solution, with a lower performance, on a cable with similar characteristics was developed.

The standard coaxial cable

The basic medium is the yellow coaxial cable with a characteristic impedance of 50 Ohm. This was the first medium defined, being initially associated with transceiver connection points with a tap connection, then, more generally, with a type *N* connector technology. As opposed to thin cable, which we shall discuss later, this cable is sometimes called thick cable. The most important mechanical characteristics of the cable are the following:

- The central conductor is made of solid copper and has a diameter of 2.17 ± 0.013 mm.
- The dielectric which insulates the two conductors is such that the desired propagation rate can be achieved and the attenuation is limited to the required value.
- The cylindrical conductor consisting of an aluminum shield (braid and foil elements) has an internal diameter of 6.15 mm and an external diameter of 8.28 ± 0.18 mm. This braid, which also acts as a screen, must be grounded at just one of its two ends (to avoid the passage of current in the cable due to masses with different potentials). The intermediate connectors should thus be insulated from the metal components on the cable path.
- The external sheath is either of colored PVC (polyvinyl chloride – yellow is recommended) with an external diameter of 10.29 ± 0.18 mm, or of fluoropolymer (for example, FEP or E-CTFE) with an external diameter of 9.53 ± 0.25 mm. It should have a black ring drawn on it every 2.5 m as a unit of measurement for the taps.
- A length of at most 500 m per segment.
- A distance of at least 2.5 m between each attachment point.
- At most 100 connections per segment.
- A minimum bend radius of 25 cm (10 inches). Note that, while it is not advisable to split the coaxial cable segment, the cable sections should have a length of 23.4, 70.2 or 117 m. These three lengths, which are multiples of 23.4 m (one, three or fives times the dimension of a bit on the cable) are such that the reflections which occur on the lines are superimposed out of phase.

The physical characteristics of the cable are as follows:

- A characteristic impedance of 50 Ohm (reminder: $Z = 138/\sqrt{\varepsilon} . \log(D/d)$).
- An attenuation less than 17 dB/km at 10 MHz and less than 12 dB/km at 5 MHz.
- A resistance for the two wires (round trip) of less than 10 Ohm/km.
- A signal propagation speed greater than or equal to $0.77c = 2.3 \times 10^8$ m/s, corresponding to a maximum period of 21.65 bit times to cross a segment.

- A cable attachment point should not give rise to a signal reflection greater than 4%.

The standard coaxial cable costs less than 5 US dollars per meter, which makes it a relatively expensive medium. This price, like the prices given elsewhere in the book, is only given for information, as an order of magnitude.

The associated connector technology is of type N (Figure 10.2). Each cable segment ends with a male connector. The segments may be interlinked by straight female–female connectors, with or without a baseplate (the baseplate is used to fix the connector to a patch-cabinet plate) or by Ts, which allow the connection of a transceiver. At each end of the complete segment a terminator ($50 \pm 1\%$ Ohm from 0 to 20 MHz and a phase shift of $< 5°$) should be screwed on for the purposes of load adaptation. There are other type N connector modules such as the straight–straight male connector, the male–female elbow (with a right angle), the male terminator, the female terminator, and the N–BNC adapter.

In most cases, the cable sheath consists of PVC for use within buildings, polyethylene being reserved for passage to the outside. PVC burns less easily than polyethylene and thus tends to limit the spread of fires. However, PVC releases toxic and corrosive gases when it is burnt, together with opaque smoke. The toxic gases include halides and may also degrade to hydrochloric acid. Its drawbacks may have non-trivial consequences for the occupants of buildings in case of fire.

Thin coaxial cable

Another type of coaxial cable was introduced in an IEEE supplement and was even incorporated in the ISO standard, namely thin coaxial cable of the RG58 type. Like the yellow cable, it has a characteristic impedance of 50 Ohm, but is much thinner, so less resistant and considerably cheaper. Its main characteristics are:

- A central conductor of electroplated copper with a diameter of 0.89 ± 0.05 mm.

- A dielectric of a quality such that the cable has the required electrical characteristics.

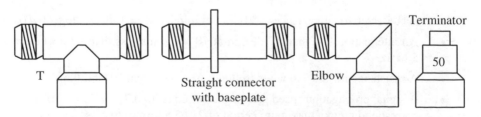

Figure 10.2   Elements of the basic BNC connector technology.

- A cylindrical conductor consisting of aluminum tape and electroplated copper braid, with an external diameter of 2.95 ± 0.15 mm.

- An external sheath of either PVC (often black) with a diameter of 4.9 ± 0.3 mm or FEP with external diameter 4.8 ± 0.3 mm.

- A maximum length of 185 m per segment.

- A minimum distance of 50 cm between two attachment points.

- At most 30 connections per segment.

- A minimum bend radius of 5 cm.

- A signal propagation speed greater than or equal to 0.65 c.

The other electrical specifications are the same as those above.

Thin coaxial cable is associated with a BNC connector technology (Figure 10.3), which is also less expensive than the type N connector technology. When using thin cable, it is general practise to run the cable right up to the machine, where the connection is then made using a T (BNC), the transceiver being built into the connector card. In this case, care should be taken to ensure that the T does not separate the cable of the BNC connector from the card by more than 4 cm, otherwise there is a risk of mismatch.

In the above, we saw that there exists a straight N–BNC connector which can be used to connect a standard coaxial cable segment to a thin coaxial cable segment. This type of connection is not described in the standard, but works provided the distances are proportionately respected. A segment consisting of cables of the two types (x meters of standard cable and y meters of thin cable) should satisfy $x/500 + y/185 < 1$.

Thin coaxial cable costs less than 1 US dollar per meter, which is much more affordable than the standard coaxial cable, making this a preferable physical medium for small installations where economy is desirable.

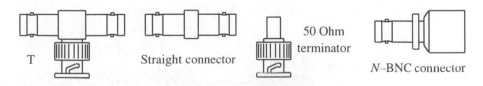

Figure 10.3   Basic BNC connectors.

Optical fibers

Ethernet V 2.0 defined point-to-point optical links over 1 km, without specifying the media from which they should be constructed. This could only be fiber optic cable.

Since the IEEE standardization has taken a great deal of time, various types of fiber and connector have been used by manufacturers. However, the optical fiber retained for Ethernet in FOIRL, then 10baseF, is the graded-index multimode silica fiber with a core of diameter 62.5 μm. The ST connector technology is recommended from 10baseF, to replace SMA. Exceeding the one kilometer limit for FOIRL, links may extend to two kilometers with 10baseF; however, in fact, manufacturers have for some years offered (non-standardized) hardware capable of supporting much longer optical lines (4 km).

In practise, fiber remains an expensive physical carrier; for example, a ten-fiber cable costs less than 15 US dollars per meter. Finally, we note that, in practise, fibers in the form in which they can be handled have a diameter of 250 μm rather than 62.5 μm. This is explained by Figure 10.4.

The main characteristics of optical fiber suitable for all Ethernet installations, bearing in mind preparations for 10baseF and FDDI, are listed below.

Multimode graded-index silica optical fiber has a core diameter of 62.5 ± 3 μm, a sheath diameter of 125 ± 2 μm, a numerical aperture of 0.275 ± 0.015, and attenuation at 850 nm of less than 3.5 dB/km, a bandwidth greater than 160 MHz.km at 850 nm (IEC 793-2 type A1b requires more: 200 MHz.km) and a propagation speed of 0.67 c (5 μs/km).

With a view to future use of FDDI, one might ensure that the fiber proposed also has the following characteristics: an attenuation at 1300 nm of less than 1.5 dB/km and a bandwidth greater than 500 MHz.km at 1300 nm. Links of a length of at most 2 km should also be used, in conformance with 10baseF (except for the passive case) and FDDI.

10baseF mentions a relatively self-evident practical detail, in that it recommends that all unused optical connectors should be covered with a cap. This provides a protection against dust and also ensures that operation of the active devices is not disturbed by parasitic optical signals. Finally, this limits the risk of someone involuntarily looking directly at the light ray from an emitter.

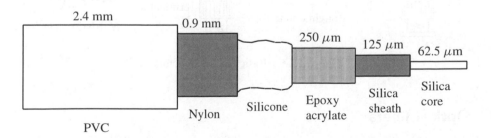

Figure 10.4   Overall structure of an optical fiber.

Twisted pairs

StarLAN already used the unshielded twisted pair, but its rate was only one tenth that of 10base5. Thus, the development of 10baseT was accompanied by a deployment of hardware.

In fact, the twisted pair is an inexpensive medium, which is easy to install and may possibly be used for other types of network, which is not the case for the thick 50 Ohm cable. Within a few years users became so infatuated with it that it became a preferred medium for Ethernet installations, and today shares with optical fiber the privilege of being viewed as a physical carrier for the future.

10baseT repeated the specifications for the twisted pair given in 1base5, namely, two UTPs with a characteristic impedance of 100 Ohm, an attenuation less than 11.5 dB (from 5 to 10 MHz) per segment, a propagation speed of 0.585 c (or 5.7 ns/m), and a maximum recommended length of 100 m per segment. However, the choice of the unshielded twisted pair is governed by the desire to take over the existing telephone cable in buildings for data communication purposes. Unfortunately, this praiseworthy intention is rarely implemented in practise, since telephone signals may have a high voltage (48 V for the bell circuits) and may perturb the data transfer if all the cables are contiguous.

In spite of everything, the quasi-universality of the UTP, on which signals for Token Ring (with maximum lengths less than for STP), LocalTalk, ISDN, ARCnet, 100baseT and FDDI make it the favored physical carrier for prewired installations. In brief, prewiring involves providing services to all the offices when the cables are laid and the wall sockets installed, independently of the immediate needs, but with a view to medium- or long-term gain. The physical topology is still a star around the plant room, even though it can be adapted by relooping the segments at the level of the patch cabinet. Provided the lengths are suitable (generally limited to 100 m per segment), the twisted pair is a preferred medium, since it can accommodate both Ethernet and rival local area networks today and FDDI tomorrow. However, when long lines are involved (to be specific, longer than 100 m), one should then think in terms of optical fiber, which has far superior qualities (low attenuation, wide bandwidth). Fiber optic cables have their place in prewiring since they often represent the most practical medium for interlinking the plant rooms in one or more buildings.

Although STPs are not well adapted in terms of characteristic impedance (150 Ohm rather than 100 Ohm), given their better characteristics they will be suitable for and will permit (using products from certain manufacturers) lengths greater than 200 m, still in 10baseT technology. We note that STP should be used to advantage, since the quality of the adaptation on twisted pair is far less than on coaxial cable. This is because a mismatch on coaxial cable generates a reflected signal whose power is proportional to the difference in impedance. This undesirable signal circulates backwards and may be superposed on the valid signals (with the frame moving in both directions on the cable, from the point of emission). However, on twisted pair, the reflected signal circulates in the opposite direction to the valid signals, and can only be superimposed after a second reflection, when its power is even weaker (function of the square of the coefficient of reflection).

By way of indication, a cable of four twisted pairs costs less than 1 US dollar per meter.

Other possibilities

Some companies have developed transmission facilities outside the specifications of the standard and its supplements. There have been two approaches in the domain of local area networks, first in response to a need for point-to-point, face-to-face links, and second, in order to provide a service for the offices in a building, based on the capillary cabling.

As far as the first requirement is concerned, solutions have existed for several years which permit links, for example, between two buildings, without the need to install any cable (which may be a crucial advantage in certain cases, such as when a road is crossed). Thus, it is possible to implement a duplex frequency-modulated microwave link at 23 GHz between two points which may be several kilometers apart, or a link using centimeter waves with the spread-spectrum technology (DS-SS, direct sequence spread spectrum; and FH-SS, frequency-hopped spread spectrum) generally with a rate of several hundred kbps. The accessible coverage is a direct function of the authorized emitted power.

In the same area, we find a laser link extending up to 1 km, with a rate of 10 Mbps or above. This type of equipment is mounted on the roof of a building or on a window sill, and must be aligned in a precise direction. It is designed to be perturbed relatively little by climatic variations, fog, rain or snow. The last technique is the only one which is not subject to authorization by public authorities or by the authority responsible for the assignment and use of frequency ranges.

As far as the second requirement is concerned, solutions are now reaching the market, although, again, a stable state has not yet been reached. However, we note that this market has a considerable potential. These future Wireless Local Area Networks (WLANs) are also referred to as Wireless In-building Networks (WINs) because they are designed for operation within buildings (Figure 10.5). The IEEE 802.11 committee is tasked to study this type of application of local area networks and the draft was due to be submitted by the end of 1994. There are three possible transmission options: wide spectrum, narrowband microwave, and infrared. For the first (most common) option, the frequency bands are 902–928 MHz, 2.4–2.4835 GHz, and 5.725–5.825 GHz (ISM – industrial scientific and medical – bands) and the distance covered may vary from 30 to 250 m or the equivalent of $\sim$4500 m^2. A direct line of sight is not necessary between the source and receiver (passes through walls). For the second option, the frequency band is 18.825–19.205 GHz, and the distance covered may vary from 12 to 40 m or the equivalent of 450 m^2. In this case also, a direct line of sight is not necessary (reflected rays can be used). These two options may operate with a star topology (whose center is a single communication device, possibly with packet switching) or from peer to peer (which corresponds to the bus, all the stations being visible to each other). This second system requires a more complex access

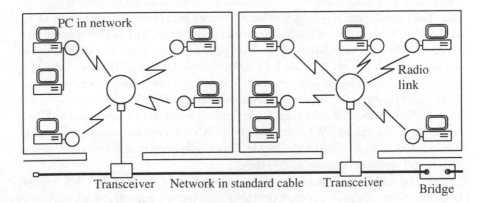

PC in network

Radio
link

Transceiver   Network in standard cable   Transceiver

Bridge

Figure 10.5   Schematic view of offices served by a WLAN.

management system than the first, based on CSMA. The last option is based on infrared emissions from 870 to 900 nm (3×10^{14} Hz). It allows distances of between 10 and 25 meters, is a point-to-point system, in most cases requires a direct line of sight between the emitter and the receiver, and is the technique most sensitive to vibrations. On the other hand, it can be used between buildings, which can only be achieved for narrowband microwave and wide spectrum using antennas.

We note that radio emissions, unlike transmissions on electrical conductors, must take place within frequency bands assigned by the official body, and are therefore reliant on the communication capabilities at the frequencies assigned, in terms of rate and coverage. Subject to improved conditions, even higher rates (100 Mbps) could be envisaged in years to come.

The IEEE 802.11 committee has selected the main technologies and types of operation envisaged for its future standard. The signal will be a radio-frequency signal rather than infrared, which tolerates the proximity of several similar systems less well and which only performs well for directed beams. The frequency band will be the 2.4 GHz ISM band, which is defined worldwide and is relatively easy to use. The other frequencies, 915 MHz and 5.8 GHz, one of which is already very busy and the other of which is too expensive in equipment terms, are not available in all countries. The radio technique used will be wide spectrum Slow Frequency Hopping (SFH) which has an intrinsic robustness to external perturbations and the ability to allow several nearby elements to operate concurrently without a specific configuration. The radio technique involves regular changes (for example, every 50 ms) of the carrier frequency according to a random or deterministic (pseudo random) sequence. Here, 75 subchannels out of a total of 83 are used normally and the remaining 8 are used for interference management. These subchannels each have a bandwidth of 1 MHz. The only other technique which does not require an installation license is the direct sequence, which, by default, uses a very small fraction of the bandwidth (the spreading factor generally lying between 10 and 100). The topology will be of the type base station – remote station, in which a cell is defined around every base station, such that remote stations may connect to the network within this cell. The peer-to-peer topology has been replaced because of its limitations as far as the evolution (extension) of the network is concerned. The access method will be of the Time-Division Multiple Access (TDMA) type, which is well adapted to the topology (this is not the case for CSMA/CA) and to the SFH radio technique. The base station is responsible for scheduling within its cell. One alternative for the MAC layer might be Group Random Address Polling (GRAP).

We note that the European Telecommunications Standards Institute (ETSI) envisages standardizing a WLAN called HiperLAN (for high-performance European Radio LAN) in the middle of the decade. This would operate in a 150 MHz band at 5 GHz and would have a rate of 20 Mbps.

The requirement which led to the development of the wireless LAN resulted from the communication needs of devices which move frequently, work situations in temporary locations and the particular case of buildings which are very difficult to cable. These technologies, which can be used to serve the stations of a group of offices, today only cover part of the function of local area networks, namely their capillary branches. The speeds available have until recently, been modest, but they have now caught up those of conventional local area networks (several Mbps) with which they can now interconnect and extend. For example, there now exist WLANs which are compatible with Ethernet or Token Ring (4 or 16 Mbps).

The future of these techniques, whose expansion is proceeding apace, should be ensured, since they can be integrated naturally into a cabling architecture while avoiding terminal links. Moreover, they provide a certain freedom as far as the devices are concerned, which now have an antenna (small size) and are no longer attached to the wall socket in a fixed fashion. Depending on the frequency of the signals used (microwave or infrared), the path of the rays may or may not pass through certain obstacles, be reflected by the walls of the building and provide a more-or-less convenient coverage of a surface area of up to 5000 m^2. The emitters and receivers are even more complex, but if one draws a parallel with the state of local area network technology at the end of the 1970s, one may have confidence in their development.

Here is a note on security and privacy. One might think that WLANs are more secure than LANs because, as they dispense with a cabling stage, they eliminate the problems associated with that medium, such as generating at times non-trivial breakdowns. On the contrary, these technologies use radio emissions which are generally undirected and are particularly sensitive to the problems of eavesdropping or protection against intruders. Therefore, some manufacturers include an encoding and encryption system in their product from the design stage, thereby limiting the risks.

Before concluding this section, let us return to the complexity of the new technologies, which will only become affordable if they become widespread. For example, the transition from Ethernet to a WIN requires a segmentation of the frames, and the transition from one network to the other requires a protocol layer extending up to level 3.

The WIN implements its own access method and its own encoding, and has to manage access problems that do not exist in the world of local area networks. For example, since radio waves may follow various paths to reach the stations from the central antenna (with reflections on walls, furniture) this generates interference, which may be harmful. Thus, the system should be able to judge the direction associated with the most direct path to each station, so that it can then try to reach each station by the best radio path.

Similarly, new requirements for the higher-level protocols emerge, which have to evolve to better incorporate the notion of mobile machines (Figure 10.6). In fact, a station linked by a radio link will not necessarily always be located at the same place, whence on the same network or sub-network. The management of its logical addressing, routing tables, and name directories must therefore support these movements, which may be frequent.

Conclusion   The original medium, the yellow coaxial cable is being progressively abandoned in favor of unshielded twisted pair and optical fiber (Figure 10.7).

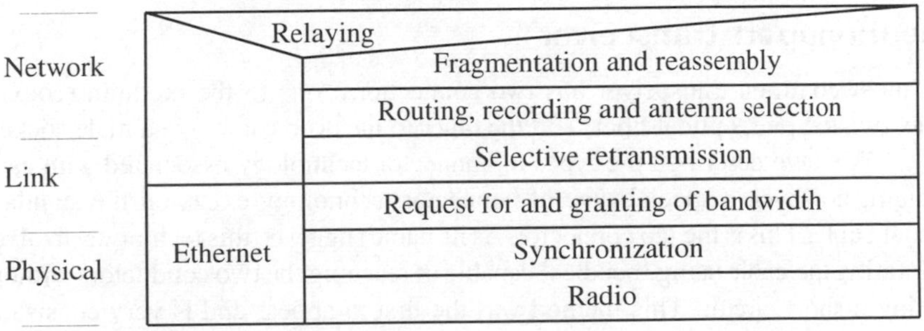

		Relaying
Network		Fragmentation and reassembly
		Routing, recording and antenna selection
Link		Selective retransmission
		Request for and granting of bandwidth
Physical	Ethernet	Synchronization
		Radio

Figure 10.6   Protocol stack needed for LAN–WIN interconnection.

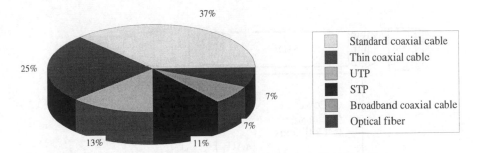

Figure 10.7   Distribution of the media for Ethernet in the USA (*Data Communications*, March 1992).

In fact, the most commonly drawn structure is constructed as a star on a fiber optic backbone with terminating cables in twisted pair serving the offices. The standard coaxial cable no longer has a great attraction, since its capabilities have been exceeded by those of fiber and its cost is too high in comparison with cabling based on twisted pair. Only qualities of the thin coaxial cable are still of interest for the particular case of small installations with a high numerical connection density, for which the bus topology is still the most advantageous.

In Part III, we shall see why the recent choices of cabling are almost all oriented towards twisted-pair and fiber optic cables.

10.2 Transceivers

The transceiver (its name comes from the fusion of the two words *transmitter* and *receiver*), called the MAU in the IEEE 802.3 document, is the active element that is connected to the cable on which it emits or receives the electrical signals. It then communicates these to the connector card via the AUI cable.

The monoport transceiver

The most common transceiver has two connections, one to the medium (coaxial cable, twisted pair, optical fiber) and the other to the drop cable, via a male socket.

We have described the types of connector technology associated with each medium, however, a special type of connector technology exists on the standard coaxial cable. This is the tap connector. As its name suggests, this technique involves perforating the cable using 'needles' capable of reaching the two conductors without causing a short circuit. This method was the first to appear and is very consistent with the spirit in which Ethernet has been developed, that is, the wish to produce a network which is simple to install (the cable laying) and easy to modify (by moving the taps almost anywhere without cutting the network). The cable was then

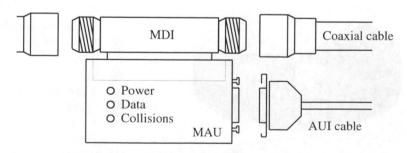

Figure 10.8   Sketch of insertion transceiver (type *N*).

seen as offering a self-service facility for communication. In Part III, we shall see that rigorous rules for installation and modification are vital to the maintenance of reasonably consistent networks. The tap technique is no longer recommended since former tapping points may age, leading to a considerable variation in impedance due to this connection mode.

The method of connection by insertion is more expensive, since it requires a severing of the cable at each site of a future transceiver, together with the incorporation of two male connectors of type N. Thus, it is more troublesome since one has to open the cable and thus interrupt the traffic during operation. However, the overall quality is better and the contact more reliable.

As shown in Figure 10.8, the MDI part of the transceiver is fitted onto the MAU and thus can be changed conveniently. The MDI is a simple connection element and can be used to adapt the transceiver to N connectors, BNC connectors or a tapping module (Figure 10.9).

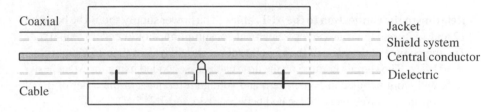

Figure 10.9   Schematic cross section of a tap on yellow coaxial cable.

The electrical characteristics

A transceiver should have the following main electrical characteristics.

Relating to the medium attachment   To minimize the variation in impedance due to the transceiver, the latter must have a resistance greater than 100 kOhm and a capacitance less then 2 pF (which covers the influence of the circuits and also that of the connectors).

We have seen that the code was of the Manchester type, where 1 is encoded by a rising edge and 0 by a descending edge. The signal emitted should have a continuous component (or offset) of -41 ± 4 mA (or between -37 and -45 mA). The alternating component should be between the offset ± 28 mA. Thus, the resulting signal should range between 0 and -90 ± 4 mA. The corresponding voltages are 0 and -2.05 V. Since the coaxial cable has a characteristic impedance of 50 Ohm the transceiver sees two sections from its attachment point, or twice 50 Ohm in parallel $= 25$ Ohm. Thus, for example, Ohm's law $U = Z \times I$ implies -2.05 V $= 25$ Ohm $\times -82$ mA. The rise time should be between 20 and 30 ns (for the 10–90% portion) and the fall time identical to within 1 ns (Figure 10.10).

Figure 10.10   Electrical signal and rise time (~25 ns) on the coaxial cable.

The continuous component of the signal (its average) is thus -1 V on emission, which is already an indication of activity since the free state of the medium (complete absence of signals) is at 0 V. Since the collision corresponds to the superposition of two signals, the resulting continuous component of the signal is therefore greater than that of a valid signal. Thus, the transceiver's collision detection threshold should be -1.56 ± 0.07 V (which reduces to a threshold of between -1.49 and -1.63 V). For 10base2, the threshold should be between -1.4 and -1.58 V.

Relating to the connection to the AUI cable   The power supply should be between 12 and 15 V, and the transceiver's electrical consumption should be less than 0.5 A. The impedance of the pairs of the 15 point socket should be less than 15 Ohm from 3 to 30 MHz. The signals emitted on the drop cable are encoded using the Manchester code with continuous component zero and voltage references of the order of ± 1 V (the gap should effectively be located between 0.45 and 1.315 V).

Crossing delay

The limits on the transceiver crossing delay are defined so that a network can be constructed based on simple rules (such as the maximum number of repeaters, coaxial segments, inter-repeater links, transceivers) without the need to recalculate the time taken to cross the network by the longest path every time (Figure 10.11).

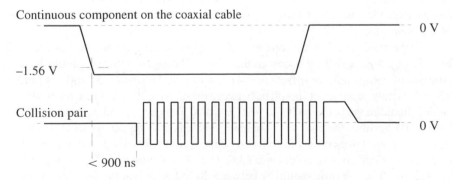

Figure 10.11   Delays in detecting a collision.

They are thus assigned the following fixed values: a delay time for transmission of the data valid in a state of continuous flow of less than 1/2 bit time (50 ns) with a loss of at most five bits in the direction from the coaxial cable to the drop cable and at most two bits in the direction from the drop cable to the coaxial cable. In fact, the transceiver is authorized to lose several of the leading bits of the preamble of the frame to be transmitted. The transmission time for a collision (naturally, in the direction from the coaxial cable to the AUI cable) should be less than or equal to 9 bit times. After this delay, of less than 900 ns the transceiver emits a 10 MHz signal on the collision pair (Control In) to the connector interface.

Jabber protection

The transceiver has a method for protecting the network against malfunctioning of the connector card to which it is attached. Thus, if the interface card requests an excessively long or uninterrupted emission, the transceiver is able to truncate this and notify the connector via the drop cable collision pair (or signal quality).

This security is called jabber protection and should be triggered after 20 to 150 ms of continuous transmission (Figure 10.12). The truncation of the emission is accompanied by a signal indicating the presence of a collision (10 MHz on the Control In pair). The truncated state should be inhibited 0.5 ± 0.25 s after the end of the emission from the connector card.

We note that this protection is fundamental since, if a defective device were to emit, for example, an infinite preamble on the cable, no machine would be able to take over and the network would be totally blocked. Moreover, in this particular case, no traffic could be detected by an analyzing device placed in observation mode.

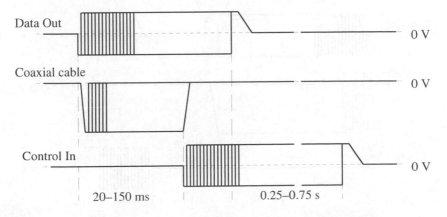

Figure 10.12   Illustration of the triggering of jabber protection.

The SQE test

There exists a test of the collision pair called the SQE test or *heart beat* (because it is very regular) (Figure 10.13). This test consists of a brief signal which is sent by the transceiver to the connector card after the emission of each frame on the collision pair (or Control In) to check that the link between the transceiver and interface is operating properly. The arrival of this signal at the card means that if the card has not received a collision indication during collision, it is because emission has passed off well and not because the collision pair is cut.

This test may be activated, if necessary, on each transceiver (usually using a jumper wire or a microswitch). The IEEE 802.3 standard, in which it first appeared, recommended that it should be activated on all transceivers except those connected to a repeater (or the equivalent: hub, active star), so that the process of counting collisions when the repeater partitions a port would not be interfered with. In practise, very few stations use this test, and it can even be deactivated on all the transceivers of the network. The SQE test should be emitted approximately 1.1 μs (from 0.6 to 1.6 μs) after the end of the frame and should last 10 ± 5 bit times (between 500 and 1500 ns). The receiving window for this signal will therefore have a length from 4 to 8 μs.

Conclusion   The transceiver is the element responsible for the emission, reception, and monitoring of the physical signals on the network (Figure 10.14). It communicates with the connector card via the AUI cable and transmits to it all the data it sees passing on the medium (up to the loss of the leading bits). Conversely, it emits the data sent to it by the connector interface on the physical medium, essentially as it is received. Its only intelligence comprises its capability to interrupt an excessively long emission and to test the validity of the collision pair after the emission of each frame.

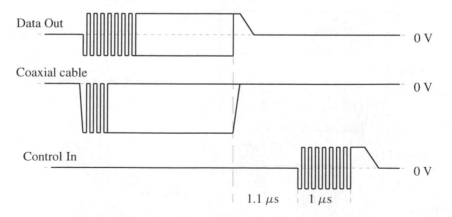

Figure 10.13   Heart beat after an emission of a correct frame.

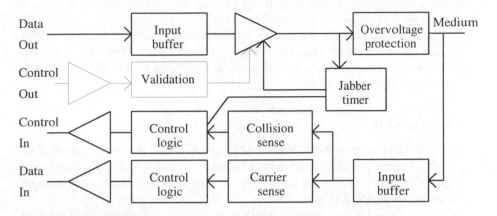

Figure 10.14   Schematic illustration of the circuits of a transceiver.

In practise, transceivers often have LEDs. These are quite useful, as they may be used to carry out elementary diagnostics when problems arise. They can indicate the state of emission, reception and collision detection, the triggering of the jabber protection or the position of the switch validating the SQE test.

Figure 10.14 illustrates the main functional blocks of a transceiver and their inter-relationship. Finally, the accompanying table gives the crossing delays for the different types of transceiver, for valid signals and for collision detection; these times may be used to calculate the round-trip delay on the network.

All the times in Table 10.1 are given in bit time (0.1 μs). Note that on the coaxial cable, this time does not include the rise time of the collision, without which a value of 17 bit times should be used. In the section on repeaters we shall see that transceivers built into repeaters often have slightly lower times.

Table 10.1   Delays of different types of transceivers (in bit time).

	10base5	10base2	FOIRL	10baseT	10baseFP	10baseFB	10baseFL
Tx	3.5	3.5	3.5	5	4	2	5
Rx	6.5	6.5	3.5	8	3	2	5
Coll	9	9	3.5	9	11.5	3.5	3.5

The multiport transceiver

The multiport transceiver is a transceiver with several male AUI connectors, generally two or four. Its internal structure simply amounts to a set of several transceivers accessing the cable at the same point. Thus, its advantage lies in its compactness and the fact that it can be used to connect more than one machine to the network at a single point, since the perturbation due to the local mismatching remains unitary. Its crossing delay is the same as that of a transceiver and, like a transceiver, it is fed by one or more drop cables.

If two terminators are directly attached to the multiport transceiver, this becomes a small virtual Ethernet, which is very practical when one wishes to establish intercommunication between two devices with female AUI connectors (repeater, bridge, router, probe).

The FanOut

The FanOut is a concentrator for male AUI ports, which also has a female AUI port. This element is capable of collecting together several (generally eight) drop cables attached to stations and connecting the whole to the network using a single transceiver (monoport) (Figure 10.15).

This is a very useful device, which makes it easy to simulate a small Ethernet network that is not attached to a true transceiver. It is even possible to cascade several FanOuts if there is a requirement for a large number of AUI connectors, thereby creating a large virtual Ethernet. The FanOut is quite common and affordable. Note, however, that it generally requires a power supply and that it has a non-zero crossing delay (less than 1 μs, but of the order of several hundred ns). This means that this time must be included in the calculation of the length of the maximum path for the network. One also needs to know the length of the AUI cable connecting the transceiver, and then to add this to that of the cable leading to the station (the sum of the two should be less than ∼45 m).

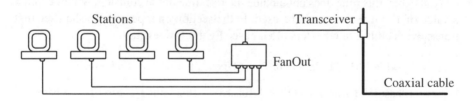

Figure 10.15 Four stations attached to the network via a FanOut.

10.3 The AUI cable

The cable linking the transceiver to the connector card (PLS) is often called the drop cable (for attachment unit interface) in the standard, and is also referred to as the drop cable (since it often descends from a transceiver placed in a suspended ceiling to a wall socket) or the blue cable (as it is usually blue).

This cable serves no purpose if the station interface has a 10base2 port (in BNC connector technology) or a 10baseT port (in RJ45 connector technology), since then the coaxial cable or the twisted-pair line leads right to the machine. Otherwise (10base5, FOIRL and 10baseF) the AUI cable is indispensable. Its maximum length authorized by the standard is 50 meters; however, caution is advisable, as some manufacturers only certify the connection of their hardware for 30 or 15 meters.

The cable has a male DB15 jack at one end and a female DB15 plug at the other (Figure 10.16). One special feature of this cable is the locking of its 15-point connectors. These are not of the screw type, as is usual in information technology, but use a slide latch and locking post. This form of locking (standardized by MIL-C-24308), which belongs to the philosophy of the initial development under which Ethernet was to be easy to manipulate, has proved to be a source of problems. It is unreliable because when the slide latch is eventually slid around the two ports it becomes twisted, and cannot provide sufficient rigidity. In answer to this problem, manufacturers have provided their interfaces with screw connectors, thereby creating an undesirable heterogeneity. We could dwell on the quality of production of the slide latch, since there are various models, some of which are relatively reliable.

The main characteristics of the drop cable (according to IEEE 802.3) are:

- Five individually shielded twisted pairs.
- A characteristic impedance of 78 ± 3 Ohm between 5 and 10 MHz.
- A total length less than 50 meters.
- A propagation speed greater than or equal to 0.65 c.
- A maximum transit time of 257 ns (2.57 bit times).
- An attenuation of less than 3 dB at 10 MHz (per pair).

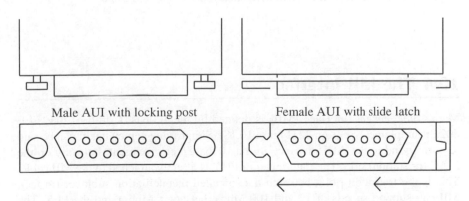

Male AUI with locking post   Female AUI with slide latch

Figure 10.16   Representation of two types of end connector.

- A total resistance for a conductor of less than 1.75 Ohm.

- Finally, the cable costs less than 4 US dollars per meter.

The definition of the AUI cable belongs to those chapters which the IEEE has supplemented with new material. Thus, the cable has changed from four to five pairs, the shielding on each pair has become accessible by the connector and the cladding ground (in contact with the global shielding) is no longer linked to pin 1 (Figure 10.17). Some connector cards designed to operate in the IEEE 802.3 world will require appropriate drop cables.

    We recall that the 'Control In' pair (or collision presence) is used by the transceiver to notify the connector card of the presence of a collision or the triggering of the jabber protection and to transmit the SQE test. In all cases, the signal emitted on this pair (2–9) has a fixed frequency of 10 MHz.

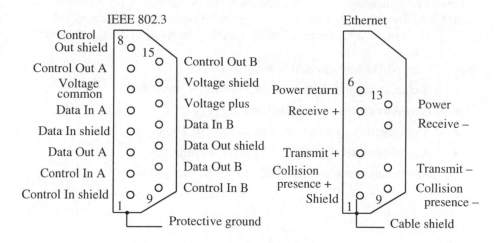

Figure 10.17   Different pin layouts for the AUI cable.

10.4 The MII interface

Media Independent Interface (MII) is defined by the 100baseT draft of the IEEE 802.3u supplement, section 22 (Figure 10.18). Simplifying somewhat, it can be said to correspond to the AUI interface in the 100baseT environment, but only on the MAC (or station) side. The transceiver or PHY is directly attached to the MII cable. This is the transition point between the so-called reconciliation sublayer (in fact, MII can support speeds of 10 and 100 Mbps, but not 1 Mbps) and the PLS. The reconciliation layer itself lies between the MAC and the PLS.

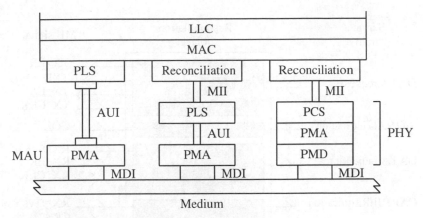

LLC: Logical Link Control
MAC: Medium Access Control
PLS: Physical Layer Signaling
PCS: Physical Coding Sublayer
AUI: Attachment Unit Interface
MII: Media Independent Interface
MAU: Medium Attachment Unit
PMA: Physical Medium Attachment
PMD: Physical Medium Dependent
PHY: Physical Layer Device
MDI: Medium Dependent Interface

Figure 10.18   Three different types of Ethernet interface.

The AUI is optional and is only specified at 10 Mbps. The MII is also optional, but is specified at 10 and 100 Mbps.

Note that the PMD layer is not used by 100baseT4, but only by 100baseX (100baseTX and 100baseFX). The PCS layer implements the 8B/6T encoding for 100baseT4 and the 4B/5B encoding for 100baseX.

On the MII link the data is transmitted in each direction by 4 bits (nibble) in parallel. Note that this is not directly related to the retransmission mode that is used on the medium.

The signals transported are MAC level transmission and reception, collision detection, carrier detection, and transmit enable. In fact, the clock signal used for the emission is also transmitted by the transceiver, as is the clock signal for reception derived from the received signal (Figure 10.19).

This represents a total of 19 different signals (8 for the data itself).

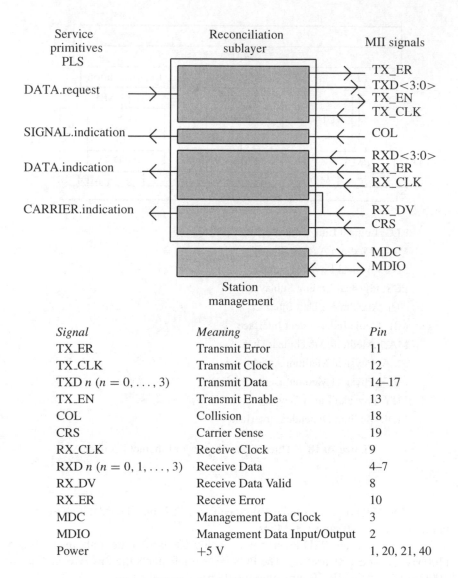

Figure 10.19   Logical and physical signals.

Signal	Meaning	Pin
TX_ER	Transmit Error	11
TX_CLK	Transmit Clock	12
TXD n ($n = 0, \ldots, 3$)	Transmit Data	14–17
TX_EN	Transmit Enable	13
COL	Collision	18
CRS	Carrier Sense	19
RX_CLK	Receive Clock	9
RXD n ($n = 0, 1, \ldots, 3$)	Receive Data	4–7
RX_DV	Receive Data Valid	8
RX_ER	Receive Error	10
MDC	Management Data Clock	3
MDIO	Management Data Input/Output	2
Power	+5 V	1, 20, 21, 40

The MII cable should not be longer than 50 cm, which gives a total of 1 m
for the two extremities of a link. The maximum delay corresponding to this total
is 10 ns per segment, but also 2.5 ns for the MII–PHY connector. Moreover, the
lengths of the MII cables have to be reduced to the lengths permitted by 100baseT
on the segments.

The connector of the IEC/SC 48B type has 40 pins on two lines and has a jack-type locking mechanism. It is female on the MAC side and male on the side of the cable attached to the PHY. The connector template should be less than 1.5 cm high and 5 cm wide.

The conductors of the MII cable should have a diameter of 0.32 mm (28 AWG) with a characteristic impedance of 68 ± 10% Ohm, and they are used at TTL electrical levels 0 and 3.3 at 5 V.

The management signals (MDIO) are used to communicate information registers which indicate, for example, the state or type of the PHY, which may result from an auto-negotiation phase, as follows:

- 100baseT4
- 100baseTX full duplex
- 100baseTX half duplex
- 10 Mbps full duplex
- 10 Mbps half duplex

We shall review these management functions in more detail in Chapter 14 in our discussion of 100baseT.

10.5 The interface card

Straddling levels 1 and 2, the connector card covers the functions of an interface with the transceiver (the PLS in the IEEE 802.3 model) and the MAC functions. The card is called the Network Interface Card (NIC).

The NIC consists of electronic circuits and carries out a fixed processing defined by the physical implantation of the components. It can be said to form part of the hardware, apart from the communication work carried out by the machine (processing according to the higher protocols) which corresponds to the execution of software code.

One of the circuits on the card is dedicated to the local area network and is specific to a particular technology. For example, chips for Ethernet have been available for a long time and can be found in interface cards and in all bridges and routers. Known circuits include, for example, AMD's LANCE Am 7990 and 79C960, Intel's 82586, 82593 and 82596, and National Semiconductor's DP83902 and 83910. Comparable dedicated circuits also exist for Token Ring, LocalTalk, and ARCnet.

As far as the physical layer is concerned, the card originally had a single AUI female port. With the arrival of 10base2, some manufacturers preferred to give their hardware a unique BNC port, while others chose to add the BNC port (which, in fact, incorporates a transceiver) next to the AUI jack. Finally, interface cards adapted to FOIRL and 10baseT are also available, and we note that it is even possible to obtain three sockets (AUI, BNC and RJ45) on a single PC card, leaving the user free to choose between these types of attachment, with a minimum number of attachment elements.

As far as the higher layers are concerned, since the card is a commonplace computer interface, it can exchange data with the computer via the machine bus. The packet formatting follows from the Ethernet technology at the MAC level and the indications are managed by the card driver.

In the case of PCs, the card exchanges data with the software driver provided by the card manufacturer, which has standardized accesses to cooperate with the various software of the microcomputer world (managers: servers and clients, emulation of passive terminals, network applications: file transfer, electronic mail, network management).

With the rapid evolution of workstations and microcomputers, the frequency of central microprocessors is increasing as are the speeds of internal buses. This is accompanied by an increasingly greater consumption of bandwidth by each machine (up to several Mbps).

Smart cards

It is important to be aware that, in most cases, the interface card is an element which imposes constraints on the use of an Ethernet network. In fact, all the elements defined in the standard, together with certain recent bridges and routers are capable of processing the network traffic, whatever the load. However, interface cards are generally incapable of emitting at 10 Mbps, even on an empty network. The maximum speed for current cards often lies between 100 kbps and 1 to 4 Mbps. The receive capacity is also limited, among other things, by the buffer capacity and the speed of transfer to the CPU card processing the protocol decoding. This brings to light the close relationship that exists between the processing capacity of the mother card's microprocessor and the amount of information the computer is able to communicate per unit time. This dependence is due to the fact that the processing for the protocols of level 3 and above is carried out entirely by software using appropriate decoding programs.

To counter this limitation, some of the decoding functions may be implemented in hardware. This is what is done in so-called smart cards. These have circuits and microprograms which are useful in the processing of protocols from the LLC or (DoD) IP level to the transport layer and thus relieve the central system of these additional tasks. However, the performance of these cards, which are clearly more expensive than conventional equipment since they are more complex, while greater, may still be constrained by the capacity for communication between the smart interface card and the mother card for data exchange at level 5 and above. Moreover, these cards cannot evolve as easily as a program module, following the modification of the contents of a field or of a procedure in a protocol, and for this reason they are less flexible in their use. The smart cards available for PCs generally handle the DoD protocols (IP, TCP) using their own microprocessor and their local memory.

10.6 Repeaters

It was mentioned earlier that the repeater is an interconnection device which is an integral part of the Ethernet network (Figure 10.20). It is defined in brief in the ISO standard (section 9) and more fully and in more detail in the supplements IEEE 802.3c and d. However, the 10baseF standard redefines this section 9 again, enlarging the application domains.

We note that the repeater is located at the level of the physical layer and thus has no knowledge of the fields of the frame which belong to the MAC level. It reproduces the frame exactly, without deciphering it and without being able to check whether or not it is valid. The segments it links together form a single Ethernet. Finally, since it is located at level 1, it cannot interconnect two segments with different speeds, such as 10base5, 1base5 (StarLAN) or 100baseT.

The simple repeater

The function of the repeater is to interconnect the medium segments in order to extend the network by linking several segments. It may have two or more ports and may or may not incorporate transceivers. Note that when it has many ports the repeater becomes the center of a star topology.

Its work thus involves transporting the Ethernet packets from the medium segment which provides them to the others. In so doing, it reshapes the electrical signals; it is also responsible for extending the fragments, completing the preambles, detecting and propagating collisions, interrupting excessively long emissions, and partitioning defective ports.

The regeneration of the electrical signals eliminates jitter and reduces noise problems by compensating for the attenuation of the signal. One reason why a segment of coaxial cable cannot be as long as the round-trip delay on the network would allow is that there is always a need to detect collisions (as required by CSMA/CD), in other words, to distinguish a valid signal from the superposition of two signals, which may have been attenuated. The repeater allows signals to recover their original level.

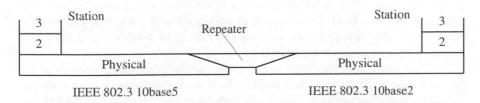

Figure 10.20   Representation of a biport repeater between standard Ethernet and thin Ethernet.

The crossing delay for a simple repeater (with female AUI ports) is 8 bit times. This becomes 4 bit times for the repeater part of a box incorporating the transceivers (the delays due to the built-in transceivers are given below).

The repeater also has to extend very short bit sequences (less than 96 bits) circulating on the network (called fragments). It is prudent to ensure that all the stations have seen these signals (carrier sense present), which is done by extending them to at least 96 bits. When these fragments are the result of collisions, their presence is not abnormal and does not signify malfunctioning.

The repeater is also responsible for completing short preambles by extending them to 56 bits and making them follow the SFD. In the case where the repeater transmits an excessively long preamble, this should be no more than six bits longer than the received preamble.

If a collision occurs on one side of a repeater, as a result of its action, or between two other stations, the repeater is responsible for detecting this collision and propagating it on the other segment. In this way, any station concerned about the result of its emission will be informed that a collision has occurred and the others will detect that the whole of the network is busy for the duration of the collision. When a collision is detected on a port, the repeater then emits a jam-type signal on the other segment(s). The jam is a sequence of at least 62 bits, consisting of 1 and 0, beginning with a 1. The emission of the jam should stop less than 5 bit times after the end of the collision. The crossing delay for a collision should be less than 6.5 bit times for a repeater with external transceivers and 19 bit times (9 extra on input and 3.5 on output) for a repeater with built-in coaxial transceivers.

Like the transceiver, the repeater has a function to monitor emissions judged to be excessively long and will interrupt its own retransmission after more than $5 + 50\% - 20\%$ ms or 40 000 to 75 000 bit times. The repeater reactivates its retransmission after 10.6 ± 1 μs. We note that the repeater's jabber protection is triggered well before the jabber protection for the transceivers, which enables the repeater to avoid cutting off the transceivers, which would block it.

Finally, the repeater may (optionally) implement a partition function, which involves deactivating a port that is judged to be a source of repeated collisions. Two conditions may trigger this protection: the passing of a threshold corresponding to a number of successive collisions; and a collision deemed to be abnormally long. The threshold for the maximum permissible number of consecutive collisions should be greater than 30 (generally chosen to be 32, or twice 16, or the equivalent of two successive *excessive collisions*). An abnormally long collision causes auto-partitioning after 1000 to 30 000 bit times (from 100 μs to 3 ms). The repeater reactivates the port after having detected an activity corresponding to approximately 500 collision free bits (between 450 and 560 bits, to be precise). In practise, all repeaters have an auto-partition function.

The term 'auto-partition' relates to the capability of some repeaters to let the user choose the state of the interfaces (activated, deactivated) using a simple access software. Transition to a silent state corresponds to a manual partitioning; the inverse corresponds to a departitioning.

Remark On reflection, it is apparent that as the repeater is responsible for extending short fragments and preambles, it cannot always respect the interframe delay.

In fact, if several frames with short preambles reach it in succession, it will have to add the complementary bits to each before retransmitting it. Forced to transport each frame in less than 8 bit times, it will not always be able to respect the interframe minimum and will therefore violate the 9.6 μs rule. A modification of the standard is envisaged (as indicated in draft 10 of 10baseF) to stipulate in section 4.4.2.1 that the interpacket gap (IPG) may be reduced to 47 bit times after the crossing of a network, because of variable network crossing delays, possible bits added to preambles and misalignment of clocks.

A new parameter which also occurs in the 10baseF standard is the Path Delay Value (PDV). This time is useful in evaluation and validation of the longest Round-Trip Delay (RTD) of a network. The PDV is divided into Segment Delay Values (SDV). One difference arises at the level of the SDV, depending on whether the segment concerned is the first segment on the path, the last segment or a segment between the two. For the calculation of each SDV, times associated with the minimum and the maximum admissible values for each segment are given in the table below. The SDV is calculated as follows: basic number + coefficient × segment length (in meters). The drop cables on the path are assumed, by default, to have a length of 2 meters, and the extra meters have to be added into the calculation.

The total PDV, the sum of the SDV should never exceed 575 bit times. The base numbers are given in bit time.

Note that 10baseFB has not been defined to constitute terminal connections (to stations or DTEs), even though some manufacturers offer this.

Table 10.2 Table of bases and coefficients for computing the maximum RTD on a given path of the network.

Segment type	Base for for first segment	Base for for intermediate segment	Base for for last segment	Coefficient (bit times)	Maximum length (m)
10base5	11.75	46.5	169.5	0.0866	500
10base2	11.75	46.5	169.5	0.1026	185
FOIRL	7.75	29	152	0.1	1000
10baseT	15.25	42	165	0.113	100
10baseFP	11.25	61	183.5	0.1	1000
10baseFB	—	24	—	0.1	2000
10baseFL	12.25	33.5	156.5	0.1	2000
ISLAN	72	86.5	209.5	0.113	100
AUI (−2 m)	0	0	0	0.1026	48

The rule is given by the following inequality (lengths of AUI cables greater than 2 m should be included in the calculation):

$$PDV = \sum SDV = \sum (base + coefficient \times length) \leq 527 \text{ bit times.}$$

Respect for the PDV, which corresponds to the delay in crossing, should be ensured in parallel with the evaluation of the interpacket gap (IPG) shrinkage, which is measured by the Path Variability Value (PVV). No path through the network should exceed these two limits.

Table 10.3 Table of values for computing the maximum IPG shrinkage on a given path of the network.

Segment type	Emitter segment	Intermediate segment
Coaxial cable	16	11
All links, except 10baseFP	10.5	8
10baseFB	—	2
10base FP	11	8

$$PVV = \sum SVV \leq 49.$$

Note that the receiving segment is not included in the calculation, so the calculation is not necessarily symmetrical.

In conclusion, this provides a convenient method for evaluating the validity of a configuration or a topology including different types of medium.

The multimedia active star

The star should primarily be viewed as a multiport repeater, the term star being derived logically from the topology created by this repeater attached to several segments.

Based on technical progress, manufacturers have done their utmost to incorporate the maximum number of facilities in a single apparatus, which is often modular and takes the form of a rack in which each card represents a type of attachment to a chosen medium. Originally, the backplane of these devices consisted of a passive bus equivalent to an Ethernet segment. Things have changed since then and several independent buses are now implemented, giving a choice of the network to which the card to be inserted is to be connected.

The following types of card are available:

- Female AUI connectors to link coaxial transceivers of type N (as on a standard repeater).
- Male AUI connectors to link stations directly (in this case, the star functions as a FanOut).

- Type *N* coaxial connectors to interlink 10base5 segments (relatively rare option).

- BNC coaxial connectors to link 10base2 segments to a T or directly at the cable end (high impedance or 50 Ohm internal terminator).

- RJ45 connectors to interlink 10baseT segments.

- 50-point Telco connectors to interlink 12 10baseT segments.

- ST or SMA optical connectors to interlink FOIRL links or synchronous optical links.

Normally, each card has several ports of the same kind, where the number of ports is generally a function of the size of the card.

Furthermore, recent developments have led to the production of cards with capabilities going beyond the simple function of access to a repeater stage. For example, there are cards which act as:

- A bridge between two ports (female AUI connectors) or between two backplane buses, or a combination of the two,

- A remote bridge between an AUI port (or backplane) and one or two sockets for remote connection (for example, RS232 or V.35),

- A router (managing protocols such as TCP/IP, NetWare, DECnet, XNS, AppleTalk, ISO) between two ports, two backplane buses or a combination of the two,

- A remote router, identical to a remote bridge with the routing function,

- A management card or SNMP probe, with an *out of band* port, generally of type DB25 or DB9 for RS232 connection.

The management card is now discussed in more detail, since its incorporation in the range of multimedia stars was associated with the qualification of smart hubs. Its main function is to permit remote monitoring of equipment with, initially, reporting of the light indicators from the front panels of these modules (self test, transmit, receive, jabber, collision, partitioning). It then proved possible to obtain statistics about the whole star (global traffic, per card, per port, error rate, load curve) and to observe and learn Ethernet addresses. This was followed by the configuration of certain parameters and the activation or deactivation of a card or port. All the supplementary functions which do not form part of the basic work of the star multiport repeater provide information about the traffic flow in various parts of the star. If the star is constructed from a number of manageable stars, the overall traffic can be monitored by the load on each card and the state of each port. In this case, it is even possible to locate a machine and even to follow the movements of stations. Used properly, the management card may prove to be a very useful tool for validating the current architecture of the network or causing it to evolve, and foreseeing the overloading of certain nodes or segments. Furthermore, these cards generally communicate their information to a PC or a Unix station on the network, but also have a serial external port (out of band) for a direct access via a modem, which is indispensable in the case of complete blockage of the network.

Finally, these stars now accommodate several technologies, and even the following cards are available for them:

- MAU Token Ring card in DB9, RJ11, RJ45 or hermaphrodite (rarer) connector technology

- Token Ring repeaters on fiber optic links in ST or biconic connector technology

- LocalTalk in RJ11 connector technology

- FDDI in single or multimode fiber with ST duplex or MIC connector technology, or twisted pair with DB9 or RJ45 connectors.

Connection between these networks and with Ethernet is made possible using module or card bridges and/or routers which are able to access different backplane buses.

One final type of common card for use with multimedia stars is (Figure 10.21):

- The terminal server in RJ45 or 50-point Telco connector technology, whose functionality is described in a later section.

To be perfectly multimedia, stars must support synchronous (10baseFB) and asynchronous transmission modes. Some manufacturers offer hardware which functions synchronously, with some standard accesses (AUI, BNC, 10baseT, FOIRL). These ranges also include solutions on twisted pair (which do not conform to IEEE 802.3) which are able to borrow point-to-point links over longer distances.

In addition to the diverse types of connection provided by multimedia stars, these stars also implement richer capabilities than a simple repeater. Independently

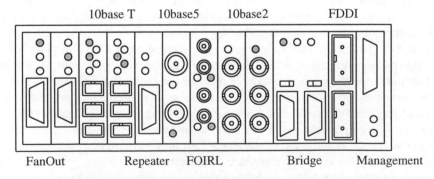

Figure 10.21   Symbolic representation of a multimedia star.

of the functions of a bridge and a router and of monitoring possibilities, the functions provided by multimedia stars include the management of point-to-point redundant links and, recently, the implementation of elementary filtering.

The point-to-point links such as the twisted-pair segments for 10baseT and fiber optic segments (FOIRL, 10baseF) may be duplicated. One of these two links is active and used operationally; the other is used for redundancy. To secure the connections between two stars it is sufficient to use two ports on each. If transceivers are used, these must then have two ports. When a problem arises on the active link, or in the active end elements, the second link replaces it and the network manager is notified via his or her monitoring system. In certain cases, the switch may be very rapid (a few bit times), since fault detection is so much easier in synchronous mode. Moreover, protection of this type can also be envisaged on coaxial cable, with duplication of the access points. This reduces to linking the star to two transceivers on the same cable. The star is responsible for detecting faults in the transceivers, the drop cable or one of the AUI cards and for executing the switch. However, in this case, the medium cannot be duplicated.

To ensure that their systems are available for even longer periods, the manufacturers offer racks with a redundant power supply and the possibility of changing the modules while leaving the whole powered up (hot swap). Thus, one may envisage building totally secure multimedia stars for the crucial nodes of the network. Breakdown does not involve any stoppage time, as once the defective element is deactivated, it can be replaced and reactivated and return to take over the link provided by the back-up elements during the breakdown.

In addition to management functions, which can be used to validate/ invalidate a port or monitor it in a particular way, 10baseT cards also offer an address filtering (source or destination). In fact, it is recognized that, in the majority of cases, a 10baseT link from a hub ends at a transceiver feeding a unique machine. Thus, an RJ45 port of the star can be associated with the address of the station attached at this point which adds security to the network by allowing only that machine to talk on that link. With the potential for filtering currently available, it is sufficient to define the type of link for each port to a unique machine or a set of machines and, in the first case, to enter the only authorized Ethernet address. The 10baseT will not only filter this port as requested, but may also indicate the illegal address which has attempted to use this port recently. Conversely, a machine attached to a port can be allowed to see only the traffic which concerns it. This is a way of limiting eavesdropping which provides surplus privacy. This new filtering functionality, which is certainly reduced but available at each port individually, provides additional security, but also requires a stricter management of the network. In fact, to make it difficult for users to use the network, one has to be able to modify the filtering addresses in parallel with the movements of machines on relocation or at the time of new installations, that is, quickly and without error.

When the multi LAN technology repeaters have several networks of each type on the backplane, it is of course possible to assign each module freely to one of the buses (or rings) of the backplane, but it is also sometimes possible to link each port of a given module to one of its internal networks. This is static per port switching.

This parametrization can be carried out directly on the module or, preferably, from the management console.

Finally, the most advanced modular designs are able to support concentration modules implementing a dynamic packet switching technology. In this case, each card inserted in the device corresponds to added dedicated bandwidth.

Stackable hubs

A new generation of hub or multiport repeater has emerged recently, which could eliminate so-called stand-alone equipment once and for all and threatens to be an advantageous replacement for modular hubs. These are stackable hubs, sometimes referred to as cascadable hubs (Figure 10.22).

These hubs may consist of a limited number of elements interconnected in a chain or star by short proprietary links (generally a few centimeters long). This means that the overall stack formed in this way can only be presented as a single repeater storey as far as Ethernet is concerned. The manufacturers offer a minimum modularity, perfectly oriented towards the most urgent requirements: numerous 10baseT ports (for example, 16 or 24 per module) with RJ45 or Telco connectors, a few AUI or optical ports for backbone links, and an optional SNMP management agent. The main aim is to preserve the main functionality and advantages of a modular chassis in a more affordable range.

Some manufacturers allow one to mix modules for different LAN technologies, where only the management is common to all. Moreover, there exist interconnection modules, such as local or remote bridges, multi-protocol brouters, and SNA gateways. Finally, we note that these devices in general correspond in a particular way to the capillary service from secondary plant rooms for a hundred attachment points.

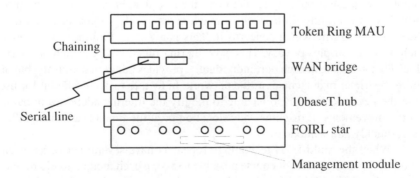

Figure 10.22   Example of a stackable hybrid Ethernet/Token Ring stack.

The passive optical star

The passive optical star (Figure 10.23) is a special instance of a star, as it has no active elements and can only process optical signals from transceivers. Its internal structure is particularly simple, since it comprises optical fibers fused together with one another so as to distribute any signal entering on one of the fibers fairly and uniformly across all the output fibers. Thus, it is a box with a number (4, 8, 16 or 32) of pairs of optical connectors (input–output), and it does not require a power supply.

Initially, the star does not have a direction of operation, but once a connection has been established the same Tx/Rx order must be respected on all the other ports.

The attenuation due to the passive star is given by the formula $2 \times C + E + 10 \log N$, where C is the loss due to a connector, E is the star's margin of attenuation and N is the number of optical ports.

The fact that it has no electronic circuits makes it very valuable for sites where the electromagnetic disturbance is large and where the safety restrictions (for example, overheating, risk of fire) are important. One example might be a tentative application as an interconnection box for a computer network in a car.

This type of technology has been in existence for some time but has only been standardized lately, since it has been included in the 10baseFP standard (Figure 10.24). However, it also has non-trivial shortcomings, since it is not easy to guarantee the detection of all collisions under all circumstances, for example in the presence of optical noise (which is inevitable). The internal structure of the star is as simple as the method of managing the signals by the transceivers is elaborate.

We have seen that, to ensure that the data it transmits is emitted without difficulty, the transceiver has to continually check the validity of its emission, which corresponds to an elementary function on coaxial cable (reception = emission), twisted-pair or point-to-point optical fibers (reception = none during the emission) but not in the case of passive optics. In fact, when the transceiver emits, it does not know either the segment length (and the associated transit delay) or the number of ports of the star (and the resulting attenuation) and, despite everything, it has to be able to interpret the signals received to judge whether a frame is its own frame and whether it is intact or superposed on another.

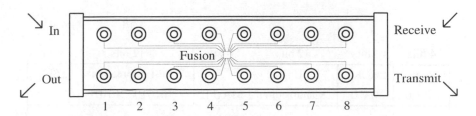

Figure 10.23   Symbolic diagram of a passive star with eight ports.

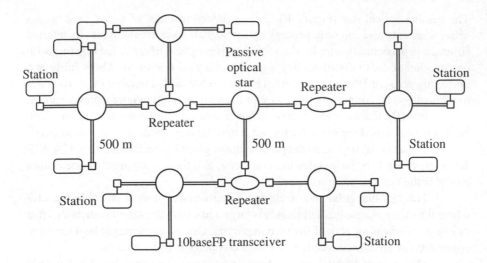

Figure 10.24   Example of a large 10baseFP network.

With a view to improving this technology, IEEE 802.3 10baseFP defined a more elaborate technique than simple transposition of the Ethernet frames on optical fiber. Here, the first 56 bits of a frame preamble are replaced by two fields of four bits (a synchronization structure, a packet header) and a unique 32-bit word, followed by at least 12 bits (always an even number) of a normal preamble (Figure 10.25). Next come the standard SFD and the frame itself. The synchronization structure is 1010 (in that order), and the packet header is a violation of the Manchester code (code rule violation: CRV) which can be used to identify it. The unique word consists of the manufacturer identifier on 12 bits and 20 bits giving the transceiver number. The least significant bit is transmitted first. Thus, the preambles transmitted by all transceivers are different.

A collision is detected in the following two cases: if the transceiver receives on its AUI cable a frame to be emitted while it is receiving (except if it is receiving the return of a previous signal sent back by the passive star), and if it receives a CRV

4 bits	4 bits	12 bits	20 bits	⩾12 bits	8 bits
Sync	PHCRV	\multicolumn{2}{c}{Unique word}		Rest of preamble	SFD
1 0 1 0	1 MV 0 1	Manufacturer	MAU ID	101010...101010	

Figure 10.25   Preamble for a frame in 10baseFP.

without having detected a silence of at least 125 ns. To detect the superposition of two (or more) simultaneous frames, use is made of the fact that each contains a Manchester code violation. After correct receipt of a start of frame the signal is sampled at 20 MHz and a check is made to ensure that the average signal is zero. Since the phasing at this frequency is not necessarily known, two sums are calculated, one between two consecutive samples and the other between two samples with one sample in between. If neither of these sums is zero a collision has occurred. This method is designed to detect 100% of collisions between two or more stations; it is proposed but not obligatory, since manufacturers achieve the same results in a different way.

Summary   We now summarize the crossing delays for all transceiver types.

Tables of the total crossing delays for a repeater with built-in transceivers (such as a hub), for a valid signal and then for a collision are given below.

Table 10.4   Delays of different repeaters for a valid signal (frame).

Transceiver type	Delays due to the transceiver Input + Output	Total time in bit times
10base5	6.5 + 3.5	14
10base2	6.5 + 3.5	14
FOIRL	3.5 + 3.5	11
10baseT	8 + 5	17
10baseFP	3 + 4	11*
10baseFB	2 + 2	4
10baseFL	5 + 5	11

*: for 10baseFP the calculation involves a repeater incorporating two transceivers and not a passive star.

Table 10.5   Delays of different repeaters for a collision.

Transceiver type	Delays due to the transceiver Input + Output	Total time in bit times
10base5	9 + 3.5	19
10base2	9 + 3.5	19
FOIRL	3.5 + 3.5	13.5
10baseT	9 + 5	20.5
10baseFP	11.5 + 1	19*
10baseFB	3.5 + 2	12
10baseFL	3.5 + 5	15

*: for 10baseFP the calculation involves a repeater incorporating two transceivers and not a passive star.

The switching hub

The most efficient solution to the new bandwidth requirements is to increase the global speed of the network without jeopardizing the architectures previously chosen. The idea is, in fact, to improve the existing MAC technology by moving from an access mode in which all the connections share the global bandwidth to one in which the total bandwidth is dedicated to each pair of items of equipment for the duration of the transmission of each packet.

Taking advantage of the star topology linked to all installations with structured cabling (twisted pair and optical fiber), it is effectively possible to guarantee that the maximum speed is available to each port for each of its communications. The hub is then called a switching hub, since it is responsible for the dynamic switching of the packets between the ports, simulating the operation of a switching matrix.

The main practical advantage of switching lies in the fact that it can make use of the majority of existing network hardware, whether cabling, connectors, all the network interface cards (and, of course, their drivers) and, in certain cases, even the multi LAN technology modular chassis. In addition, the concept of packet switching is applicable to all shared LAN technology, whether Ethernet (recently including 100baseT), Token Ring, LocalTalk or FDDI. However, the popularity and vulnerability of the CSMA/CD access method has made this requirement urgent on Ethernet, in order to help users who are already in a difficult situation with overloaded networks.

No LAN standard deals with packet switching yet, although this is nevertheless a completely separate new technology with its own qualities and characteristics. We note in passing that the switch is an intermediate hardware element between the hub and the multiport bridge. Like a hub it has a large number of ports, but operates like a bridge in that it works on the MAC addresses. Given that it operates at the MAC level, we shall not describe it in further detail until Chapter 11, on interconnection hardware.

10.7 Test equipment

Various types of hardware may be useful for testing a network, during receipt or when dealing with a breakdown. Some hardware has been specially developed for local area networks, other hardware is general purpose.

The oscilloscope

This traditional device is used to visualize the signals directly in the coaxial cable or on the twisted pairs of the drop cables. When it has a resolution greater than 10 MHz, it can be used to check the shape of the signals, the rise and fall times and the interframe gap. Its main advantages are that it can be used to visualize packets

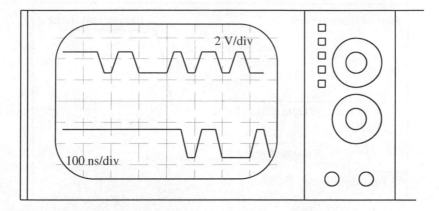

Figure 10.26   Ethernet signals on an oscilloscope screen.

passing through an active hardware element of the network (transceiver, repeater, bridge, star) and can measure the crossing delay for the device (Figure 10.26).

It is easy to find tap points for the electrical signals, whether on the coaxial cable, the twisted pairs of the AUI cable or the 10baseT lines, which can be used to establish the observation directly on the medium or between the MAU and the PLS without disturbing the communications. Measurements on the optical transceivers are usually made through the intermediary of the drop cable. Finally, one particular application is the qualification of the retransmission of intensive traffic by an interconnection device, where one seeks to detect irregularities such as bursty emissions which are detrimental for the other hardware.

Since it is a laboratory tool, one always needs to have available a minimum quantity of minor measurement hardware associated with the oscilloscope: a probe, crocodile clip, drop cable splitter and BNC and type N connectors.

The coaxial reflectometer

The reflectometer for coaxial cable measures the variation of the impedance along a medium segment (it does not cross the repeaters) (Figure 10.27). Its operation is based on the periodic emission of calibrated peaks at one end and the observation of the amplitude of the reflection of this signal in time. This measurement is known as Time-Domain Reflectometry (TDR). Note that the reflectometer screen is graduated in mρ/DIV rather than in Ohm and only measures differences in impedance.

These reflected peaks are processed in order to determine the impedance graph for the cable over its whole length. Thus it is possible to detect any abnormal variation which could lead to malfunctioning, to check that the maximum reflection rate of 7% at an arbitrary point (connection of a transceiver) or 4% at the straight connector points studied is not exceeded. The graph can also be used to locate the

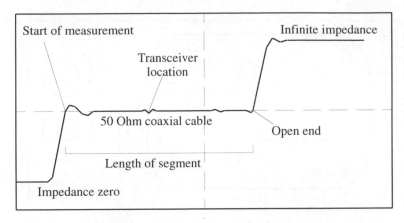

Figure 10.27   Example of a screen of a coaxial reflectometer.

positions of cuts, junctions, and transceivers relatively exactly. If the opposite end is not fitted with a 50 Ohm terminator, the important reflection at this point can be used to obtain a reliable estimate of the length of the segment measured.

A regular measurement campaign, for example every two years, may be used to monitor the aging of the medium, its hardware and its attachment points.

For increased freedom in measurement activities and operations one should choose a battery-operated device. Since the reflectometer generates electrical signals and quantizes their reflection on return, all the transceivers connected to the segment studied must be disconnected during the measurement so as not to disturb either the reflectometer or the attached stations. The greatest risk is that the emissions from the transceivers will lead to a deterioration of the reflectometer, if the latter does not have appropriate protection.

The optical dBmeter

The optical dBmeter has the simple function of measuring the power of a light signal reaching it. Thus, it can be used to evaluate the attenuation of a fiber optic link, with a view to checking that the maximum attenuation between the two ends authorized by the standard (9 dB for FOIRL) is not exceeded (Figure 10.28).

Good quality work requires the choice as light emitter of a stable calibrated source (not an active transceiver for example) operating in the same frequency range as the network hardware to be installed (850 nm for Ethernet, 1300 nm for FDDI). The measurement is relative, that is, the attenuation due to the fiber is evaluated by taking the difference between the power received directly behind the source and the power of this same signal after it has crossed the link in question. Current hardware can usually store the first value as a reference, so that the display then gives the difference directly.

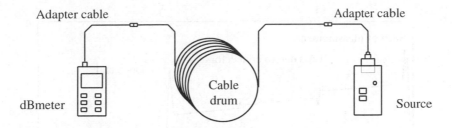

Figure 10.28 Configuration for measurement of the attenuation of an optical fiber.

Since the connector technology for the optical source and the receiver cannot be universal (given the heterogeneity of this area) adapter cables are usually needed. Thus, it is important to carry out the reference measurement with the attachment cables which will be used subsequently.

The receiver indicates the power in dB (hence the name dBmeter) or in mW. The signal frequency used should also be indicated (820, 850, 1300 or 1550 nm) for greater accuracy.

Some emitters can accommodate different sources, each operating at a specific wavelength and being either an LED or a laser. The laser, which delivers a considerably greater power than the LED, is used for the measurement of very long lengths. In a practical way, the source and the dBmeter are both small battery-operated devices (which can be held in the hand) which are robust enough that they can be moved without difficulty.

We stress that this is an elementary measurement which cannot be used to locate a fault when the link is defective, but only gives a global figure. We shall see below that there exist instruments capable of analyzing the quality of the optical fiber in a much finer manner.

The optical reflectometer

The optical reflectometer operates on the same principle as the coaxial reflectometer but, of course, using light signals (Figure 10.29). It produces Optical Time-Domain Reflectometry (OTDR), measuring the reflection rate (or variation of index) along the fiber by emitting periodic peaks from one end. The result is a graph showing the attenuation due to the fiber at all points, which gives, among other things, the total length of the link.

Unlike measurement using the dBmeter, reflectometry gives information about the quality of the fiber over the whole path, except at the output end, where the reflection rate on the open connector is generally sufficiently large to mask any defect at this point. This device can be used to evaluate the attenuation per kilometer, visualize the quality of the attachments (pair of connectors) and the splices and locate these precisely. Like measurement using the dBmeter, it is preferable to carry out

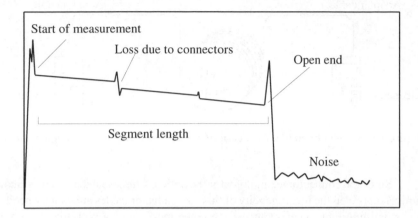

Start of measurement

Loss due to connectors

Open end

Segment length

Noise

Figure 10.29   Example of the screen of an optical reflectometer.

the reflectometry at the same frequency as that of the active elements which are to be used (850 nm for Ethernet).

Specifically, the gradient of each section easily gives the attenuation as a function of the length (for example, 3.5 dB/km with the 62.5/125 μm at 850 nm); the difference between the two sides of a pair of connectors gives the attenuation due to this attachment (strictly, the stable tangents to each side should be used). One effect that is rapidly encountered is the dazzle in each large perturbation, such as that produced by a connector. Since the reflectometer's receiver is saturated by the returning signal (comparatively much larger than the simple reflection due to the fiber itself), measurement near a connector is not reliable. To obtain a better resolution, one should choose a shorter peak (long peaks being reserved for measurements over long distances, which require more power). However, the measurement will still be partially masked around a strong source of reflection. This implies that the first and last connectors cannot be qualified, since a stabilized part of one of their sides is missing. To counter this disadvantage a trailer (extra length of fiber) can be inserted in front of the link to be studied, and possibly after it. This makes it possible to measure the end connectors since one then has a stable line segment, obtained before and after the fiber, on the screen. It is then possible to evaluate the total attenuation, although less accurately than using a dBmeter. Note that, since the majority of optical links are bi-fiber links, the two fibers may be looped together for measurement at the far end using a jumper wire; thus, it is possible to check the two distant connectors even if one does not have a trailer. However, measurement from the other end is still useful for checking the two other connectors.

In practise, the reflectometer is a top-of-the-range device, whose sources are often in the form of inter-changeable slide valves, each with a unique fixed operating frequency.

In conclusion, we note that there exist elementary optical reflectometers called fault finders which give a graph very similar to that of a reflectometer, without being able to provide a reliable measurement of the attenuation. Since only the distance from the source of the observed reflection can be retained, they have to be reserved for use in an emergency (intervention in the case of breakdown), and cannot be used to qualify the optical fiber.

The tester for twisted pairs

The tester for twisted pairs is a small, easily transportable device (it fits into the hand). This is a more recent tool than the previous ones, being directly linked to the development of local area networks. It is a tool in full evolution which incorporates an increasing number of functions. Originally, the only measurements it was capable of taking related to twisted pairs. It could give the approximate length of the segment (using TDR) and indicate whether the segment was open or short-circuited or whether the pairs were crossed. The result is displayed in English (in text mode, without graphics) on a liquid crystal display (Figure 10.30).

Today, it is adapted to standard and thin coaxial cables (type N and BNC), to the shielded and the unshielded twisted pair (hermaphrodite and RJ45 connectors) and, indeed, to the palettes of patching modules. It is able to test several pairs at a time, check their order and detect crossings, measure the in-loop resistance and store the reflectometry curves obtained and print them or transmit them to a PC. It can generate Link Test Pulses to validate the ports of a 10baseT hub, and is capable of measuring the network activity using a bar graph, generating alarms when events occur and dialing via a modem. Associated with a small RF receiver box, it can be used to track the path of the cabling in walls and suspended ceilings.

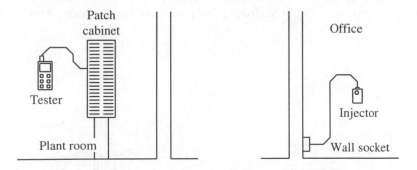

Figure 10.30   Test of a cabling link using a tester and an injector.

The Ethernet test set

The Ethernet test set is a simple, portable tool which implements part of the MAC layer. Thus, it can be used to carry out tests involving the emission and receipt of frames in the Ethernet format, in order to validate a network infrastructure including all types of medium, transceivers, repeaters, bridges and AUI cables.

The main desirable capability is the possibility of creating an automatic echo mode between two connection points. The two sets of the pair are generally assigned in a master–slave relationship. The master regularly generates frames (possibly numbered), which the slave receives and replies to with identical frames. The master set is responsible for checking that no frames are lost. This test is used to check a chain of devices on the route of the packets. Since no protocols above the MAC level are involved, this qualification is purely Ethernet. We note that for the traffic to pass through the bridges, the source and destination of the frames must be distinct (use of emission in multicast is possible, but not always desirable). Passage through routers is rarely possible because the contents of the MAC frames generated are meaningless in most cases. Since the presence of traffic on the medium does not always facilitate implementation of this echo mode (partly because of collisions), the use of test sets may be restricted to during receive operations on empty networks.

In addition to their ability to carry out an exchange in echo mode (Figure 10.31), these test sets can provide other functions such as the test of the drop cable (continuity and insulation of each pair, determination of the type: Ethernet V 2.0 or IEEE 802.3) or the test of the transceiver with qualification of the electrical levels of emission, reception and detection, the delay in triggering the jabber, and the presence or absence of the SQE test. This collection of tests may be very useful when dealing with a network one of whose elements is conjectured to be defective. The Ethernet test set can be used to carry out a series of tests of the units. Some test sets offer the possibility of evaluating the round-trip delay for a network, either from a point, by the emission of a frame which is reflected against one end in an open circuit, or between two test sets with the voluntary generation of a collision. These measurements are generally less precise than those of a reflectometer, but quickly give an order of magnitude measurement. Finally, the test set can also generate a given rate of traffic (from a few percent to the maximum) with frames

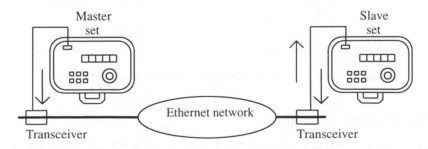

Figure 10.31   Pair of Ethernet test sets in echo mode.

of a parametrizable length, emit defective packets (too long, too short, with a bad CRC) or create collisions.

Some manufacturers offer Ethernet test sets with three AUI sockets (two of which are used to test the AUI cable from end to end), a BNC connection (for testing the transceiver outside the network when it can be attached by the AUI socket and the coaxial cable at the same time) and, sometimes, tap points on the drop cable pairs (this last option is essentially adapted to qualification operations in the laboratory using an oscilloscope).

The test set should be able to count all the frames received, the collisions and the faults. Since the device is relatively rudimentary, it is expected to be precise, reliable and easy to use and install. As we shall see in Part III, it is a very useful piece of hardware in repair work, when it can be used to validate one or more network access points. Note that the test set operates with frames whose fields are only important at the MAC level, and that the data field is generally just a sequence of bytes, independent of any protocol. Conversely, the test set is able to count the frames circulating in the network and recognize whether or not they are intended for it, although it cannot provide more information.

Although it is not an Ethernet test set, we now include a rapid description of the tool called a frame killer. This uncommon device is designed to inhibit all traffic going to or coming from a particular group of stations. It carries out a test on the MAC-level address field and systematically generates a collision with the frames to be eliminated. In this way it blocks all undesirable traffic.

The operation of this device is restricted to the interdiction of all dialog for stations, in the period before it can be located precisely to deal directly with its user. By preventing it from communicating with the rest of the network one seeks to limit the disturbance it causes (for example, broadcast avalanche). Note that, since the test is carried out at the MAC level, the frame killer must be located in the same network as the machine in question and not beyond a router or a gateway.

The analyzer

The Ethernet analyzer is the most complete MAC-level test equipment, which is still portable for use in repair work. It should be able to operate on the Ethernet fields for both reception and emission.

Moreover, over successive evolutions, the analyzer has acquired an understanding and a knowledge of the most common higher protocols, and can deal with all the fields of the frame (from the preamble up to level 7). It has also become programmable, which opens up a wealth of possibilities for implementation.

The analyzer should be able to measure the network traffic precisely and display the total number of frames, errors and collisions received, their rates per second in the form of an instantaneous value, and an average, together with the maximum rate recorded (associated with the time this occurred). It should also be able to capture complete frames, construct the list of addresses of machines using the network and decode the frames as finely as possible while automatically managing the standard protocols (TCP/IP, DECnet, XNS, IPX, ISO, and so on)

(Figure 10.32). It will also be required to emit frames whose format and various higher-level fields will be defined by the user or recovered by capture on the network. All these tasks should be executable within as broad a range of speeds as possible, both during reception and counting and during emission, so that the use of the analyzer is independent of the measurement conditions. For example, the analyzer will be required not to lose traffic in reception, even when the load is very high, whether valid frames, very short frames (a few bytes), excessively long frames or collisions. In all cases, the counters should be exact so that the measurement is truly reliable and can be used with confidence. Similarly, in emission, the analyzer should be able to generate a maximum level of traffic, even with short frames (64 bytes). Even more demands will be placed on it if this device is used in assemblies for qualifying network hardware.

On this subject, we note that there are several ways of counting the traffic as a percentage (Figure 10.33). If one considers the frame with all its fields (preamble, addresses, type, data and CRC), the maximal traffic in short frames (64 bytes + 64 bits = 576 bits) is 85.7% ($= 14880 \times 576/10^7$), while, if one ignores the preamble, the short frame comprises 64 bytes and the maximal traffic represents a usage of 76.2% ($= 14880 \times 64 \times 8/10^7$). This explains why, excluding device faults and limitations, not all analyzers count in exactly the same way. Still on this subject, some analyzers include in their evaluation of the traffic (as a percentage or in kbps) all the bits read, whether they are part of a frame structure or isolated. The resulting information is sometimes very useful, as in the case of an infinitely long preamble which would occupy the medium without representing traffic in terms of frames per second.

The possibility of programming these devices with a few lines of code or a sequence of test conditions means that they can be used in an automated and diverse way. For example, it is possible to trigger an arbitrary action (alarm, storage, capture, emission) when different events occur, such as the receipt of certain special packets, the passing of a threshold or the elapsing of a timer. Applications can therefore be developed by users focusing on their own needs.

Finally, the industry has recently begun to produce analyzers with analytical

```
frame 3111    9 Sept 92      16h27'34"42536             length 60   no error
Ethernet : Dest :   Sun-07-51-17  Source  : HP-23-45-81  Type : DoD_IP
   IP Version : 4  Header length bytes : 20  Type of service : routine
         Total length : 41  Ident : 37562  Flags : May Frag Last Frag
         Frag offset: 0    Time to live : 30       Next protocol : TCP
         Chksum : OK 00-19 Source : 154.27.2.154  Dest : 154.27.35.48
   TCP Source : 1023    Dest : RWHO_RLOGIN      Sequence no : 142578296
         Acknowledge : 765774905     Data Offset : 20  Flags : ACK_PSH
         Window : 4096       Chksum : OK      Urgent point : not used 0
```

Figure 10.32   Example of a screen showing a decoded header.

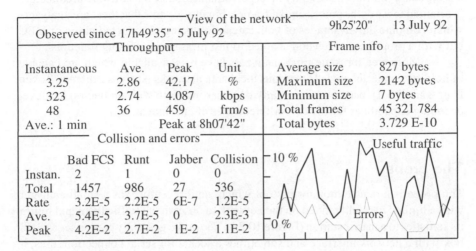

Figure 10.33   Example screen of analyzer statistics (unit for errors: occurrences/frame).

capabilities and a certain autonomous reasoning power. Expert systems have been coupled to the functionality of the devices so as to relieve the novice user of level 2 or 3 repair tasks. Thus, these new analyzers claim to be able to detect defective frames at the MAC level or in the network layer together with certain anomalies such as the duplication of logical addresses. Although this new facet is a noteworthy introduction, one should not expect too much from a PC with an analyzer card and an inference motor, which, in any case, cannot determine the topology of your network or the characteristics of the traffic of the stations.

In practise, there are two main categories of Ethernet analyzer, one based on slot-in cards (in long format) for PCs (possibly portable), the other based on proprietary hardware, which is therefore closed. In the first case, either the card is 'smart' with its own microprocessor and RAM (a few Mbytes are needed) and capable of carrying out certain processing directly on certain packets received and stored in its memory, or it is a simple Ethernet card and all the processing is the responsibility of the microcomputer host. Up to now, this second type of card has not been able to offer the visibility capabilities of dedicated cards, which are sometimes expensive but have a high performance. The advantages of the analyzer in the form of a PC card lie first in its apparently few restrictions, in that it interfaces with any portable micro with a (long) extension slot that is not necessarily reserved solely for the Ethernet analyzer function and, second, in its openness to MS-DOS software (spreadsheets, graphics), since after processing the data is returned to the PC platform and can be stored in standard files. These files can then be recovered by a word processor, a spreadsheet or a commercial graphics program. Moreover, manufacturers sometimes offer users the possibility of enriching certain decoding themselves by accessing the source code. The advantage of the analyzer developed on a proprietary platform lies mainly in its performance, since its hardware architecture is oriented towards the processing of frames. Finally, we note that there are analyzers which combine the advantages of both categories, being constructed based on a PC but with a proprietary extension adapted to fast message processing functions.

Moreover, for some time, analyzers have been available which are capable of holding connector cards for various local area networks (such as Ethernet, Token Ring and FDDI), but which have only one user interface with unique higher-level decoding capabilities for the two or three types of attachment.

The probe

The probe is a remote monitoring tool which, until recently, was a small analyzer with a limited capability, fixed on the network to observe the traffic there and return its statistics to a master station (Figure 10.34). The probe generally comprises a small box with a network interface and sometimes a socket for serial connection; thus, it does not have a screen or any form of display. This implies that a non-trivial part of the processing is carried out at the level of the management station (calculation, averaging, storage, display).

The main data concerns network load statistics and graphs, covering valid frames, errors, and collisions over periods of various lengths. This includes the storage of maximal values, the evaluation of mean rates and peaks for each category of frame, together with a listing of the Ethernet addresses of active stations with their corresponding traffic and error rate. These figures are communicated regularly to the monitoring station, either by the network, if this is not defective or out of service, or by the intermediary of a serial link between the probe and the station.

Probes have evolved with the development of management protocols such as SNMP of the TCP/IP family. They still collect statistics on the network traffic, as an analyzer might, but they no longer simply present them in the manufacturer's format and now follow the SNMP standard and certain groups of the RMON (remote monitoring) MIB specifically defined for this purpose. The groups of RFC 1271 are statistics, history, alarms, hosts, host_top_N, traffic_matrix, filters, packet_capture,

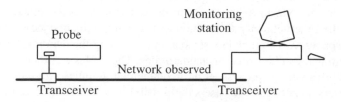

Figure 10.34   Monitoring system comprising a probe and the master station.

and events. These groups correspond to relatively rich analytical and observational capabilities, which also consume processing power, hence the need for a dedicated CPU. These standards also classify the errors in detailed categories (Table 10.6).

In addition, SNMP defines the values to be monitored in the form of variables in a tree structure, the whole being defined in libraries called Management Information Bases (MIB). The manufacturers have naturally added to the amount of data that their probe can capture by adding proprietary MIBs to those already defined (MIB-I, MIB-II, and RMON).

Finally, we note that if the network implements the dynamic packet switching technology at certain nodes, the probe becomes somewhat less interesting, since each port of the switch only allows traffic to pass which is either explicitly destined for interfaces connected behind this port or is in diffusion. Thus, a probe alone on a switch port will only see the traffic in diffusion. This remark also applies to any network which is micro-segmented by numerous local bridges.

Table 10.6   Standard transmission characteristics.

	Length < 64 bytes	Correct length	Length > 1518 bytes
Correct FCS	Undersize	Packet correct	Oversize
Bad FCS	Fragment	Bad CRC/misaligned	Jabber

Management hardware

Here, we distinguish between the agent which accumulates the measurement data (such as the probe) and that which processes and analyzes the data and presents them to the person responsible for monitoring the network. This last element actually constitutes the management tool with which people communicate.

Several classes of device are capable of transmitting the data relating to the traffic they observe to a management center. This includes hardware dedicated to the monitoring function (probe, analyzer) or hardware involved in the network architecture (repeater, hub, star, bridge, router, terminal server, file server, peripheral server) which is equipped with sufficient intelligence to send statistical reports to a master station.

All these elements accumulate information about the parts of the network in which they are located and send their data stream to one or more concentration points whose job it is to synthesize all the data. The management station receiving the data streams first has to be able to understand them, which is not a self-evident matter. In fact, the proprietary formats of the messages exchanged for management of the hardware devices have given way to certain standard protocols. However, each manufacturer is able to record special information which it then includes in its database, in an extension of the standardized framework. For example, if the management station is meant to cover a large number of makes of hardware, it should be able to decode the packets of each and associate a meaning with each counter (knowledge of a private MIB).

If possible, the management station will present results of the analysis of the contents of all the message in graphical form, associating graphs of various loads, changes in colors when certain thresholds are passed and requests for acknowledgment when warnings are issued. One possible method of navigating through the various layers of description avoids submerging a whole screen, in the case of a heavily populated network, and represents the network in a hierarchical fashion.

In addition to simply listening in to the packets of management information circulating on the network, monitoring systems should also be able to interrogate (poll) the machines managed to retrieve the desired counters at the appropriate time. They should also be able to parameterize certain acquisitions by defining the measurement periods, the addresses observed, the protocols concerned, the levels of alarms or notification on the traffic, the percentage of frames in diffusion, the errors, the collision rate, and so on.

In addition, a hierarchy of management stations may be developed with several successive levels of information retrieval. In this light, one can envisage that a single console may receive the synthesized overview from several machines, which themselves receive the information from smaller management systems. At each stage, the concentration of reports on the state of part of the network should be handled in such a way that only relevant new details are retained and only important or significant warnings are passed on. The objective remains the same, that is, to be able to monitor the network, whatever its size, from a single screen, while ensuring that no notable events are missed and without being submerged by a chain of alarms triggered by a single event.

When choosing a device of this type, care should therefore be taken to ensure that the tool is easy to use (or as undaunting as possible) to eliminate the risk of being faced by a sequence of indications with an impenetrable meaning. One should also look for a system with a rich knowledge of hardware from different manufacturers (possibly developed in collaboration), and which can be updated by adding modules describing recent or additional databases. The underlying standardized protocol should be SNMP today and possibly CMIP or SNMP v2 in the near future.

In fact, SNMP was not originally designed for such generalized and complex uses as those for which it is effectively employed today. It was to be a rudimentary and temporary solution. Consequently, its simplicity and intrinsic shortcomings (lack of security, low performance on important data, limited error management, no report for hierarchical or distributed configuration) have begun to become truly restrictive and must be overcome. SNMP v2 represents a recasting of this management protocol, which is applicable to network and application-related devices and to computer systems, and which supports other protocols in addition to those of the TCP/IP world. It covers the functionality developed for Secure SNMP and, of course, the description of objects by the MIB.

Chapter 11

Interconnection possibilities

- MAC bridges

- Connection to networks of other types

- Terminal servers

Up to now we have described the components which may constitute an Ethernet network, together with those which can be used to test it. Given the inherent limitations of the technology, in terms of the area covered and the number of machines, interconnection requirements appeared at a very early stage.

The first requirement was to extend an existing network or to interlink several more-or-less adjacent networks. Various types of hardware meet this requirement, including bridges, routers, and gateways. Repeaters and stars, which cannot extend the coverage of a single network, do not fall in this category, even when they can be used to exceed the standardized distances.

Bridge processing is at level 2 (more precisely, at the MAC level), and thus achieves a more than satisfactory performance (its functionality may be encoded entirely in hardware). The bridge has the advantage of being totally transparent as far as the use of the network is concerned. Its disadvantage is inherent in its function, namely that it cannot be used for logical segmentation of interconnected networks and therefore propagates the problems on all the networks attached to it.

The router provides connection at level 3, where the routing information is normally found. Its processing depends upon the encapsulated protocols and thus may be less extensive, in terms of its knowledge of protocol classes (mono- or multiprotocol). Since its work is much more elaborate, it is partially handled by software, which, several years ago, was an indicator of a modest performance. Its advantages lie in its independence from the lower layers, since it may have all types of network interface (Token Ring, FDDI, serial lines). It is not transparent and has to be addressed before it can be crossed.

The gateway is concerned with links at the level of the higher layers and remains a specific hardware device. When it acts on application data (level 7), it may be developed on any protocol stack on each side of its interfaces.

Readers will have understood that the devices do not all meet exactly the same requirement, even if they all involve interconnection. Their respective advantages inevitably mean that they are each preferred in different situations.

These three types of hardware are relatively old and only their performance has evolved at different times. Bridges were the first to provide suitable capabilities, followed by routers. Gateways, being specific devices, are somewhat separate.

11.1 MAC bridges

We have already seen that an Ethernet network was limited in its extent (once the maximum number of repeaters had been installed) and in the total number of machines. With the deployment of Ethernet technology, the desire to extend a network or to interlink several networks soon arose and led to the definition of an element called a bridge. For many years, bridges existed and operated well without being standardized. The IEEE 802.1 standard was issued in 1990 and the previous hardware has undergone very minor evolution. This standard was updated by the ISO version: IS 10038.

The bridge can be used to interlink two (or sometimes more) networks via female AUI slide-latch sockets; constraints such as the round-trip delay remain local to each network (Figure 11.1). However, the whole operates as a single network, since the crossing of the bridge is transparent to the users. The bridge also has an action on the traffic and does not allow all the frames reaching it to cross. In fact, it is capable of learning which machines are located behind each of its ports and of filtering (not allowing to cross) a frame whose destination belongs to the same network as the emitter. This functionality is made possible by observation of the frame addresses.

The bridge is said to be local when it interlinks segments of adjacent local area networks. Conversely, we shall see that the remote bridge interlinks distant local area networks by using the intermediary of a serial line.

The bridge is said to be located at the MAC level because its processing and understanding of the frame are based on the interpretation of the packet at that level. Thus, the bridge rejects any frame which is erroneous from the MAC point of view, including excessively long and excessively short frames, frames which do not consist of a whole number of bytes, and those with a bad CRC (the repeater does not do this). Frames which are meaningless to it are not processed, either for learning or forwarding. If a received frame is valid, the bridge learns its source address, which amounts to storing the pair (source address, number of port at which received). Thus, it knows from then on that the station which emitted that frame lies behind the port through which the frame reached it. This information is stored in its learning table, which the bridge will use for any forwarding decision. Simultaneously with the learning, the bridge processes the frames reaching it. If the destination address of the frame received on the port N is not in its table it retransmits (forwards) the frame on all the ports other than N. If the address of the frame is in its table and associated with port N, it discards the frame from its processing procedure, since, in the meantime, the frame will necessarily have reached the destination station, which is on the same network. Finally, if it finds the address in its table, but associated with a port other than N, it forwards the message on this port only. This whole process is called natural filtering or filtering by learning (Figure 11.2). It is standardized by the IEEE under the name of transparent bridging. All Ethernet bridges must implement this filtering function, as a minimum.

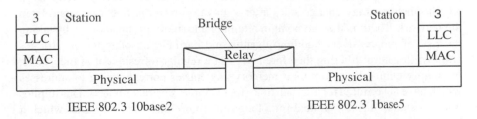

Figure 11.1   Example of a bridge between Ethernet and StarLAN.

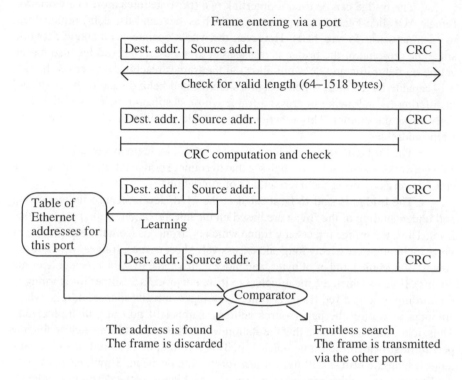

Figure 11.2   Stages in the natural filtering operation on one side of a biport bridge.

Depending on the hardware, the learning of an address may take place immediately, or after one or more frames have passed (this last case is rare and undesirable). In the best of circumstances, the frame that is used to update the learning table is subject to filtering with the new table, which amounts to saying that a frame with identical source and destination addresses will never cross a bridge. For most bridges, the device will let the first frame through, but not subsequent frames.

The learning function associated with natural filtering is not simply additive, that is, it does not accumulate the addresses observed indefinitely in its tables. In fact, such behavior would be a handicap in the case of evolving networks in which machines may change sides after a move or even disappear for good from the network. There is then no point in retaining a memory of the address, by taking the risk of progressively building gigantic and partially obsolete tables. Bridges employing natural filtering therefore carry out a regular refreshment of their table, by simply eliminating from their memory any entries corresponding to addresses which have not emitted for a certain time (for example, several minutes). This implies that if a station has not emitted for a long time (more than the delay after which it is forgotten), the frames destined for it will be forwarded by the bridges on all their ports, like packets with an unknown destination. Another condition which results in the modification of the learning table is the change of side of an address (a physical address previously seen on a port of the bridge is later detected on another port). In this case, too, the bridge updates its table as a function of the recent information. However, if the address changes sides regularly and relatively quickly, some bridges then refuse to register the address, considering this to be an abnormal situation.

We note that, in the case of several networks interlinked by several bridges, it is not crucial for a bridge to be able to differentiate between every existing network. It is sufficient for it to have a local view and, without risk of upsetting the operation of the network, it may confuse all the networks which are finally linked to it through the same port.

IEEE 802.1D represents the bridge as shown in Figure 11.3. This figure picks out the vital functional blocks for the bridging function (the two MAC entities and the MAC relay entity) and the supplementary blocks (the LLC entities and the higher layers). The MAC level is implemented for observation of the traffic and to forward frames, while the level above is used for communication between bridges.

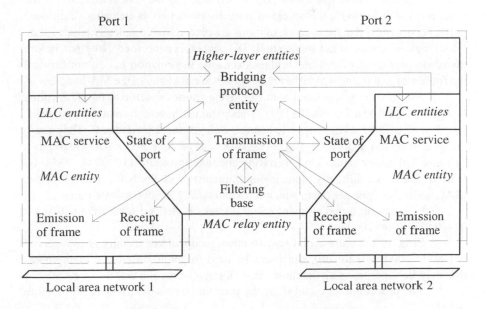

Figure 11.3   Architecture of a biport bridge.

The spanning tree

The vulnerability of the transparent bridge to loops is a crucial problem which was settled by the implementation of an interaction between bridges and a capability to detect and eliminate looped paths. In fact, the loop, if it is not detected, causes the bridge learning tables to lose all their validity and gives rise to a continuous circulation of the frames which then fill all the linked networks. We note that the solution chosen to resolve the loop problem by deactivating ports on certain bridges is simple, but not optimal. In fact, it would be more effective to distribute the traffic on the different possible routes, thereby increasing the global bandwidth of the interconnections.

Nevertheless, the manufacturers of transparent bridges soon implemented a version of the spanning tree algorithm (the term 'spanning tree' refers to a loop-free topology extending over all the interconnected networks). However, as soon as the IEEE 802.1D committee had finalized the Spanning Tree Protocol/Algorithm (STP/A) all the manufacturers rallied to it, with the concomitant advantage that bridges of different makes take part in the same exchanges to establish the desired tree. DEC's implementation, which was very common, is also supported by certain interconnection equipment.

In summary, the STA's function is to define one of the bridges of the architecture as the root bridge and to establish a ramified topology based on this, without loops, of course. The loops are suppressed by deactivating certain bridges and all the networks are thus attached to the root bridge by a unique path (see changes from Figure 11.4 to 11.5). On each network, one of the bridges is chosen as a designated bridge, this being the bridge that leads to the root bridge. Similarly, each designated bridge has a root port which leads to the root bridge, while the other ports which provide this access to more distant networks are called designated ports. Ports involved in the creation of loops are placed in a completely passive state (blocking), except as far as listening to BPDU packets is concerned. Note that, before the configuration stabilizes, the bridges exchange information but do not forward the frames of real traffic which they receive and do not yet learn the MAC addresses.

For this, the bridges communicate using frames specific to the STP, called Bridge Protocol Data Units (BPDU). These frames have a format of type IEEE 802.3 or IEEE 802.2 (LLC type 1, connectionless, unacknowledged). They use a group destination address 01-80-C2-00-00-00 and an SAP = 0×42 (which has a symmetrical binary value). On Token Ring, the function address 03-00-00-00-80-00 is used (due to the difficulty of managing multicasts with the NIC). The bridge has MAC addresses (one per port), which it uses naturally as source in its frames.

In addition, a management group address is defined for all the networks: 01-80-C2-00-00-10.

Finally, for future evolutions, 15 other group addresses have been reserved (01-80-C2-00-00-01 to -0F), which can be used to define different bridging areas that may be superposed on the same network interconnection architecture.

The procedure for establishing the spanning tree is described below in more detail.

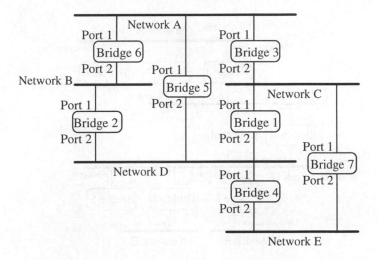

Figure 11.4   Example of networks bridged before the spanning tree is established.

Choice of the root bridge

When it is energized, or when it is isolated (in the absence of any external information), any bridge thinks that it is itself the root bridge. It therefore periodically (every 2 seconds) broadcasts frames on the networks to which it is attached, indicating that it is the root and giving its 8-byte identifier. This identifier consists of the priority and the MAC address of the bridge (it is recommended that this should be the address of the port with the smallest number). The frames are sent to all the bridges, but do not cross them. The bridge chosen is that with the highest priority, that is, whose identifier has the smallest value. This root bridge is therefore a designated bridge for the LANs to which it is connected.

Whenever a bridge receives a BPDU from a root bridge which is effectively superior to it, it stops emitting its own messages and echoes those coming from the root on the networks behind it. In these messages it indicates the identifier of the bridge it considers to be the root and uses the STP parameters implemented by the latter.

Choice of the root ports

Once the root bridge is determined, the other bridges of the network will propagate this information on the networks to which they are attached and position their ports in such a way that the root port is that which is on the side of the root bridge, while the others are designated ports (Figure 11.5).

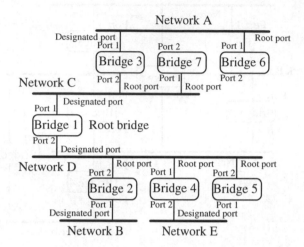

Figure 11.5 Example of a tree-like topology emanating from the root port.

Choice of the designated bridges and ports

On each distant network (on which the root is not directly connected) the bridges will inform each other of the bridge identifier for the bridge that they have chosen as the root and of the cost of the path they propose to this root bridge. After a joint survey of the root, the bridge proposing the least expensive path will win. This cost is normally proportional to the sum of the inverses of the speeds of the networks crossed, or the sum of the delays in emission. The other bridges will place their port in a passive (or blocked) state so as to eliminate loops (Figure 11.6). The ports are chosen using a system of preferential selection based on the priority, then the number.

For this calculation, it is recommended that the cost of each network should be 1000/(speed in Mbps of the connected network), which gives: $\approx$ 4000 for a serial link at 256 kbps, 250 for Token Ring at 4 Mbps, 100 for Ethernet, 62 for Token Ring at 16 Mbps and 10 for FDDI or 100baseT.

In the case of a dispute, when the bridges propose the same path cost, the decision is based on the priority level of the bridges (that is, on the identifier) and, in the case where a bridge has several ports connected to the network, the port with the smallest identifier is chosen. Note that all the ports of a bridge should have an identifier consisting of a priority and their number.

In the previous, somewhat simplified example, we used the number of the bridge as the identifier and we supposed that the costs of all the networks (and the costs of the associated ports) were identical.

All in all, the ports move between four different states, plus a deactivated state. The listening and learning states are transitory phases.

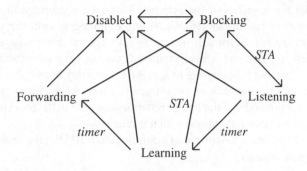

Figure 11.6   Diagram of port states.

Once the port is declared to be part of the spanning tree topology, the transition from the listening phase to the learning phase and then to the forwarding phase takes 15 seconds in each case, or a total of 30 seconds.

The transition to the deactivated state is not part of the STP, but may be imposed by the management system.

Bridge Protocol Data Unit   The two types of message emitted by the bridges to manage the spanning tree are the configuration BPDU and the BPDU indicating modification of the topology. They all have a frame format conforming to the structure shown in Figure 11.7.

The MAC source address is that of the emitting port of the bridge. The LLC header includes the DSAP and SSAP = 0×42 indicating the STP.

The configuration BPDUs are emitted periodically by the root bridge on its networks. The bridges receiving them in turn forward them on all the networks they feed, and thus propagate the identifier of the root bridge, while incrementing the path cost as a function of the last network crossed (path cost of the receiving port). Thus, these BPDUs leave the root and are echoed on each branch of the tree, up to the extremities. Note that they transport the parameters imposed by the root, including the maximum age of a message, the interval between hellos and the delay in forwarding.

n bytes	3 bytes	35 or 4 bytes	*p* bytes
MAC header	LLC1 header	BPDU	MAC postfix

Figure 11.7   General structure of a BPDU.

The messages emitted by the root have an age of 0 and are forwarded with this same age along the branches of the network. However, if a bridge of the network temporarily receives no further BPDUs, it will continue to emit the same packet periodically (every two seconds), increasing the age of the message relative to that from which it is derived. Thus, it indicates that its original information is not perfectly up to date, but is beginning to age. After the delay of *max age* (20 seconds recommended) the information coming from the root where these BPDUs were constructed is suppressed and the bridge redefines the path to the root (path cost and root port) based on other indications which it receives.

Figure 11.8 shows the format of a configuration BPDU; the individual fields are constructed as follows.

- **Flags**

- **TCA (most significant bit): Topology Change Acknowledgment** Bit positioned by the root bridge to acknowledge receipt of a message notifying a topology modification and indicating that the emitter should stop sending other messages of this type.

- **TC (least significant bit): Topology Change** Bit positioned by the root to inform the bridges that a change has occurred and that the forward delay should be used for the timer of fast aging for the learning table (15 seconds instead of 5 minutes).

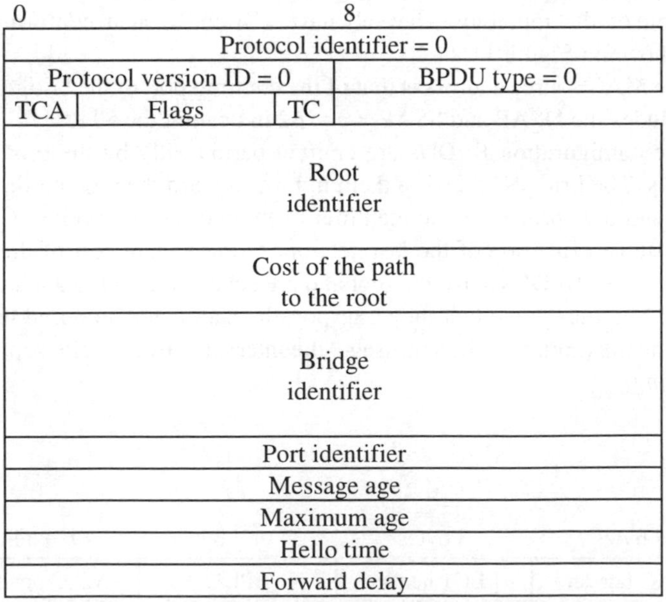

0		8	
Protocol identifier = 0			
Protocol version ID = 0		BPDU type = 0	
TCA	Flags	TC	
Root identifier			
Cost of the path to the root			
Bridge identifier			
Port identifier			
Message age			
Maximum age			
Hello time			
Forward delay			

Figure 11.8 Format of a configuration BPDU.

- **Bridge identfier**
  - Priority of the bridge (two most significant bytes): 32768 by default, from 0 (high) to 65535 (low).
  - MAC address of the bridge (six least significant bytes).
- **Port identifier**
  - Priority of the port (most significant byte) to force the selection of the port in the case of a double connection: 128 by default, from 0 (high) to 255 (low)
  - Port number (least significant byte).
- **Root path cost** Cost of the path to the root: from 1 to 65535. Recommended value = $\sum$ 1000 Mbps/speed of networks crossed.
- **Message age** Delay which has arisen between the receipt of the last source BPDU carrying information from the root and the emission of the present BPDU which is derived from that. This delay may be overestimated by 1 second at most (4 seconds is an absolute maximum) but should never be underestimated.
- **Max age** Maximum age that a message may have, once stored, without being updated, after which it should be discarded: 20 seconds recommended, value of from 6 to 40 seconds imposed by the root bridge.
- **Hello time** Minimum interval for periodic transmission of information from the root: 2 seconds recommended, from 1 to 10 seconds.
- **Forward delay** Delay serving as timer between the stages of listening and learning and then of forwarding and also as the age of aging during the changeover phase, value imposed by the root bridge: 15 seconds recommended, from 4 to 30 seconds.

When the bridge does not choose the default values indicated above it should, however, respect the following inequalities:

$$2 \times (\text{Forward Delay} - 1 \text{ second}) \geq \text{Max Age}$$
$$\text{Max Age} \geq 2 \times (\text{Hello Time} + 1 \text{ second}).$$

Note: the durations are encoded in units of 1/256 s.

The BPDUs indicating modification of the topology are emitted by a port when it detects a change in the network, such as the non-receipt of periodic configuration BPDUs on one of its active ports, or when it becomes the root itself (Figure 11.9). The bridge then emits this indication to the root bridge and the information is propagated, in the opposite direction to the configuration BPDU, from the periphery to the center of the network. The root bridge acknowledges this message with a configuration BPDU (with the Topology Change bit activated), and all ports receiving it reduce the age of the dynamic entries in their learning table. Normal operation is resumed as soon as the topology change bit of the flag field of the following BPDU is reset to zero.

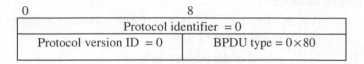

Figure 11.9   Format of a BPDU notifying a change of topology.

Other parameters, such as the crossing delay for the bridge, are defined by the standard:

- **Maximum bridge transit delay** Maximum acceptable delay in forwarding a frame, after which it should be discarded: 1 second recommended, 4 seconds absolute maximum.

- **Maximum BPDU transmission delay** Maximum delay in transmission of a BPDU by the bridge: 1 second recommended, 4 seconds absolute maximum

- **Hold Time** Minimum interval between the emission of successive BPDUs on a port: 1 second.

Finally, the standard specifies that the maximum recommended diameter for the architecture is seven bridges. This means that at most seven bridges can be crossed when passing between two different networks; this is equivalent to a maximum diameter of eight networks.

The filters

In addition to the natural filtering function, some so-called programmable bridges offer client-defined parametrization of filters. The number of these filters is generally a multiple of eight, and they can be applied at one or more ports, on input or output.

There are several categories of filter, such as those which involve the modification of the natural filtering by the forcing of static addresses in the learning table or the prevention of the insertion of a given address. It is thus possible to give an incomplete definition of a permanent address to be fixed in the learning table, which may, for example, only involve the manufacturer part (first three bytes). These static filters always correspond to a test on the destination field of the frame in transit. However, another category of filters can also be used to define tests on the source address of frames, on the type/length field or on any other byte sequence. In fact, serious programmable bridges can be used to read and test any field, defined by its offset (from the first byte of the frame), its length, a binary mask (used to ensure that only the desired bits are taken into account) and a reference value. In the case of equality with the reference value, the action may be to forward the frame and not the others or, conversely, to discard the frame and not the others, to associate it with a priority level within the bridge, or simply to count the frame and leave the behavior of the bridge unchanged.

These different categories of filtering are applied in serial and in a well-determined order (Figure 11.10). Natural filtering (possibly modified by the addition of static addresses) is generally the first test performed. It is followed by the test of the source address, that of the type field, and finally, the establishment of the correspondence with a given bit sequence.

We note, in passing, that this filtering capability enables the bridges to work on fields of a level greater than two. It is easy to see that the bridges are then capable of eliminating frames in general IP broadcast (it is sufficient to take the IP destination

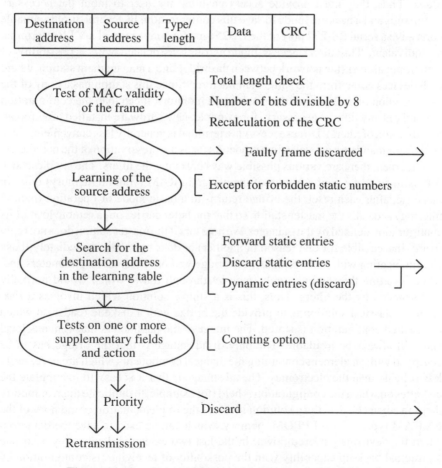

Figure 11.10 Stages of filtering in a programmable bridge.

address and compare it with 255.255.255.255). However, since the filter is always fixed, it cannot, for example, take into account a variable-length header, and thus its domain of application remains limited.

Here is one last point on the subject of the intelligent filtering of certain devices which are able to discard frames according to the consistency of their fields. Thus, bridges may reject frames whose type field does not have a meaningful value (such as 0000), frames with an unauthorized source or destination address (for example, manufacturer field set to 00-00-00) or frames passing on a MAC level protocol which they do not support (such as the Loopback). This is a plus, because the bridge does not forward these frames, however minor their illegality, but one should bear this in mind when carrying out tests with an analyzer, which generates valid frames (MAC level) that are not necessarily perfectly rational (at the LLC or network level).

Unlike simple bridges which do not implement natural filtering, programmable bridges can modify their operation according to the parametrized filters. Thus, they must provide access enabling the user to input the necessary commands and a back-up mode to save this configuration. In general, programmable ports have a serial RS-232 port of the DB25 type for connection of a VT100 terminal or equivalent. This direct access mode is often associated with a possibility of communication via the network between the bridge and a management station, where both devices come from the same manufacturer. Since this station has a copy of the configuration of each port of the machines it monitors, it can load the configuration remotely at any time, if necessary (for example, new hardware installed after repair, modification of filters). Direct access via a terminal is generally less convenient, since all the commands are passed in line mode. As far as the preservation of the parameters is concerned, there are various possible ways of saving the filters. The simplest such way is to store the configuration of the bridge in RAM (volatile memory) only. In this case, after each reset, the bridge returns to a basic mode of operation (natural filtering) and calls the master station so that the latter carries out a remote load of its configuration defined by the manager. We note that if the master station does not reply (being inaccessible for one reason or another) or does not reply immediately (busy communicating with other bridges), the bridge will have lost all its parameters and, while awaiting the station's reply, may let through traffic which would normally be forbidden by the filters. Thus, this is a simple solution which involves a risk. Another classical solution is to provide the bridge with a diskette reader on which the desired configuration is stored. The image of the parameters thus remains local and will always be available. The only disadvantage is that the bridge has to be equipped with an element containing mechanical components which are necessarily less reliable than the electronics. The advantage is that it is easy to manipulate the diskettes on which the configuration is held (for example, to duplicate them or modify them in advance). The third solution involves the implementation of memory of the NVRAM type or flash EPROM memory, which can be used to save the data even when the device is powered down. In the last two cases the device may associate an internal back-up capability with the possibility of receiving its configuration by remote loading.

As we noted earlier, bridges are relatively old elements, but their capabilities have evolved considerably. The first devices had quite modest filtering and forwarding rates, but their use could not be considered to be truly transparent since they could easily lose part of the signal sent to them. The interconnection of segments by bridges was essentially imposed by an inescapable requirement (to extend a network, to enable two networks to intercommunicate). Conversely, today, the choice of a bridge may result from a desire to reduce the traffic of a large network by segmentation (using the natural filtering function), in the implicit hope that the set of all the networks interconnected by bridges will function better than the original heavily loaded network, which of course implies a reliance on the device capabilities.

The multiport bridge

In the case of multiport bridges, the mode of operation is more or less identical to that of a biport bridge. The main difference is that the learning table has to contain two fields per entry, namely the Ethernet address and the port on which it was seen. In fact, it is not desirable for an unknown address on the receiving port to be transmitted to all the other ports. Instead, the correspondence should be sought and broadcast should only take place after a fruitless search of all the addresses stored by the bridge.

The multiport bridge is nevertheless subject to a constraint on its processing capability which is a direct function of the number of bridges. In fact, although a biport bridge should theoretically be able to filter twice 14 880 frames per second and be able to transport up to 14 880 frames per second (in the worst case, a network will be saturated by short frames with a non-local destination), the N port bridge should be able to filter $N \times 14\,880$ frames per second and transport $(N/2) \times 14\,880$ frames per second.

Although some local bridges now manage to process the maximum Ethernet traffic, that has not always been the case; in fact, it requires a well-adapted hardware architecture. Thus, bridges should not only increase the number of interfaces, but should also, as far as possible, be capable of not losing frames because of overflow (which would imply a lack of reliability).

The MAC bridge based on the PC

At the bottom of the range in terms of performance are local bridges, developed based on PC hardware, which have been supplemented by two Ethernet cards. These devices have the advantage of being affordable and easy to modify (hardware and software). However, their capabilities are often too limited to permit the intercommunication of two networks with a medium-to-high load. Thus, they are reserved for relatively undemanding applications.

However, these devices have recently undergone an evolution with the support for serial links offering low-cost WAN connections and the routing of various common protocol stacks.

The switching MAC bridge

Some bridges have a special hardware structure based on dynamic frame switching. These bridges (which are necessarily multiport bridges, if they are to be of real interest) are capable of creating (virtual) connections between two networks independently of the traffic of the other networks, and this for the duration of the transmission of a frame. This switching takes place in parallel; each Ethernet network attached to this bridge is guaranteed not to experience a degradation in the performance of the interconnection hardware with the load of the other networks. As an intermediate device between hubs and bridges, the switching bridge (or switch) has already been discussed with repeaters. It is described more fully below.

The switching bridge exploits the star structure of the twisted-pair and fiber optic hubs to cause an evolution of the access method whereby a signal emitted by any one of the network stations is reproduced on all the segments, and thus reaches all the ports so that it becomes an operation in which the frame received by the hub is only routed to its unique destination, without consuming the bandwidth of the other ports (Figure 11.11). In fact, in the first case, the traditional hub shares the total bandwidth by simulating a bus and occupying the bandwidth of each machine when one of these emits. In the second case, the switch dedicates the whole bandwidth to each port and may route several frames simultaneously.

Hardware or software architecture

Packet switches may be implemented in various ways. The distinction between hardware and software switches is that between switches based on a hardware architecture developed specifically for the switching function and those based on one or more general-purpose processors (CISC or RISC) executing a code sequence describing the bridging function.

At any given time, several frames may cross the switch simultaneously, using circuits established for the duration of their passage only.

Hardware switches include specific VLSI integrated circuits, which handle the packet forwarding function on the contents of the MAC source and destination

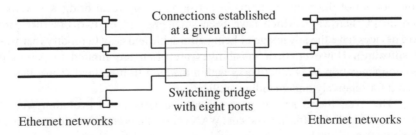

Figure 11.11   Symbolic diagram of a switching bridge with eight ports.

addresses optimally. Their structure is inevitably distributed because these circuits are present in every port, and hence in multiple instances. Their advantage lies in the performance of which they are capable. Their main disadvantage is the limited capacity for evolution, since, by definition, they are unable to evolve to the role of router.

Software switches execute a program which may evolve naturally to bridging (including support for the spanning tree or various types of filtering) or multiprotocol routing. Conversely, their global capabilities are limited by those of the central CPU, and their performance (bandwidth and transmission delay) depends in a non-trivial manner upon the total load to which the switch is subjected.

Switches may use a true switching matrix on a backplane or a distributed architecture (consisting of specific components) around a high-speed internal bus; their global performance may increase with the number of ports supported.

There are two address processing modes, namely the on the fly mode, where the packet is forwarded as soon as its MAC destination address (first field) is read, and the store and forward mode, where the packet is stored in its entirety on receipt before being re-emitted. The advantages of the first mode are clearly its rapidity and regularity (very low transit delay, independent of the frame length), while the second mode can be used to eliminate all faulty packets, including those which have been involved in a collision. The software architectures mentioned above are generally associated with the second mode of operation.

Finally, for those wishing to orient their equipment to a hub switching in which all Ethernet accesses may access all the 10 Mbps, or to the function of a high-performance multiport bridge, the switch will support address tables of varying size. If few addresses are known to the port, it is known as (dynamic) port switching; if a large number of addresses are known it is called segment switching. Note that the concept of switching, where the bandwidth is guaranteed by the user, is only really applicable for a port switching limited to one (or more) Ethernet machines by connection to the hub. Segment switching is the equivalent of a high-performance multiport bridge. Table 11.1 lists the various characteristics of a switch.

Performance

The crux of the evaluation, testing or qualification of a bridge is the verification that it is intrinsically (without the addition of a filter) functioning well. The traffic level at which frames start to be lost will then be measured in frames per second. In most cases, this limit is given in frames per second and not as a percentage of the traffic or in bytes per second. This reduces to saying that the operation of the bridge is generally decorrelated from the length of the frames to be processed, which is not surprising, since the action of the bridge is only triggered by the first two fields (the MAC addresses), which are fixed.

To give a purely indicative figure, a bridge capable of transporting 2000 frames per second may prove insufficient in certain cases (heavy loads), although if it can forward 5000 frames per second it will be suitable for most applications (Figure 11.12). However, for several years, hardware (sometimes expensive) has

Table 11.1   Characteristics of a switch. Each line gives the two possible options. The lines are mutually independent. In each cell, the advantages are shown in roman print and the disadvantages in bold.

Criterion	First option	Second option
Type of equipment	*Modular chassis* Evolutive number of ports **Sometimes too many possibilities**	*Standalone box* Typically affordable **Non-evolutive configuration** **Limited-speed interswitch connection**
Architecture	*Hardware* High-performance (specific VLSI) **Functionality limited to** **switching only**	*Software* Easy evolution to bridging, routing and filtering. **Performance function of the traffic**
Internal structure	*Distributed/multi-processor* Better global performance **Complex equipment structure**	*Centralized* Simplicity of switch concept **Poor performance, a function of** the **global load on the equipment**
Distributed internal structure	*Distributed* Better global performance independent of the total load **Complex internal operation**	*Hierarchical* Simpler internal structure **Performance a function of the master** **Unique failure point**
Switching core	*High-speed bus* Evolutive number of ports Support for various LANs **Complexity transferred to** **interfacing components** **to the high-speed bus**	*Switching matrix* Performance independent of traffic Internal components operating at the unit speed of the links **Configuration limited by no. of ports** **Limitation to a single technology**
Processing	*Store and forward* Check before forwarding Mandatory if ports with different speeds exist **Transit time ≥ frame length**	*On-the-fly* Transit time min. and constant **No check of the packet** **Dependence on network access delay**
MAC addresses per port	*Small number (port switching)* Guarantee of switching services for each station of the network Reduced domain of action of the MAC **Implicit micro-segmentation**	*Large number (segment switching)* Connection of existing segments 1st natural stage of migration **MAC defects persist** **partially on each segment**

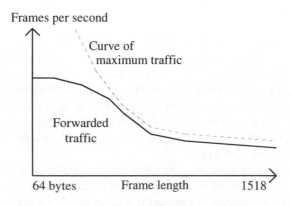

Figure 11.12   Typical performance of a bridge during forwarding.

been available which is capable of working with the whole Ethernet bandwidth without loss (maximum = 14 880 frames per second). This is top-of-the-range equipment which is reserved for specific requirements and exacting conditions.

Furthermore, not all bridges react in the same way to heavy traffic (greater than their forwarding capability). The best succeed, in all circumstances, in transporting the maximum number of frames per second, corresponding to their threshold for no losses, while the worst collapse as the load rises and then only transport traffic equivalent to a fraction of their maximum bandwidth.

In the same spirit, some bridges have the property that they smooth the load at the element level, that is, they re-emit a more homogeneous (from the point of view of the interframe gap) traffic than that input. Others, on the other hand, will tend to transmit the frames in bursts, even if the traffic reaching them is homogeneous, when they approach their loss threshold.

The crossing delay for a local bridge is generally between 100 and 200 μs plus the frame-reading delay. Some bridges, generally high-quality ones, have a quasi-constant crossing delay, while others exhibit a variable crossing delay depending on the load to which they are subjected. As in the previous case, regularity is a desirable quality; however, the delay required to cross the bridge does not hinder the flow of the network traffic, although it is often an indicator of the internal operation (sporadic forwarding being generally linked to the approaching saturation of the processing capabilities).

Finally, it should be mentioned that the addition of parametrizable filters generally degrades the performance of the bridge. This is mainly true for filters which do not use the learning table (since the implementation of static addresses, or the prohibition of some addresses, only modifies the behavior of natural filtering slightly). In fact, since the internal architecture is oriented towards the processing of address fields, it is adapted to fast management of the learning table (observation, recording, establishment of correspondence), although searches of another field (type/length or arbitrary bit sequence) are not always as immediate. Thus, these tests, which may be implemented by a conventional architecture, degrade the filtering rate in proportion to the number of filters implemented. In all cases, we would expect the filtering capabilities of a bridge to decrease as little as possible when filters are added.

Remote bridges

The remote bridge is an element which may be used to interlink two (or more) Ethernet networks separated by a serial link over any distance. On each network a remote bridge forms the interface between the local area network technology and the modem, linking it to one or more serial lines.

This type of face-to-face operation (per pair, in the case of two interlinked networks) is sometimes called a half bridge, since it is the whole which has the functionality of a local bridge, namely discarding of faulty frames, natural filtering, loop detection by the STP, and so on.

Thus, in most cases, the remote bridge has a female AUI socket and one to eight sockets for serial lines. There exist bridges with multiple Ethernet interfaces, but these must then be able to carry out the function of a local bridge between these AUI ports and of a remote bridge to the remote bridge links.

The serial lines are mainly special purpose lines, whose speed may vary from 9600 bps to 256 kbps (or, more recently, 2 Mbps); links at 64 kbps are very common. Note that these links have a bandwidth considerably lower than that of a local area network, which leads to a limitation on the exchanges between distant networks made possible by bridges. A very large transfer will take considerably longer if it has to pass over a serial line than if it only crosses local bridges. Another important consequence is that remote bridges are not subject to the same performance constraints as local bridges. If they still have to be able to read all the packets in transit on the Ethernet network (which corresponds to a filtering rate of the order of the maximum speed of Ethernet), there is no point in their being able to re-emit more than a few thousand packets per second (forwarding rate). In fact, the serial lines remain the main bottleneck. To put a rough figure on it, a line at 256 kbps can only transport 500 short frames (64 bytes) per second, while the Ethernet port can deliver 14 880 frames of this type per second.

These lines are generally of the RS-232 (V.24) type, but may also be V.35 or RS-449. The associated connectors are of the DB25, American V.35 and DB37 type (Figure 11.13).

As serial interfaces are less demanding than the Ethernet interface, some remote bridges are extensible and can include several serial sockets, while retaining the same hardware base and thus the same processing capability. Serial interfaces may be in the form of multiport cards or small modules.

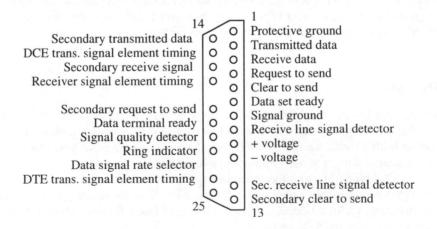

Figure 11.13   Connector signals for the RS-232 interface.

The protocols used in these serial lines have, up to now, almost always been proprietary, although they are often inspired by High-Level Data Link Control (HDLC) and are therefore incompatible. This has meant that the hardware at each end should come from the same manufacturer. Thus, if two companies, with their own range of remote bridges, wished to become interconnected, at least one of them would have to use a different make of hardware. Meanwhile, IEEE 802.1 G is working on this technology. At present, certain protocols which are almost standardized are becoming common. One example of this is the Point-to-Point Protocol (PPP), which was approved in 1989 by the IETF and which should replace the Serial Line Interface Protocol (SLIP) which was dedicated to the transport of IP packets. There are other alternatives, such as X.25, TCP/IP (where the packet is encapsulated in IP) and the new Frame Relay. We note, however, that in all cases these protocols consume part of the bandwidth for transporting their information (header, length, control sequence, and so on).

In practise, as remote bridges have not been subject to the same speed constraints as local bridges, they offer all the programming capabilities, similar to those of local bridges. Associated with this parametrization, in most cases they have a back-up system on diskette.

Finally, remote bridges may use several links in parallel to connect two sites. These lines may be used in a joint manner, which has the advantage of increasing the global speed and the security of the link (with the disadvantage of often being slightly more expensive than a line at twice the speed). The DLS protocol may be used to manage the sharing of the load between these paths.

Distributed load sharing

Abbreviated to DLS, this (non-standard) protocol is also called Load Balancing, and is used to distribute the load over several links from a single bridge, where these links may be parallel or lead to the same point by different paths. For this, the lines are grouped within logical circuits.

When attached to remote bridges, DLS is able to calculate the cost (inversely proportional to the speed) of a route between two bridges. It adds the weight of each section crossed and can thus obtain an estimate of the global capacity of each possible route to a target point. After that, it distributes the traffic across each path in relation to its caliber. Since the distribution is fair, if two lines of the same speed are placed in parallel, the load will be distributed with 50% on each. If one of the two lines has a bandwidth double that of the other, the traffic will be divided in the ratio 2/3 to 1/3.

In the case illustrated in Figure 11.14, the existence of a loop (bridge 1, bridge 2, bridge 3) will trigger the transition of bridge 2 to the passive state. The networks A and B will then be connected with a bandwidth equivalent to $\sim$ 176 kbps (128 + 48) and a cost of 5682 (1/(1/7813 + 1/208 330)). If bridge 1 breaks down, the STP will reactivate bridge 2 and the 9.6 kbps back-up line will determine the cost of the link between the cable segments (1000/0.0096 = 104 167). Note that an Ethernet segment also has a cost; thus, the link between bridges 1 and 2 is at 10 Mbps, that is with cost 100.

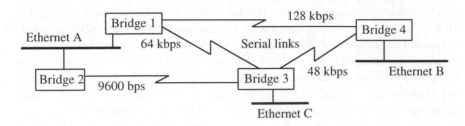

Figure 11.14   Two Ethernet segments linked by a redundant network of serial lines.

Since the packets may follow several totally different paths, on which the constraints are different, there is nothing to say that they will arrive in the order in which they were emitted by the originating bridge. As we have seen, this is unimportant for some protocols, which are able to re-sort the packets on arrival, although it may be a source of connection loss for protocols which do not delay each receipt and wait for the traffic in the order in which it is emitted. Thus, bridges which are capable of using several different paths offer the possibility of forcing the First In, First Out (FIFO) order to be respected. This can be done by assigning a group of destination addresses to each interface.

The modem

Since the remote bridge necessarily accesses the serial line by a modem, a number of the characteristics of this type of device are described here.

The modem is generally located at the limit between the area belonging to the user and the carrier's area (possibly national). It is used to connect two terminal communication elements by a two-wire link or a long four-wire link, by transforming the serial digital data into analog signals adapted for transmission over long distances using modulation. The line belongs to the network provider if it passes into the public domain, but may be private if it remains within the user's site.

Modems are said to be synchronous or asynchronous, depending on whether they are capable of transporting clock information in parallel with the data. There are also so-called baseband modems, which are generally reserved for short distances or low speeds and do not really apply true modulation to the signal before it is transmitted.

The 'leased lines' offered by the national service provider includes: telephone links (up to 9600 bps and 14 400 bps with modems conforming to the CCITT recommendations V32 and V32bis, respectively), analog links (from 1200 to 128 kbps, now almost abandoned), and links from 2400 kbps to T1/E1 (1.5/2 Mbps) (soon to be even faster: E3/T3 (34/45 Mbps)).

Moreover, in recent years, the application of data compression algorithms to transmission on serial lines has become common, and it is possible to pass the equivalent of 38.4 kbps, asynchronously on an analog telephone line (V42bis protocol is recommended, including data compression of the type MNP class 5).

11.2 Connection to networks of other types

MAC bridges, as described above, are directly linked to a technology, or more precisely, to a particular MAC layer (that of Ethernet, in our case). This leads us to believe that a bridge cannot naturally interconnect two networks with different MAC layers.

This has been true for a long time, since the interconnection hardware for two networks of different technologies has to do more than simply forward the MAC fields after having read and checked them. However, bridges capable of interlinking Ethernet, Token Ring and FDDI networks have been available for some years. These are actually bridges, since they have no knowledge of the layers above (LLC or network), although they are still more complicated than Ethernet–Ethernet bridges.

Ethernet–Token Ring bridges

Products are available which are capable of transporting frames between these two different network technologies, although it should be borne in mind that this is not an easy task.

At the physical level, the differences in the speeds, the encoding methods and the bit order do not give rise to insurmountable problems. But at the MAC level things are more difficult, with frame fields which only exist on one side of the bridge (AC, FC, FS), the management of the token, which is meaningless for Ethernet, incompatible minimum and maximum permissible frame lengths and, by default, a type of non-transparent bridging on Token Ring. In fact, the bridging on Token Ring is governed by the source-routing algorithm, in which the stations themselves seek to determine the best path across the networks and bridges to the destination station. Thus, the frames transport routing information (bridging information, in fact) so that they can be switched when crossing bridges. All these differences mean that not all traffic can cross the Ethernet–Token Ring bridge with ease, and so this device can only be adapted to certain exchanges using one or more given protocols.

Given the difficulties of application and the limitations of this type of bridge, it is really only useful for transporting non-routable traffic between Ethernet and Token Ring. The use of a router, without this constraint, is much more natural.

Ethernet–FDDI bridges

Like the Ethernet–Token Ring bridge, the Ethernet–FDDI bridge is more than a simple MAC bridge. It has to manage the differences between the two technologies, although, first, there are fewer (not always source routing) and, second, the need for this category of interconnection hardware is greater. In fact, the installation of a main artery in FDDI, acting as a backbone for multiple Ethernet networks (which serve the buildings), requires the interlinking of these two types of network (Figure 11.15). A number of options are now possible, namely routers (which we shall discuss later) or bridges. As far as bridging is concerned, there are two options: bridging by encapsulation or translation bridging (IEEE 802.1 H describes this mode). The router has advantages in terms of security, since it retains a logical separation between the networks and sub-networks attached to it, although the bridge has the advantage that it does not nominally intervene in the communications. This choice, as will be shown in the following section on routers, should be made as a function of the needs, constraints and objectives.

Over time, the performance of specific electronic circuits has improved considerably, and has allowed the development of devices with an interconnection function for Ethernet and FDDI networks which is transparent to the machines (as is the case for a simple Ethernet bridge). We note that the management of address tables on FDDI, with a speed of 100 Mbps, is constrained to being carried out with extremely short delays. This second transparent model is called translation bridging, since the MAC fields of the input frames are repositioned in the output frames. Of course, the FDDI frames have fields that do not exist in Ethernet, but several types of frame have been identified (Ethernet V 2.0, IEEE 802.3, IEEE 802.2, LLC with SNAP) which can adapt the padding needed for certain fields. Finally, the problem of maximum frame lengths is partially resolved by a few devices and for some protocols. Thus, there exist Ethernet–FDDI bridges capable of segmenting an IP frame with more than 1500 bytes of data circulating on the ring. These 'smart' bridges reconstruct the header of each segment in a way that is consistent with the protocol used. This is a considerable functionality, but one which falls outside the scope of bridging. In the near future, Ethernet–FDDI bridges should also be able to apply this sort of segmentation to ISO or IPX frames.

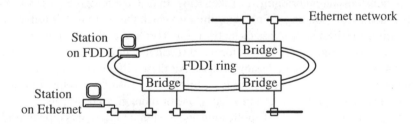

Figure 11.15   Architecture with an FDDI backbone and stations on the ring.

Routers

The router is an interconnection device that uses the logical address information contained in the headers of levels above Ethernet to switch packets within a set of networks (Figure 11.16). In fact, most (but not all) protocols have ways of

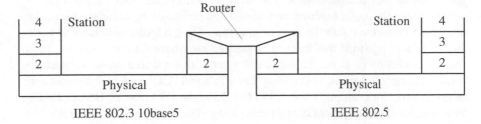

Router

4	Station					Station	4
3							3
2			2	2			2
	Physical				Physical		

IEEE 802.3 10base5   IEEE 802.5

Figure 11.16   Example of an Ethernet and Token Ring router.

identifying the machines independently of their attachment, using a logical address. This description is placed in the network layer. In addition to the level 3 source and destination addresses, the protocol defines the so-called routing parameters, such as the default gateway, the maximum number of routers that can be crossed before reaching the destination, the choice of a route according to type of service (small delay, high speed, high reliability). It is these fields that the router will use to switch and re-emit the frame. It should be noted that in its work, the router is led to modify the physical-level frame. It will change the layer 1 addresses and replace them by its own address as source and the station address as destination, if the latter is on a network attached to it or by the address of the next router to be passed through. This is a fundamental concept, which means, for example, that the observation of MAC level frames leaving a router is of no interest, since they then all have the same source address because the frames entering have the same destination address.

The monitoring of the traffic on the networks between which routers have been installed requires observation tools to visualize the level-3 fields.

Finally, as routers have a knowledge of the different possible routes between the logical networks attached to them, it is advantageous for them to be able to intercommunicate to exchange their tables or information on the availability of a route at a given time. This means that they are able to work in a concerted manner to choose the fastest channel, distribute the load over various serial lines, modify the interconnection technology if loops are detected or switch to a back-up link if the main link fails. So-called routing protocols have been defined to encode these exchanges of data between routers; these incorporate an algorithm (sometimes relatively complicated) for modifying the tables and propagating recent information. In fact, on networks with a large number of interconnection devices, it is crucial to be able to ensure the evolution of routing when incidents occur without losing too much time and without creating an oscillatory phenomenon involving the circulation of contradictory packets on the network. One should not forget that each element only has a knowledge of its own interface, and has to reconstitute the overall configuration of the global network from the information reaching it.

To ensure maximum security, all the routing tables may be predefined and fixed. In this case, the routing is no longer dynamic but static, and only evolves when routes which the manager wishes to incorporate in his or her network are added.

Since the router function lies at level 3, it processes the decapsulated packet and is not concerned with the type of interface. Thus, a router may have virtually any interface, provided this transports the packets whose format it knows. Thus, routers can easily be made multimedia devices with local area network interfaces for, for example, Ethernet, Token Ring, LocalTalk and FDDI, and wide area network interfaces for, for example, E1 & E3 (T1 & T3 in the USA), X.25, HDLC, LAPB, PPP, and, more recently, SMDS and Frame Relay. The serial ports are of the RS-232, X.21, V.35, G.703, and, more recently, High Speed Serial Interface (HSSI) type.

This capability to function with various types of low-level technology implies an ability to truncate excessively long packets, and reconstruct the header of each segment produced. In fact, the networks do not all support the same maximum packet size and the router may very well route frames exceeding the maximum length of the destination network. Since it understands information relating to level 3, it will be able to intervene actively in fields containing, for example, the total length of the datagram or the fragment offset.

The routers now available are almost all multi-protocol, with the ability to handle successive frames corresponding to the main protocols such as IP (DoD), CLNP (ISO), DECnet (Digital), IPX (Novell), AppleTalk (Apple), VINES (Banyan), and XNS (Xerox). They also support a number of routing protocols such as the Routing Information Protocol (RIP), Border Gateway Protocol (BGP), Exterior Gateway Protocol (EGP), Open Shortest Path First (OSPF), Interior Gateway Routing Protocol (IGRP), and ISO's ES–IS and IS–IS.

In addition, since some protocols have no well-defined routing information at level 3 (LAT, SNA, NetBIOS), it should be possible to transmit these frames unchanged, that is, to bridge them. Thus, the router should be capable of carrying out the bridging function in parallel with the processing of routable protocols. This explains the term bridge–router, or brouter, which is found in the technical literature and denotes devices capable of implementing bridging and routing functions. Like bridges, these devices can accept filters, taking advantage of their knowledge of the level above.

We note that the operation of a router depends entirely upon its use (prefixes to the logical network and sub-network addresses to be communicated, choice of the routing system, contents of the routing table if a static method is chosen, and so on). This means that it is vital to program the router to adapt it to the desired function, and that the device should be able to save this configuration, otherwise it will be useless. Thus, routers have a port for connection of a VT100 console, so that the commands to implement the different types of routing can be typed in directly. But they can also be accessed via the network (for example, using the Telnet protocol) and generally in a more user-friendly manner. In addition, they store their configuration locally (diskette or non-volatile RAM) and can also receive their parametrization via the network. This remote loading via the network may be carried out using the FTP protocols (which provides some security since FTP relies on TCP and IP) or TFTP (unguaranteed, because the lower layers are UDP and IP) with a possible call to

BOOTP. Finally, many have the facility for modification of their software by remote loading, in a similar manner to the acquisition of the configuration. Two cases must be distinguished. The first comprises devices whose code is stored in ROM, PROM or EPROM (and cannot therefore be altered) but which can execute procedures stored in RAM. The second comprises devices whose code is stored in non-volatile RAM or EEPROM, and which implement a complete upgrade by means of remote loading. The first case still requires a change of ROM if the router is not to restart with an old version after a reboot, while the second solution involves the risk that the hardware may become unusable if the transfer cannot proceed in a single integral action. In fact, if a power failure occurs, the code having been only partially loaded, no more attempts will be permitted and the circuits will need to be physically changed.

The IP router

Let us consider the specific case of an IP router, in order to give examples of the processing carried out for routing.

The IP router is undoubtedly the most common router, given the popularity of the DoD protocol stack. Its function is to enable (at least) two different logical networks to intercommunicate by translating the physical addresses of the frames it has to transport. Logical networks are distinguished by the first part of the logical level addresses (IP).

There are various classes of IP address defined by the apportionment between the number of bits giving the network number and the following bits which give the number of the host in that network (Figure 11.17). Each network number is

Class A (from 0.0.0.0 to 127.255.255.255)

0	Network identifier 7 bits : 126 networks	Host identifier 24 bits : 16 777 214 machines

Class B (from 128.0.0.0 to 191.255.255.255)

10	Network identifier 14 bits : 16 382 networks	Host identifier 16 bits : 65 534 machines

Class C (from 192.0.0.0 to 223.255.255.255)

110	Network identifier 21 bits : 2 097 150 networks	Host identifier 8 bits : 254 machines

Figure 11.17   The three main classes of IP address.

assigned uniquely by a centralized official body, the Network Information Center (NIC). However, note that the use of addresses which have not been assigned is not dangerous as long as the traffic remains confined and there is no risk of giving rise to conflict or confusion with the machines of the network that officially holds the network number used.

An additional concept allows each group of users with an official address to divide their domain locally into sub-networks. This is based on the use of a sub-network mask (see Figure 11.18). This mask consists of a sequence of 32 bits, and can be used to distinguish between the bits which form part of the sub-network address (corresponding to the bits of the mask set to 1) and those which identify the host (the bits of the mask set to 0). See RFC 950 for more details.

For a station or a router, the sub-network field is treated as though it were associated with the Internet part. Thus, the traffic between two stations in different sub-networks will necessarily have to be routed.

Note that, since IP addressing is user defined, it is not necessarily associated with the physical topology. Thus, machines on a single Ethernet cable may be divided into two logical subsets (each with a different network number). Stations belonging to different networks will then have to pass through a router to communicate, even if the stations and the router are all attached to the same Ethernet network. Conversely, a single IP network may consist of several Ethernet networks, some of which may be remote (provided only repeaters, bridges, and remote bridges are used).

The values corresponding to a sequence of 0s or 1s in the network part, the sub-network part and the station number have particular meanings and should be reserved for this application. The 0 (sequence of bits set to 0) is used to implicitly denote the entity (IP network or sub-network) in which one is located, the host in question. The sequence of 1s (for example, 255 for a byte) corresponds to broadcast and denotes all the networks, all the sub-networks, all the hosts or the whole system (in case of the address 255.255.255.255). Some implementations of IP give the sequence of 0s the meaning of broadcast, which could be a source of confusion and lead to major problems. Finally, the address 127.X.X.X corresponds to a looping internal to the station and does not affect the network.

The basic task of the router is to transmit the packet to be routed, modifying the physical addresses to ensure that it is routed to its destination (which is given by the IP address). Here is a simplified description of how it does this.

Internet part		Local part	
10	Network identifier	Sub-network identifier	Host identifier
2 bits	14 bits	5 bits	11 bits

Figure 11.18 Example of partitioning by the mask 255.255.248.0 (21 bits set to 1, then 11 bits set to 0).

Station A wishes to emit a frame to station B. It only knows the IP-level logical address of the latter. Perhaps with the help of the sub-network mask, if it has one, station A determines whether station B is on the same network (or sub-network) as itself. If this is not the case, it refers to its routing table to find which router is the transit point for this network. If it does not find this explicitly it will send this frame to the default router. Thus, station A's connector card deposits the frame, as illustrated in Figure 11.19, on the physical network. When it receives it the router will read it, interpret it and re-emit it on station B's network.

If the router is not directly connected to B's network, it too will have to pass through one or more intermediate routers, and the frame will bounce from router to router until it reaches its destination (Figure 11.20). On each occasion, the physical addresses change and certain parameters such as the number of jumps taken are modified. Thus, it is conceivable that on the path leading to the target machine, the frame is obliged to pass through a network of a different technology, which would force one of the routers to segment the packets and to reconstruct the header of each segment produced.

Unlike bridges with a relatively limited overall view of the networks, the router has to know which direction to take to return to a particular logical network. Today, IP networks of nearly all countries are interconnected and permit international exchanges by the intermediary of a sequence of routers. The complexity arising from the ability to manage such configurations has forced the existing routing protocols to evolve with the size of the networks. Some complete high-performance products are now available and the constitution of large-scale compositions can be envisaged.

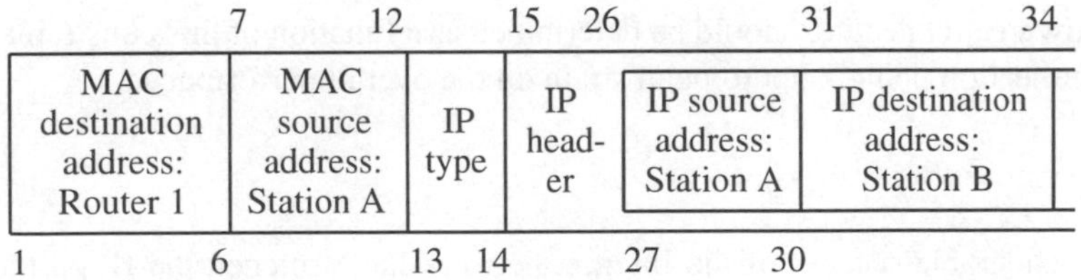

	7	12		15	26		31		34
MAC destination address: Router 1	MAC source address: Station A	IP type	IP header	IP source address: Station A	IP destination address: Station B
1		6		13	14		27	30	

Figure 11.19   IP frame encapsulated in Ethernet with the numbers of the bytes.

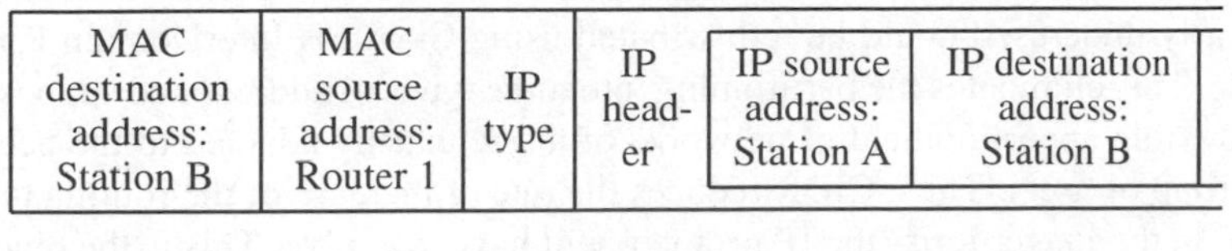

MAC destination address: Station B	MAC source address: Router 1	IP type	IP header	IP source address: Station A	IP destination address: Station B

Figure 11.20   Frame leaving the router for its destination.

Protocols such as IGRP or OSPF try to ensure the reliability of the global network, and treat modification or evolution information cautiously to ensure stability. In addition, they are also able to evaluate the capabilities and cost of each network in a refined way, and to track the state of adjacent or nearby routers and thus provide dynamic management of a large number of devices.

Before ending, note that a multi-protocol router is capable of processing IP frames, as just mentioned, and also other protocols simultaneously. Moreover, it can bridge certain frames and, like bridges, see its natural behavior modified by the addition of specific filters relating to the fields of the network layers it supports. Unlike the bridge, the router, which is responsible for the decomposition of network protocol headers, is able to find a particular field independently of the encapsulation of the lower levels. Thus, if the frame is encapsulated directly in Ethernet or in IEEE 802.3 followed by IEEE 802.2, the IP header does not begin at the same offset; but this will not affect filtering required of a router.

Finally, the router has sufficient knowledge to analyze the validity of a packet and reply to it autonomously if it can (for example, search for correspondence between logical and physical address) or even discard it and inform the sender (if the packet destination is unknown, if it has exceeded the maximum number of jumps permitted for its journey).

Just as some bridges have sight of the layer above, some IP routers support the TCP protocol and are capable of implementing filters similar to those of bridges (forwarding, discarding, priority transfer) on the value of transport-level fields.

It should be stressed that, unlike the bridge with which it often competes, the router links two segments that remain disjoint at the logical level, although the bridge gathers them into a single network. Consequently, the possible problems of a network do not necessarily disturb the nearby networks, as they would in a configuration consisting of non-programmed bridges (natural filtering). Thus, it follows that the router carries out elaborate but not complex processing, and that the dimensions of its hardware architecture should be determined as a function of this constraint if the interconnection point is not to put a strain on the overall performance.

IPng

The considerable success of the Internet network has stretched the IP protocol to its limits. In fact, IP is approaching exhaustion of its addressing potential. The 32 bits provided for this field for logical identification of terminal equipment and the associated partitioning structure did not anticipate such a growth.

There are two possible solutions. For the medium term (ten years or thereabouts) some of the address bands which have already been allocated but are clearly underused could be redistributed using Classless InterDomain Routing (CIDR). This eliminates the partitioning into three types of address and supports the more flexible apportionment of networks of a size exactly adapted to the needs of each group of users. Thus, CIDR reduces the rate of increase of the routing tables.

In the longer term, the IP protocol will have to evolve. This is the objective of IPng (IP next generation) which is intended to replace IP. But, in addition to extending the addressing capacity of the network layer, IPng will also overcome the defects and gaps of IP and be adaptable to new requirements (such as mobility).

Thus, the specifications for IPng should meet a certain number of crucial technical requirements. These correspond to a continuity in the evolution of IP, to the elimination of a number of shortcomings or, primarily, to the support for new capabilities, associated with the current and future size of the Internet, and the new connection modes resulting from recent technical advances.

- The ability to manage at least 10^9 networks and 10^{12} terminal devices (stations) and, preferably, the ability to manage 1000 times these minimum values (for the case of a non-optimized distribution); this can essentially be done using 16-byte addresses.
- Use of conservative routing methods.
- Support for various interconnected network topologies.
- Optimal exploitation of high-performance networks with a simple and strict header structure (accelerated processing with a header without checksum, divided into multiples of four bytes).
- Introduction of a clear and realistic method of migration from IP.
- Provision of a reliable and robust service.
- Independence from the physical network (in addition, the flow label may correspond to the ATM virtual circuits).
- Provision of a datagram-type service (connectionless oriented).
- Support for auto-configuration of addresses.
- Guaranteed security for certain operations (specific mechanisms for authentication or encryption at the network level).
- Unique global addressing for each device (even with topological structuring).
- Based on open, publicly accessible standards (RFC).
- Support for group broadcast (multicast).
- Provision for evolution with extensible headers for the implementation of options (new and additional functions).
- Support for various classes of service (QoS with the flow label).
- Support for the mobility of devices and their connection to the network.
- Incorporation of control protocols similar to those of IP (ping, traceroute).
- Support for encapsulation in various IPng protocols (tunneling).

The new IP protocol will be called IPv6. In fact, the Internet Assigned Number Authority (IANA) has assigned version number 6 to IPng, being an evolution of the present IP protocol which has version number 4.

Gateways

Gateways are interconnection devices which carry out their processing on the layers of levels greater than 3 (from 4 to 7). Thus, for a gateway to operate at level N, it must be able to decode the lower layers (from 1 to N) of the communication systems to which it is attached, which will enable it to obtain the level N message by successive decapsulation. It should then be able to transport the data for this message (which it understands) between its two (or more) communication interfaces and execute the encapsulation steps associated with the port on which it is to emit. Thus, the gateway can interlink two different networks at all levels, provided that on either side the packets transport information from the same unique application process.

It can be seen that its function is more complicated than those of the devices discussed up to now, which were limited to a view of the first three layers only. In addition, since the requirement met by the gateway is always special, the machine may be a business computer programmed as a function of the protocols used and the applications to communicate. Since it is generally not a machine whose architecture was developed for this function only, its performance in terms of frames forwarded per second may be noticeably lower than that of routers or bridges.

Conclusion   In certain situations, repeaters have been replaced by bridges, which represent more complex interconnection devices supporting the natural filtering function and which can be used to extend Ethernet installations over several networks. As the technology has evolved, bridges have proved able to take on the task of repeaters, with the advantage of achieving a performance close to the maximum physical level speed. Today, routers are also able to segment networks from a logical point of view. However, since these interconnection devices operating at levels 1, 2 and 3 are the only elements which handle routing data (in the broad sense), they will continue to coexist and there is no risk of their being supplanted by another device operating on the higher layers.

11.3 Terminal servers

Among the various devices studied so far, the terminal server is slightly separate, since its primary function is not to support the operation of one or more networks, but to use them. The terminal server is a device capable of concentrating several terminal links (mainly of the asynchronous type, with speeds of a few kbps each) and passing these through a network with a sufficiently high speed, such as Ethernet.

On one side the terminal server has an Ethernet port, generally involving a 15-point AUI socket, while on the other side, it has a certain number of sockets (often a multiple of eight, up to 128) for passive terminals. The links may be of the RS-232 or RS-423 type with a speed of up to 38.4 kbps per port, and the connector technology is of the 50-point Telco, DB25, RJ12 or Modified Modular Jack (MMJ) form.

Thus, its work is first to transport the packets coming from the terminals on the network to their destination (which, in most cases, is a mainframe or another terminal server) and, second, to switch the packets received from the network towards the terminals for which they are destined. To carry out this transport the server encapsulates the messages in Ethernet frames, but it is also obliged to use an additional layer, which will contain the information relating to the exchange (identification of the terminal and the host computer, connection characteristics). Two protocols are used for this, namely DEC's Local Area Transport (LAT) and TCP/IP. Today, almost all terminal servers are capable of working with both protocols, even simultaneously. As far as LAT is concerned, we note that it is a non-routable protocol, which has to be transported by bridges or requires the activation of the bridging function on the routers.

Terminal servers may themselves use the network to find their configuration or their system software on a server at boot time. For this, they use the TFTP protocol with BOOTP or RARP, or the MOP protocol for remote loading of the files and data vital to their operation.

In addition, these terminal servers may also be used to interlink modems or printers, and sometimes have parallel link type ports (Centronics) for this (Figure 11.21). Over time, the basic function has been supplemented by other capabilities, such as the possibility of several simultaneous sessions in LAT and/or TCP/IP on each terminal, and terminal servers have acquired an increasingly higher performance.

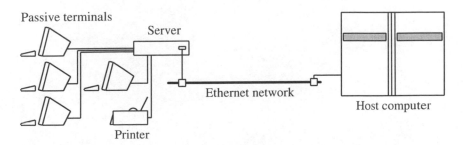

Figure 11.21   Schematic diagram showing the typical use of a terminal server.

Chapter 12

The main figures to remember

Here is a recap of the main physical and numerical constraints associated with Ethernet together with a number of figures that can be deduced:

- A speed of 10 Mbps in serial mode (except for 1 Mbps in 1base5 and 100 Mbps in 100baseT).

- An emission time of 0.1 μs per bit (at 10 Mbps). On a standard coaxial cable, a bit occupies 23 meters and a short frame (counting all fields) would be 13.3 km long.

- A propagation speed ranging between 0.77 c (2.3×10^8 m/s) on standard coaxial cable and 0.59 c (1.77×10^8) on twisted pair.

- At most four repeaters (hence five segments) on the path between two stations.

- At most three non-IRL segments may be present on the path between two stations.

- On a path between two stations which includes four repeaters, each optical segment of the IRL type should be less than 500 meters long for FOIRL, 10baseFB and 10baseFL and less than 300 m long for 10baseFP (when the segment corresponds to two links).

- On a path between two stations which includes three repeaters (hence four segments), no FOIRL segment should have a length greater than 1 km for 10baseFL and 10baseFB or 700 m for 10baseFP. For terminal links (to DTE) these lengths are 400 m and 300 m, respectively. In the case of 10baseFP, the segment again corresponds to two links, one on each side of the star.

- The AUI cables around a 10baseFL or 10baseFP segment should never exceed 25 m, so that the sum of the lengths of the AUI cables at the two ends of a single segment should never exceed 50 m.

- A length of 500 meters per segment of standard coaxial cable (yellow).

- A length of 185 meters per segment of thin coaxial cable. These two restrictions are due to the maximum permissible attenuation along a segment: 8.5 dB at 10 MHz and 6 dB at 5 MHz. Above these values, collision detection cannot be guaranteed as easily, since the signals may be too strongly attenuated.

- A distance of at least 2.5 m between each transceiver on the standard coaxial cable (yellow).

- A distance of at least 50 cm between each 'T' on the thin coaxial cable.

- At most 100 stations per segment of the standard coaxial cable (yellow).

- At most 30 stations per segment of the thin coaxial cable.

- At most 1024 stations per Ethernet network. This constraint does not derive from the previous two. In fact, a segment including 100 repeaters could feed 100 other segments, and hence $100 \times 99 = 9900$ stations. This limitation is intended to reduce the congestion probabilities.

- The frames have a length between 64 and 1518 bytes (60 and 1514 bytes excluding the CRC).

- A minimum interframe gap of 9.6 μs (at 10 Mbps).

- A maximum traffic of 14 880 short frames per second (at 10 Mbps).

- A maximum traffic of 812 long frames per second (at 10 Mbps). This is calculated as follows: $10^7/(64 + 8 \times N + 96)$ where N is the number of bytes in the frame, including CRC (thus N ranges from 64 to 1518).

- Up to 16 successive collisions for the transmission of a frame, with up to 10 increments of the delay interval.

- A crossing delay for a transceiver of less than 3 bit times for emission and 6 bit times for receipt.

- A crossing delay for a repeater of less than 7.5 bit times per frame.

Table 12.1 summarizes the various characteristics associated with each possible type of medium in Ethernet (we distinguish between two main categories: multi-access technologies and topologies with point-to-point links).

The number of connections on a 10baseFP segment depends upon the number of ports the passive star has. The attenuation over a segment should not only be less than 26 dB (maximum) but also greater than 16 dB (minimum). Note that in 10baseFP a segment includes two optical links and the star linking them, where the link with its connectors has an attenuation of less than 6 dB and the star has an attenuation of between 16 and 20 dB.

Table 12.1   Summary of the restrictions according to medium type.

Type of medium	Number of connections	Segment length	Attenuation per segment	Propagation speed	Max. delay per segment
10base5	100	500 m	8.5 dB	0.77 c	2165 ns
10base2	30	185 m	8.5 dB	0.65 c	950 ns
10broad36		3.6 km	36 to 52 dB	0.87 c	14000 ns
10baseFP	33	2 × 500 m	26 dB	0.66 c	5000 ns
FOIRL	2	1 km	9 dB	0.66 c	5000 ns
1base5	2	250 m	6.5 dB	0.59 c	4000 ns
10baseT	2	100 m	11.5 dB	0.59 c	1000 ns
10baseFB	2	2 km	12.5 dB	0.66 c	10000 ns
10baseFL	2	2 km	12.5 dB	0.66 c	10000 ns
100baseT4	2	100 m	12.5 dB	0.585 c	570 ns
100baseTX	2	100 m	5.2/10 dB	0.6 c	556 ns
100baseFX	2	400 m	11 dB	0.66 c	2040 ns
AUI	DTE/MAU	50 m	3 dB	0.65 c	257 ns
MII	DTE/PHY	0.5 m			2.5 ns

The length of a 10baseT segment depends upon the cable capacity and may exceed 100 m.

Note that the physical size of an Ethernet element and the number of elements in it are limited, first, by the round-trip delay and, second, by the narrowing of the interframe gap. Any configuration should be validated against these two factors.

Chapter 13

Critical situations

Ethernet technology has limits other than those described in the standard, in terms of traffic and efficiency. A network with several hundred truly active machines, each claiming a fraction of several percent of the bandwidth, should be viewed as a large network. It will have load peaks, which will generally cause the communication performance to fall, and which are associated with high error and collision rates.

As the size of the network and the number of machines attached increase, a load which is sufficient to place the mode of operation beyond the preferred scope will be attained. It will then be necessary to consider inserting bridges in place of repeaters at the main interconnection nodes. A threshold of 40% is often cited as being the maximum load below which Ethernet operates well and above which problems become more frequent and bothersome. This is a global figure, which has no precise meaning if one does not know the configuration of the network in question. Another, more meaningful indicator of how well the network is operating is the relative collision rate, in terms of occurrences per frame. This is normally less than 1/1000, but depends heavily upon the emission mode of the elements (regular, in slots, in bursts) and on their number and disposition (on the distance separating them). When the collision rate increases, the performance is degraded, retransmissions become more frequent and the timeouts of the higher protocols are put through their paces. Moreover, if a defective element (for example, one which fails to obey the Ethernet rules) disturbs the network, its action may translate into an increase in the collision probability and the faulty device will be detectable using an analyzer to monitor the collision counter.

It will have become evident that an assessment of the state of operation is no easy task and that the best indicator is necessarily relative to a previous state. Thus, regular, periodic observation accompanied by the generation of a number of statistical reports is recommended. The results may then be used as a reference to evaluate the health of the network in question at a given time.

In the great majority of cases, small Ethernet networks linked by bridges or switches may form a communication system which is sufficient for the whole enterprise. In fact, they form a chain, each link of which provides good working conditions (availability of almost the whole bandwidth). The requirements for exchange between these interconnected networks are theoretically less important than the local traffic in each network. This is a direct consequence of the division of the networks into coherent user groups. However, special situations may arise in which the Ethernet technology is under dimensioned. For example, a configuration consisting of a high-performance server feeding more than ten demanding client stations (for example, diskless) may generate peaks of almost 10 Mbps, placing the network in a stress zone in which all users suffer. Nevertheless, we stress that it is rare for the limitation to be due to the network rather than to the capabilities of the server.

Ignoring the problems inherent to Ethernet technology, such as collisions, short frames and misaligned frames, there exists a particularly awesome phenomenon known as a broadcast storm. This is triggered by the higher-level protocols (levels 2 or 3) and the associated routing functions, which, in certain, partially inconsistent configurations (sometimes due to different implementations), propagate the same message from one machine to another by duplication. Each machine capable of understanding this message becomes involved in the movement and contributes to the useless loading of the network. These frames, whose destination address is a general broadcast address, cross the bridges (local and remote) and may rapidly saturate a whole network or all the networks.

These phenomena, which are difficult to control once they are triggered, can be combated, first, by limiting the number of machines with a dubious or illegal configuration (at the level of the higher protocols) and, second, by filtering broadcast frames when they cross bridges and, of course, when they cross routers. However, these incidents in which the network traffic becomes chaotic are very difficult to eliminate completely in large networks; at best they can be limited or confined.

Chapter 14

Technical developments

- Switching

- Ethernet at 100 Mbps

- IsoEthernet

- Full duplex

- Daisy chain

Several trends are currently in evidence:

- Those which correspond to an improvement of products supporting the Ethernet technology by incorporating richer functions in equipment with a higher performance.

- Those which lead to an evolution of the technologies and protocols now in place with the development of new functionalities and additional capabilities within which Ethernet networks are incorporated.

The first category includes:

- Techniques already used by some manufacturers which have finally been standardized (passive and active optical star).

- New, more practical and less expensive media (infrared transmission, radio waves, unshielded twisted pair for high speeds).

- Longer permissible lengths (within the limit of the time budget, or in full duplex) on twisted pair and optical fiber.

- Hubs with a backplane containing several Ethernet buses and other LANs, where each card may optionally be connected to any bus, and/or each port may be connected to one of the internal buses independently of the other ports.

- Extensive filtering and security functions associated with each port of a star.

- The general implementation of dynamic packet switching technology in the main nodes of the network to increase the global bandwidth as required without necessitating a modification of the other equipment.

- Increasingly important capabilities for analyzing and monitoring the network elements and the global traffic (systematic integration of an SNMP agent or an RMON probe).

- Natural extensions to the standards offering higher speeds (such as Ethernet at 100 Mbps).

In the second category, Ethernet at 10 Mbps will only be one module among all the available telecommunication technologies. Ethernet will then occur as the final link for all users, the minimal channel of which is vital to all terminals. This would mean, for example, that twisted-pair links (of the 10baseT type) would link the stations to the concentrator, with each actually offered 10 Mbps of bandwidth (the management of the overall traffic would be performed at the centre of the network using a different technology, such as dynamic packet switching, FDDI, or more probably, ATM). These links to each unit would support the transport of isochronous traffic together with computer data.

Note that, within a certain framework, the two directions come together and the near future will probably lie somewhere between these two trends.

Finally, in the section on media, readers will have noticed the description of radio and infrared links under local area networks. This type of communication could replace the stage of service by capillary cable if wireless techniques are as reliable and effective as they appear, and if the prices fall sufficiently.

14.1 Switching

Since dynamic packet switching constitutes one of the most undeniably progressive evolutions of existing LAN technologies, in what follows it is described from the point of view of the associated services. The associated equipment was discussed in Chapter 11, on interconnection hardware.

Functionality of the switch

Switching provides a coherent set of services and capabilities which correspond to a true evolution of the existing technologies. On this subject, note that switched Ethernet offers a functionality very similar to that promised by the arrival of ATM (but still in a spirit of continuity to the benefit of users): guaranteed bandwidth per port, management of congestion, traffic priorities, plesiochronous traffic, multicast channels, and a virtual network concept.

Furthermore, dynamic packet switching is applicable to all technologies using a shared access method, in that it offers to dedicate the entire bandwidth to each port. This is true for Ethernet (at 10 or 100 Mbps), Token Ring, FDDI, ARCnet and LocalTalk. Moreover, switching can be combined with other advances (such as 100baseT). It is even indispensable in the full-duplex case.

Performance

It is vital that the intrinsic performance of the switch should be perfectly transparent as far as its usage is concerned, that is, the internal bandwidth should be at least equal to the sum of the speeds of all the ports which are able to enter into communication simultaneously. In the case of a 10baseT switching hub with N ports, the bandwidth should be greater than $N/2$ times 10 Mbps, measured in terms of bits per second, but also, and most importantly, in terms of packets passed per second (pps): $(N/2) \times$ 14 880 pps. In fact, the switch, like the bridge or router, works on the headers. Thus, its task is directly proportional to the number of MAC headers to be processed per second. Of course, this result should be independent of the global load on the switch.

Management of congestion

One of the new aspects which have appeared with this switching technology is that the N to 1 fluxes have the property that they may give rise to congestion (Figure 14.1), then to overflow, while one of the switch's specific tasks is to eliminate this kind of problem. Consequently, for a switching technology to be complete it is essential that it should manage extreme situations in a consistent manner to ensure that no packets can be lost by the switch (under any conditions) and to provide a fair distribution of the access of the N stations to the server. In addition, several priority levels may be used which share out the bandwidth, giving priority to applications judged to be critical.

Thus, some manufacturers offer a back pressure algorithm which informs emitters that they are involved in an over-run phenomenon and that their transmissions will be limited. This MAC mechanism should be perfectly compatible with the LAN technology used and applicable to all types of traffic, that is, protocol independent. Congestion management can also be perceived as an extension of the service offered by collision management (and its backoff-algorithm) (Figure 14.2). In the Ethernet framework, one way of implementing such a mechanism may involve occupying the medium on the ports responsible for the congestion (ports receiving more traffic than can be effectively emitted to the addressees) so as to regulate the bandwidth of the latter. The aim is to establish a correspondence between the sums of the input and output bandwidths for each stream. When an over-run occurs the switch will then instantaneously fix the emissions on certain ports, so as to recover a fluid traffic flow; this should be done without causing frame loss and with at most a few collisions. Then the switch makes full use of the CSMA/CD, but does not act as a simple NIC, since it authorizes itself to continue its emission to achieve the desired effect, independently of the Ethernet rules and timers.

In Token Ring and FDDI, bits A and C may be used to indicate that the addressee is present, but not ready to receive the frame which should be re-emitted.

In the case of a switch, when a packet is lost when receive buffers overflow,

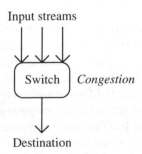

Input streams

Switch   *Congestion*

Destination

Figure 14.1   Congestion condition.

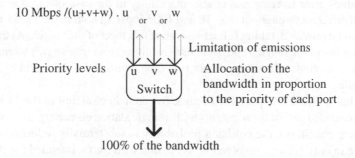

Figure 14.2   Regulation of the congestion situation.

no indication is sent to the emitter and only the first connection-oriented layer (*a priori*, the transport layer) will be able to detect the loss by timeout on the non-acknowledgment, and recover by re-emission. However, this implies a perceptible delay at the user level (generally of the order of a few seconds) and, possibly, an aggravation of the congestion phenomenon, as all the packets emitted since the first unacknowledged packet will be retransmitted (those within the sliding window), although most of these may have reached the addressee normally.

We note that the hub (multiport repeater) manages the congestion phenomenon simply using the CSMA/CD access method, where the occurrence of a collision tells the emitters concerned that their emission could not be carried out properly and did not reach the addressee. Of course, the hub only has 10 Mbps of global bandwidth. This is because the switch imposes strict limits on the MAC layer collision domain behind each of its ports to which it has to be able to provide the same service as the latter.

Privacy

Packet switching is naturally associated with an increase in the security of exchanges, since the communications are only visible from the ports of the emitter and receiver. The implicit disadvantage is that it becomes very difficult to observe the global network traffic, as was previously possible using an analyzer placed anywhere on a segment. Thus, the only solution involves built-in monitoring equipment with direct read access to the bus or the matrix at the heart of the switch.

Crossing delay

The fact that a central switch is used (whether it be a true switching matrix or a system emulating the function of one) means that a low and predictable propagation time across the switching hub can be offered. This delay may be fixed if on-the-fly operation is used, that is, always on the same number of bytes, or linearly proportional to the length of the frame if a store and forward mode of operation is used. This mode enables error filtering and is also mandatory in the case of input and output ports with different throughput (e.g. 10 and 100 Mbps). In both cases an isochronous service can be provided, taking full advantage of this facet of the switch. At this point the broadening of the range of possible uses resulting from true switch technologies is evident; uses now include support for real-time, multimedia voice and (above all) video traffic.

This is effectively possible because the domain of action of the MAC layer may be reduced to very short segments with a single station on each (port switching). Under these conditions, the collision probability is substantially reduced (since an interface can only become involved in a collision with traffic intended for it, which is unlikely), and the medium access delay is therefore zero in most cases. In this case, the whole chain linking two stations has the synchronicity property needed to support multimedia or real-time traffic.

Note that, for video compression using MPEG, for example, the 10 Mbps provided by an Ethernet channel is generally sufficient.

Multicast frames

Shared technologies with multiple access (rings, bus, chain, and star) implicitly allow the broadcasting of a message with a single emission, since all frames emitted are seen by all network ports. The use of multicast or broadcast packets to reach a group of addressees simultaneously has naturally become central to most communication systems (TCP/IP, DECnet, NetWare, NetBIOS, and so on). However, in a switched environment, broadcast traffic has the disadvantage that it consumes bandwidth on all ports.

The principal objective is to avoid the need to modify the normal procedures for existing protocol stacks and, at the same time, to benefit from recent advances. Thus, switching should be accompanied by the ability to emulate an interface identical to that for which the application has been developed.

Thus, multicast channels may be defined corresponding to specific groups between which broadcasts may take place. We stress that the multicast frame, which on a shared network necessarily reaches the group of equipment which can recognize it, has to be specifically multiplied and forwarded to the desired connections, in the case of a switched network. In this case, multicast packets only occupy part of the bandwidth on the ports effectively concerned with this traffic.

Virtual networks

The concept of virtual networks (virtual LANs) is a very practical tool, when defining a structuring of the set of stations connected to a switched network. It corresponds to a logical partitioning of a (possibly important) network into groups and sub-groups with consistent, hierarchical access, independently of the geographical distribution (Figure 14.3). The concept of virtual networks is also an extrapolation of multiple backplane networks

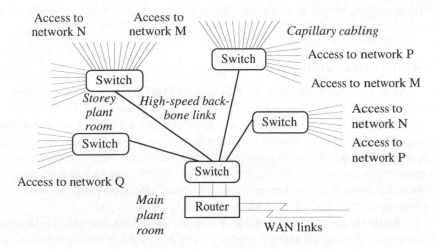

Figure 14.3   Physical infrastructure segmented into virtual networks.

for a single chassis, since it is possible to create an evolving number of different networks.

This segmentation may be made as a function of the company structure (departments, services, divisions, and so on) or based on criteria for access to the same network servers and/or resources. It can often correspond to the partitioning into networks with different addresses or to the subnetting plan. However, it brings with it a decorrelation between membership of a network and/or a computer environment and the location within the company site. Thus, virtual networks permit an integration of itinerant accesses within a routed infrastructure, without the need to modify any network protocol parameters.

In all cases, the virtual network concept facilitates all accesses to the network since each port can be associated with an arbitrary group by simple parametrization, if necessary for a short period. Thus, levels 1 and 2 of the network become a flexible and modular resource, allowing all the configurations desired by the manager. Above this infrastructure, the level 3 interconnection devices (multiprotocol routers, since bridges have lost their *raison d'être*) retain their segmentation function associated with the applications and the protocols used.

Simplification of the MAC structure

In addition to the guaranteed speed per port, packet switching corresponds to a homogenization of interconnection devices of the bridge and hub type. In this sense, switching may be viewed as the extension of the prewiring concept to active MAC devices. In fact, when levels 1 and 2 of a network consist of interconnected switching hubs, they form a simplified infrastructure, on which station accesses may be freely associated with any specific group of users. Thus, the number of networks may evolve according to user needs, while their geographical coverage may evolve as a function of user movements.

Switch–router complementarity

The switch is a level 2 device in the OSI model (MAC level, to be more precise), whereas the router operates at level 3 (network) and possibly at the MAC level (bridge). In all cases, the switch should be viewed as a building block for the construction of a MAC infrastructure capable of supporting a number of distinct logical networks, which may be conveniently defined, independently of the physical location of the ports, using virtual networks. The number, extent and arrangement of these networks may evolve, while at the same time supporting a structured partitioning of the set of all users into several hierarchical levels.

While the switch is a forwarding device, the multiprotocol router is primarily an interconnection device which is used to control and establish the communication between logically distinct segments. *A priori*, a router should not be regularly required to support full-bandwidth interconnection channels, since this would imply that the distribution of machines is inconsistent with that of the exchanges. This simple packet forwarding task falls to the switch. On the other hand, the router has a much more detailed view of the traffic, and may use this knowledge to manage connections subject to constraints on the applications or on the areas to which the users belong.

Thus, the stratification which exists in the world of local area network devices is enriched by a new stratum corresponding to switches, which are placed between traditional hubs and various multiport repeaters on the one hand, and multiprotocol brouters on the other. This increase in complexity of the general equipment is accompanied by an improvement in global performance, with each level of device being associated with a specific requirement. We stress that the switch is not intended to replace the hub or router, but to supplement the global architecture by addressing the performance requirement for packet forwarding (with increasing bandwidth) and the management of virtual networks.

Migration

Since packet switching can be incorporated in a natural manner in existing networks, it is very natural to evolve a network flexibly by successively migrating the most exacting computer islands (client servers and segments) or those which are most restricted by the limitations of the shared technologies. This does not involve a sudden challenge to previous IT investments, but the gradual toppling of greedy connections on a network element, which will slowly eliminate congestion problems.

It is also very important to work progressively from the heart of the network, which supports the highest speeds, to the departmental backbones and subsequently to the peripheral segments.

14.2 Ethernet at 100 Mbps

At present, there are two ways of multiplying the bandwidth of Ethernet accesses by a factor of 10 without challenging the frame format, and thus also user applications.

100baseT

The first solution, in terms of continuity of evolution, is 100baseT (Figure 14.4), which is similar to 10baseT but with a ten times greater speed. This technology has the advantage that it retains most of the characteristics of Ethernet on twisted pair, which is now well known and validated on a large scale (almost 30 million devices connected).

100baseT retains the original access method: CSMA/CD with its merits (simplicity, efficiency, rapidity) and its shortcomings (non-deterministic), collision management, the format and length of frames and addresses, and even baseband emission. This very conservative approach has meant that 100baseT technology can be incorporated under a working group of the committee for IEEE 802.3 supplement u (initially, it was envisaged that an additional IEEE 802.14 committee would be created), and thus it has the appearance of an extension of Ethernet rather than a rival technology or a replacement.

The standard was issued in 1995, while the stable draft standard issued in late 1994 already provides for interoperability of the hardware of manufacturers involved in the Fast Ethernet Alliance. These manufacturers (and there are many) have perceived the interest of a traditional high-speed technology which could operate hand-in-hand with existing computer equipment and applications, including drivers and adaptors.

This alliance brings together many manufacturers and protagonists in the LAN world, who together produce more than 60% of all Ethernet devices. Software houses also form part of this grouping.

The conservative aspects of 100baseT also enable users whose cabling is adapted to the limited requirement of 10baseT (only two pairs per port) to migrate to 100 Mbps without having to update their installation. In fact, 100baseT includes a description of the use of a medium comprising two Unshielded Twisted Pairs (UTP)

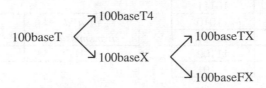

Figure 14.4   Physical levels of 100baseT.

of category 5 (data quality) with a length of 100 meters. This is 100baseTX, which retains the Physical Medium Dependent (PMD) layer of FDDI. For UTP cabling of categories 3 or 4, 100baseT requires 4 pairs (twice that of 10baseT) and proposes a new technology, 100baseT4. Note that we are no longer dealing with standard or thin coaxial cables, and shall only consider so-called 'structured cabling': twisted pairs and optical fibers.

In addition, the maximum coverage of a network without bridges falls to 400 meters (200 meters on twisted pair) rather than the 4 km allowed by the 10baseFB supplement. In fact, while 100baseT offers a tenfold increase in speed without major modifications, it also requires an equivalent reduction in terms of distance (the round-trip delay being proportional to the emission delay for a short frame). Similarly, the interframe gap becomes 0.96 μs and the maximum performance is 148 809 pps per port.

100baseTX

100baseTX uses the cable type of FDDI's TP-PMD: UTP category 5 (IEC 11801), also called Data Grade TP (DTP) and Shielded Twisted Pair (STP) such as IBM's type 1, using two pairs of a length limited to 100 meters: one pair for emission and one for receipt.

100baseTX uses 4B/5B conversion (which includes an intrinsic consistency check, and raises the bit rate to 125 Mbps), followed by stream cipher scrambling and MLT-3 encoding (three levels multiline transmission) (Figure 14.5).

Data	Symbol
0	11110
1	01001
2	10100
3	10101
4	01010
5	01011
6	01110
7	01111
8	10010
9	10011
A	10110
B	10111
C	11010
D	11011
E	11100
F	11101

Interstream padding	Code
I : Fill	11111

Delimiters	Code
Start of stream	
J	11000
K	10001
End of stream	
T : Terminator	01101
R : Reset	00111

Invalid transmission	Code
H : Halt	00100

Figure 14.5   Table of legal values for the 4B/5B encoding.

4B/5B ensures that all symbols corresponding to numerical data include at least two changes of state (bit set to 1), and never more than three bits with the same value are emitted successively (which would correspond to two bits set to 0). The scrambler is responsible for distributing the signal energy across the whole spectrum. MLT-3 uses three physical levels to reduce the main signal frequency to 31.25 MHz (over a four-bit period).

The pairs used are still 1–2 and 3–6, for perfect compatibility with existing Ethernet cabling certified at 100 Mbps, rather than the pairs 1–2 and 7–8 used in FDDI's TP-PMD. UTP category 5 cables and STP cables must have an attenuation less than 10 dB for UTP5 and 5.2 dB for STP at 16 MHz, a propagation speed of 0.6 c, and a maximum round-trip delay of 1112 ns per segment.

Table 14.1   RJ45 pinout assignment for 100baseTX port.

Pins	Signal on station or repeater port side without crossover	Signal on repeater side with internal crossover
1 and 2	Tx+ and −	Rx+ and −
3 and 6	Rx+ and −	Tx+ and −

100baseT4

100baseT4 applies to all cables consisting of four UTPs of category 3, 4 or 5, still with a length of 100 meters. It employs an 8B/6T conversion (8 bits for 6 ternary symbols) and uses pairs 3 and 4 to transmit at 25 MHz on each (two pairs common to both directions) and a different pair in each direction for receipt and collision detection (see Figure 14.6).

It is recommended that the pin layout for ports on the hub side should incorporate the necessary crossovers so that a single straight cable can be used to link the transceiver to the repeater (as in 10baseT).

The RJ45 connection compatibility (ISO 8877) is retained and the MDI uses all the pins.

It can be seen below that 100baseT4 does not pretend to evolve towards full-duplex operation. In fact, two of the four pairs are already used in bidirectional mode.

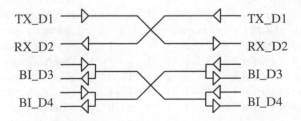

Figure 14.6   Transmission on three pairs, two of which are bidirectional.

Table 14.2 RJ45 pinout assignment for 100baseT4 port.

Pins	Signal on station or repeater port side (without crossover)	Signal on repeater side with internal crossover
1 and 2	Tx_D1+ and −	Rx_D2+ and −
3 and 6	Rx_D2+ and −	Tx_D1+ and −
4 and 5	BI_D3+ and −	BI_D4+ and −
7 and 8	BI_D4+ and −	BI_D3+ and −

The three SOSB symbols constitute the Start of Stream Delimiter (SSD). Note that the complete preamble still consists of the equivalent of eight bytes.

Since the number of bytes in the original frame is arbitrary (between permitted limits of 64 to 1518 bytes), the last byte of the frame, DATA_N, may be on any one of the three pairs, at random: TX_D1, BI_D3 or BI_D4 (see Figure 14.7).

This 100baseT4 technology is important in that it means that 100baseT is not restricted to UTP category 5 installations. Cables of category 3 or 4 have a propagation speed of 0.5852 c, a maximum round-trip delay of 1140 ns per segment

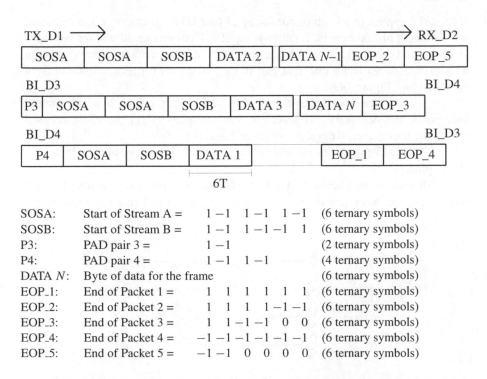

SOSA:	Start of Stream A =	1 −1 1 −1 1 −1		(6 ternary symbols)		
SOSB:	Start of Stream B =	1 −1 1 −1 −1 1		(6 ternary symbols)		
P3:	PAD pair 3 =	1 −1		(2 ternary symbols)		
P4:	PAD pair 4 =	1 −1 1 −1		(4 ternary symbols)		
DATA N:	Byte of data for the frame			(6 ternary symbols)		
EOP_1:	End of Packet 1 =	1 1 1 1 1 1		(6 ternary symbols)		
EOP_2:	End of Packet 2 =	1 1 1 1 −1 −1		(6 ternary symbols)		
EOP_3:	End of Packet 3 =	1 1 −1 −1 0 0		(6 ternary symbols)		
EOP_4:	End of Packet 4 =	−1 −1 −1 −1 −1 −1		(6 ternary symbols)		
EOP_5:	End of Packet 5 =	−1 −1 0 0 0 0		(6 ternary symbols)		

Figure 14.7 Decomposition of the transmission of a frame on the three pairs.

and an attenuation less than or equal to 12.5 dB from 2 to 12.5 MHz (where the latter is the highest fundamental sequence). Note that a ternary symbol effectively lasts 40 ns so that, on a pair, a period comprises 80 ns or more.

100baseFX

100baseT may also be applied to 100baseFX optical fiber for lengths up to 400 meters. In this case also the physical level is that of FDDI MMF-PMD.

4B/5B encoding is followed by non-return to zero inverted. The maximum attenuation is 11 dB for 62.5/125 μm multimode fiber. The maximum round-trip delay is 408 bit times or 4080 ns.

The maximum length of 400 m, which is less than the normal limit of 2 km for multimode fiber, may appear to be one of the main shortcomings of the 100baseT technology (lack of support for usual structured cabling rules). However, it can be circumvented if one dispenses with the constraint on the round-trip delay, for example, using a full-duplex mode which will probably be available in the near future.

The two technologies, 100baseTX and 100baseFX, are grouped together under the name 100baseX. They are inspired to a large extent by the ANSI standards, and make it possible to use the available electronic components without requiring specific development work.

In 100baseX the whole Ethernet frame (including the MAC field) is viewed as a 100baseX stream or PDU. This is delimited by a start of stream delimiter (J-K) and an end of stream delimiter (T-R). Only data symbols are found between these two extremes. The interframe gap is transmitted in idle code.

Auto-negotiation

The 100baseT standard defines a certain upwards compatibility, since the 100baseTX PHY (the equivalent of the transceiver) can also operate in 10baseT. This type of capability is communicated, on the one hand, between the PHY and the reconciliation sublayer through the MII and, on the other hand, between two PHY, lying opposite each other, by the medium.

In fact, the MII interface permits the exchange (read and write) of management data between the PHY and the station management entity. This information consists of 32 registers, of which only the first eight are defined explicitly by 100baseT. The following eight registers are reserved and the last 16 are dedicated to the manufacturers. All the registers have 16 bits. The first eight registers have the meaning shown in Table 14.3.

Only the first two registers (control and state) are base registers which are necessarily implemented by all PHYs. The contents of the control register (register 0) and the status register (register 1) are shown in Tables 14.4 and 14.5, respectively. Bits 0 to 7 of register 0 are reserved, all the other bits of register 0 can be read or written. All the bits of register 1 are read only.

Remote faults may arise under four conditions:

- Test of remote fault operation.
- Loss of the link.
- Jabber.
- Failure to detect a valid link by more than one PMA in parallel (10baseT, 100baseTX, 100baseT4).

Table 14.3 Meaning of auto-negotiation registers.

Register address	Register name
0	MII Control
1	MII Status
2 and 3	PHY identifier
4	Auto-Negotiation advertisement
5	Auto-Negotiation Link Partner Ability
6	Auto-Negotiation Expansion
7	Auto-Negotiation Next Page Transmit

Table 14.4 Control register.

Bit	Name	Meaning of 0	Meaning of 1
15	Reset	Normal operation	PHY reset (< 0.5 s)
14	Loopback	Disable loop back mode and isolate the medium	Isolate the medium and enable loop back mode Tx→Rx
13	Speed selection	10 Mbps	100 Mbps
12	Auto-Negotiation Enable	Disable Auto-Negotiation Process	Enable Auto-Negotiation Process
11	Power Down	Normal operation	Power down
10	Isolate	Normal operation	Electrically isolate PHY from MII
9	Restart Auto-Negotiation	Normal operation	Restart Auto-Negotiation Process
8	Duplex mode	Half duplex	Full duplex
7	Collision test	Disable COL signal test	Enable COL signal test

Table 14.5   Status register.

Bit	Name	Meaning of 0	Meaning of 1
15	100baseT4	PHY not able to perform 100baseT4	PHY able to perform 100baseT4
14	100baseX full duplex	PHY not able to perform full duplex 100baseX	PHY able to perform full duplex 100baseX
13	100baseX half duplex	PHY not able to perform half duplex 100baseX	PHY able to perform half duplex 100baseX
12	10Mbps full duplex	PHY not able to operate at 10 Mbps in full duplex mode	PHY able to operate at 10 Mbps in full duplex mode
11	10Mbps half duplex	PHY not able to operate at 10 Mbps in half duplex mode	PHY able to operate at 10 Mbps in half duplex mode
5	Auto-negotiation terminated	Auto-negotiation process not completed	Auto-negotiation process completed Registers 4, 5, 6, 7 valid
4	Remote fault	No remote fault detected	Remote fault condition detected
3	Auto-negotiation ability	PHY not able to perform auto-negotiation	PHY able to perform auto-negotiation
2	Link status	Link is down	Link is up
1	Jabber detect	No jabber condition detected	Jabber condition detected
0	Extended capability	Base register set capabilities only	Extended register capabilities

The next two registers (2 and 3) are used to communicate numbers identifying the PHY precisely: the OUI, the manufacturer's model number and the number of the revision. Only 22 bits of the OUI are taken into account; the first two bits need not necessarily be transmitted as 0 (since they have special meanings: unicast/multicast address and local/universal address) (Figure 14.8).

All the management registers are communicated by the MII MDIO signal, where the frames have the form shown in Figure 14.9. In this figure, Z indicates a high-impedance state. The physical address (PHYAD) corresponds to the number

15
0 15
0
Register 2
Register 3
Organizationally Unique Identifier
Manufact-urer's model number
Revision number
1
24 5
0 3
0

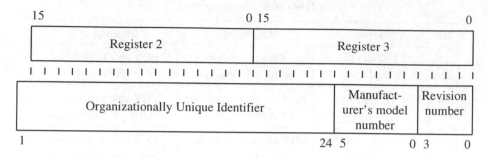

Figure 14.8 Decomposition of registers 2 and 3.

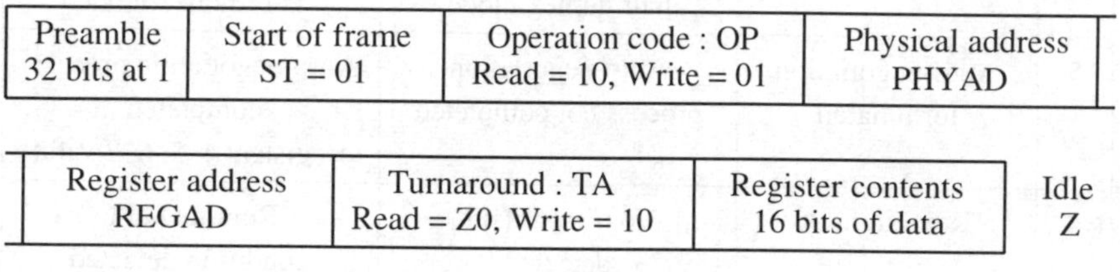

Preamble
32 bits at 1
Start of frame
ST = 01
Operation code : OP
Read = 10, Write = 01
Physical address
PHYAD
Register address
REGAD
Turnaround : TA
Read = Z0, Write = 10
Register contents
16 bits of data
Idle
Z

Figure 14.9 Management frame.

LLC
MAC
Reconciliation
MII
PCS
PMA
PMD
Auto-neg
PHY
MDI
Medium

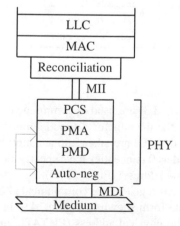

Figure 14.10 Position of the auto-negotiation functions in the model.

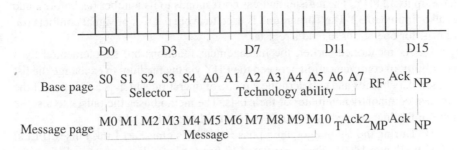

Selector, of 32 possible message types, the following are already defined:

    0 = reserved for future developments

    1 = IEEE 802.3

    2 = IEEE 802.9a

    31 = reserved for future developments

Technology ability (technologies supported), 5 independent bits are defined:

    A0 = 10baseT

    A1 = 10baseT full duplex

    A2 = 100baseTX

    A3 = 100baseTX full duplex

    A4 = 100baseT4

RF: Remote Fault

    0 = no remote fault

    1 = indication of remote fault

Ack: Acknowledge

    0 = acknowledgment of receipt not yet received

    1 = acknowledgment of receipt of message after 3 successive consistent receipts

NP: Next Page

    0 = last page

    1 = another page follows

Message, 2048 possible messages, of which the first codes are:

    0 = reserved for use in a future auto-negotiation

    1 = zero message (during an exchange with Next Page)

    2 = UP message with Technology Ability extension follows

    3 = Two UP messages with TA extension follow

    4 = UP message followed by the code for remote fault

    5 = message followed by 4 others encoding the OUI

    6 = message followed by 4 others encoding the PHY_ID

    2047= reserved for use in future auto-negotiation

T: Toggle, inverse of the value of the toggle for the previous message

Ack2: Acknowledge 2

    0 = inability to conform with the previous message

    1 = will conform with the previous message

MP: Message Page

    0 = Unformatted Page (UP)

    1 = Message page

Figure 14.11   Encoding of pages in FLP.

of the PHY with which the management entity wishes to correspond. An entity may have up to 32 PHY. The register address corresponds to its number (as before), and is also limited to 32. The Turnaround is used to avoid the risk of signal conflicts (on return) for operations to read a register.

As mentioned earlier, the management functions are supplemented by a possibility of communication between the PHY via the medium to exchange the list of their capabilities and to determine a mode of operation which is a function of the greatest common denominator of their lists. The method uses the pulses to test the state of the link defined by 10baseT or Normal Link Pulse (NLP).

During the auto-negotiation phase the PHYs emit Fast Link Pulses (FLPs) in bursts (Figure 14.10). These consist of 17 fixed pulses 125 μs apart and 16 pulses which may be inserted between these fixed pulses to encode the 16 bits of the word (or page) to be transmitted (see complete structure on Figure 14.11). A pulse in an even position represents a 1, no pulse in an even position represents a 0. The FLP bursts are emitted periodically every 16 ms until the end of the auto-negotiation procedure. Each burst lasts 2.125 ms and consists of peaks separated by at least $62.5 \pm 7 \ \mu$s.

A 10baseT device or transceiver will see the FLP sequence as a simple Link Test and will reply with a Normal Link Pulse (periodic peaks every 16 ± 8 ms, in the absence of traffic). In turn, receipt of the NLP by the 100baseT PHY will force the activation of 10baseT operation.

To obtain the greatest common denominator, the following ordering of the technologies supported has been defined (in decreasing order): 100baseTX full duplex, 100baseT4, 100baseTX, 10baseT full duplex, 10baseT half duplex.

Note that 100baseT4 comes before 100baseTX since it covers a greater variety of twisted-pair media.

Devices

100baseT defined two types of repeater (or hub) (Figure 14.12). The first, the class II repeater, is associated with a well-defined connector technology (one of the physical signaling systems: 100baseTX, 100baseT4 and 100baseFX); the second, the class I repeater, may have ports of different types.

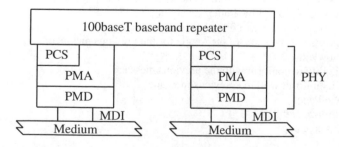

Figure 14.12   Decomposition of the 100baseT repeater.

Table 14.6   Maximum propagation delays (in bit time).

100baseT repeater	For a valid signal	For a collision
Class I	104	64
Class II	46	46

Of course, the class I repeater is slower (RTD of 168 bit times) and so a network can only have a single class I repeater on a path between two stations. The class II repeater is less flexible but faster (RTD of 92 bit times) and up to two repeaters of this type may occur on the path between two stations (see maximum network length on Figure 14.13).

Every user with twisted pair cabling comprising either four pairs per port or two pairs per port if the cable is IBM STP or UTP category 5, can look to a migration to 100 Mbps without apprehension (provided the connection compatibility follows the same criteria). He or she may insert a number of 100baseT ports in his or her network and progressively exchange the network interface cards of the PCs or stations requiring the greatest bandwidth. These NICs may possibly be hybrid cards

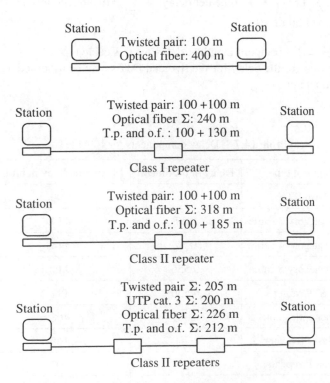

Figure 14.13   Example of 100baseT network diameters.

capable of operating at 10 or 100 Mbps, with automatic recognition. In fact, we have seen that the 100baseT standard provides for the fact that the end machine should be able to detect the speed it can use on the Ethernet network and switch to 100 Mbps as soon as its port is effectively attached to a 100baseT port (or 200 Mbps full duplex in the near future).

The carrying over of the main characteristics of 10baseT also enables us to envisage developments similar to those already witnessed, such as the possibility of replacing shared access by switching to provide a bandwidth of 100 Mbps per port, or operation in full duplex mode (2 × 100 Mbps), which could shortly be standardized. Of course, the latter is only possible in a switched environment and for 100baseX solely.

In fact, the 100baseT technology is almost inevitably associated with dynamic packet switching. Indeed, a bridge, or preferably a central switch, is vital when passing from 100 Mbps ports to standard Ethernet ports. Consequently, this conversion is directly associated with the cohabitation of two rates during the progressive migration phase.

100baseT specified a method of calculating the longest path similar to that of 10baseFB. The components are shown in Table 14.7. The rule is summarized by the following inequality

$$\begin{aligned} \text{PDV} &= \sum \text{LSDV} + \sum \text{repeater delays} + \sum \text{MII cable delays} + \text{DTE delay} \\ &\leq 511 \text{ bit times} \end{aligned}$$

where LSDV = 2 × segment length × delay for this cable type.

The value of the delay for the two end DTEs may be modified as indicated by the manufacturer.

Table 14.7 Delay components for 100baseT.

Segment type	Delay in bit time/m	Maximum delay in bit time
Two DTE	–	100
UTP category 3 cable	0.57	114
UTP category 4 cable	0.57	114
UTP category 5 cable	0.556	111.2
STP cable	0.556	111.2
Fiber optic cable	0.501	408
Class I repeater	–	168
Class II repeater	–	92
MII	1	

100VG-AnyLAN

The 100VG-AnyLAN technology, which denotes 100 Mbps on voice-grade twisted pair cables that support all LAN technologies (in fact, Ethernet and Token Ring), was introduced by Hewlett-Packard (Figure 14.14). It represents an ambitious proposal for an evolution of Ethernet, since, apart from the physical layer, it will involve a change in the access method to eliminate the probabilistic aspect and a merging of the two most common types of network. However, it retains a shared access method, sharing the bandwidth over all the accesses by time-division multiplexing.

Nevertheless, it should be stressed that the compatibility with Ethernet and Token Ring applications does not imply that 100VG-AnyLAN will be able to act as a gateway between these local area networks. In fact, interconnection elements, of the bridge or router type, will be needed systematically to access the traditional networks.

The first consequence of these differences has been the assignment to a new IEEE committee, 802.12. This, despite the fact that originally (in 1992) the project, then called 100baseVG, only concerned Ethernet.

A new deterministic access method has been introduced: the polling round robin or the Demand Priority Access Method (DPAM), which eliminates the penalizing phenomenon of collision. With this method, the hubs manage the network. After a learning phase, the root hub (highest in the tree structure) records the requests from the stations (requests to emit in response to its polling) and lets each of its accesses speak successively (by stopping sending the idle signal on their links). Of course, the hubs connected downstream do the same. Note that the UpLink port of a downstream hub is specifically designed for cascaded connection. The packet received by the hub is immediately directed to its destination, which implicitly corresponds to the privacy and security capabilities developed in recent years on 10baseT hubs and switches. One of the ports may also be placed in 'promiscuous' mode, so that it receives all the traffic for observation. Furthermore, the efficiency of this method has made it possible to achieve an effective speed close to 100 Mbps. Finally, this method should also have short delays in comparison with those of a token passing method.

The frames may equally well be in the Ethernet (in fact IEEE 802.3) or the Token Ring format, which makes 100VG-AnyLAN a 'universal' technology, but also shows the distance separating these conventional LANs, just like FDDI several years ago.

Two different priority levels may be associated with the traffic (normal and high), which makes it possible to incorporate synchronous traffic in the data communications and at the same time guarantee a given bandwidth for this type of communication. The Target Transmission Time (TTT) means that an upper bound can be placed on the access delay and a constant average speed can be guaranteed. However, traffic with normal priority is automatically assigned a high priority after a waiting time of 200 to 300 ms.

The 'intelligence' of the 100VG-AnyLAN hub includes the ability to modify

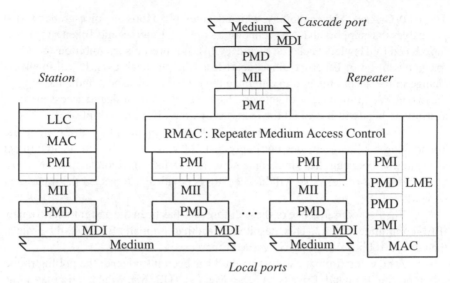

PMI: Physical Medium Independent
MII: Medium Independent Interface
PMD: Physical Medium Dependent
MDI: Medium Dependent Interface
LME: Layer Management Entity

Figure 14.14   Decomposition of the 100VG-AnyLAN elements: station and repeater. The four connections shown between the PMI and the MII correspond to the four channels of the physical architecture.

its behavior on request, to monitor the traffic as a function of the packets and transmission requests and assemble more detailed management information than in the case of a simple 10baseT hub.

In terms of cabling, 100VG-AnyLAN can operate on twisted pair or optical fiber. Fiber allows lengths of 1 km for Ethernet and 2 km for Token Ring. On UTP category 3, 4 or 5 cables, four pairs are needed to reach 100 m, against two pairs for STP. Note that, for UTP5 and STP, a length of 200 meters per segment would be possible. The draft also describes the use of UTP cable with 25 pairs.

100VG-AnyLAN uses a 5-bit conversion of type 5B/6B, which requires three mapping tables to ensure that the signal is balanced in terms of 0s and 1s, and an upstream scrambler. There exist 6-bit codes with two 1s and four 0s, which are said to be of weight two (and unbalanced), codes with three 0s and three 1s, which are said to be balanced, and codes with two 0s and 4s, which are said to be of weight four (also unbalanced). These processes run on each pair as shown on Figure 14.15 and give the pattern structure of Figure 14.16.

The bits are transmitted on the four pairs in full duplex mode, with an offset of half a sextet between pairs 1 and 2 and pairs 3 and 4. Thus, each pair operates at 30 Mbps, with a main frequency at 15 MHz, similar to that of 10baseT (10 MHz). A future increase in the speed on higher-quality cables can therefore be envisaged. We note that the proposed physical layer has a high performance but is complicated; it uses a 5B/6B code and NRZ on four pairs (in half duplex) instead of two (in simplex) to multiply the bandwidth of 10baseT by 10. However, VG cables with two pairs should make it possible to achieve speeds of 50 Mbps.

The connector technology is again RJ45 (ISO 8877) where the MDI uses all the pins (Table 14.8).

Table 14.8   RJ45 pinout assignment for 100VG-AnyLAN port.

Pins	Signal on station side or on that of repeater Uplink port	Signal on side of repeater Downlink port
1 and 2	TPIO:0 + and −	TPIO:3 + and −
3 and 6	TPIO:1 + and −	TPIO:2 + and −
4 and 5	TPIO:2 + and −	TPIO:1 + and −
7 and 8	TPIO:3 + and −	TPIO:0 + and −

Each link should have a characteristic impedance of 100 ± 15 Ohm from 1 to 15 MHz, a propagation speed of 5.7 ns/m (0.585 c) and an attenuation less than or equal to 14 dB from 100 kHz to 15 MHz.

The number of bytes of the frame transmitted is arbitrary (within the range of validity) and the end of the frame (last sextet) may occur equally well on any one of the four pairs.

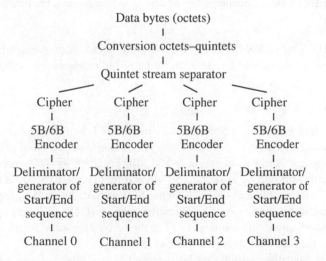

Figure 14.15   Partitioning of the data transmission. The scrambler uses the generator polynomial $x^{11} + x^9 + 1$.

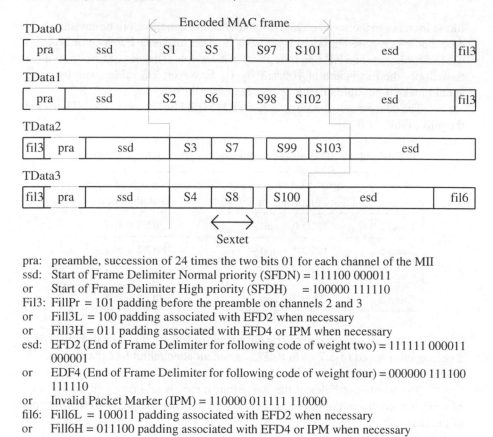

pra: preamble, succession of 24 times the two bits 01 for each channel of the MII
ssd: Start of Frame Delimiter Normal priority (SFDN) = 111100 000011
or Start of Frame Delimiter High priority (SFDH) = 100000 111110
Fil3: FillPr = 101 padding before the preamble on channels 2 and 3
or Fill3L = 100 padding associated with EFD2 when necessary
or Fill3H = 011 padding associated with EFD4 or IPM when necessary
esd: EFD2 (End of Frame Delimiter for following code of weight two) = 111111 000011 000001
or EDF4 (End of Frame Delimiter for following code of weight four) = 000000 111100 111110
or Invalid Packet Marker (IPM) = 110000 011111 110000
fil6: Fill6L = 100011 padding associated with EFD2 when necessary
or Fill6H = 011100 padding associated with EFD4 or IPM when necessary

Figure 14.16 Decomposition of a 64-byte frame across the four pairs.

100VG-AnyLAN hubs can be cascaded in up to three levels, which permits a geographical coverage of up to 600 m for a twisted pair network with no bridges.

Evolution

A priori the transition from a conventional Ethernet or Token Ring local area network based on structured cabling to 100VG-AnyLAN does not present a problem. Four pairs per port are vital for operation at 100 Mbps (except on STP), otherwise only half the bandwidth will be available (50 Mbps if there are only two UTP pairs).

Once the problem of the medium has been settled, the existing topology (tree or ring structure) and the existing structured cabling (UTP, STP and optical fiber) can be retained, and it only remains to swap the active elements (interface cards and hubs, not forgetting interconnection devices).

This migration, which may be progressive, will enable the attached stations to access a very comfortable bandwidth, while retaining the associated network software. In addition, 100VG-AnyLAN provides plesiochronous transport of traffic for future multimedia applications.

Conclusion

For managers confronted with the requirement for higher speeds on their Ethernet networks who wish to improve the architecture, the choice has been difficult up to now. Until now, they might have envisaged eliminating the bottlenecks by inserting a technology with a higher performance in the infrastructure, such as FDDI; but this amounted to a wager on the future of a new network.

Today, 100baseT and 100VG-AnyLAN provide access to 100 Mbps, either by a simple evolution of the speed of Ethernet or by correcting the main shortcomings of the access method. These two concurrent offerings provide for re-use of the

Table 14.9   Comparative table for the main 100 Mbps technologies.

Technology	Ethernet	100baseT	100VG- AnyLAN	FDDI
Standard/draft	IEEE 802.3	IEEE 802.3u	IEEE 802.12	ANSI X3T9.5
Bit rate	10 Mbps	100 Mbps	100 Mbps	100 Mbps
Access method	CSMA/CD	CSMA/CD	Demand priority	Token passing
Characteristics	Probabilistic	Probabilistic	Deterministic	Deterministic
Frames transported	Ethernet	Ethernet	Ethernet Token Ring plesiochronous	FDDI: asynchronous and plesiochronous
Types of medium	Coaxial cable Twisted pair Optical fiber	Twisted pair Optical fibre	Twisted pair Optical fiber	Optical fiber Multi/single mode twisted pair
Twisted pair segment length	100 m 250 m realizable	100 m	100 m (200 m possible)	100 m
Multimode optical segment	2 km	400 m	1 km 2 km (Token Ring)	2 km
Repeaters/series	4	2	5	[500]
Network diameter	4 km (+ AUI)	400 m	1 km (Ethernet)	100 km
TP network	500 m (+ AUI)	200 m (+ 5 m)	600 m	200 m
2 twisted pairs	UTP 3/4/5	STP and UTP5	STP	STP and UTP5
Supplement	10baseT	100baseTX	–	TP-PMD
Transmission mode	1 Tx and 1 Rx	1 Tx and 1 Rx	2 p. full duplex	1 Tx and 1 Rx
Coding used	Manchester	4B/5B + MLT-3	5B/6B	4B/5B + MLT-3
Main frequency	10 MHz/pair	31.25 MHz/p.	30 MHz/pair	31.25 MHz/p.
4 twisted pairs		UTP 3/4/5	UTP 3/4/5	
Supplement		100baseT4	–	
Transmission mode	N.A.	3 pairs data + 1 pair collision	4 pairs full duplex	N.A.
Coding used		8B/6T	5B/6B	
Main frequency		25 MHz/pair	15 MHz/pair	

existing cabling in the case of twisted pairs and optical fibers and the transport of frames in the standard format.

100baseT has the appearance of a natural evolution which retains the characteristics of Ethernet, while 100VG-AnyLAN is much more ambitious in that it incorporates the Token Ring technology and defines the transport of plesiochronous traffic.

14.3 IsoEthernet

Another evolution of Ethernet involves the incorporation of support for synchronous channels, that is, the transport in parallel with the standard traffic of asynchronous data of one or more channels in which the transit time and the bandwidth are fixed and bounded. This type of local area network, called ISLAN (IsoLAN for isochronous) falls under the IEEE 802.9 committee with Supplements a, b, c and d. IEEE 802.9 describes data rates of 4 and 20 Mbps (3.584 and 19.968 Mbps, to be precise).

Supplement a deals with the IsoEthernet PHY at 16 Mbps, while Supplement b deals with AU to AU internetworking (AU: access unit, that is, an IsoEthernet hub). Supplements c and d deal with the Managed Object Conformance Statement (MOCS) and Protocol Implementation Conformance Statement (PICS). We note that the end station becomes the Integrated Services Terminal Equipment (ISTE).

More precisely, IsoEthernet offers two services: a primary service (Multi-service) retaining the usual 10 Mbps but with an extra 6 Mbps full duplex channel (like the WBC offered by FDDI-II) and a secondary, all isochronous service with a 16 Mbps full duplex channel, which can be used, for example, for video. In all cases, IsoEthernet, like FDDI, uses a 4B/5B encoding which is more efficient than the Manchester code. To achieve synchronous operation, IsoEthernet is based on a periodic emission of cells or cycles every 125 μs. These cycles, which consist of 512 symbols (5B) corresponding to 256 bytes, are the result of a multiplexing of the various channels transported.

Thus, the multi-service mode of operation incorporates (see Figure 14.17):

- A half-duplex Ethernet packet channel (P-channel) at 10.016 Mbps
- An isochronous full duplex channel (C-channel or 96 dedicated B channels) at 6.144 Mbps
- A full duplex channel (D-channel) at 64 kbps
- A full-duplex maintenance channel (M-channel) at 96 kbps
- A full-duplex frame-synchronization channel at 64 kbps.

This amounts to a total of 16.384 Mbps. All these channels are multiplexed in each cycle, representing, 313, 192, 2, 3 and 2 symbols per cycle, respectively.

As far as the all-isochronous service is concerned, it comprises:

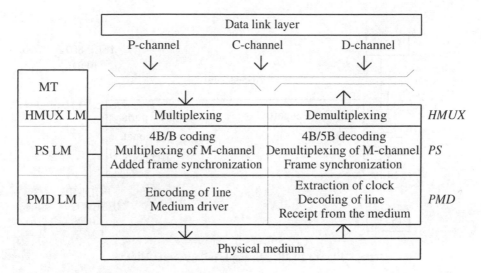

HMUX: Hybrid Multiplexer
PS: Physical Signaling
PMD: Physical Medium Dependent
MT: Management

Figure 14.17   *Decomposition of the physical layer (HMUX, PS, PMD).*

- A full-duplex isochronous channel (C-channel or 248 dedicated B-channels) at 15.872 Mbps
- A full-duplex channel (D-channel) at 64 kbps
- A full-duplex maintenance channel (M-channel) at 96 kbps
- A full-duplex frame synchronization channel at 64 kbps
- An empty (idle) channel at 288 kbps.

In both cases, with a 4B/5B and NRZI encoding, the total speed of 16.384 Mbps becomes an effective speed of 20.48 Mbps on the medium. This also gives a main frequency of 10.24 MHz, which is almost the same as in standard Ethernet with a Manchester encoding. This means that it is possible to retain the same implementation rules as for 10baseT, namely 11.5 dB maximum attenuation from 5 to 10 MHz on a twisted pair link and a maximum delay of 1000 ns. However, the isochronous constraints impose additional limits on a complete path, as indicated in the table in the section on repeaters in Chapter 10.

The M-channel is managed at the Physical Signaling level between the Layer Management and the corresponding PHY blocks.

IEEE 802.9a describes all the LAN functionality, but also that of the PABX type, which makes IsoEthernet the only LAN service with such an isochronous capability. In fact, the Access Unit (or repeater) may have isochronous IEEE 802.9

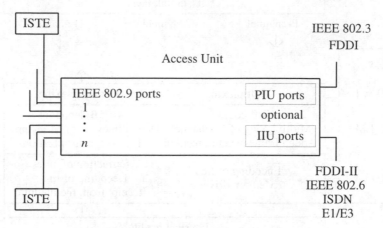

Figure 14.18   Example of an Access Unit.

ports and also, optionally, Ethernet packet or FDDI ports (PIU: Packet Interface Unit) and isochronous ISDN, DQDB, FDDI-II, ATM, E1/T1 or E3/T3 ports (IIU: Isochronous Interface Unit) (see Figure 14.18).

It is apparent that such a device must incorporate a switching capability, embodied in the Packet Switching/Multiplexing Unit (PSMU) and the Isochronous Switching/Multiplexing Unit (ISMU).

The IEEE 802.9 standardization is effective, but it does not appear to have been followed by product announcements. IEEE 802.9a and b, scheduled for issue in 1995, are more encouraging, since they permit a flexible integration into the Ethernet architectures. In fact, the multi-service mode includes a standard 10 Mbps channel and functions on the same type of cabling. However, as we have seen, terminal equipment is notably different from and much more complex than the usual hubs.

Nevertheless, this is a very complete technology which provides a perfect answer to the requirement to integrate synchronous traffic in data communication infrastructures.

14.4 Full duplex

One relatively simple evolution of Ethernet, though it gives a non-trivial performance improvement (factor of 2), involves using the point-to-point 10baseT or 10baseF (active) links in full duplex mode (Figure 14.19). This solution requires minimal modifications to the interface cards (the non-detection of collisions by the MAC layer) and is not accompanied by any new constraints on the most common cabling systems (twisted pairs and optical fibers). Conversely, the physical links are used more effectively, since each segment is capable of transporting signals in both directions simultaneously. This full duplex operation makes it possible to achieve 20 Mbps per link, although it can only be implemented in practise if the hub is actually a dynamic packet switch, capable of handling several frames simultaneously. In this case, the network offers a maximum speed of 20 Mbps for each access (10 Mbps for receipt and also for transmission).

Moreover, the full-duplex technology is also applicable to the 100 Mbps Ethernet: 100baseT (100baseTX or 100baseFX, but not 100baseT4, since the receive and transmit channels must be different), and to Token Ring and FDDI, still with dynamic switching concentration elements.

In addition, the full duplex mode eliminates the limitations due to the RTD and permits the establishment of links of a length greater than the maximum prescribed in the standard (4 km for Ethernet at 10 Mbps, 400 m at 100 Mbps). Thus, single-mode optical fibers can be put to optimal use over large distances (greater than 50 km with the most powerful emission and detection components).

Finally, the standardization of the full-duplex mode in Ethernet 10 Mbps does not appear to be entirely up to date, while it could soon apply to 100baseT or Token Ring (DTR: Dedicated Token-Ring).

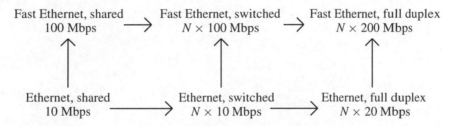

Figure 14.19   Summary of the possible evolutions of the Ethernet bandwidth.

14.5 Daisy chain

Finally, another solution derived from Ethernet on twisted pairs has been proposed by a number of manufacturers which involves chaining the elements, rather than arranging them in a star around the hub as in the standard topology. We note that certain implementations of StarLAN (1base5) already had this capability at 1 Mbps. This non-standardized method allows one to install a minimum length of physical medium (if the user does not envisage structured prewiring) or to re-use the cables of a LocalTalk network. Approximately ten accesses can be chained in this way.

PART III

Engineering and maintenance of a network

Introduction

At the beginning of the 1980s, Ethernet networks were installed to meet immediate needs, using existing hardware, with no great concern for the installation rules, the possibilities for evolution, access to the cabling or conformance to laying procedures. The coaxial cable had to run near the machines, being as accessible as possible so that a tap could be inserted wherever it was desired to feed the newly arrived station (see Figure III.1). Often, security constraints were satisfied simply by ensuring that the braid at one end of the cable was grounded.

As Ethernet has evolved, the size of the networks to be installed has increased (see Figure III.2), and laying rules have been issued. Adherence to these major directives has become crucial to the facilitation of large-scale operations, the acquisition of homogeneous installations and the application of re-usable methods. Thus, the lifetime of a local area network, from its design to its obsolescence, has been divided into stages, which has made it possible to divide the work into elementary tasks that are easier to handle and to impose an organization on the activities relating to the installation of a LAN. In addition, as each task corresponds to a simple, well-defined objective the ideas and documents generated at the time of an implementation are then readily available for use in other studies.

In Part III, we shall touch on the main aspects of each phase, giving examples where necessary (these are sometimes special cases which may not be well adapted to other conditions). The emphasis is on a description of the work to be carried out at each stage and the presentation of a form of solution which readers may choose to follow more or less faithfully.

Practical details will also be presented so that readers can then make their selection from all the techniques currently on the market.

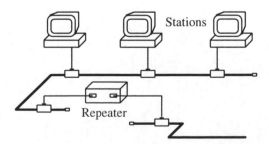

Figure III.1   Small easy-to-install Ethernet network.

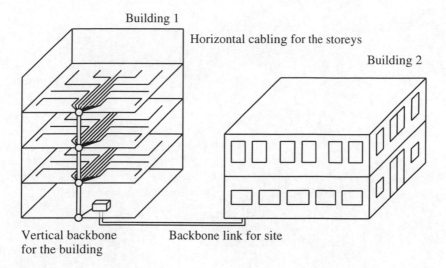

Figure III.2 Network relying on a complete cabling of the buildings on a site.

Chapter 15

Stages

- Study

- Installation

- On-site monitoring

- Acceptance operations

- Evolutions and modifications

- Maintenance operations

- Management

- Security and privacy

Global observation of the process of the creation of a local area network from its installation to its death/replacement/obsolescence, rapidly shows that it is possible to distinguish relatively specific tasks. These relate to feasibility and study stages, the description of a real solution, installation and implementation, on-site monitoring and, finally, the validation of the installed network (generally called acceptance).

More precisely, in the case of an important mission, the following phases may be involved:

- The brief preliminary design phase comprising the presentation of various possible solutions, accompanied by a comparative study, the selection of one of these and the technical justification of this choice, a brief description of the solution arrived at, an evaluation of the possible implementation planning and the associated global cost, together with an estimate of the margins of uncertainty at this stage of the project and the basic elements (delays and prices) that have been used in the calculations.

- The detailed preliminary design phase comprising a more complete presentation of the solution chosen and its variants, together with useful details, explanations and justifications (choice of hardware), a more precise evaluation of the delays and costs, covering any additional work required (electricity, masonry) and the availability of the entities involved. The detailed preliminary design also involves the compilation of a technical dossier for the work consisting of useful plans (cable measurements) and assessments of quantities (connectors and patching).

- The production of the detailed technical specifications follows the detailed preliminary design phase; these specifications are intended to provide all the information needed to carry out the work effectively. They cover the fundamental functionality required, the capabilities desired and the choices of hardware. The description of all positions of active elements of the network, the possibilities for drawing cables in the rooms and corridors concerned, the media lengths and the numbers of each useful component are determined at this stage. The overall work may be partitioned into batches so as to distribute the tasks according to their common denominator. Thus, there may be a cabling batch, comprising the laying of the media and involving the laying of cable runs and ducts and the necessary removal of suspended ceilings and raised floors, and so on. A second batch may concern connectors and patching, involving all the tasks of installing sockets and patching modules, together with installation of all the jumper cables. Another batch may be concerned with active elements, including tests of each unit, their installation and attachment. The detailed technical specifications are usually accompanied by functional diagrams and work plans, which include all the diagrams and charts providing an unambiguous description of the work to be carried out.

- The enterprise consultation document is generated as a specific proposal to the enterprises to which it is envisaged the work will be subcontracted. Thus, it covers all the elements of the detailed technical specifications which may help the company to estimate the cost and, ultimately, carry out the work, if it is retained. The first part of the consultation document is thus extracted from the detailed technical specifications and merely covers the technical points relevant to a costing of the installation. The rest of the document consists of financial and administrative clauses governing the project management.

- The overall job control phase, constituting what is commonly called on-site monitoring or follow-up. This task is directly concerned with the problems raised by the installers which sometimes have repercussions on the technical choices. It includes monitoring the whole cabling operation, quality control for the work, the arrangement of on-site meetings, the preparation of associated minutes and the signing of interim reports. The main aim is to ensure that the network installed is laid in conformance with the security rules and the technical directions established in the detailed technical specifications. It also involves taking informed decisions should practical questions not envisaged in earlier preparative phases arise.

- The acceptance of and detailed accounting for the work corresponds to the acceptance of the results of the installation work (signing of the definitive acceptance document) and the release of payment to the contractor. The description in what follows the acceptance of and detailed accounting for the work is decomposed into several different stages according to the level of observation. A document giving a precise description of the work will be requested from the contractor. This document will include, for example, the cable paths drawn on building plans, the contents of the plant rooms, details of the connector system, an explanation of the labeling used and its contents, the characteristics of the hardware and cables used, and the results of measurements and tests.

- The dossier of work performed constitutes the end of the installation. It may consist of a compilation of all the technical and administrative documents described above, supplemented by the summary of each stage and the inclusion of any elements which may be of relevance later when carrying out repairs or when an extension is required.

We note that certain stages may be superfluous in the case of limited installations. However, these seven phases should primarily serve as a model leaving everyone to establish his or her own personalized process.

Other entities may be involved once the network is in place and operational. These include repair operations, since not all the elements are infallible, and activities relating to modification and extension (which are similar). These last two are generally inevitable once the network becomes several years old.

The operational stage is not really part of the overall activity, since, if all is well, the network should satisfy the users at this stage and require only a small amount of additional activity. It has only been shown in Figure 15.1 to make the diagram more readable.

The term 'management' covers a number of aspects, which it is advisable to distinguish between in order to determine the inherent requirements of an installation and to better judge the capabilities of the products offered. Thus, there may be a management function for the network hardware (configuration, monitoring and maintenance) and for the communication software (version management, consistency checking), a management of the network traffic (choice of interconnection elements, implementation of filters), a management of the invoicing for the network services provided to users, and so on. In the section on management, we shall see how these objectives may be divided into separate tasks.

Since the skills required for installation, acceptance or repairs do not necessarily lie in the same area, it is therefore preferable to dissociate each action from the overall process and to assign it to the group of people who can best handle this matter and resolve any related problems which may arise. Chapter 16, on human resources, deals with this aspect in more detail.

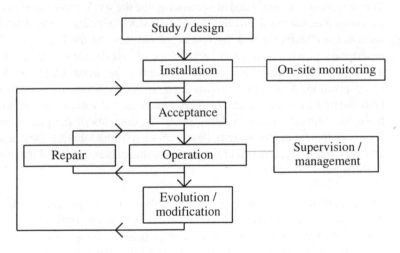

Figure 15.1   Decomposition into various stages.

15.1 Study

The first stage naturally involves studying an installation request (Figure 15.2). Care should be taken throughout this work to ensure that the solution envisaged

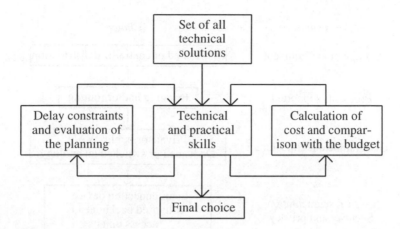

Figure 15.2   The three main components involved in the selection of a solution.

corresponds to the requirements expressed by the future users. Those responsible for the study should seek to restrict themselves to answering the request, even though this may include proposing global solutions which they would like to see as an option.

Given that Part II essentially dealt with technical aspects relating to the operation of an Ethernet network, the knowledge of real installations has not been discussed in detail until now. Thus, specific practical aspects are described which are useful when equipping sites with data communication capabilities. More refined appraisals are then considered, covering, for example, the choice of topology, the medium, the technology, and the type of patching. This will be followed by assessments of the cost and time needed for all these operations.

The information now given relates to hardware aspects of the installations, which are equally linked both to the technology of the local area network envisaged and to the laying rules used by those responsible for the cabling in the buildings.

Design

The design of the network involves the definition of the architecture to be implemented, that is, primarily, the choice of technologies for the physical, MAC and network levels, the schematization of the global network topology and the enumeration and specification of the nodes and interconnection devices (Figure 15.3).

If the architecture consists of several local area networks on distant sites which are to be interconnected, a WAN will be necessary; this will have to be studied in this stage at the earliest. The criteria will be the estimated cost, the bandwidth offered and the flexibility of this (as a function of the type of traffic or of availability

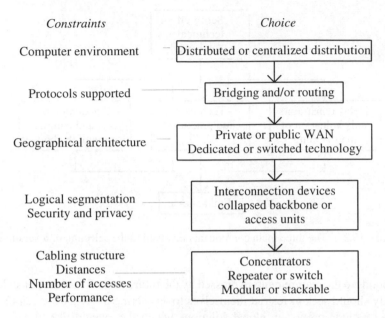

Constraints   *Choice*

Computer environment — Distributed or centralized distribution

Protocols supported — Bridging and/or routing

Geographical architecture — Private or public WAN / Dedicated or switched technology

Logical segmentation / Security and privacy — Interconnection devices collapsed backbone or access units

Cabling structure / Distances / Number of accesses / Performance — Concentrators Repeater or switch Modular or stackable

Figure 15.3   Progression in the design of an architecture.

criteria), and the degree of privacy and security required. The choice may be from among specialized links (totally dedicated to a user), public or private packet switching networks (X.25 or Frame Relay), ISDN, the public switched telephone network, or a combination of these technologies which provides greater security or answers a need for additional bandwidth to cope with overflow situations.

The choice of the protocol(s) used will be determined by the set of computers to be attached. Unless the enterprise has decided on progressive homogenization of its network protocols (for example, OSI), the applications and computer systems to be connected will determine this choice.

The MAC level technology should be selected from among the most common LANs and MANs. Even though only Ethernet, Token Ring and FDDI may appear to be in the running (the latter appears to be losing momentum), it remains to define the general network topology and the machines of which it will be composed.

Depending upon the size of the site and the buildings, it is the cabling which will dictate the position of the plant rooms as a function of the realizable cable lengths. In fact, since twisted pair is used almost systematically for all recent capillary services, the distance between a socket in an office and the arrival of the cable in the plant room should be strictly less than 100 meters (a distance of 80 meters is often used, for security; this leaves a margin for the patch cords on either side). The network topology to be implemented at the end of the infrastructure will generally be a LAN (Ethernet or Token Ring) with a broader or narrower bandwidth. For example, in Ethernet, 1, 10 or 100 Mbps are shared between all attachments to the plant room, dedicated station by station or even switched between ten or so machines with a minimum share to each port.

The number of these plant rooms and their distance apart will determine the choice of the backbone topology. If the distances require it, (single-mode) optical fiber will be used. Finally, the speed, the redundancy requirement, the number of different logical networks and the criteria for evolution will favor a given technology. Taken together, the possibilities include LANs (as before: Ethernet and Token Ring, at various speeds, shared or switched, half duplex or full duplex), MANs (principally FDDI), various proprietary solutions and, soon, ATM.

Although the router remains totally indispensable in response to interconnection requirements (including LAN–WAN access) it would be wise not to place a router, or even a 'collapsed backbone', at the center of a homogeneous infrastructure, whose main requirement is only a relatively simple forwarding or high-performance switching function.

Cabling

The cabling of a local area network, which involves the installation of medium segments in the rooms to be served, comes under the management of the building work, just like electrical cabling and telephone cabling. The Ethernet installation rules should thus be compatible with the working methods used in these areas. However, local area network technologies are much more recent than the supply of electricity or telephony, and therefore a certain number of procedures to which the network will have to conform, unless all the previous choices are to be called in question (paths, ducts), are already in place.

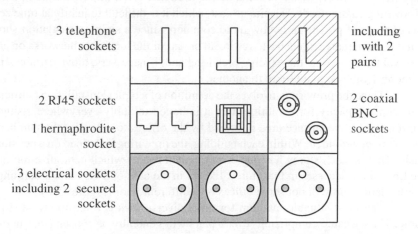

Figure 15.4   Example of a multi-usage wall box.

Since the cabling of local area networks could easily be studied and then carried out by the same entities responsible for drawing the electrical cables or telephone pairs, it is natural to think in terms of joint laying operations in which cable runs are installed in parallel routes, wall boxes include electrical, telephone and computer sockets and plant rooms contain both telephone hardware (for example, PABX) and network hardware (hub, bridge, router) (Figure 15.4).

Since the electrical cabling generally carries much higher voltages than cabling for the telephone and local area networks, it will generally be installed in a separate cable run, but may end in the office in a modular box combining all the types of wall socket needed by the user. The other two types of cabling, for telephone and data communication, have similar characteristics and may thus be laid side by side.

Prewiring

In the same way as for electrical and telephone networks, cabling for local area networks may be provided in advance with a service distributed homogeneously in all the rooms which are likely to be used as offices at some time. In fact, the number of electrical and telephone sockets in a room or office is generally chosen independently of the precise needs of the future occupants, with provision being made to accommodate the needs in the great majority of cases. However, these desirably universal installations are a preparation for the changes which will take place in the building with removals and the movement of personnel, furniture, and partitions.

Thus, the concept of prewiring had its origins in the need to lay media segments uniformly in the rooms of an enterprise. This cabling can be defined before the need is expressed and may, from its design on, support certain technical advances. Thus, the prewiring is necessarily a homogeneous cabling which usually exceeds the extent or density of the installation required at a given time, with the intention of covering future needs. Despite its cost, which it is difficult to justify at time zero, this concept of prewiring is now quite common, since a simple calculation shows that it is often more expensive to rewire all or part of the local area networks on each removal than to re-use the existing prewiring and, if necessary, move certain active elements from one plant room to another.

Thus, the prewiring involves the definition of a typical installation (sufficient and with a capacity for evolution) that it is hoped to apply everywhere, using as reference unit, the surface area occupied by the offices to calculate the number of sockets to be provided. Within each building, the prewiring is defined on a per storey basis. That is, each storey has one or more plant rooms which centralize the links feeding all the accesses in that storey. Except in the case of a very small building, a single plant room will not serve offices on a different floor (Figure 15.5).

The most suitable medium for these diverse uses is often the twisted-pair cable. Thus, a cable comprising several pairs will generally be chosen (four in most cases) which ensures that one cable will be suitable for most technologies. In fact, local area networks implemented using twisted pairs rarely need more than two pairs

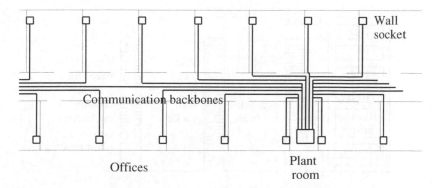

Figure 15.5 Synopsis of the capillary path of the prewiring, ending in a plant room.

(one for emission, one for receipt). Since the physical performance of the cable cannot evolve with future technologies, a compromise is sought in which a cable with a reasonable capacity satisfying the known needs is chosen, in the hope that future technologies will be compatible with this medium (which is quite common). When a coaxial access is needed, a balun is used; this is a small special-purpose element which adapts the impedance of the twisted pair for the desired access (50, 75 or 93 Ohm).

Other media are conceivable, but only optical fiber is sometimes used to extend networks beyond the maximum length of a twisted-pair segment (usually 100 meters), or for cable runs near electrical cables. This is reserved as the medium for the main artery or the communication backbones, and is only used to serve terminals under exceptional circumstances.

The cables run in cable paths or ducts, which should preferably be metallic for the purposes of electromagnetic shielding. These cable paths leave the plant room for the offices (for the capillary service) and for the other plant rooms (for the communication backbones).

The offices are located around plant rooms, which are placed at the center of the star followed by the cabling topology. This means that when installing prewiring it is vital to find a certain number of plant rooms or, if this is not possible, sites reserved for patch cabinets. Each of these plant rooms should be less than 100 meters from the wall sockets of the offices it services (depending upon the cable path: up into suspended ceilings, down into skirting boards, in a zigzag, and so on) (Figure 15.6).

Each plant room contains the patch cabinets which bring together the entry of all the cables from the offices served by the room, the active hardware of the local area network(s) together with the patch cabinets of the communication backbones between the different plant rooms. Note that the communication backbones, which correspond to the artery concept, may be constructed from twisted-pair, coaxial cable

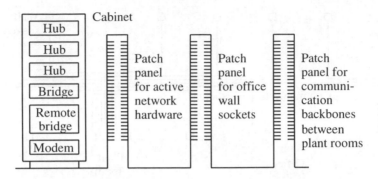

Figure 15.6   Equipment in a typical plant room.

or fiber optic links. In fact, one of the three types will be chosen, depending upon the distance criteria, the risks of perturbations and the requirements for intermediate connections.

Thus, the plant room can be used to connect all the conductors of the media segments within the building (via the patch panels). In addition, it harbors the active devices attached to the network, since the rack cabinets can accommodate stars and hubs and also the interconnection devices (bridge, router, modem).

For practical purposes, it should have an air vent, or better still, ventilation, if it houses active devices, and it should have a minimum floor area (5 m^2 is often thought to be an acceptable value). One should not forget that engineers should be able to move freely between the patch panels to work there and that the active elements should be accessible from both sides (front and back), which means that the two doors of the cabinet should be freed.

The telephone

Telephony, which has long since proved the concept of prewiring, with a quasi-systematic service to the offices, and which uses a medium based on twisted pair, can easily be mixed with the computer-related prewiring (Figure 15.7).

In reality, we have seen that the physical medium dedicated to data communication should have capabilities exceeding the simple criterion for voice transport. However, nothing prevents us from passing telephone signals on so-called data grade twisted pairs. At a slightly greater cost, this makes it possible to homogenize the cables laid for the prewiring and obtain a global set of links which can be shared as desired between the telephone and data communication needs. Note that, in fact, the classical unshielded twisted pairs have a characteristic impedance of ~600 Ohm at voice frequencies (1 kHz).

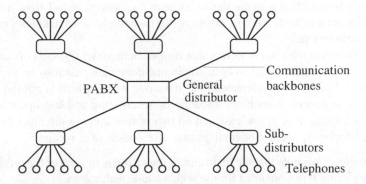

Figure 15.7   Schematic architecture of a telephone installation.

Moreover, the distribution via interlinked plant rooms and the use of a patching system are also traditional as far as telephone installations are concerned. In addition, it is apparent that the different patching methods using connection modules applied to local area networks are generally inspired by elements developed for telephony.

All the telephone links are concentrated in a central point, ending in the PABX, and they may pass through communication-backbone cables based on multiple pairs.

We stress that the association of telephony and data communication within a single prewiring installation is very important and creates few additional constraints. Thus, it is a reasonable solution as far as the implementation of a complete infrastructure is concerned (new rooms or renovation) which has the advantage that it brings together almost all the cable laying operations.

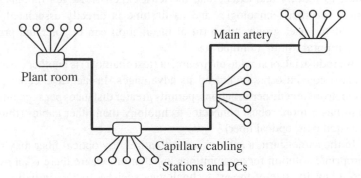

Figure 15.8   Schematic architecture of a data communication installation.

As shown in Figure 15.8, the architecture of data communication networks can easily be matched with the star structure of a telephone installation, since it has less constraints at the level of its topology (the communication backbones may form a star, chain or tree).

However, one has to ensure that the patching system (panels of connection modules) is as well suited to data communication manipulations as to those of telephony. In fact, most telephone lines have two wires, which is not the case for local area networks; branching, disconnection, rerouting and test operations take place on a single pair in one case and on two or four pairs in the other case. Note that, in telephony, fax or modem lines may also consist of two pairs.

Conclusion   We note that the main aim of prewiring is to combat the proliferation of all the cable types intended for use with a single technology.

Initially, prewiring was reserved for enterprise sites (offices and computer rooms), then it was applied to other categories of building, such as universities, airports and hospitals, and so on. Today it forms part of the infrastructure of these buildings and may be proposed as a fixture when they are fitted out.

Note that buildings which are entirely prewired are sometimes referred to as 'smart buildings' to stress that they can be adapted to many different uses, almost independently of the technologies and topologies desired. This represents a return to the area of home automation, in which a dwelling place is equipped with this same 'intelligence' capable of transporting all types of information (digital data, sound, pictures, video, alarms and detectors, electrical commands).

Other solutions

Prewiring is presented as the ideal method, however, the choice of prewiring with the laying of twisted-pair cables is not always the best solution for small installations (with only a few offices).

In fact, a simple thin coaxial cable running between ten locations in one room (machine room or small computer center) is still the fastest network to implement, the easiest to modify and extend and the least expensive. Even though it cannot be adapted to other technologies and its lifetime is directly associated with the presence of the user group, this form of installation can be tolerated provided it remains temporary or of a limited size.

An industrial, or similar, environment (test chamber) is another case in which the standard coaxial cable retains all its advantages. In fact, it is better protected against electromagnetic perturbations, permits greater distances per segment, is more solid, and has a more robust connector technology than other cables (thin coaxial cable, twisted pair, optical fiber).

In the same spirit, a network served entirely by optical fiber may represent the appropriate solution for an ambitious installation, where there is an overriding desire to adapt to state-of-the-art technologies such as FDDI (initially). When a decision is taken to opt for a medium with a very long lifetime, greater prudence is called for, since the technologies are evolving rapidly and it is very difficult to know today what the optimum medium for networks will be twenty years hence.

In fact, while 62.5/125 μm graded index silica optical fiber is the almost universal high-quality fiber today, single-mode fiber, which offers a far greater bandwidth, will probably replace it soon. However, the fact is that technical advances may result in developments relating to operational frequencies. Thus, after ten years, a situation may arise in which a building is fully prewired based on optical fiber of a type which is then obsolete.

Here, we stress that one should not seek a cabling or prewiring with an excessively long lifetime. If an installation effectively lasts for ten years without needing a common modification (laying of new media, change of lengths, modification of patch panels) it will probably have reached the end of its life after that time. Thus, it is wise when evaluating the cabling budget to think in terms of a lifetime of between five and ten years.

The figures in Table 15.1 are only given for indicative purposes, to permit a rapid (and relatively coarse) evaluation and for use in comparative calculations.

Table 15.1   Average price of cabling for different LAN technologies.

Medium type	Price of medium (US dollars per meter)	Price of two terminal connectors, (US dollars)
Ethernet Standard coaxial cable	3.6	16 Type N
Ethernet Thin coaxial cable	1.2	5 BNC
Ethernet Four screened twisted pairs	1	3 RJ45
Ethernet AUI cable	4	48 DB15 with slide latch
Token Ring Two shielded twisted pairs	1.4	21 Hermaphrodite
IBM SNA RG62 coaxial cable	0.8	5 BNC
LocalTalk One twisted pair	0.8	1.6 RJ11
Optical fiber 50/125 62.5/125 100/140	5 Bi-fiber cable	30 24 SMA ST

Precautions

Whichever cable is chosen, one important criterion that is independent of its electrical characteristics and its transmission capacity is its behavior in case of fire. The cable should not catch fire easily, it should not release toxic gases, thick smoke or high pollutants. These strictures are dictated by safety aspects, since the cables run in occupied buildings, and taking environmental considerations into account. For example, cables with PVC insulation may be banned under certain conditions, although PTFE is acceptable.

Regular efforts are made to improve the safety of those working in rooms in which transmission cables are laid. New materials are being studied and developed as part of a trend to minimize their effect in an accident situation.

Flat cables

It is sometimes said that standard cabling, like prewiring, cannot cover all the user requirements. In fact, delivery to the station may be more-or-less easy.

If the machine to be attached is located by a wall, near a block of sockets, an 'extension cable' (AUI cable, attachment cable, jumper cable) is all that is needed to connect the station to the socket. From the practical point of view, this solution does not present a problem, since the 'extension cable' runs along the wall, possibly behind a table. On the other hand, if the room is large, the station may be located on a table in the middle of the room, far away from the wall blocks. Since the laying of a cable from the table to the wall carries a risk of deterioration for the cable, the machine connectors and the wall block, and is an inconvenience for the occupants of the room, one may consider laying the cables under the carpets.

Recently, a number of companies have produced somewhat different types of electrical and computer cables which are flat enough that they can be installed under carpets (for convenience, carpet squares should be used). These include shielded and unshielded paired cables (not twisted) with two or four pairs together with coaxial cables and fiber optic cables. This could be thought of as providing a convenient way of extending the prewiring to the site of each machine, since the flat cables are easy to lay in a manner which supports evolution, in that the links can also be moved, extended and shortened.

This section concludes by inviting readers to consider this particular type of solution for requirements which are difficult to meet by the usual methods (large office, small networks in rooms which are difficult to cable, temporary installations). However, this medium should be primarily reserved for short links: capillary cabling.

Connector system

In all cases, whether of a medium based on twisted pair, coaxial cable or optical fiber, the connector system is fundamental as far as reliability is concerned. In fact, it is generally the only part that may be subject to frequent manipulations, of varying degrees of brutality.

This end component should be chosen to be well made if one wishes to avoid problems with the connection quality over time. Of course, the products from the main well-known manufacturers are more expensive, but the materials used are of a higher quality and the connectors are better finished. Consequently, they are more robust and age less rapidly.

For example, one might require the AUI sockets to be cabled according to the standard (five individually shielded pairs, plus a global shielding) and to be mounted in metal covers, and that the pins should be full and soldered. These prescriptions are taken from the recommendations of the IEEE documents, and may be useful to anyone wishing to avoid, as far as possible, operational faults due to the connector system.

It has already been stressed that, in general, a great many of the problems one may meet with a network are associated with the physical medium. Since the cables are generally immobilized and unassailable (overhead ducts, suspended ceiling, raised floor), the only components which can be damaged are the accessible ones: connectors, jumper cables, and attachment cables. Thus, one should ensure that the connectors are not badly made or excessively fragile.

Modular sockets

As far as prewiring is concerned, all the cables arrive in the office at the level of one or more wall-socket boxes. These boxes may combine all the data communication and telephony requirements of a standard user. They may equally well accommodate sockets for local area networks or telephones. However, the adaptability of the prewiring may make it necessary to change the socket type when the occupant changes. In fact, if the cabling is to be re-used to support a new technology without too much difficulty, it is vital to modify the connector system available in the offices so that it corresponds to user needs. The same twisted pair cabling may effectively support the telephone, a serial link, Ethernet 10baseT, Token Ring or AppleTalk, but the corresponding sockets are different (T-shaped, DB25, RJ45, hermaphrodite, RJ11).

However, some manufacturers produce modular sockets (consisting of a fixed part housing the end of the cable and an interchangeable part adapted to the technology supported by the prewiring). This second part might be used to distribute the four available pairs across two sockets (as for IEEE 802.3, 10baseT which only requires two pairs), and may even incorporate one or two baluns providing coaxial connections at 50, 75 or 93 Ohm, or even twinax (IBM) (Figure 15.9).

This philosophy appears very consistent with the concept of prewiring, in which the installation put in place at a given time has a certain durability in that it can be adapted to the level of the topology (using jumper cables in the patch cabinet), to the level of the technology using the active elements in the plant rooms and to the level of its access points by providing the requisite type of socket. Of course, the characteristics of twisted pairs (or another medium used) will not evolve easily, and the same applies to the number of links leading to each office.

Modular systems may be used equally well both for wall sockets available in offices and for the patching facilities provided in the plant rooms. This makes it possible to adapt the cabling directly to the active devices using only attachment cables with identical connectors at each end. However, the usefulness

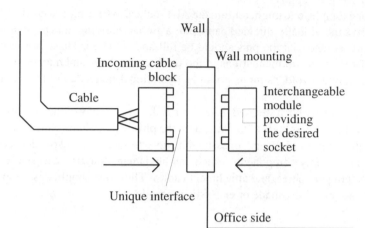

Figure 15.9   Simplified schematic of a connector system using modular wall sockets.

of a modular connector technology is primarily reliant on its simplicity as far as the end user is concerned, since generally, patching systems may use a homogeneous connector system for all the cables.

When the cabling includes coaxial cables, coax–twisted pair or even coax–coax baluns may be used to offer an impedance different from that of the actual cables laid at the level of the access points.

It should be stressed that modular sockets extend the adaptability of prewiring to the terminal connector technology. This in no way hinders their integration into a standard cabling (laying of the medium as a function of the needs, precisely recorded at a given time).

Patching

The primary function of patching is to permit the modification of the path of a physical link by manipulating the jumper cables located on the desired trajectory. In fact, in the case of prewiring, but also more generally, the cables laid are not linked directly to the active devices (Figure 15.10). If this were the case, it would imply that the physical installation were completely fixed and totally devoid of logical structure. Consequently, it would be very difficult to maintain (repair, modification, extension).

For many years, cables laid have been attached in a group to a distribution panel or patch panel, which presents all the conductors in an accessible manner. This arrangement has become indispensable and, as we shall see, the method used can improve the efficiency of the maintenance teams. Each incoming cable can be given a label on the front face of the modules, making it easy to identify the line one is looking for.

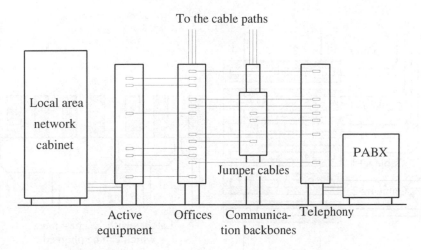

To the cable paths

Local area
network
cabinet

PABX

Jumper cables

Active   Offices   Communica- Telephony
equipment   tion backbones

Figure 15.10   Example of the arrangement of patch panels.

A plant room may include three distribution panels: one concentrates the modules linked to all the cables of the capillary service to the offices which end in this room; the next corresponds to links between this plant room and other similar plant rooms (links by communication backbones); while the last provides access to the active devices located in the plant room. The contacts between the cables leading to these distribution panels are provided by jumper cables (attached lead). If it is desired to separate the cables dedicated to telephony from those dedicated to data communication, another distribution panel has to be added next to the first. On the other hand, if desired, one can opt for a patching system suitable for both types of application. This option has the advantage that there exists a global pool of conductors between the plant room and each office, which can be accessed to meet the telephony and network requirements of each occupant. Since the assignment is not fixed by the technology, it is easy to imagine that the distribution will permit numerous combinations.

The modules connected to each distribution panel may be of different colors according to the function chosen for the panel (Figure 15.11). For example, the modules linked to office sockets may be blue, while those linked to active devices (hub, PABX) will be yellow, those corresponding to communication-backbone links will be green, and those which are cabled entirely to the ground will be black, and so on.

To merge the data communication cabling with the telephone cabling effectively at the patch-panel level, it is important to have a patching system that allows access to a pair as well as to the whole of the cable. In fact, while a cable with four pairs satisfies nearly all the requirements generated by local area networks, a single pair is sufficient to feed a telephone point. However, if the number of

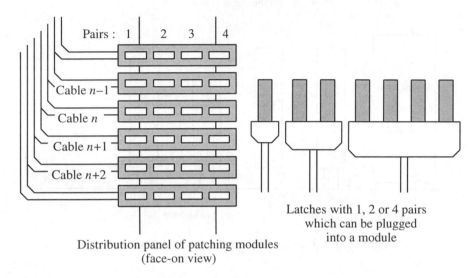

Distribution panel of patching modules
(face-on view)

Latches with 1, 2 or 4 pairs
which can be plugged
into a module

Figure 15.11 Schematic representation of connection modules and associated latches.

attachments increases above that provided for, the greater flexibility obtained will enable full use to be made of all the cables. In this connection, note that an Ethernet 10baseT link, like Token Ring, only requires two twisted pairs, while LocalTalk only uses a single pair.

By collecting together the maximum number of logical links within each cable, near optimal use of the prewiring can be achieved. Note also that systems with modular wall sockets will carry the greater part of the infrastructure.

Electronic patching

There is a way of avoiding large numbers of jumper cables hanging between the distribution panels, which inevitably involves risks of poor contact and essentially requires a documentation of the patching regularly implemented.

This method involves replacing all the distribution panels of a plant room by a high-dimensional switching matrix, the sole purpose of which is to connect an office socket to a port of an active device on request. The matrix will therefore include a large number of inputs and outputs (several hundred), and will be managed by software that can be used to determine the current configuration at any given time.

While this solution is certainly very nice and gives concrete expression to a pleasing concept, it is really only useful when the workload represented by the patching process becomes too heavy. In fact, if the network does evolve greatly, interventions to attach a station or connect a machine which has moved will correspond to a few manipulations per month and will scarcely justify the acquisition of a system with such a potential.

The applications for which this type of product is intended are, on the one hand, installations of large, very dynamic networks (in which the machines move frequently) and, on the other hand, cases where the manager is not on site and has to reconfigure the patching from a distance. In the first case, it is preferable to automate part of the operations to make them less laborious and safer, and at the same time, to ensure the availability of up-to-date documentation describing the current system state. In the second case, if the engineer cannot move around the site rapidly, he or she will also be able to modify the patching instantaneously to meet user needs.

Simulation software

One last tool, whose existence one should be aware of when designing an important local area network, is simulation and modeling software. This type of software is used for virtual operation (on a screen) of a certain number of interconnected networks and their associated technology.

The given items, which are easy to determine at this stage of the project, include the network technologies (Ethernet, Token Ring, FDDI or others), the topologies, the segment lengths and the number of segments. The capabilities of the interconnection devices are already less easy to determine; for, clearly, evaluations are only of interest if they can be used to validate a solution before the infrastructure is effectively put in place or to evaluate the health of an existing network. Finally, one must also enter as parameters the number of stations it is intended to connect, the quantities of information that it is assumed will cross these networks and the structure of the induced traffic (periodic, regular, slotted, bursty). One should try, for example, to define the servers of other groups of machines explicitly (source of important stream). This may lead one to think that the use of this software, which is sometimes highly instructive, should, above all, be highly precise and meticulous if it is intended to achieve significant results. The presentation of the envisaged network model on which the simulator is to work itself represents a non-trivial task.

Conclusion   To help those responsible for a study, we shall now recall the figures which can be used to evaluate the round-trip delay on an Ethernet network and to validate a configuration on paper.

In Part II it was clearly explained that the time taken to cross an Ethernet network must be limited to avoid the danger of being unable to detect all collisions; thus, it is vital to check that the installation envisaged conforms to this RTD criterion. When things are still simple and only coaxial cable and fiber optic FOIRL links are used (the limitations are derived directly from the maximum number of repeaters and segments and the maximum permissible segment length), the arrival of other elements makes the calculation more complex, as is made clear later.

The round-trip delay for active elements includes the crossing delay for a signal in one direction and that for a collision in the other.

Table 15.2 complements the method of calculation described in Chapter 10 (section on repeaters).

Table 15.2   Table of crossing delays for all types of media and elements.

Elements crossed on the network	RTD for unit	Total number of elements on path	Total delay due to this type of element	Max. RTD per segment
Standard coaxial cable	8.66 ns/m	m	ns	4330 ns
Thin coaxial cable	10.27 ns/m	m	ns	1900 ns
Fiber optic FOIRL	10 ns/m	m	ns	10000 ns
Fiber optic 10baseFL	10 ns/m	m	ns	20000 ns
Fiber optic 10baseFB	10 ns/m	m	ns	20000 ns
Fiber optic 10baseFP	10 ns/m	m	ns	10000 ns
Twisted pair	11.3 ns/m	m	ns	2000 ns
AUI cable	10.27 ns/m	m	ns	514 ns
Coaxial transceiver	1525 ns	ns	ns	
FOIRL optical transceiver	700 ns	ns	ns	
Synchronous optical transceiver	300 ns	ns	ns	
Passive optical transceiver	1000 ns	ns	ns	
10baseT transceiver	1400 ns	ns	ns	
FanOut	300 ns	ns	ns	
Internal repeater + transceiver	< 3750 ns	ns	ns	
Repeater	1450 ns	ns	ns	
10baseT hub	3750 ns	ns	ns	
Synchronous active optical star	1400 ns	ns	ns	

Total delay $< 46\ \mu$s

15.2 Installation

The installation should adhere to certain rules which ensure that the network will function correctly and will be maintainable. Several of these guidelines are taken from the note IEC 907 (International Electrotechnical Commission), *Local area network CSMA/CD 10 Mbit/s baseband planning and installation guide*. The gist of this technical report is summarized here and advice adapted to the IEEE supplements and to new advances in technology is also given.

Coaxial cable

- The coaxial cable should be grounded by the braid (external conductor) at one end only. The grounding should be implemented using copper wire with a cross section of at least 4 mm^2. This implies that all the other elements of the N or BNC connector system (T, straight connector, terminator) should be protected and insulated (for example, by a plastic sleeve).

- It is always preferable for the cable segment to be constructed from a single production batch so that the sections are more homogeneous (if the cable sections all come from the same manufacturer, this may ensure that the propagation speed will not vary by more than 0.5% between segments).

- The minimum bend radius of the standard coaxial cable is 25 cm once laid and 20 cm during the installation.

- The minimum bend radius of the thin coaxial cable is 5 cm.

- If the cable has to be suspended, it should be tacked down at least every 3 meters.

- It is recommended that the cable should be placed at least 10 m from major sources of radiation (such as lift contactors, electric arc welding sites, generators).

- Pay attention to the damage to which the coaxial cable may be subject during laying: deformation (traction, twisting, torsion, bruising, very short radius), abrasion, severance, cracking. One of the main sources of deterioration during drawing the cables is the presence of sharp edges on the cable path.

- For paths in suspended ceilings, it is advisable to remain less than 3 m from the floor, whenever possible.

- For paths in suspended ceilings or raised floors it is preferable to have a hatch at most 30 cm from the points of possible intervention: on transceivers, connectors and load adapters.

- The crimping of N or BNC connectors should be finished well (no wires from the braid visible, no crushed sheath, no loose connectors or connectors with play).

- The N connectors should only be tightened by hand.

- Note that, since the useful frequency band for Ethernet is limited to 20 MHz, there is no need to use the connector technology approved for more robust applications (military).

- If the presence of a 30 V AC voltage between the braid and ground is detected after laying, this is an indicator of a fault in the installation and analysis is required before proceeding further.

- In time-domain reflectometry the maximum admissible reflection at a point is 4% (care should be taken to ensure that the transceivers are not emitting during the measurement).

- The maximum admissible reflection at any point is 7%.

- Before grounding, the insulation resistance between the braid (external conductor of the cable) and the ground should be greater than 200 MOhm. This measurement should be carried out using a megger at 500 V with all the transceivers disconnected.

- There should not be a short circuit between the two conductors. However, the loop resistance of a coaxial cable segment should be less than 10 MOhm/m (at 20° C).

- The loop resistance of the cable with the transceivers should be less than 5 Ohm.

- The transceivers should be installed on reference rings drawn every 2.5 meters on the standard coaxial cable.

- One might suggest that transceivers should not be placed at segment ends. In fact, this would mean that it would be possible not to superpose the variation in impedance due at the attachment point (T or tap) on that of the straight link and the load adapter. Thus, a minimum section (2.5 m in 10base5, 50 cm in 10base2) should be left between the last transceiver and the load.

- If the path is such that lightning protection cannot be guaranteed, if the zone is perturbed by electrical noise, if the temperature is too high, if the bend radii extend to 3 cm or if the constraints relating to safe operation of the link are fundamental, then optical fiber should be chosen.

The AUI cable

- It is desirable that the AUI cable should be fixed so as not to pull on the slide-latch lock (reputed to be fragile and unreliable).

The twisted-pair cable.

- The wires of each twisted pair of the cable should not be inverted between the patching and the wall socket. Similarly, the pairs should not be inverted among themselves as this might harm the operation.
- The 10baseT jumper cable in the office should be placed where it is not in the way, to ensure that there is no risk of pulling out the relatively fragile RJ45 sockets.
- It is recommended that the twisted-pair cables should be placed in shielded cable paths dedicated to data communication and, if possible, almost a meter away from high-voltage cables and sources of electromagnetic radiation.

Fiber optic cables

- Optical cables should not be subject to excessive traction when they are laid, and one should ensure that the bend radii indicated by the supplier are respected, otherwise the fibers may be irremediably harmed.

The active elements   An equipotential link for the power supply transformers should be provided if network elements are to be installed in zones fed by medium voltage (> 450 V eff).

General   Demand labels on the cables and the patch plates (Figure 15.12). The labeling should be clear and consistent, and the labels should be solidly fixed and have a high physical resistance.

In the case of a twisted-pair cable leading to a plant room, an indication of the plant room may be omitted if it appears superfluous (for example, only one plant room per storey). On the other hand, in the case of a coaxial or fiber optic cable, the technology used might be indicated (Eth for Ethernet, TR for Token Ring, and so on), together with the logical type of the network supported (for example, MN for main network or MgtN for management network).

The more important the network installed is to be, the greater is the attention that should be paid to the quality of implementation, since the network will certainly have to live with this installation for several years. Many problems of a physical level may certainly result from overhasty choices or botched operations.

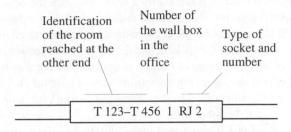

Identification of the room reached at the other end

Number of the wall box in the office

Type of socket and number

T 123–T 456 1 RJ 2

Figure 15.12   Example of a label for a patching module.

Finally, to simplify the work of the installer and minimize the choice available to him or her at the last moment, the detailed technical specifications produced should be as precise and consistent as possible. For example, it is not easy to find out that a path cannot be used as specified because it is already full of cables, but one of the tasks of the person responsible for the dossier is to establish realistic specifications, which may call for a number of on-site visits, as necessary, and reference to those who know the site or the building best (the electricians or the works department). Thus, the person responsible should be encouraged to carry out preparative groundwork to avoid being forced to modify his or her plans during the work itself.

15.3 On-site monitoring

This phase has several objectives. The main aim is to ensure that the rules laid down in the schedule of conditions or the detailed technical specifications are adhered to, and that the network installed effectively corresponds to that defined on paper. For this, one has to consider all the technical points where the installer has a margin for maneuver, so that each solution chosen by the latter is appropriate, even when it is a minor detail (position of the distribution panels, color of the connection modules, type of labeling).

The second important aim is to ensure that the laying methods are adhered to, in relation to the security of the operators, the non-degradation of the cables and equipment installed and the global neatness of the whole project.

Finally, monitoring of the progress of the work will enable one to identify any slippage in the planning at the earliest possible time, and to anticipate the consequences of a delay at this stage (ordering of materials, date of payment, call for additional teams).

The first subject is fundamental to subsequent peaceful operation of the network. It is easy to appreciate that any maintenance or extension task may become a real headache if, during the course of the work, it is discovered that the network in question does not conform to the descriptions in the detailed technical specifications.

In fact, every action should be preceded by a study to check the actual state of the network. The points requiring vigilance are the choice of the hardware (the cables and their physical characteristics, the cable paths and the associated nuts and bolts, the rack cabinets, the make of the sockets, and the plugs), the effective cabling (in the cabinets, in the sockets, adherence to the patching plan) and the way in which these cables are manipulated during laying operations. One should not forget that a cable (coaxial, twisted pair or fiber optic) may be damaged during installation without the damage being immediately noticeable.

The second subject is concerned more with the person responsible for the security and others dealing with the cabling (telephone, electricity, alarm) that occupies the same paths as those used by the networks. In both cases, it is a matter of integrating the laying of a data communication infrastructure without violating the security rules for the building or the site, and without impeding the other installers or damaging their installations, while even seeking to make use of the existing cabling using the labeling templates or existing routes in the suspended ceilings and ducts. This may provide a better view of the operation of laying the network, which is sometimes seen as an intrusion by those responsible for maintaining the other cabling systems (old and thus understood well).

Finally, the third point is only mentioned here for information, since it adds little to the quality of the implementation, but rather forms part of the project management, in that it provides specific information about the progress of the laying and installation phase.

Here is an example of the great attention that must be paid throughout the on-site monitoring phase. The 10baseT lines linking the PC interface card to the wall socket should consist of four twisted pairs (two pairs may suffice if they correspond to the pins of the emission pair 1–2 and the reception pair 3–6 of the RJ45 socket). However, if the installer lays flat cable, which is apparently identical (apart from the fact that the cable is slightly thinner since all the conductors are run in parallel), transient problems may then affect the network operation. In fact, above a length of several meters, this type of cable is no longer suitable for communication at 10 Mbps, and intermittently generates errors which may appear as a function of the frame length or the density of transfers. The manifestations of the problem will then be wrongly associated with a particular protocol or type of exchange since this protocol uses longer packets than others. The repair crew then becomes involved in useless and time-consuming research procedures, simply because the cables installed were not those required. A similar thing may occur for other cables and hardware components of the network.

15.4 Acceptance operations

The acceptance operation involves checking an installation, or a meticulous follow up of the progress of the laying operations, either by tests and subsequent checking or a combination of the two.

Often, the physical acceptance, concerning the transmission medium and the terminal elements (connectors, patch plates), is distinguished from the logical or functional acceptance which involves ensuring that the network is operating effectively. In fact, the different stages of the acceptance operation correspond to descriptions at various levels in the schedule of conditions. Thus, the functional acceptance which tests the overall capabilities of the network (non-exhaustively in most cases) ensures that the system provides the required global capabilities. The acceptance of each individual unit may qualify the elements as a function of the required characteristics. Careful and continuous on-site monitoring is the best way of monitoring the overall quality of the infrastructure installed. Let us not forget that a major part of the installation will be hidden during the acceptance procedure (in suspended ceilings, raised floors, attachment plates, patch cabinets).

As shown in Figure 15.13, at the time of a large-scale installation, it is best to decompose the acceptance operation into a number of elementary tasks. This decomposition may be carried out logically, proceeding in the opposite direction to the definition. To follow this method, at each stage of the definition a list of the tests that can be used to validate the functionality described has to be drawn up. The more one advances into details of the solution in place, the more the tests or associated checks will concern specific (and generally smaller) elements.

On the other hand, if the test is of a low level, it is realistic to carry out an

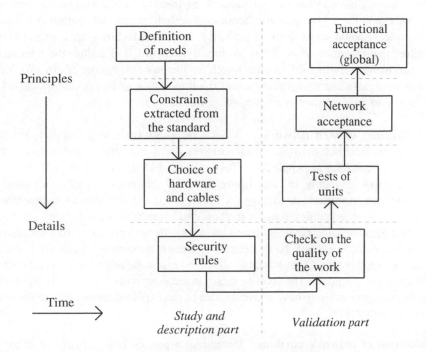

Figure 15.13   Progress of the definition and test stages, by level.

exhaustive check, although as the level of functionality increases the test will become more global, and thus incomplete, and constitute no more than an indication.

Finally, note that, as far as the progression of time is concerned, the definition stages run from the most general to the most specific, although this order is inverted in the acceptance phases (from the element to the whole).

By way of example, the phases of a typical large installation are now described.

Global operation of the network   The test of the primary operation of the network as a whole will necessarily be at the application level. It may involve:

- Tests of file transfer between workstations (for example, with FTP)
- Opening a session on a remote host
- Emulating a terminal on a remote microcomputer (Telnet in text or terminal mode, Xwindow in graphics mode)
- Access to a server and attempts to share resources (database, peripherals).

If the network includes interconnection devices, attempts may be made to pass traffic through these (bridges, routers, gateways), since these may not have been qualified beforehand on a per unit basis (following the steps described below).

For each test, the framework of the expected results (maximum time taken, admissible number of lost packets, periodicity of measurements, and so on) corresponding to the global acceptance threshold which will permit definitive acceptance should have been established beforehand. Since this preparation requires the implementation of test platforms (from which to deduce the reference measurements), it will facilitate the search for the probable source of any problem which may arise and an appreciation of the importance of this problem, and will allow one to move towards a resolutory approach.

Qualification of each network   A network corresponds to a complete entity, such as an Ethernet network or sub-network, or a network or sub-network of any other technology (AppleTalk, Token Ring, FDDI). The test will involve representative elements of the future set of user machines (PC terminals, workstations, mainframes). Changes will be carried out between these machines to qualify the speed achieved under the best conditions (for example, only one pair of active elements) and the degradation caused by the background traffic, simulated using test equipment, will be evaluated. To obtain maximum benefit from these tests, the simulated background traffic should be as similar as possible to real traffic (variable and irregular). The level of these tests corresponds to the MAC layer. As before, it is preferable to have a precise idea of the expected results before the real tests are undertaken.

Validation of network portions   Definition: a portion of a network is either a coaxial cable segment with its transceivers or a point-to-point link, or a hub or a star with its links.

The test may be performed with two test sets, which will verify that the network is operating properly at the physical level (media and active elements) from an AUI port. The speed to which each portion is subjected may be the theoretical maximum speed (14 880 frames/s for short frames, 812 frames/s for long frames). At this level, it is also possible to test the transmission of defective frames, the propagation of collisions or the partitioning capability. The tests may be exhaustive and involve the checking of the operation of each access point on each segment.

Cable and connector characteristics   The measurement at this stage involves coaxial or optical reflectometry, which validates the physical characteristics of the medium (measurements of total lengths for confirmation, determination of the attenuation at the operational frequencies for comparison with the figure given by the standard, observation and adaptation of the impedance, localization of perturbations). The optical and twisted-pair jumper cables may also be inspected, to determine a correspondence with the optical-fiber type used in the network infrastructure (diameter, numerical aperture), to monitor the connector technology for the RJ45 sockets (wire color, pin number) and to check that twisted pairs and, if necessary, shielding, are effectively present. At this stage, the measurements are necessarily exhaustive. In fact, if a medium segment were defective, it would be more complicated to repair after the installation of the network was complete (for example, if it were discovered at the time of the final acceptance) than at this stage.

Quality and security of the work, physical details   Quality assurance monitoring will take place as the work proceeds. This concerns the crimping of connectors, laying of the medium, cleanliness of the installation and adherence to rules laid down in the schedule of conditions, including the labeling of cables and sockets, the color of connection modules and the position of wiring cabinets and active elements. Care should also be taken to ensure that the quantities of commodities ordered but not installed (jumper cables, 10baseT transceiver cables) correspond to the schedule of conditions. It is also important to take security aspects into consideration. Finally, the physical details to be reviewed at this stage include the contractor's choice for each element (cable, connector, socket), and accessory equipment (in a cabinet: ventilation, lighting, power supply facilities as a function of the network devices), and so on.

A visual check as part of the on-site monitoring with a regular presence throughout the laying operations will make it possible to provide useful advice at the appropriate time. This will also enable one to ensure that the recommended arrangements are followed and, possibly, to keep a check on the planning. Care should be taken to ensure that methods which are visibly unsuitable should be corrected at the earliest possible time (especially when these may lead to irremediable damage to certain elements).

In the case where the installer himself (herself) tests the physical level (described above), it is wise to monitor the approach he (she) follows when taking the measurements. One's confidence in the results will depend closely upon the test method used. In the same spirit, a measurement performed counter to certain rules or methods may provide unusable results, since it will not give a true or representative numerical indication.

15.5 Evolutions and modifications

The modification phase is generally similar to a small installation task, so it will give rise to the same methods and procedures. Depending upon its importance, care should be taken to produce the preliminary and subsequent documents in the same format as for a typical installation.

It is fundamental that evolutions of the whole network, or of some of its segments, be accompanied by the immediate updating of all documents associated with the network (plans, general and detailed synopses, list of stations, plan of patch cabinets, and so on). Without this, the documentation describing the installations rapidly becomes out of date and loses all its reference value. In fact, the network is 'alive' in the sense that it grows, changes and evolves as new items reach the market. Thus, even when the dimensions of the cabling were chosen to be sufficient to accommodate all modifications without requiring extension, the set of active access points will alter.

The monitoring of the network thus constitutes a single integral task, responsibility for which should be well defined in order to avoid 'free-for-all' intervention on the network. One natural consequence of this is the need to identify a single spokesperson for the network. He or she will be responsible for following all the procedures relating to intervention (generation of progress reports, updating of cards showing the patching, informing users of outages, and so on). Thus, in parallel with the installation of a network, it is fundamental to define the human structure which will take responsibility for each of its stages. When defining the possible ways of intervention, care should be taken to ensure that this does not lead to any conflict between those involved and that their areas of action do not overlap.

It is clear that a simple intervention in the network is an operation that anyone can undertake. Changing the point at which one is plugged in, modification of the patching by the introduction of jumper cables or the extension of a thin coaxial cable segment are all practical actions that everyone apparently understands and is capable of. However, they may have disastrous consequences for the rest of the network. The machine which is moved without the person responsible having been informed may have unwittingly changed logical networks. Blind manipulation of patching may put a user in the dark, or even cut the access to an element that is crucial to others (router, gateway, server). Extension of an existing cable inevitably leads to a temporary cut on connection and, if one is unaware of the length already laid, may result in transient perturbations (whose probability is a function of the traffic and the frame length) which are difficult to detect when their cause is unknown.

15.6 Maintenance operations

Intervention for maintenance

In the case of breakdown, or where there is doubt about the operation of the network or a particular element of it, the intervention team is called to resolve the problem. The fundamental task of this team is to get the network working again with a minimum delay so that users are not affected for too long a time.

In fact, as networks are now integral parts of the office automation environment, they have become vital to the smooth running of some departments. Thus, the objective is simple: to cure or reduce the problem as rapidly as possible. This implies acting methodically and progressively, carrying out all the stages of the repair process in a proper manner.

On the other hand, the repair team must avoid aggravating the problem, for example, by making it definitive or by interrupting ongoing activities before the results of the intervention have been anticipated. This action should have a simple aim (to test the operation of a single element, replace a component, introduce a partial modification to a configuration). The possible results of this action should be anticipated beforehand, so that a conclusion can be drawn rapidly. The team should also ensure that a backup machine can be introduced at any time, should the tests not be successful. This will avoid the accumulation of several modifications, since explanation of any cure soon becomes laborious. In summary, methodical procedures should be adopted.

As shown in Figure 15.14, it is vital to know just which point the repair procedure has reached at any given time. One needs to know what has been analyzed and ruled out and what has been and may be involved in measurements still to be taken, and to be able to identify the part that remains to be dealt with. Moreover, it is practical to be able to determine, at any time, the time spent in each stage and the time it will still take either to complete the repair or conclude the analysis. This enables one to make a reasonable choice of the tests to be undertaken, or to put in place a provisional, degraded but adequate, configuration. In fact, the determination of the area which may be affected may lead the repairer to prefer a partial modification to the network configuration, rather than to risk inconveniencing the users for too long a period.

Repair methods

In a repair operation, the problem detected by the user may be the consequence of a fault of any kind. It may involve a hardware fault, an error in the software parametrization (level 3 and 4 protocols) or a configuration which is ill adapted to the network.

It is vital to be able to determine the type of anomaly rapidly, so that one can work on a broad spectrum of faults. Although there is no substitute for experience as far as this task is concerned, certain arguments may help one to determine the reason for the user's unhappiness.

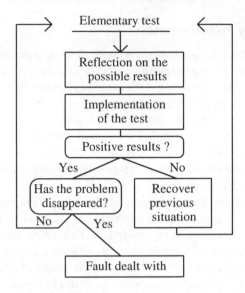

Figure 15.14   Methodical approach to repairs.

The first phase involves translating the fault as described by the user into network-technology terms. There are two main categories of fault phenomenon:

- A global or specific decrease in performance, with a noticeable variation in the speed, collision rates or number of errors.

- An intermittent, periodic or continuous, but clear fault (given that certain periods of the day are particularly heavily loaded: 9–11 am and 3–5 pm), where the problem can be reproduced with varying degrees of difficulty. Moreover, this fault may affect all or part of the network, and thus the relationship between the problem and the stations affected should be investigated. Breakdowns may:
  — be associated with a machine or a place (which means that the machines and the cabling part can be separated)
  — concern one machine, a particular group of machines or all the machines (the link or the difference between the machines affected should be investigated: hardware side – manufacturer, model, attachment type, physical position; software side – network system used, communications configuration (server, diskless or dataless station, distributed application), software version)
  — occur for a particular type of traffic or for all exchanges (traffic characteristics, protocols and applications used, routing of the exchange, server or gateway used, frame length)

— be perceptible in communications with the outside or only in internal communications, in one or both directions (implication of the interconnection devices in the problems detected).

Thus, discussions with the user should be held to identify the relevant elements, including those relating to the hardware, the protocols, the software (applications), and the configuration. What the user says should be recast to associate the breakdown with as precise a category as possible.

One approach involves taking a logical route and following it as closely as possible. We shall describe two examples of ways in which this may be done.

Method 1 Begin with the element with the least restrictions which is the nearest to the manifestation of the fault (when this is localized). If this element is ruled out, gradually broaden the range of devices and components to be considered. This will give a progressively larger set, which will inevitably lead to questions about the source of the fault. For example, one might follow a sequence implicating the state of the following items of equipment in the order given in Figure 15.16.

- The AUI connector technology of the NIC and the NIC itself
- The AUI cable
- The medium segment (its connectors and its grounding)
- The repeater or the hub (its AUI cables and transceivers)
- Other network segments (and their repeaters)
- The local bridge or router (and the networks interlinked by these)
- The remote bridge or router

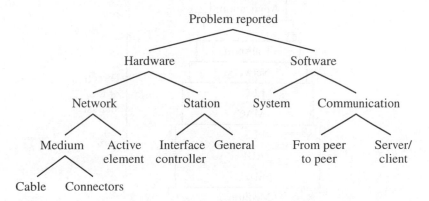

Figure 15.15 Example of the classification of sources of problems which may affect the network.

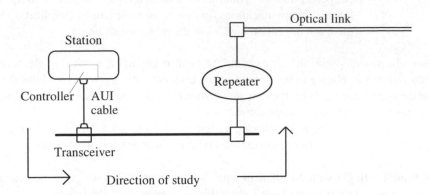

Figure 15.16 Sequence for the case considered.

- The modem or the serial line
- The network of the remote site.

Method 2 Begin with the physical layer and move up through the OSI layers at each stage (which implies testing the most elementary things before the most complex). As before, we can give an example of a logical sequence of points to be considered. Investigate whether the problem may reside in (see Figure 15.17):

- The bottom of the physical layer: the AUI, N, BNC, optical or patching connector technology; the medium segments, whatever they may be (adaptation, parasitic reflection, length); the transceivers

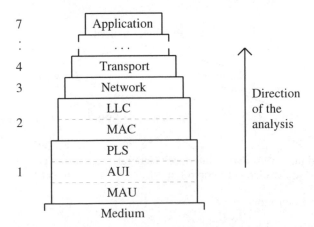

Figure 15.17 Progression through the layers of the OSI reference model.

- The PLS level (repeaters, hubs, multimedia stars)
- The MAC level (NIC, bridge, and also the configuration authorized)
- Levels 3 and above (router, gateway, protocols used in the exchanges, routing protocols)
- Level 7 (application, software used, server used).

At each stage, one should check that the point in question is operating properly in conformance with the standard. If, at each stage, care is taken to eliminate the element tested, one will finally discover the origin of the fault (see diagram on Figure 15.18). When checking a particular component, it is simplest, when possible, to replace it by a reference element; otherwise, the performance of the component should be quantified in a sequence of tests.

Returning to the scheme described at the beginning of the section, recall that the most complicated breakdowns to resolve are those which combine various causes whose manifestations are similar enough to be confused. It may then be quite difficult to establish operationally that the source of a fault has been effectively identified, while at the same time the problem has apparently not disappeared. However, a methodical approach should help one to progress gradually towards the solution.

Test devices are not always crucial, but they simplify the work considerably, since, apart from the stations and the machines using the network effectively, they can be used to evaluate the elements at the physical level.

The most useful of the devices described in Part II are:

- The coaxial reflectometer for installations in which the cabling is mainly based on coaxial cable
- The twisted-pair tester for infrastructures comprising twisted-pair cables (shielded or unshielded), including prewired sites
- The optical dBmeter and the associated calibrated source, which are simple and practical tools for checking fiber optic links
- The pair of test sets for carrying out tests at the MAC level
- The LAN analyzer to observe the traffic and decode all the protocols (level 1 to 7).

The merits of these devices are reviewed in more detail in Chapter 17 (documents and necessary hardware).

15.7 Management

At the beginning of Chapter 15 (the stages) it was shown that the management of one or more networks could be split up into elementary tasks. Let us now try to perform this segmentation in a logical manner (Figure 15.19).

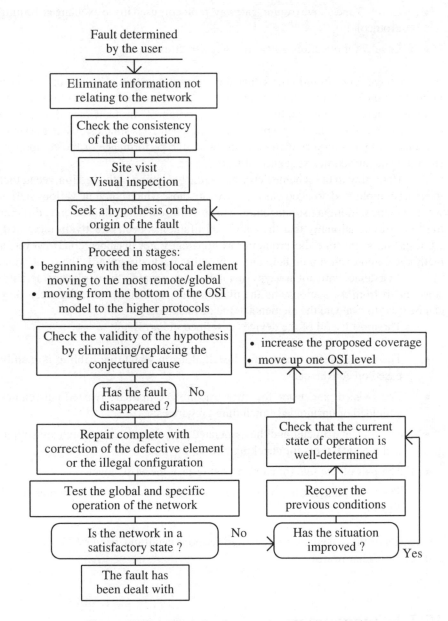

Figure 15.18   Example of a procedural repair method.

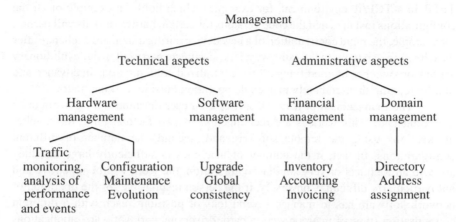

Figure 15.19   Division of the management into sub-domains.

Two fundamental aspects surface after a fundamental study: these are technical subjects associated with the hardware and software used in the operation of the network or conversely, used by the latter as a means of communication; and subjects of an administrative nature, associated with the tool, which is the network. The technical aspects concern both the management of the hardware as a whole and the software installed, and the monitoring of the traffic using all the means of observation available today. Here, we have chosen to collect together tasks concerning the hardware and the data that they may provide about the state of the network. In fact, the useful data for monitoring comes from all the network devices, whether they be effectively active elements in the network (hubs or managed stars, local and remote bridges, routers) or simple workstations with an agent (process designed to provide indications about the traffic seen at a point, at a master station). Thus, the hardware management will separate the monitoring function, which we shall describe later, from the mission of organizing the hardware as a whole.

The latter should include the configuration of the parameters of programmable devices (activation, deactivation of ports, implementation of filters, and of well-defined routing, choice of the address of the master station to which statistics and alarms are to be directed), together with the monitoring of these devices to ensure that they are operating properly and calling for maintenance when necessary. The selection of the parameters may involve collaboration with the entity responsible for the administrative aspects and management of the logical domains. The function also includes monitoring of the hardware together with updating of the hardware (insertion of modules in or removal of modules from a rack, changing the backplane of a bridge, increasing the memory of a router) and the software (changing versions in ROM or RAM or on disk), when required. Do not forget that many 'smart' devices permit remote loading of their configuration or operating code. Thus, the mission of organizing the hardware as a whole should incorporate the management of a station with appropriate communication protocols (Telnet, FTP, TFTP, in a TCP/IP environment, for example) which holds an example of all the configurations installed and the code versions for certain hardware. This will permit, for example, the rapid configuration of a new device during a standard exchange after the detection of a fault. In the same way, it is possible to carry out major evolutionary actions or switches by modifying all the centralized configurations in advance and rapidly loading them remotely in a single operation outside working hours.

The management of network software on user machines may constitute an important task. This work is a direct function of two factors. First, the number of positions using the remote software and, second, the number of different configurations. In fact, if the number of machines is sufficiently large and they all have an identical or very similar configuration, the work will be repetitive and not particularly difficult. Conversely, if the person responsible for the operation of network software has to manage several tens of positions, each with a different configuration (type of interconnection card, driver, network software, applications installed, operating system), each intervention will be a unique case and will require specific knowledge. Thus, the monitoring of a set of microcomputers using a network manager may become a real headache if each user is free to load whatever programs he or she wishes. It would therefore be prudent to introduce a number of rules limiting the possibilities and one might even provide a model of a typical implementation. However, this ideal configuration which the person responsible would like to see become general should be sufficiently open and effective as to be acceptable.

The administrative aspects are less linked to the telecommunications technologies, since they put in place monitoring and management procedures and provisions relating to the enterprise's investments in an attempt to ensure that these are profitable in the medium or long term. This branch may include invoicing for services provided by the existing infrastructure or the operational monitoring to the departmental users of data communication. The cost to be attributed to a connection will then have to be evaluated, depending upon the technology used, but also on the servers which the users wish to access or the means of interconnection with other networks they would like to use. Thus, the administrative section is responsible for managing the access rights to each service as a function of the quotas. It will also be necessary to monitor the use made of the network and its added values so that the dimensions of the latter can evolve in a close relationship with the demand. Once again, periodic and serious forecasts, based on various measurements and observations, can be used to provide the best service to users by giving them practical and reliable communications techniques.

Thus, ISO has defined five major management domains:

- Security management, covering security and privacy aspects in the network.
- Performance management, covering the collection of statistics and monitoring of the operation.
- Configuration management which defines how configuration and software updating should be managed.

- Fault management, which describes how to manage faults and alarms.

- Accounting management which is concerned with practical aspects of the management of the equipment as a whole.

Monitoring

We shall define monitoring (or remote monitoring) as a means of observing the network, with no possibility of modifying the behavior of the devices. Management incorporates a greater functionality, as in addition to the generation of traffic-related indicators, it offers the possibility of acting on certain elements of the network.

For a number of years, a summary of the operational state of the network has been available to the user on a station bringing together all the information transmitted by the observation devices (probes or so-called 'smart' multimedia stars). While, initially, machines with the ability to monitor the traffic and produce a summary for an administrator were components of the network dedicated to this function alone, these are tending to fall into disuse, given that all recent top- or middle-of-the-range hardware now incorporates a monitoring capability in addition to its intrinsic function.

There are several categories of management system, including general systems (standardized or *de facto* standard), systems associated with one or more low-level technology, systems associated with a network manager and, finally, manufacturer and proprietary systems.

The category of general management systems includes:

- SNMP, a *de facto* standard protocol from the TCP/IP world, which is associated with numerous MIBs to handle each particular technology or type of network hardware.

- SNMP v2, which considerably improves upon SNMP in that it covers all types of resource (applications, systems, and so on) and no longer network resources alone, although its deployment is not yet assured.

- Common Management Information Protocol and Services (CMIP/CMIS), defined by the ISO, which are intended to form the future universal management system (exists today over LLC: CMOL and over TCP/IP: CMOT).

This kind of system may be capable of interrogating the various layers of the communications protocol stack of the machine containing it, and of sending information about the circulation of data at each level to a central node.

The category of management systems associated with a given physical technology includes:

- IEEE 802.1B for all local or metropolitan area technologies defined by the IEEE, such as IEEE 802.3 (Ethernet), IEEE 802.4 (Token Bus), IEEE 802.5 (Token Ring) and IEEE 802.6 (DQDB).

- NMT for Token Ring, which constitutes the 'intelligence' of a Token Ring network, that is, the vertical layer in which the functions for monitoring the proper operation of the network and for recovering the ring in case of error are implemented.

- SMT from ANSI X3T9.5, which is the management protocol for level 1 to LLC, provides services similar to NMT and is defined solely for the FDDI technology.

These protocols form part of the development associated with a network technology; their role is to monitor the operation of the physical and MAC layers and quantify the traffic passing through these. They understand the importance of the procedures taking place (inherent to the technology) and are able to call some of these when necessary. The management system is then able to determine the state of a medium segment, a port, a machine or the whole network. One of the functions, returned to below, is the ability to reconstitute the network topology by interrogating its component elements.

It is important to note that there also exist management systems associated with Network Operating Systems (NOSs) such as Novell's NetWare Management System, which are always evolutions of the monitoring system originally associated with the NOS. These management systems, which essentially center on the monitoring of exchanges between client PCs and the server, have acquired the ability to receive other types of information such as SNMP traps or NetView packet reports, and even to interrogate agents. However, their main merit is their mastery of the protocols associated with the relevant NOS and thus their detailed understanding of the exchanges and their meaning. Today, this management software derived from the functions of the NOS is tending to become closer to major management systems, but may retain its property of analyzing the communications inherent to the manager.

Finally, in proprietary open SNMP platforms, we find:

- Hewlett-Packard's OpenView (for HP and Sun Unix stations and for PCs with MS-Windows)
- Sun Microsystem's SunNetManager
- IBM's NetView/6000
- Bull's ISM
- Novell's NMS
- Cabletron's Spectrum.

Note also one of the most important platforms in the IT world:

- IBM's NetView, which is capable of managing all SNA networks and their devices and which, consequently, represents the most common system, but can also manage non-SNA elements via service points.

Old systems had the advantage of being able to provide all the indications available to the hardware, since they were defined by the actual hardware manufacturer. However, they were often closed to the machines of other manufacturers, which implement a different, and incompatible communications protocol. An understanding of SMT and NMT messages is also built in, if a capability to follow the behavior of FDDI and Token Rings dynamically is required. Similarly, the STP packets circulating between the bridges enable the management systems to follow the modifications of the topology.

However, we stress that the SNMP protocol discussed in the previous chapters is currently the *de facto* standard for monitoring and management. When the parametrization or action (command *set*) functions are not implemented, SNMP is primarily a monitoring system. SNMP is found at the level of repeaters, hubs, multimedia stars, routers, and Unix stations. Probes, whose function is to implement a very complete management protocol, thus appear to be useful at the heart of a network.

Although the alternative from the ISO world may be a competitor for SNMP in years to come, CMIP has not yet been developed as expected. Once again, the advantages of the TCP/IP family have been crucial; in short, a proposed protocol may initially be insufficiently ambitious and not conform to ISO (although it may be interfaced to it) while at the same time being very real and validated by numerous implementations. Moreover, SNMP could make room for SNMP v2 even before CMIP can break through.

Elsewhere, ISO has defined a standardization framework for management systems defining five different domains of action, monitoring or measurement, namely:

- Security
- Performance
- Configuration
- Faults
- Management and accounting.

These effectively correspond to the main axes covered at least partially by the open platforms now available. Note that the management is a particularly vast domain in which intense development is now taking place.

SNMP

The management protocol for the TCP/IP stack currently has a fundamental attraction since the great majority of manageable devices support SNMP. Customers may have shown a sufficiently urgent need for manufacturers to decide in favor of a non-ISO solution, despite the already long-standing desire to move towards an ISO standardized world.

SNMP is a relatively simple protocol in comparison with CMIP, thus it is not too greedy in terms of resources for the machine in which it is housed, and evolves with the definition of new information bases, each adapted to a particular area.

SNMP operates with a certain number of agent elements, charged with recovering information about the traffic as seen from the device in which they are implanted, and with a central station which concentrates the data. Strictly speaking, the station is the network management system and may spontaneously interrogate the agents or accumulate the messages sent. In the second case, it must be defined for each agent as the specific destination of notification packets emitted by that agent.

SNMP is based on the use of the UDP and IP protocols and requires these to be implemented in each agent. One should bear in mind that the ability to be manageable is independent of the primary function of a device. Thus, a bridge or repeater will be able to communicate with the management station using a protocol suite up to the transport level, but will retain an interconnection task at the MAC or physical level, respectively (Figure 15.20). Despite the fact that a hub is able to decode an SNMP/UDP/IP frame, its behavior must remain unchanged and it will continue to reproduce the defective frames reaching it and to propagate collisions, and so on. The implementation of additional layers is exclusively dedicated to exchanges of management information. In Figure 15.21, the three Ethernet, IP and UDP layers return information to SNMP, which can communicate this information using the same stack. This is a special case, since SNMP can only monitor one layer, for example, Ethernet, in the case of a repeater, and possibly a layer which does not belong to the UDP/IP stack (internal functions to the workstation, use of microprocessor capabilities, and so on).

However, a knowledge of the IP, UDP and SNMP protocols is crucial, as far as the managed device is concerned, to enable it to encapsulate the counters in a standard format and send them on the network to one or more master stations. Depending upon the richness of the implementation, one may find a TCP/IP environment associated with the monitoring function which incorporates remote login via Telnet to connect itself directly to the device in text mode and to access all the counters directly available via SNMP using simple commands (tree of choices or rolling menu) (Figure 15.22). Similarly, capabilities for remote loading of the configuration may

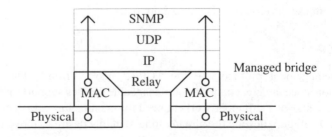

Figure 15.20   Data flow on interrogation of the MAC or physical layers.

Management tools
Management protocol
SNMP
UDP
Useful protocols
IP
Ethernet
Information from managed objects
Exchanges with the management station

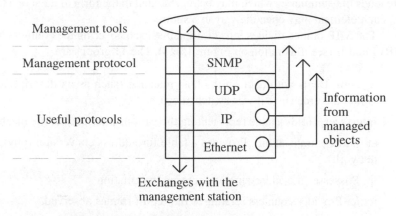

Figure 15.21 Protocol layers vital to a managed node.

be found in the case of a programmable device (smart hub, bridge, router) based on a transfer protocol of the FTP or TFTP type.

For information, we shall describe the structure of an SNMP encapsulated on Ethernet (with UDP/IP). Therefore, this includes the MAC level prefixes and suffixes and possibly those for the LLC, network and then transport levels. At the heart of the SNMP Protocol Data Unit is the linkage of variables carrying all the counters requested by the interrogating station. Each counter is defined by its identification and value.

All the data known to SNMP is stored in a tree structure so that the counters can be classified according to domain. To access the standard Management

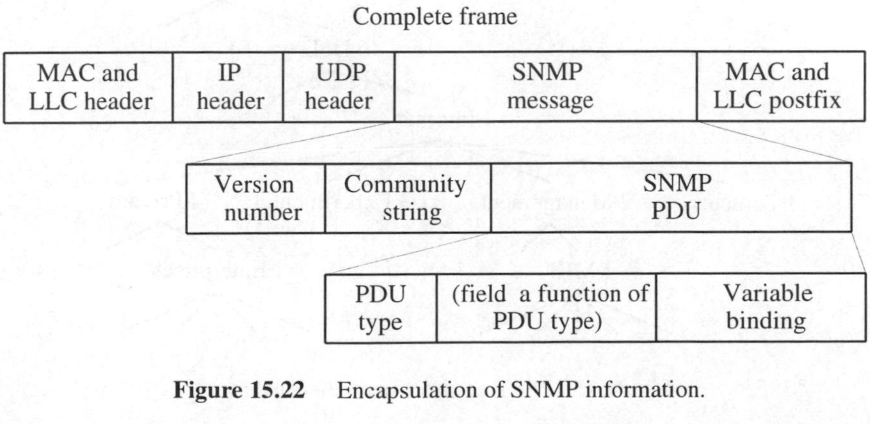

Complete frame
MAC and LLC header
IP header
UDP header
SNMP message
MAC and LLC postfix
Version number
Community string
SNMP PDU
PDU type
(field a function of PDU type)
Variable binding

Figure 15.22 Encapsulation of SNMP information.

Information Base (MIB) one already has to pass along branches 1.3.6.1.2.1. Then, one reaches the summaries which may be represented in the form of a list or a table. Thus, each element may open the way to a subtree.

The MIB branch divides into 11 domains, each covering the counters listed in MIB I and II (see illustration on Figure 15.23). The 11 groups are:

1   System. Deals with data on the host machine (such as its description, its name, the time since it was switched on).

2   Interfaces. Holds a table representing the various interfaces of the machine.

3   at (address translation). Provides a table for address conversion (physical–network).

4   ip. Possesses the addressing and routing information.

5   icmp. Provides counters relating to the ICMP frames observed.

6   tcp. Contains summaries of the TCP packets seen together with a table of the machine connections under this protocol.

7   udp. Contains summaries of the UDP packets seen together with a table of the connections open under this protocol.

8   egp. Used by routers to communicate with autonomous systems.

9   cmot. Holds the data associated with CMIP over TCP/IP.

10   Transmission. Collects together the objects depending upon the various media.

11   snmp. Holds traces relating to the operation of SNMP.

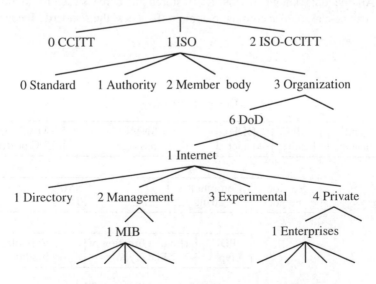

Figure 15.23   Tree structure of the database.

The 'Enterprises' branch (1.3.6.1.4.1) contains the manufacturers of the network worlds and all the extensions specific to each enterprise (private MIB). In fact, since the standard MIB does not cover all the existing hardware possibilities, the manufacturers always make all their counters accessible to SNMP, but via special database developments. However, to be able to interpret the information contained in a private MIB, one must have the descriptor for and know the significance of the information held there, and thus be in possession of the MIB specifications provided by the manufacturer. Files giving the state of each manufacturer's extensions are generally publicly available.

The commands used to obtain the figure acquired by an agent are of the *get* type. Thus, using an argument indicating the element targetted, one can pass through the tree structure down to the branch of interest. Additional commands may be used to reach the preceding or following element directly using the last position of the pointer without redefining the complete path. However, certain actions require the writing of a value in the agent tables. In this case, the command *set* is used, with the position of the variable as the argument, and the value to be given to it as the parameter. In a similar manner to reading, writing may be performed by moving from one element or continuing without redefining the description of the whole path.

Regular monitoring of the network will also allow one to provide elements contributing to the security of the network and to ensure a certain privacy in the communications. The observation of all changes in the topology or in the accesses will allow one to detect an unauthorized connection immediately. Of course, this involves considerable work because the network is live, in that machines are connected and disconnected several times a day and new stations appear regularly; however, without this monitoring the network may be exposed to a number of changes which become more important as the expanse of the network increases. In fact, as soon as a network is linked to remote networks, the risk of a malicious user being able to reach your station is no longer negligible. Then, your data may be read, copied or damaged and third parties may take advantage of the performance of your systems. To avoid such troubles, try to construct a communication unit which is secure and protected, in which attempts should be made to detect any intrusion or illicit action rapidly.

15.8 Security and privacy

This section deals with the security which can be put in place around a network together with privacy problems associated with the use of a local area network.

Security

Security involves protecting oneself against loss of data caused by a network fault or guarding against degradations in the working conditions due to a temporarily poor communications quality. As in mini- or microcomputer science, the tool represented

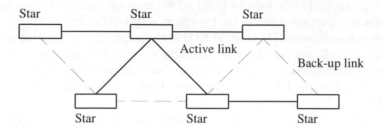

Figure 15.24 Example of redundant topology with automatic deactivation of loops.

the local area network is today so well integrated in the professional environment that it has become an indispensable cog. Thus, the momentary disappearance of transmission capabilities or the deterioration of the performance of these may hinder employees or make them unproductive for the duration of the fault.

With the advent of local area networks, it is wise to measure the degree to which the data communication tool is embedded in the day-to-day work, so that this instrument can be dimensioned as a function of its performance. Thus, when one realizes that a network has become an unavoidable link in a chain of procedures vital to the enterprise, it is urgent to ensure that this network is sufficiently well monitored and can be backed up with the least possible delay.

There are several ways of reinforcing the security of a network; one is almost universal and involves duplicating it, while another, more elaborate method requires a detailed study of each element.

Simple redundancy is often easy to conceive of, but not easily applicable to local area networks. In fact, while it is easy to provide duplicates of all active devices (repeater, hub, bridge), where each has a twin placed alongside it, it is already more complicated to switch all users with access to a certain coaxial cable quasi-simultaneously to the duplicate cable. Similarly, some devices, such as hubs controlling 10baseT lines or routers which have a necessarily unique configuration, can be replaced with varying degrees of difficulty. However, whether things are self-evident or a certain preparation is required, a switch to the redundant element is always possible. Note that the concept of prewiring is particularly suitable for this principle of duplication, since each medium link is used by one user only (point to point). Transition to a back-up link could take place without interrupting the rest of the network. Conversely, coaxial cable appears as an obstacle to security, since a momentary stoppage of all communications when a major fault occurs on the cable cannot be avoided.

The second option involves designing a secure network automatically, for example, by opting for duplicated synchronous optical links between plant rooms or multimedia stars with redundant power supplies which still retain one or two empty connection modules on the star ready to take the relay from a defective element, or by dimensioning the capillary cabling with sufficient generosity that it is possible to use a free port whenever a segment or a socket fails. Finally, this solution corresponds to a meticulous study of what is on the market, in an attempt to combine the advantages of each manufacturer to develop the most reliable network possible. Thus, one may find devices capable of supporting a looped connection between all the stars which only activate the links as a function of faults detected (see Figure 15.24).

Redundancy of the serial links between remote sites is easy to achieve, with the remote bridges and routers managing all the active lines and extracting the maximum bandwidth. In the case of a line fault the only consequence is a reduction in the total speed.

Privacy

Privacy represents the ability to keep a data set which has to be transmitted over the network secret. The only people who can read the data should be the authentic addressees. Detailed analysis of the technical data of Part II shows that it is unlikely that a technology such as Ethernet on coaxial cable will fall under the area of free access, and hence free from all constraints of limited diffusion, protected access and the exchange of passwords or keywords. Of course, Ethernet can be adapted, but it was not originally designed with these necessary protection elements. In fact, a clandestine read on the coaxial cable is undetectable if it is always silent and very difficult to locate if the machine grants itself the physical and logical addresses of another (apart from the conflicts this may cause if it uses these at the same time as the original machine). In the case of 10baseT technology, using smart hubs, a machine cannot therefore be connected to an arbitrary port of the hub without being detected, but, in general, some part of the network, such as the main artery, is still in coaxial cable. If the malevolent person is sufficiently well equipped, he or she may place a small radio receiver near the coaxial cable or the twisted-pair segment, without needing to find an official socket. The electrical conductors radiate and thus make it easy to capture the signal, with a view to reconstituting the frames. Only optical fiber is perfectly silent, although it is still possible to obtain a small portion of the signal in transit by bending it sufficiently for certain rays to leave the silica duct. However, this becomes highly specialized work.

If one imagines a spy station having found an access point, this may explicitly read all the frames circulating on the network. In fact, many NICs offer the possibility of reading the frames which are not directly addressed to them. Thus, it only remains to decode the protocols one after the other, from the bottom up, to obtain the application-level message. Thus, access protection on a machine by a request for a password on login is of no use, since the password circulates in clear on the network, often character by character. We are only left with the encryption of the data when it enters the communication system (via the application layer) or the exchange of access keys which can be used to ensure the privacy of exchanges.

When privacy is an important criterion, there are a number of options which allow one to reinforce it, although they do not guarantee it completely:

- Use of optical fiber rather than coaxial cable, for long links between repeaters, bridges or routers.

- Use of passive optical stars (inaccessible) rather than active stars, whenever possible.

- Installation of hubs with an observation monitoring option (on the MAC source address), scrambling capabilities (on the MAC destination address) and management capabilities, rather than elementary hubs or, worse still, FanOut.

- Segmentation of a large network into small interconnected networks or, more generally, use of the dynamic packet-switching technology, preferably of the port switching type (which carries out a natural filtering on the destination address and possibly on the source address).

- Interconnection of the networks by routers (with protected configuration) rather than by MAC level bridges.

- Controlled or restricted access to active devices and plant rooms (protected plant rooms).

To conclude this overview, recall that it is wise to force all users right from the start to follow a certain number of strict measures (sometimes limiting) when using the network. For example, they might be asked to declare the access they require to a particular server, the new network software they are installing or details of their communication (disk backups, copying of files, graphical transfers or simply exchanges of pages of text). This information is often useful and it is almost impossible to reconstitute it simply by observing the communications on the network. On the other hand, those responsible for the interconnection devices should take care to configure the equipment so that only useful traffic that has been officially declared can be passed. This filtering may be carried out on the physical or logical addresses, on the type of level 3 protocol, on another field in the frame or, again, on associations with the number of the port at which the packet enters or leaves.

Chapter 16

Human resources

- Useful knowledge

- Day-to-day procedures

It will have become apparent that the main aim of this book is to teach about the technical and practical elements which will be useful to those confronted with the world of local area networks (and, in particular, Ethernet). However, some notes about the individuals involved in this capacity are also in order.

16.1 Useful knowledge

As shown, each stage requires different skills. While the study and design stages require a knowledge of the existing standards to retranscribe the needs expressed by the requesting entity, practical experience acquired during previous implementations is a *sine qua non* for on-site monitoring.

Thus, the principal components of each stage and the skills brought to bear by those responsible are reviewed briefly (see Table 16.1). Each step is described in slightly greater detail to show the qualities needed and the essential aptitudes.

16.2 Day-to-day procedures

Each phase in the processing can be schematized using a certain number of procedures, where it is most important to proceed methodically at all times. Although it is not easy to describe the attitude to be adopted to a question or general problem relating to local area networks, certain indications can be given.

The study stage

This stage is marked by the great freedom available to the person responsible for the study, since he or she is relatively free to move towards any particular type of technology. The only constraints are that a solution should be provided which meets all the needs expressed. In fact, in each case, several more-or-less appropriate answers may be found.

When a new dossier is opened, it is important that the person responsible for the network design should not start from scratch by reinventing procedures and working methods. It is thus advisable that he or she should ensure that the study phase is essentially repetitive, even if it thereby loses part of its attraction. The resulting organization will inevitably bring a speed-up in the processing and make the set of networks installed more homogeneous. Continuing in this way, one might go so far as to define an in-house doctrine which advocates the topology, the technologies, the media, the connectors, the quantities, the suppliers, and so on. This will make the study work almost automatic, once the structure of the rooms and buildings has been matched with the possibilities offered by the doctrine.

Thus, it is clear that one fundamental aspect of the work carried out during any study or analysis of a network configuration is use of the documentation. One

Table 16.1   Components and skills required.

Stage	Main actions	Useful knowledge and skills	Suitable profile
Study (description of the project)	Understanding of the needs expressed, translation into terms of real solutions	Relevant LAN standards, inherent technical constraints, association between the theory and specifics	Engineer or manager responsible
Definition (editing of the schedule of conditions)	Selection of the topology and the medium, choice of hardware	Knowledge of what is on the market, validation of the chosen solution	Engineer or manager responsible
Installation (on-site monitoring)	Verification of the quality of the installation	Practical details, professional experience (cabler)	Specialist worker
Acceptance operations	Qualification of an installation	Real operation of the network equipments	Engineer or manager responsible
Evolution and modification	Small implementation, brief acceptance	Standards/ documents, predefined procedures	Technician
Maintenance	Repairs	Mastery of existing facilities, and study method	Technician for level 1 and MAC level, engineer for overall views
Administration	Monitoring, supervision, management, parametrization	Capabilities of hardware installed, configuration of the whole network	Technician for the monitoring, engineer for the configurations

needs to know how to use the existing dossiers, and all the evolutionary stages which the project design will pass through must be laid down in practical and clear documents, which, in turn, should be easy to consult and re-use in the future.

The installation stage

This stage consists of precise specification work, which should be implementable without modification, if possible and work to follow-up and monitor the operation. The first point requires rigor together with a good knowledge of the problems which may be caused by the buildings or structures that will house the cables and connectors. This means that editing the detailed technical specifications is only of value if one can be almost certain that all the potential obstacles have been listed and that the solution determined has been adapted to this context.

The second point is the counterpart of the first, in other words, if the study work and the work to list the difficulties due to the surroundings noted during visits is successful, it should be sufficient to monitor the progress from a distance, ensuring only that the directions in the schedule of conditions are properly taken into account. Conversely, if the level of detail and realism of the detailed technical specifications is inadequate, it will be necessary to maintain a regular presence on the site in order to be able to answer the questions which the installers will not fail to ask when faced with unforeseen complications.

In both cases, a practical nature is called for, with rapid, but rational reaction to potential pitfalls which may arise at any time. In this way, the more skilful personnel will be able to save time and materials during the laying.

The acceptance stage

The acceptance operation is carried out to ensure that the installation conforms with its description in the schedule of conditions. If one has total confidence in the sub-contractor, the acceptance may be reduced to something very minor (counting of the equipment, visual check). But this also means that one is certain that the network installed will be capable of meeting the needs, despite the fact that it has not even been tested. In reality, it is always sensible to check the operation of the network before signing the agreement.

However, while the low-level (physical, MAC) tests are simple, the higher-level trials should be developed as a function of the configuration of the network and of future uses.

At the physical level, the test of all the media should be performed using an appropriate tool (coaxial or optical reflectometer, twisted-pair tester). At the MAC level, the tests should also be exhaustive and should validate the wall sockets and the media segments, and then the networks and their active elements, by an exchange of several tens of thousands of frames. Thus, it should be possible to compose the list of trials completed in a relatively systematic way.

At levels three and above the tests should prove that the network actually provides the required communication capabilities. This now involves a quantification of quality which did not exist for the lower levels, whose results are generally of the form accepted/rejected. Thus, one has to know how to judge the validity of a transmission from the delay it entails and be able to interpret the gravity of a fault reported by a layer 3 or 4, and distinguish between problems due to the computer system and those due to the network. All this knowledge can only be acquired through experience and practical use of communication systems. It is imperative that the person responsible for defining the acceptance test suite should be familiar with both the computer environment which will crop up on the network, and with the communication software which forms the interface with Ethernet.

The repair stage

Recall that the main aim of this stage is to restore the normal communications functions to the users as soon as possible, even though the repair may be provisional.

As for acceptance, there are two aspects to maintenance, depending on the OSI level investigated. The low levels can be tested and eliminated once and for all by a few simple manipulations (including a test of the medium and the replacement of a number of active elements). These interventions fall wholly within the competence of a team of technicians.

On the other hand, complex breakdowns, such as the degradation of the communication quality (if, for example, equipment is still communicating with each other, but less well than before), may occur at all levels, even at the application level (above the actual communication system). Then, global skill is needed to work towards the origin of the fault. If no-one possesses these skills, the problem will have to be studied by a number of individuals whose areas of competence are partially overlapping and complement one another.

In summary, it may be said that the knowledge required for maintenance ranges from the characteristics of the cables installed to the facilities provided by the communications software and, at the same time, covers a command of the topology and configuration of the interconnection devices. If the network is effectively very extensive, several people will be required to contribute according to the area involved as the research progresses.

Chapter 17

Documents and materials

- Documentation

- Test equipment

Up to here, procedures which permit a methodical approach from the design of a network to its installation have been described. However, studies must be prepared with the usage of reference documents, designing decisions should be made with writing of related dossiers, and tests or acceptance operations should be conducted using suitable measurement apparatus.

Thus, certain documents and materials must be brought together in order to carry out a complete installation operation under the best conditions.

17.1 Documentation

Several types of document are useful when dealing with and monitoring local area networks. These include the purely technical documentation:

- Norms, standards and drafts describing the technologies used or envisaged
- Reviews, notes and specialized works explaining particular aspects which concern us
- Catalogs of the hardware offered by manufacturers, giving the precise characteristics and capabilities of the elements studied,

and the documentation associated with the installation:

- The original request, the schedule of conditions, the complete description of the whole installation, the acceptance schedule (when the laying of the network is complete)
- Evolutions, summaries of extensions and modifications
- A compilation of all the repairs carried out, giving, in each instance, the symptoms and the cause detected or the result of the analysis.

All these documents are useful and may be used to facilitate and improve proceedings. It is advisable to make them accessible to those likely to have to use them, whether to re-use them to refer to or to find information about the existing installation. In all cases, it is preferable that this documentation should circulate and be used profitably rather than lie dormant in a cupboard until it becomes obsolescent.

Reference documents

This category of document covers the official standards (such as those of the ISO), the standards of (generally national) research bodies (such as the IEEE), the drafts which usually precede these standards and the *de facto* standards defined by one or more manufacturers (IBM, DEC, Apple, and so on) or by a state organization (such as the DoD).

During the study and design phase, this type of work should be used to ensure that the edicts of the standard are adhered to. In this way, one can ratify the principal broad outlines of the installation prepared (topology, lengths, number of attachment points, and so on).

During the phases of industrial consultation and installation acceptance, these documents will be used to validate the work carried out (protection, insulation, quality of the grounding) and to check the conformance of the cables and hardware used (sizes of the conductors, attenuation of the segments at the operational frequency).

Books and reviews

In addition to the reference documents, there are also popularizing publications which analyze or explain a system or a protocol. These commercially available books are of variable quality, but generally have the advantage of not drowning the reader in a mass of detail of no concern to him/her, as is the case with a standard in which no points can be poorly defined. There are also complete, well-written books which can be used as an introduction to a technology. However, a search for rigor should preponderate if one is to rely on this type of written support.

In large companies, notes for internal use may provide an analogous source of knowledge, by introducing the reader to a particular technical area and providing useful explanations.

Note that these works, unlike norms and standards, may become obsolete after a few years, since the technologies implemented for a given use may have evolved considerably during this period.

Reviews have an even shorter lifetime and are only really instructive at the time of their appearance. However, the more a magazine is oriented towards a particular area of research, the longer the information remains significant. Conversely, the more the magazine focuses on the technologies, products and materials reaching the market, the more its durability will be reduced.

Reviews have the advantage that they follow the evolution of devices most closely and have an overall, essentially impartial view. Articles contrasting different solutions will encourage readers to ask themselves questions and answer with a personal opinion based on various sources of information. On this subject, it is advisable to obtain more than one magazine, and not to hesitate to buy foreign issues (American in particular).

Manuals and instructions for use

Every piece of hardware is sold with documentation of some sort. Unless this is totally devoid of interest, one should try to keep it as long as the hardware is in place.

If the element concerned is relatively simple (for example, a transceiver or a rudimentary repeater) and the manufacturer did not think it appropriate to include figures characterizing the hardware in the document, the manual will be of no use whatsoever. In all other cases, some information at least will be useful, and it is advisable to archive a copy of the manual.

In fact, it is in these documents that you will find estimates of the crossing delay for the hardware (particularly if this is better than that required by the standard), the lengths of media that can be attached and the manufacturer's recommendations for using the hardware under the best conditions (cable type, connector type, need for external ventilation, electromagnetic environment). One might also look for global characteristics such as the dimensions, the power consumption and the operating temperatures.

The instructions for use or the manufacturer's catalog may also provide information about the options available for this hardware, and the date at which it is intended to modify or update it (additional software option, module for other types of access, change of backplane). Finally, if it is a relatively complicated device (manageable hub, programmable bridge, router) the technical documentation will serve as a reference, since the configuration system and command language are non-standard and the manufacturer's documents are the only sources in this area. This will include how to become connected (parameters of the VT100 console or definition of the management PC), the list of commands and their action, the accessible counters and their meaning, and so on. Even when the hardware can be managed via SNMP it generally has a direct access mode (serial socket) with a special dialog mode. Moreover, private MIB extensions can only be understood and used with the manufacturer's notes and descriptions. Thus, it is best for the person responsible for the monitoring, maintenance or configuration of the hardware to have read all the documentation thoroughly at least once.

Monitoring documents

From the original expression of requirements prior to the study to the final acceptance dossier, all the documents accompanying the phases of the network's development should be kept together. Thus, as the project progresses, one accumulates a reference document retracing all the changes made from the original request onwards. Each file contains the level of detail fixed at that stage, the progress of the implementation work or the qualification results obtained. The schedule of conditions provides a complete description of the operation, the acceptance schedule (whole network laid) confirms the required functionality, and so on.

There are two uses for this document. The first corresponds to a search for precise information on what was provided for or implemented (and which must, of necessity, be described there). This information may be useful in a repair operation (precise location of a cable or transceiver in a suspended ceiling, existence of a backup link), when an extension is required (knowledge of the exact length of a segment, position of the ends) or when studying a transformation (re-usable sections, free capacity in the patch panels). The other function this document may have is to serve as a basis for similar implementations in other buildings or on other sites. Then, if the needs of the occupants are similar, it is sufficient to take the existing documents and adapt them to the case in hand. The task will thus be less arduous and better structured from the beginning, but care should be taken to ensure that the work remains perfectly consistent with the new conditions.

Some of these documents will gain from being computerized (placed in a word processor coupled with graphics software). Thus, modules or the whole structure of important documents can be re-used and adapted to handle other similar matters, thereby saving a significant portion of the work. On the other hand, the cabling schemes and network summary will be easier to modify, and will be able to follow the real evolution of the network with regular updating. In fact, the advantage of computer support is quite clear when one needs to duplicate or manipulate the information.

Evolution cards

Once acceptance has been confirmed, so that the life of the network with its modifications and extensions can be followed, a trace of each action should be kept, together with a note of its consequences on the network monitoring documents (discussed above). This is crucial if the documents and plans are not to become obsolete and unusable within a few years. In fact, if they do not include all the changes that have taken place, they no longer represent reality and can no longer be trusted.

This concept of an up-to-date document is very important as far as the work of network maintenance teams is concerned. The value of such a scheme depends closely upon the quality of its updates. Like the documents produced at the time of the installation, modification cards can be computerized. It is most important to keep all the general documents up to date.

For minor matters (extension by a few access points, change of an active element or replacement of an interconnection device), the card may consist of a single sheet summarizing all the stages and the actions undertaken. It should include the following data:

- The entity requesting the modification (name and coordinates of the interlocutor)
- The date the request was transmitted to the relevant operational team
- Information identifying the network uniquely (technology, position, category, number)
- Description of the actions required (quantity, location)
- Person or team effectively responsible for the modification
- Sequence of actions undertaken
- List of hardware installed (type, serial number, location)
- Tests and acceptance methods and results
- Test tools used (type, serial number)
- Dates of the end of the work and completion of the intervention (signature of receipt)
- (Possibly) sub-contractor used.

In all cases, it is best to give the matter an identifier, for example, by assigning a card number.

Collation of these extension or modification cards allows one to finalize the original documentation for the network, update it and to ensure that it retains its value, which is vital to its durability.

Maintenance cards

The maintenance card is intended to provide a clear trace of each repair operation. These cards may then be used to analyze a particular type of breakdown, to improve the procedures for searching for faults or to assess the quality of the work performed by the maintenance teams. In all cases, this written trace, which can easily be archived, can be used to follow the behavior and evolution of a data communications installation.

This amounts to a formalization of the repair work, which slightly increases the work involved in dealing with incidents by making all interventions official, but which is totally indispensable for large installations (more than a few tens of workstations). The maintenance card should, preferably, consist of a single sheet and include the following main items:

Information relating to the discovery of the problem

- The date the problem was detected (and possibly the time)
- Identification of the user or group that noted the fault (allegiance, hierarchical position, phone number, office, building)
- A description of the breakdown or fault (manifestation, repetitiveness, machine concerned, network used, network technology)
- The initial surmises and deductions, whether the user has tried to solve the problem (description of attempts, results and comments) or reference to a previous defect dealt with in the past.

Information about how the incident was dealt with by the entity responsible for the maintenance

- Date and time responsibility for the repair was assumed
- List of actions performed and tests carried out, showing the repair method used
- Conclusion and explanation of the results obtained, leading to the source of the fault or the reason for the malfunctioning (hardware responsible, incorrect parametrization, illegal configuration, over-demanding application)
- Identification of person(s) carrying out the repair (phone number), list of test equipment used (type, serial number)
- Date and time the intervention was completed.

Note that it is preferable to be able to identify each breakdown by a unique number, which can be assigned when the user requests assistance.

An example of an intervention card for an incident or a repair is shown below.

Repair no:	**Intervention card**	Maintenance contract no:	Date of commencement
Symptoms of the problem:			
Interlocutor:		Department:	
Service:	Building:	Office:	Phone:
Precise location of the network		Network identification	
Technology used	Ethernet Token Ring	LocalTalk FDDI	SNA (IBM) DSA (Bull)
Type of connection to the medium	Coaxial cable Twisted pair Fiber optic	Connection device used	Repeater Bridge Switch Router
Maintenance team:			Date and time:
Description of the stages in the repair and the method used	1 2 3 4 5 6 7		
Test equipment used	type: SN:	type: SN:	type: SN:
Result of the fault		Determined origin of the fault	
Fault code:		Total time spent:	

In addition, a fault code (bottom left) may be assigned, after examination, for every breakdown; this will simplify the processing of incident cards, for example for a statistical analysis. For information, there now follows a list of codes indicating the causes of breakdowns on an Ethernet network. The code consists of a letter describing the symptoms of the fault and a number identifying the defective element:

A   Clear and definitive hardware fault

B   Clear, but non-definitive hardware fault (blocked state)

C   Transient repetitive hardware fault

D   Transient momentary hardware fault

F   Hardware wrongly configured or parametrized

G   Equipment unsuitable for function

0   No element identified (that is, the problem did not recur or unsuccessful intervention)

1X   Fault linked to the medium

    10   Standard coaxial cable (thick)

    11   Thin coaxial cable RG58

    12   AUI cable (drop)

    13   Twisted-pair cable 10baseT

    14   Fiber optic cable

    15   Patch cord

3X   Fault linked to the connectors

    30   Type N connector

    31   BNC connector

    32   DB15 AUI connector

    33   RJ45 connector

    34   Optical connector (ST, SMA, SC)

    34   Patch panel

5X   Fault due to an active device

    50   NIC card

    51   Coaxial transceiver (N and BNC)

    52   10baseT transceiver

    53   Optical transceiver

    54   Multiport transceiver

    55   FanOut

    56   Biport repeater

    57   10baseT hub

    58   Multimedia star

    59   Passive optical star

7X   Fault in interconnection device

    70   Local bridge

71   LAN switch

72   Remote bridge

73   Local router

74   Remote router

75   Gateway

76   Modem (and dedicated line)

77   Repair beyond the competences of the maintenance team

Note that only numbers beginning with an odd digit have been used, so as to leave the manager the freedom to introduce additional codes relevant to his/her installation (if this includes networks other than Ethernet, FDDI, Token Ring, LocalTalk, and so on). For example, the following codes might be used:

60   FDDI concentrator

61   FDDI by-pass

80   Ethernet–FDDI bridge

81   FDDI–FDDI bridge

The clear aim of this coding scheme is to represent the progress of the complete repair in as synthetic and concise a way as possible. If need be, it could be associated with additional documents describing each action of the procedure.

Finally, precise and thorough editing of the intervention reports may help one to implement a form of preventative maintenance, simply through an analysis of the figures for recent months. Simple statistical calculations will bring to light the least reliable elements, the most fragile types of network and any hardware configurations which have disastrous repercussions on the traffic flow. Capture of the report information in a database, together with the use of automatic processing tools capable of providing a periodic synthesis of the actions and their assumed cause, may rapidly become highly efficient methods of investigation.

Thus, in parallel with the network management, intelligent use of the incident cards may provide all the pertinent information about the quality of each device and its operation. This requires the collation of the incident cards for all breakdowns that have occurred, making evident the symptoms together with the cause determined or the result of the analysis.

17.2 Test equipment

The various items of test equipment and the measurement tools were described in the last part of Chapter 10. Some of these are almost indispensable and their purchase should be provided for from the start; others are useful at certain times and should be associated with a category of well-defined tests.

Indispensable tools

Depending on the types of medium used and the extent of the network, certain pieces of equipment soon become indispensable to the maintenance of the network and to the monitoring of its operation (Figure 17.1).

The twisted-pair tester

If the network is based on building prewiring, and thus primarily uses the twisted pair, the twisted-pair tester will serve as a universal tool. It can in fact be used to qualify each pair (length, attenuation, crosstalk), to follow the cable path in wiring ducts and suspended ceilings, to test the ports of a 10baseT hub, and even to measure the traffic on a network.

It can be adapted to different types of twisted pair using various connectors (RJ45, RJ11, hermaphrodite, DB25, latch of patching module) and also to different types of coaxial cable (BNC, type N). It can output its measurement results on a printer and communicate with a PC.

This small portable and practical device is still being actively developed and regularly acquires new functions, such as the execution of all the tests adapted to the chosen medium type, with automatic comparison with the values recommended by the standard. Unfortunately, this means that its use may become somewhat complicated, given the number of menus available.

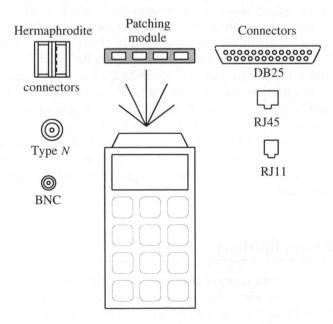

Figure 17.1   Illustration of the capabilities of a tester.

Finally, it is advisable to master the initiation of each test and the choice of parameters (medium propagation speed, test frequency, pin number, sensitivity of the measurements) before the actual operations, so that the desired characteristic can be studied effectively.

The coaxial reflectometer

If the network being maintained is based on coaxial cable (standard or thin), the coaxial reflectometer is the ideal tool for monitoring the quality of the cable impedance along its whole length (Figure 17.2).

The coaxial reflectometer is a very common dedicated device whose function is to determine the impedance curve along the medium. This curve can be used to locate points of variation, such as transceivers, straight connectors or defects (damaged cable, bend radius too small). The coaxial reflectometer can also be used to check the terminator and that its value is correct. Note that, for the measurement of distances to be reliable, the zero must be set exactly and the signal propagation speed on the medium (which is not the same on standard and thin coaxial cables) must be entered.

Finally, to avoid deterioration of the reflectometer's receiver, it is always advisable to use a reflectometer after all the machines have been disconnected from their transceiver on the segment.

The twisted-pair tester described above can also be used to carry out a reflectometry test, but it can only give its distance from a short circuit or an open circuit. In general, it is only capable of displaying the impedance curve with low accuracy, if at all. In this case, it is said to be used as a fault locator.

The test set

If it is required to test the network above the simple physical level, the test set is the simplest tool for this function. It is easy to handle and can be used to perform elementary actions such as counting frames, errors, and collisions circulating on a

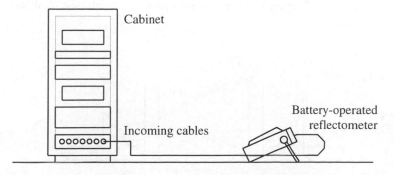

Figure 17.2 Practical measurement arrangement.

network, to emit well-defined traffic (regular, consisting of identical frames), or to initiate echo mode between two sets (one master, one slave) (see Figure 17.3). These measurements rapidly provide information about the operation of the access point(s) tested, and can be used to check the transceivers, cable segments, and repeaters. While all this is being carried out it is impossible to obtain information about the contents of the frame MAC field (addresses, type, protocol or even length).

This type of instrument is intended for use in the acceptance of virgin networks, since then the echo mode can be used without hindrance from other traffic. Conversely, when using a test set on an operational network (involving real useful traffic), care should be taken to ensure that the users are not disturbed, since its emission capabilities are relatively large. Great attention should also be paid to the function of systematic collision creation, which can easily block a network.

One way of connecting the test set without disturbing the networking too much involves linking the former to a FanOut which has previously been inserted between an existing transceiver and a station's NIC. However, one should check that one is not at the end of the network, since the FanOut has a non-negligible delay.

Furthermore, recall that certain test sets can be used in pairs to measure the Round-Trip Delay (RTD) over the whole network or between two particular points. This test is less precise than that which can be performed with a reflectometer on a coaxial-cable segment, but it has the undeniable advantage that it can be carried out on a whole network which is ready to use (or even operational, if one is not concerned about blocking the traffic for a few fractions of a second). In fact, since the test involves determining the delay between the emission of a frame and the receipt of the collision caused at the other end, the measurement effectively relates to the passage through the receivers and the multimedia stars crossed. Moreover, in reality, it corresponds to simulation of the worst case (a frame sent from one end, whose collision must reach the originating station before the latter has completed its transmission).

The optical dBmeter

This comprises a pair of devices which can be used to take a rapid measurement on an optical link. They provide unique information, namely, the total end-to-end attenuation on a link.

Figure 17.3 Echo mode between two network sockets.

Fitted with a suitable source, the dBmeter can be used to emit a calibrated signal at the operational frequency (850 nm for 10baseF) in a fiber (possibly passing through jumper cables) to ensure that the power budget authorized by the technology used is adhered to (9 dB for FOIRL, 12 dB for 10baseFB).

This type of equipment is now common, because it is simple to use, robust and very practical. However, care should be taken to ensure that the jumper cables used to adapt between connectors consist of a fiber identical (diameters, numerical aperture) to that measured. If this is not the case, differences in diameter may give erroneous results, such as an increase in the power received after having crossed the fiber. Generally, it is always advisable to follow the direction of increasing diameters (which means that rays are not lost if the numerical aperture also increases every time). However, for the 'filling' of the fiber to stabilize, it is best if the jumper cables are not too short. In the other case (decreasing diameters), a portion of the luminous power is lost in each pair of connectors, independently of the attenuation due to the trajectories in the fibers themselves. In all cases, the reference measurement (which gives the 0 dB) should be performed by placing the jumper cables to be used during the trials between the source and the dBmeter.

Note the following figures:

Power budget for a link in	FOIRL	9 dB
(always at 850 nm)	10baseFB	12 dB
	10baseFP	26 dB
	10baseFL	12 dB
Maximum attenuation due to the fiber	3.75 dB/km	at 850 nm
(and for FDDI	1 dB/km	at 1300 nm)
Decay due to the connectors	0.5 dB	ceramic ST
(typical values)	1 dB	plastic ST
	1.5 dB	SMA
	0.35 dB	MFO
	0.4 dB	FC
Attenuation due to a passive star	16 dB	minimum
	20 dB	maximum

In addition, one should not forget to provide for a safety margin, preferably leaving at least 1 dB, to ensure that as the components age and the connectors foul up, the link will not become unusable too rapidly.

Sophisticated measuring devices

In the case where the installation to be monitored is large or the constraints on the down time are substantial, it is better to use more complex hardware with a higher performance so that a greater range of interventions can be covered.

The network analyzer

The analyzer is the most complete network measuring tool from the MAC layer upwards. In fact, although it cannot test the physical level, it has a knowledge of all the levels from the link layer upwards.

The analyzer can provide precise and complete statistics about the traffic circulating on a network. It can monitor a particular machine, a specific exchange or a given protocol exactly. It can also record the trace of frames and calculate the distribution of traffic according to address. It can also decode the contents of packets as a function of its knowledge base, which extends up to level 7.

Thus, it is the universal tool which, once programmed, can adopt the behavior of a test set or be substituted for a probe (without necessarily providing identical means of interrogation). It may concentrate on the traffic of one station to determine whether its average error rate is acceptable or observe a router to ensure that no illicit configuration is implemented. In terms of the range of its capabilities, the analyzer is truly flexible and open to multiple uses.

However, for peaceful operation, care should be taken to use a really reliable and high-performance analyzer (necessarily expensive). Otherwise, one should first evaluate the capabilities of the analyzer using other tools to determine its limits and behavior in each mode, in case these are violated. In fact, it should be pointed out that certain devices sometimes count the traffic right up to their limiting thresholds and then only count a part, while others lose a small percentage under all conditions, where this percentage increases progressively with the load. Similarly, some devices, when they are unable to count all the frames, indicate this with a warning, although the majority do not inform the user. Finally, there also exist devices with a counter for frames seen even though they could not be captured; the validity of this counter must also be checked.

Some capabilities, such as the maximum number of stations which can be monitored concurrently, the overall size of the buffer holding the trace of the last frames seen or the number of statistical samples that can be held in memory during a long accumulation, are described in the documentation. Here again, care should be taken to parametrize the analyzer as a function of its limits in order to obtain the desired results.

In conclusion, we stress that the analyzer is a very useful complete tool, although for it to be used intelligently and for the operator to obtain the maximum from it, one should be aware of its capabilities.

The probe

The probe is a node, whose only task is to accumulate monitoring measurements about the traffic on the network segment in which it is located and to transmit these to a management system. Although similar to those of the analyzer, the capabilities of the probe are sometimes lower, not necessarily in terms of speed, but, more often, in terms of capture, storing and decoding of an arbitrary protocol. We also note that the probe can only emit information packets to the master station and cannot generally generate traffic simply to load the network.

As stated in Chapter 10, the probe became of less interest when most network equipment learnt to handle SNMP. Thus, from repeaters to routers, all devices are capable of playing the role of SNMP agent in addition to their own function. Since these devices are spread throughout the network, whose repeating, bridging and routing nodes they form, they are well placed to provide statistics about the segments on which they are located. In this context, the probe was only of interest for small networks with no manageable equipment, or in the case where there is an ostensible desire to separate the functions of frame propagation and observation of the resulting traffic. Note that the load generated by the probe during its exchange with the master station is usually negligible, which is almost self evident since this amounts to a synthetic summary of the traffic seen. This can sometimes be a very important advantage.

More recently, the probe regained its importance with the definition of specific very extensive RMON (remote monitoring) MIBs, which require a large, dedicated processing capability (usually a RISC CPU with a few Mbytes of RAM). Thus, these MIBs cover all aspects of monitoring and the accumulation of statistics (with history depending on the traffic type, list of all the stations categorized, classification of the most talkative stations, presentation in the form of an intercommunication table/matrix of exchanges) together with the capture of packets using filters and the definition of thresholds for triggering alarms or operations. Furthermore, so that their hardware base can be better exploited, these probes may have several interfaces, and sometimes even provide the same services as a fixed multiport analyzer, including frame decoding by protocol (with the help of the master station and associated software).

Management hardware

Manufacturer's management systems which recover the data from the probes or other manageable equipment are evolving regularly. The reason for this change is that the quantity and level of detail of information is increasing noticeably with every new equipment release.

At present, management systems are still limited to certain areas of monitoring and to areas of (remote) configuration which are often more restricted and provide a presentation via a graphical interface over an open platform. Given the colossal development required, there are few of these open platforms on the market and their number will probably not increase. The manufacturer software available for the open platforms enriches the knowledge base by the addition of a private MIB and brings a graphical view, configuration capability and monitoring tools.

However, one should not forget that some of the devices now installed were designed outside the specifications of SNMP and all other management standards, and correspond solely to proprietary requests; this is especially true outside the LAN field. Although they do not fall in this category, SNA devices supporting NetView present the same difficulties as far as SNMP is concerned.

If one wishes to retain otherwise thoroughly satisfactory equipment of this type for a few more years, one must either use a proxy agent to act as a gateway or converter for requests and responses or find a commercially available management system which, in addition to being able to interrogate recent elements interfacing with SNMP, is also able to communicate with certain rather older devices. In some cases, the solution will be a proprietary management system which has evolved with the inclusion of new capabilities (for example, processing of packets in the SNMP format); in other cases, it will comprise recent software which also takes account of part of already existing systems.

The optical reflectometer

The optical reflectometer is a very expensive tool, thus it will be reserved for the particular needs of a team which is either involved in multiple measurement interventions on fiber optic cables, or which is responsible for qualifying active devices operating on optical fiber. Its purchase is justified in these two cases because other instruments (for example, the dBmeter and the associated source) are incapable of providing the same information. The handling of the optical reflectometer is subject to a number of constraints. The first requires a mastery of the device's operation with an understanding of the importance of all the modifiable parameters. The second is linked to the fact that measurements can only be used for reference if they are performed under reproducible conditions.

Two categories of option can be distinguished, namely, those arising during measurement and those corresponding to a logical processing applied to the curve obtained. The first category includes the power of the emitted peaks, which should be chosen as a function of the length of the fiber to be measured and the desired resolution. It also includes the limit for the length scale (distance from which the reflectometer does not retain a trace) and the number of samples used and averaged by the device to produce the curve. The second category corresponds more to display criteria or to calculations performed on the picture obtained from the reflectometry. One might estimate the attenuation due to a pair of connectors or the attenuation per kilometer of a section, change the vertical scale or record the measurement on disk. Of course, the parameters of the first category are the more important, since only they influence and modify the measurement at the time it is acquired.

As far as the measurement conditions are concerned, it is vital to have perfectly reliable adaptation jumper cables. In fact, since the reflectometer has a fixed connector, it is sometimes necessary to adapt it to that of the fiber to be measured. For this, one uses a jumper cable with one connector corresponding to that of the reflectometer and the other to that of the fiber to be tested. This implies the insertion of a length of fiber which is not necessarily identical to that which is to be measured. Here, the important thing is not so much that it should be adapted (diameters and numerical aperture), but that its quality should be such as not to attenuate or perturb the pulses emitted and the reflections returned. Nowadays, some reflectometers have a removable, interchangeable connector on the source. This simplifies matters considerably, but extreme care must be taken not to dirty the end of the fiber leading from the emitter.

The TCP/IP station

The TCP/IP station, chosen here by way of example, represents a real machine with a common stack of higher protocols. For convenience, it is assumed that it is portable (for example, notebook, with appropriate software).

As a test tool, the TCP/IP station is used to check that real traffic can circulate effectively between two access points, generally separated by at least one interconnection device (see Figure 17.4). It has the advantage over other tools in that it implements communication processes very similar to those of future end user machines.

In the case of a file transfer, the quality of the transmission is thus measured as a rate (volume in bits/total time for the operation) or in terms of the number of packets lost or the number of errors. These last two quantities may be given by a function such as *netstat* or *Etherfind* under Unix, or by reading the report from an analyzer placed in parallel on the network during the exchange. For the measurement to be sufficiently representative, it must last for a certain time. Thus, one should choose a file of at least 1 Mbyte for the transfer, to ensure that the measurement does not depend upon the conditions at a single moment, but is a proper estimate of the normal capabilities of the network. The result of the test using FTP will be judged as a function of reference measurements, which can be used to determine the rate under optimal conditions (on a short, empty segment). Note that if the two stations are placed side by side, alone on a small network or on a fictitious network, the number obtained for the rate (number of bits sent divided by the transfer delay) will most certainly depend upon the capabilities of the NIC used and not on the bandwidth available on Ethernet (almost 10 Mbps under such conditions). Moreover, one needs to know the margin tolerated around the ideal element in order to decide whether the test is conclusive or proves the existence of a defect.

Another type of test may be performed using the command *telnet*, which can be used to obtain locally a connection equivalent to that of a terminal. This checks, first, that the connection is possible and, second, that the transit delays are not a hindrance, since all the screens received pass over the network. If it is desired to

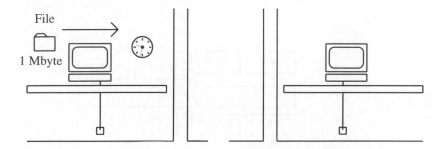

Figure 17.4 Measurement of the time taken to transmit a file over the network.

subject the network to a severe test, the connections may be tested under Xwindow (using an X terminal) by replacing the pages of text by graphical windows which are much more greedy in terms of bandwidth.

A simpler function that is faster to implement is the simple *ping*, which corresponds to the exchange of a packet (under the ICMP protocol) in each direction between two machines. This command is used to try to access a machine from a connection point being tested.

In the three cases, using a TCP/IP station, it is possible to pass through routers and thus reach all accessible networks. However, this means that the configuration of the test machine which moves should be updated in a consistent manner. Thus, care should be taken to ensure that the software configuration of the machine includes an IP address belonging to the sub-network in which one is situated, and that the declaration of the routers also follows.

Here, we see an advantage of the *telnet* command, which, when a remote machine cannot be reached using a *ping*, enables one to move from machine to machine or from router to router and to continually check the routing tables until the blockage point is found.

There now follows a short aside on the ARP protocol to explain the fact that, during the first interrogation attempt using the *ping* command the first packet may normally be lost. In fact, it should come as no surprise that the first frame emitted with a view to an exchange is unanswered, if it is the only frame which does not receive an echo.

The ARP protocol has the task of finding the physical address from the logical address (which the user generally uses to denote his/her correspondents). It is called whenever the IP layer of a machine receives data from higher protocols to be emitted to a station whose Ethernet address it does not know (see Figure 17.5). At the request of IP, ARP emits a broadcast frame at the MAC level, including the IP address sought and the coordinates of the machine which originated the interrogation. However, when IP calls ARP, it loses the packet to be transmitted and only retains the IP address sought. Thus, if this is the first frame of the *ping*, it will never receive an echo. Then, if the machine concerned is effectively accessible, it will recognize its

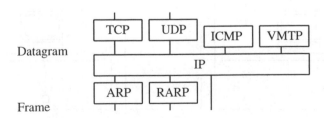

Figure 17.5   Relationship between the DoD protocols.

logical address and answer the ARP address placing information in the empty fields. On receipt of this information, the enquiring machine will store the correspondence between the IP and Ethernet addresses in its ARP table; IP will be able to follow the following packets without difficulty, requiring at most one access to this table.

Discussion of the TCP/IP station concludes with the remark that a simple portable PC with a standard Ethernet interface and appropriate emulation software can be used to perform various types of level 3 tests, and to measure the network performance in a mode almost identical to that of the real working environment of the users.

The optical set

Assembly equipment for optical connectors, which can be used both to assemble and also test connectors, falls slightly outside the measuring-device area.

Since the crimping operation for optical connectors is relatively delicate, one might seek to form an in-house skill center or opt to sub-contract this type of intervention to specialist teams with long experience of the manipulations required. It is only sensible to choose the first solution if the specialists are regularly called in to carry out this kind of operation (at least ten times a year).

Qualification hardware

The qualification and validation of hardware is slightly outside the area of test and measurement. This activity should be undertaken from the study stage for a network, in order to develop the global solution as a function of the equipment which will be involved.

In fact, even though all devices claim to meet the standard, not all devices have the same capabilities, whether in terms of performance or of the capacity for evolution. Thus, it is often useful to examine the products on the market before making one's choice. This becomes all the more important as the investment becomes larger.

Selection of equipment

Whether for active network devices (repeaters, hubs, stars), interconnection devices (bridges, routers) or, more simply, cabling components (plug, socket, cable, duct, patching system, jumper cable), the best choice of a specific element, a manufacturer or a particular source will follow a serious comparative evaluation of the qualities of the element. Prior to the establishment of the detailed technical specifications, the results of qualification tests will determine the products upon which an effective implementation of the network will depend.

This test and validation function for hardware for local area networks may be undertaken by a specialist team centralizing all the qualification needs of the enterprise; otherwise, if no such structure exists, responsibility for it may fall to the editor of the detailed technical specifications.

Table 17.1 Classification of equipment according to two criteria: OSI level and number of ports.

	Monoport device	Biport device	Multiport device
Physical level	Transceiver	Repeater	Hub Multimedia star
MAC level	Test set	Bridge	Bridge/switch
Network level and above	Analyzer probe	Router gateway	Router gateway

Test platforms may be installed during a large project, with a view to reproducing realistic conditions for the operation of the future network using a representative model of the whole communication chain envisaged.

Often, the experimenter will have to compare devices in order to select one, without having access to an appropriate qualification method. In this case he/she will have to develop test procedures adapted to his/her objective and to the equipments to be validated. Here is some general advice which may help in this task.

First, he/she must identify the essential characteristics of the device; attempts should be made to restrict these to, for example, ten points. He/she will then be able to rank these in order of importance (bearing in mind the possible real conditions under which the element may be used). He/she will then have to construct the trial configurations which will enable him/her to carry out the measurements successfully and to evaluate the desired capability effectively (see Figure 17.6). He/she will have to ensure that he/she is actually measuring the desired characteristic and that the latter is not hidden by the performance of another element of the chain or by the test device itself. The more test equipment he/she has, the easier he/she will find it to develop the assembly; however, rigorous qualification does not necessarily depend upon an abundance of devices. It is often the method that determines the quality of the measurement, and one should not forget that it is vital to be fully aware of the capabilities of the measuring devices and their limitations.

Although each category of equipment is quite different, the test and evaluation methods do have points in common. These may be classified as follows. The set of tests will be put together based on two criteria. Very globally, monoport devices will be assessed using incoming or outgoing traffic, biport devices will be subjected to transfers, which may be bidirectional, and multiport devices will be subjected to multiple simultaneous transfers. The physical-level elements will be qualified according to their respect for the characteristics described in the standard, MAC-level devices will be judged according to their performance, and equipment at level 3 or above will be evaluated according to the richness of the capabilities offered.

For example, to evaluate local Ethernet bridges or routers, one should first try to verify the filtering and retransmission rates given in the manufacturer's documentation. For this category of test, the following points may be measured:

- Initialization time when switched on
  Variation of this delay as a function of the network load.

- Observation of the traffic emitted by the isolated bridge (STP frames).

- Crossing delay
  Minimum crossing delay (regular low load)
  Crossing delay under heavy load (at the limiting threshold)
  Regularity of the crossing delay for heterogeneous traffic.

- Curve of maximum transfer (homogeneous frames, fixed-length frames)
  Abscissa: frame length of the traffic to which the bridge is subjected
  Ordinate: maximum load supported without loss (in frames/s) (usually the upper limit on the performance of a bridge is given in frames/s, almost independently of the frame lengths: from 64 to 1518 bytes).
  Measurement of the percentage of the traffic lost when the load crosses the threshold.

- Study of the variations in the maximum transfer rate for heterogeneous traffic
  Bursty traffic, with a mean value below the loss threshold
  Traffic consisting of frames with different destination addresses
  Traffic partially intended for a local destination.

- Measurement of the transfer rate for bidirectional traffic.

- Validation of the 'natural' filtering
  Number of frames used in learning (0 or 1)
  Reaction to a frame with broadcast source address (meaningless)
  Effect of changing from one side of an emitting machine to another.

Readers will naturally appreciate that the most important of these criteria is the maximum retransmission rate and its stability under arbitrary traffic (heterogeneous, irregular). A bridge which collapses when subjected to an excessively heavy load (percentage of losses increasing considerably after the threshold is crossed) should be avoided.

Finally, for a programmable device, one might also test:

- The accuracy of the bridge counters and the difference from reality
  for a weak or average load (supported)
  for traffic including defective frames
  for the maximum load before the threshold is crossed
  for a load above the threshold
  for heavy traffic with a local destination (no retransmission).

- Changes in the performance after implantation of filters (evaluation of the new limiting threshold for short-frame traffic)
  for a single loaded filter (various types of filter to be tested)
  for the maximal combination of filters.

The diversity of measurements envisaged is such that it is left to the reader to develop the series of tests best adapted to his/her needs and environment, based on the few ideas presented above.

If no test method can be implemented, one should rely on reviews and evaluations given in the specialist technical press. The fact that test methods are generally described in parallel with the results means that one should only believe measurements performed consistently and rigorously. However, note that the most common products are generally of high quality, since they have passed the selection process of several large clients to achieve top positions in the market place. Moreover, the size of the manufacturer ensures that its products and their follow-up have a minimum durability. Conversely, the cheapest products rarely lack faults.

Those wishing to test and qualify network equipment should be aware that some trials require particular measuring devices in addition to the test tools discussed above. The main ones are discussed below.

The oscilloscope

The oscilloscope is a basic device for measuring the time taken to cross an arbitrary element; it can be fitted on a coaxial cable segment, a drop cable or a twisted pair. Thus, it is indispensable for the qualification of physical-level equipment (transceivers, FanOut or repeater) whose emission levels and reception thresholds have to be checked. In fact, it conveniently gives signal voltages, displays the rise and fall times and shows their regularity. All these parameters should respect the figures given in the standard. Moreover, it is essential for measuring the crossing delay of most equipment and can be used to monitor the regularity of retransmissions by equipment using visual comparison of the traffic entering and leaving it. To detect frames and identify them on input and output, it is advisable to use traffic consisting of frames with slightly different lengths.

The oscilloscope can also be used to sample the electrical signals of optical devices (transceiver, repeater) just before the stages of emission or receipt. In this case, one has to be enterprising and competent enough to open the box and work directly on the electronic circuits without risk of causing their deterioration.

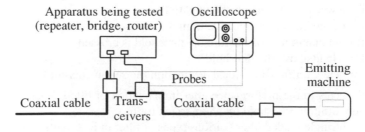

Figure 17.6   Configuration for measurement of the crossing delay.

The multiport analyzer

Several multiport analyzers are now available commercially. These generally have an Ethernet and a Token Ring port (see Figure 17.7). However, some also have an FDDI, 100baseT, ARCnet or LocalTalk interface and/or a serial V.24, V.35, ISDN, X.25 or (more recently) ATM link. If the ports listed above are numerous, the device will have a modular construction (for example, on a PC base) such that each attachment card can be purchased separately.

The main advantage of this device lies in the fact that the software processing the protocol suite is unique and, hence, the user interface always remains the same whatever type of connection is used. Moreover, if one invests in supplementary decoding modules or in proprietary add-ons to interpret the contents of the packets, this will be executable independently of the NIC. Thus, the tool can be viewed as an almost universal analyzer, in which only one piece has to be changed to adapt to current needs.

Finally, there also exist top-of-the-range analyzers which can activate two of their physical ports simultaneously and operate on the two interfaces in parallel (acquisition of traffic, emission of frames, statistics for each network). This function is typically used to check the work carried out by an interconnection device (repeater, local bridge, router, gateway). In fact, it is easy to monitor the retransmission of each packet by observing the data present on input to and output from the device. When these devices accept access cards for different networks, they can be used to test the operation of all the interconnection equipment (remote bridge, bridge between two types of LAN, multimedia router) and to qualify these in a practical and rigorous manner. One other use may be to employ the two connections on a single network

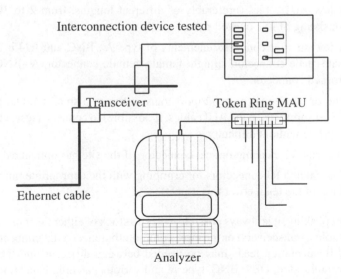

Figure 17.7   Schematic illustration of a biport modular Ethernet–Token Ring analyzer.

to load it in one area with the frames one desires and to observe its behavior under this emission by another access point.

The optical attenuator

There is a tool for testing the transmissions on optical lines by artificial simulation of a decay, namely the optical attenuator. This relatively simple instrument can be used to establish a predefined attenuation between two connectors and so to measure the level of decay up to which active equipment placed at the ends can continue to communicate. This kind of apparatus is ultimately intended mainly to check that the devices operating on optical links are able to read their respective signals correctly when the maximum attenuation is inserted between them.

Conclusion

Whatever test devices the intervention or qualification team has at its disposal, it should also have a set of small items of equipment which will always be useful. These include:

- A pair of reliable IEEE 802.3 transceivers (tested beforehand) with removable and, if possible, interchangeable PMA (BNC, double BNC, double type N or tapped).
- 10baseT transceivers and, if necessary, optical transceivers.
- A few 2.5 m sections of standard coaxial cable with connectors at each end, plus a long section to insert a decay if required.
- A few sections of thin coaxial cable with connectors at each end.
- Straight RJ45–RJ45 lines and a few crossed lines (12–36 for 10baseT).
- A few AUI cables (preferably of different lengths, from 2 to 30 meters), consisting of five twisted pairs.
- A few smaller connector elements of type N, BNC and RJ45: T, straight male–male connector, straight female–female connector, N–BNC adapter, crossed connector.
- One or two biport or quadriport transceivers or a small FanOut (using the power supply from the AUI cables, if possible) to connect a test set, analyzer or probe without difficulty.
- Material for cleaning optical connectors if the site has optical cables.
- Coaxial and RJ connectors for crimping with the appropriate pincers (if the skills of the team cover this aspect).

Generally speaking, it is always possible to keep a stock of either the most vulnerable (jumper cables, transceivers) or the most common (balun, coaxial connectors) basic elements. If adaptation leads may be needed between different interfaces (RJ11, RJ45, hermaphrodite, DB9, BNC, type N and various patching panels) it is best to carry at least one sample of each type, or even the whole range if this is not too large.

Bibliography

3Com (1990). *LAN Security, the Business Threat from Within*. 3Com

ADC Fibermux (1992). *Backbone Applications Guide*. ADC Fibermux

ADC Fibermux *LAN Hub Applications Guide*. ADC Fibermux

Apple Computer Inc. (1992). *Planning and Managing AppleTalk Networks*. Addison-Wesley

BICC (1989). *FDDI, Business Communications for the 1990s*. BICC

Chipcom (1993). *ATM, The Frontier of Networking*. Chipcom

Cisco (1992). *Internetworking Technology Terms and Acronyms*. Cisco

Cisco (1995). *ATM Internetworking*. Cisco

Codenoll (1990). *The Fiber Optics LAN Handbook*. Codenoll

Comer D. (1988). *Internetworking with TCP/IP, Principles, Protocols and Architectures*. Prentice Hall

Davidson J. (1988). *An Introduction to TCP/IP*. Springer-Verlag

De Pricker M. (1995). *Asynchronous Transfer Mode, Solution for Broadband ISDN*. Prentice Hall

Digital (1982). *Introduction to Local Area Networks*. Digital

Digital (1983). *DIGITAL Network Architecture, A Self-Paced Course, Student Workbook*. Digital

Digital (1990). *Fiber Distributed Data Interface, System Level Description*. Digital

Digital (1991). *A primer to FDDI, Fiber Distributed Data Interface*. Digital

Fiber Channel Association (1994). *Fibre Channel, Connection to the Future*. Fiber Channel Association

GN Nettest (1994). *ATM Realities, Challenges and Solutions*. GN Nettest

Hall J. (1993). *LinkVoice, Technical Service Guide*. ascom Timeplex

Hegering H.-G. and Läpple A. (1994). *Ethernet, Building a Communications Infrastructure*. Addison-Wesley

Hewlett-Packard (1992). *Introduction to SONET*. Hewlett-Packard

Held G. (1994). *Token-Ring Networks, Characteristics, Operation, Construction and Management*. Wiley

Hughes LAN Systems (1994). *ATM in Local Area Networks*.

Hunter P. (1994). *Network Operating Systems, Making the Right Choices*. Addison-Wesley

IBM (1989a). *Token-Ring Network, Architecture Reference* 3rd edn. IBM

IBM (1989b). *Local Area Networks, Concepts and Products* 2nd edn. IBM

IBM (1992a). *Token-Ring Network, Supplement for Operation with Unshielded Twisted-Pair Lobes*. IBM

IBM (1992b). *APPN Architecture and Product Implementations Tutorial*. IBM

Kapoor A. (1992). *SNA, Architecture, Protocols and Implementation*. McGraw-Hill

LANNET (1993). *High Speed Switched Networking*. LANNET

Lynch D. C. and Rose M. T. (1993). *Internet System Handbook*. Addison-Wesley

Macchi C. *et al.* (1987). *Téléinformatique, Transport et Traitement de l'Information dans les Réseaux et Systèmes Téléinformatiques et Télématiques CNET/ENST*. Dunod

Madge (1994). *LAN Emulation over ATM*. Madge

Madge (1995). *ATM at the Desktop.*

Malamud C. (1992). *Stacks, Interoperability in Today's Computer Networks*. Prentice Hall

Martin J. and Leben J. (1992). *DECnet Phase V, An OSI Implementation*. Digital Press, Prentice Hall

McNamara J. E. (1985). *Local Area Networks. An Introduction to the Technology*. Digital

Miller M. A. (1992). *LAN Protocol Handbook*. M&T Books

Netlink (1993). *Manager's Guide to SNA Internetworking*. Netlink

Netrix (1994). *The Guide to International Networking*. 95 Netrix

Network Peripherals (1992). *FDDI Performance in a SunOS Environment*. Network Peripherals

Perlman R. (1992). *Interconnections, Bridges and Routers*. Addison-Wesley

Proteon (1992a). *Networking in the IBM Environment*. Proteon

Proteon (1992b). *OSPF, Routing TCP/IP Networks*. Proteon

Proteon (1992c). *Source Routing Transparent Bridging (SRT)*. Proteon

Proteon (1992d). *Spring 1992, Harvard Benchmark Test*. Proteon

Pujolle G. (1984). *La Télématique, Réseaux et Applications*. Eyrolles

Racal Data Communication (1990). *Networking Dictionary*. Racal Data Communication

RAD (1994). *Token Ring Design Guide*. RAD

Sidhu G. S., Andrews R. F. and Oppenheimer A. B. (1990). *Inside AppleTalk* 2nd edn. Addison-Wesley

Smith P. (1993). *Frame Relay, Principles and Applications*. Addison-Wesley

Spider (1989). *Packets and Protocols*. Spider

Stalling W. (1988). *Local Network Technology, Tutorial* 3rd edn. Computer Society, IEEE

Stalling W. (1993a). *Local and Metropolitan Area Networks* 4th edn. Macmillan

Stalling W. (1993b). *Networking Standards, A Guide to OSI, ISDN, LAN and MAN Standards*. Addison-Wesley

Telco Systems (1992). *Asynchronous Transfer Mode: Bandwidth for the Future*. Telco Systems

Telenex Corp. (1991). *An Introduction to Useful Frame Relay Testing*. Telenex Corp.

Wellfleet (1992a). *Internetworking in the IBM Environment*. Wellfleet

Wellfleet (1992b). *Simplifying LAN–WAN Integration*. Wellfleet

Wellfleet (1993). *Integrating SNA and Multiprotocol LAN Networks*. Wellfleet

WilTel (1993). *Fast Forward, Putting ATM to Work Today*. WilTel

Xyplex (1992). *Standard-Based Routing*. Xyplex

Standards

ANSI (1986). *X3.139-1987*. FDDI Token Ring Media Access Control (MAC)

ANSI (1989a). *X3T9.5/87-10*. FDDI Hybrid Ring Control

ANSI (1989b). *X3T9.5/88-155*. FDDI Single-Mode Fiber Physical Layer Medium Dependent (SMF-PMD)

ANSI (1992). *X3T9/92*. FDDI Station Management (SMT)

ANSI (1994). *TP-PMD/312*. FDDI Twisted Pair Physical Layer Medium Dependent (TP-PMD)

ANSI (1995). *X3.269-199X* Fiber Channel Protocol for SCSI

Apple (1991). *A Standard for the Transmission of Internet Packet Over AppleTalk Networks*

Apple (1992). *MACIP – IP Transport over AppleTalk*

Apple (1994). *Interim Inter-switch Protocol (IISP) Specification, Version 1.0*

ATMForum (1994a). *ATM Physical Medium Dependent Interface Specification for 155 Mb/s over Twisted Pair Cable*

ATMForum (1994b). *User–Network Interface (UNI) Specification Version 3.1*

ATMForum (1995). *LAN Emulation Over ATM Specification, Version 1.0*

Bellcore (1993a). *TA-NWT-000436* Digital Network Synchronization Plan

Bellcore (1993b). *TA-NWT-001113* Asynchronous Transfer Mode and ATM Adaptation Layer (AAL) Protocols Generic Requirements

CCITT (1988). *Réseaux de Communications de Données: Services et Facilités, Interfaces Tome VIII Fascicule VIII-2 Recommandations X.1 à X.32*

CCITT (1992). *Digital Subscriber Signaling System No. 1 (DSS 1) Data Link Layer Recommendation Q.922*

CCITT *ISDN Data Link Layer Specification for Frame Mode BearerServices*

Cisco (1990). *HSSI: High Speed Serial Interface Design Specification*

Cisco (1991). *An Introduction to IGRP*

DEC (1982). *AA-N149A-TC* DECnet DIGITAL Network Architecture (Phase IV) General Description

DEC (1983). *AA-X435A-TK* DECnet DIGITAL Network Architecture (Phase IV) Routing Layer Functional Specification

ETSI (1992a). *ETS 300 211/2/3/4/5/6* Network Aspects (NA); Metropolitan Area Network (MAN) Principles and architecture, Media access control layer and physical layer specification, Physical layer convergence procedure for 2.048 Mbit/s; 34.368 Mbit/s; 139.264 Mbit/s; 155.520 Mbit/s

ETSI (1992b). *ETS 300 217-1/2/3/4* Network Aspects (NA); Connectionless Broadband Data Service (CBDS) Parts 1, 2, 3, 4

FCSI (1994). *FCSI-001-Rev 1.0* FCSI Profile Structure

FRF (1993). *Frame Relay User-to-Network SVC Implementation Agreement*

IEC (1989). *IEC 907* Local area network CSMA/CD 10Mbit/s baseband planning and installation guide

IEEE (1985). *IEEE Std 802.5* Token Ring Access Method

IEEE (1990a). *IEEE Std 802* Local and Metropolitan Area Network IEEE Standard Overview and Architecture

IEEE (1990b). *IEEE Std 802.1E* System Load Protocol

IEEE (1992a). *IEEE 802.1B* LAN/MAN Management

IEEE (1992b). *IEEE P802.3p/D3* Layer Management for 10 Mb/s Medium Attachment Units (MAUs), Section 20

IEEE (1992c). *IEEE P802.3q/D2* GDMO Revisions to Layer Management (Section 5)

IEEE (1992d). *IEEE P802.3?/D3* CSMA/CD Management (Section 19)

IEEE (1992e). *IEEE Std 802.10* Interoperable LAN/MAN Security (SILS), Secure Data Exchange (SDE)

IEEE (1993a). *IEEE Std 802.3j* Fiber Optic Active and Passive Star-Based Segments, Type 10BASE-F (Sections 15–18)

IEEE (1993b). *IEEE 802.5Q/D5* Token Ring access method and physical layer specifications

IEEE (1993c). *IEEE 802.5p/Draft 6* Changes and Additions to ISO 8802-2 for the Route Determination Entity

IEEE (1993d). *IEEE P802.10e and f* Secure Data Exchange (SDE) Sublayer Management, Recommended Practice for SDE on Ethernet V2.0 in IEEE 802 LANs

IEEE (1994a). *IEEE P802.3u/D3* MAC Parameters, Physical layer, Medium Attachment Units and Repeater for 100 Mbit/s Operation

IEEE (1994b). *IEEE P802.9a/D4* Integrated Services (IS) LAN: IEEE 802.9 Isochronous services with Carrier sense multiple access with collision detection (CSMA/CD) Media access control (MAC) service

IEEE (1994c). *IEEE 802.9b/D4* Functional Specification for AU to AU Internetworking

IEEE (1994d). *IEEE P802.12/D4* Demand Priority Access Method and Physical Layer Specifications

IEEE (1994e). *IEEE Std. 802.9* Integrated Services (IS) LAN interface at the Medium Access Control (MAC)and Physical (PHY) layers

IEEE (1995). *IEEE P802.11/D2.0* Wireless LAN Medium Access Control (MAC) and Physical Layer (PHY) Specifications

ISO (1988a). *ISO 8473 and Add. 3 1989* Data communications – Protocol for providing the connectionless-mode network service

ISO (1988b). *ISO 9314-3* Fiber Distributed Data Interface (FDDI), Part 3: Physical Layer Medium Dependent (PMD) requirements

ISO (1988c). *ISO 9542* Information technology – Telecommunications and information exchange between systems – End system to Intermediate system routing exchange protocol for use in conjunction with the protocol for providing the connectionless-mode service (ISO 8473)

ISO (1989a). *ISO 9314-1* Fiber Distributed Data Interface (FDDI), Part 1: Token Ring Physical Layer Protocol (PHY)

ISO (1989b). *ISO 9314-2* Fiber Distributed Data interface (FDDI), Part 2: Token Ring Media Access Control (MAC)

ISO (1992). *ISO 10589* Intermediate system to Intermediate system intra-domain routing information exchange protocol for use in conjunction with the protocol for providing the connectionless-mode Network Service (ISO 8473) ISO (1993a). *ISO 8802-3*. Information technology - Local and metropolitan area network – Part 3: Carrier sense multiple access with collision detection (CSMA/CD) access method and physical layer specifications

ISO (1993b). *ISO 10038* Local area networks – Media access control (MAC) bridges

ISO (1994a). *ISO 8802-2* Information technology – Telecommunications exchange between systems. Local and metropolitan area network – Part 2: Logical link control

ISO (1994b). *ISO 880206* Local and Metropolitan area networks - Part 6: Distributed Queue Dual Bus (DQDB) access method and physical layer specifications

ISO (1994c). *DIS 11801* Generic cabling for customer premises cabling

Novell (1992). *107-000029-001* IPX Router Specification

Novell *Netware Link Services Protocol (NLSP) Specification*

RFC (1980). *RFC 768* User datagram protocol

RFC (1982). *RFC 826* Ethernet Address Resolution Protocol: Or converting network protocol address to 48 bits Eth

RFC (1987). *RFC 1009* Requirement for Internet gateways

RFC (1988a). *RFC 1038* Draft revised IP security option

RFC (1988b). *RFC 1042* Standard for the transmission of IP datagrams over IEEE 802 networks

RFC (1988c). *RFC 1055* Nonstandard for transmission of IP datagrams over serial lines: SLIP

RFC (1988d). *1058* Routing Information Protocol

RFC (1989a). *RFC 1088* Standard for the transmission of IP datagrams over NetBIOS networks

RFC (1989b). *RFC 1089* SNMP over Ethernet

RFC (1989c). *RFC 1095* The Common Management Information Services and Protocol over TCP/IP (CMOT)

RFC (1989d). *RFC 1118* The Hitchhiker's Guide to the Internet

RFC (1989e). *RFC 1132* A Standard for the Transmission of 802.2 Packets over IPX Networks

RFC (1990a). *RFC 1139* An Echo Function for ISO 8473

RFC (1990b). *RFC 1144* Compressing TCP/IP headers for low-speed serial links

RFC (1990c). *RFC 1155* Structure and identification of management information for TCP/IP-based internets

RFC (1990d). *RFC 1156* Management Information Base for network management of TCP/IP-based internets

RFC (1990e). *RFC 1157* Simple Network Management Protocol (SNMP)

RFC (1990f). *RFC 1185* TCP Extension for High-Speed Paths 1185

RFC (1990g). *RFC 1189* The Common Management Information Services and Protocols for the Internet (CMOT/CMIP)

RFC (1991a). *RFC 1180* A TCP/IP Tutorial

RFC (1991b). *RFC 1201* Transmission of IP Traffic over ARCNET Networks

RFC (1991c). *RFC 1208* A Glossary of Networking Terms

RFC (1991d). *RFC 1209* Transmission of IP datagrams over the SMDS Service

RFC (1991e). *RFC 1213* Management Information Base for network management of TCP/IP-based internets: MIB-II

RFC (1991f). *RFC 1219* On the Assignment of Subnet Numbers

RFC (1991g). *RFC 1223* OSI CLNS and LLC1 protocols on Networks Systems HYPERchannel

RFC (1991h). *RFC 1231* IEEE 802.5 Token Ring MIB

RFC (1991i). *RFC 1234* Tunneling IPX traffic through IP networks

RFC (1991j). *RFC 1236* IP to X.121 address mapping for DDN

RFC (1991k). *RFC 1237* Guidelines for OSI NSAP allocation in the internet

RFC (1991l). *RFC 1240* OSI connectionless transport service on top of UDP

RFC (1991m). *RFC 1242* Benchmarking Terminology for Network Interconnection Devices

RFC (1991n). *RFC 1243* AppleTalk Management Information Base

RFC (1991o). *RFC 1245* OSPF protocol analysis

RFC (1991p). *RFC 1246* Experience with the OSPF protocol

RFC (1991q). *RFC 1257* Isochronous Applications do not require Jitter-Controlled Networks

RFC (1991r). *RFC 1287* Towards the Future Internet Architecture

RFC (1992a). *RFC 1293* Inverse Address Resolution Protocol

RFC (1992b). *RFC 1296* Internet Growth (1981–1991)

RFC (1992c). *RFC 1332* The PPP Internet Protocol Control Protocol (IPCP)

RFC (1992d). *RFC 1356* Multiprotocol Interconnect on X.25 and ISDN in the Packet Mode

RFC (1992e). *RFC 1374* IP and ARP on HIPPI

RFC (1992f). *RFC 1377* The PPP OSI Network Layer Control Protocol (OSINLCP)

RFC (1992g). *RFC 1483* Multiprotocol Encapsulation over ATM Adaptation Layer 5

RFC (1993a). *RFC 1390* Transmission of IP and ARP over FDDI Networks

RFC (1993b). *RFC 1392* Internet Users' Glossary

RFC (1993c). *RFC 1418* SNMP over OSI

RFC (1993d). *RFC 1420* SNMP over IPX 1420

RFC (1993e). *RFC 1469* IP Multicast over Token-Ring Local Area Network

RFC (1993f). *RFC 1490* Multiprotocol Interconnect over Frame Relay

RFC (1993g). *RFC 1504* AppleTalk Update-Based Routing Protocol: Enhanced AppleTalk Routing

RFC (1993h). *RFC 1516* Definitions of Managed Objects for IEEE 802.3 Repeater Devices

RFC (1993i). *RFC 1553* Compressing IPX Headers Over WAN Media (CIPX)

RFC (1994a). *RFC 1577* Classical IP and ARP over ATM

RFC (1994b). *RFC 1583* OSPF Version 2

RFC (1994c). *RFC 1626* Default IP MTU for use over ATM AAL5

RFC (1994d). *RFC 1634* Novell IPX Over Various WAN Media (IPXWAM)

RFC (1994e). *RFC 1638* PPP Bridging Control Protocol (BCP)

RFC (1994f). *RFC 1661* The Point-to-Point Protocol (PPP)

RFC (1994g). *RFC 1680* IPng Support for ATM Services

RFC (1994h). *RFC 1695* Definition of Managed Objects for ATM Management Version 8.0 using SMIv2

RFC (1994i). *RFC 1700* Assigned Numbers

RFC (1994j). *RFC 1715* The H Ratio for Address Assignment Efficiency

RFC (1994k). *RFC 1735* NBMA Address Resolution Protocol (NARP)

RFC (1994l). *NBMA Next Hop Resolution Protocol (NHRP)*. Draft

RFC (1994m). *IP Next Generation Addressing Architecture*. Draft

RFC (1994n). *Simple Internet Protocol Plus (SIPP): Addressing Architecture*. Draft

RFC (1995a). *RFC 1752* The recommendation for the IP Next Generation Protocol

RFC (1995b). *RFC 1754* IPATM WG ATM Forum Recommendations V1

RFC (1995c). *RFC 1755* ATM Signaling Support for IP over ATM

RFC (1995d). *RFC 1771* A Border Gateway Protocol 4 (BGP-4)

RFC (1995e). *RFC 1791* TCP and UDP Over IPX Networks With Fixed Path MTU

RFC (1995f). *RFC 1795* AIW DLSw RIG: DLSw Closed Pages, DLSw Standard, Version 1.0

RFC (1995g). *RFC 1808* Internet Official Protocol Standards

RFC (1995h). *RFC 1812* Requirements for IP Version 4 Routers

RFC (1995i). *RFC 1821* Integration of Real-time Services in an IP-ATM Network Architecture

RFC (1995j). *RFC 1831* RPC: Remote Procedure Call Protocol Specification, Version 2

RFC (1995k). *RFC 1832* XDR: External Data Representation Standard

RFC (1995l). *RFC 1883* Internet Protocol, Version 6 (IPv6) Specification

RFC (1995m). *RFC 1884 IP, Version 6 Addressing Architecture*
RFC (1995n). *RFC 1885* ICMP for the Internet Protocol Version 6 (IPv6)
RFC (1995o). *Remote Network Monitoring Management Information Base*. Draft
RFC *Data Link Switching: Switch-to-Switch Protocol*
SMDS Interest Group (1991). *SIG-TS-001* SMDS Data Exchange Interface Protocol,
    Revision 3.2
Xerox (1981a). *XSIS 028112* Internet Transport Protocols
Xerox (1981b). *XSIS 038112* Courier: The Remote Procedure Call Protocol
Xerox (1982). *AA-K759B-TK* The Ethernet, A Local Area Network, Data Link Layer
    and Physical Layer Specifications, Version 2.0
Xerox (1984). *XSIS 078404* Clearinghouse Protocol

Glossary

Access procedure Procedure or protocol used to obtain access to a shared resource. In a local area network, the shared resource is the medium.

Acknowledgment Positive acknowledgment in a transmission procedure.

ACSE Association Common Service Element, lower part of layer 7, standardized by ISO 8649 (service) and 8850 (protocol) or CCITT X.227. This service element is used to enable applications (such as FTAM) to establish and break logical connections with similar entities. Its position is shown in Figure G.1.

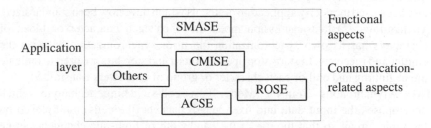

Figure G.1 Cross section of level 7 and positions of several blocks.

Address Sequence of bits (six bytes for Ethernet) which identifies the source or the destination of a data packet.

AFNOR Association Française de Normalisation. French standardization body, member of the ISO.

Analyzer Device for monitoring and measuring the signal or the information exchanged on a transmission channel. In telecommunications, the different types of analyzer check the structure of the data in addition to the signal itself and are able to decode the contents of the packets.

ANSI American National Standard Institute. US standardization body, member of the ISO.

AppleTalk Communication protocol covering layers 3 to 5 defined by Apple for its networks, based on LocalTalk, Ethernet (EtherTalk) or Token Ring (TokenTalk). The AppleTalk address, represented in decimal, consists of 24 bits, 16 for the network number and 8 for the node number. The corresponding Ethernet type field is 809B.

APPN Advanced Peer-to-Peer Networking. Architecture implemented by IBM to interlink its small and medium-size system (AS/400, PS/2) within the SNA framework.

ARCnet Attached Resources Computer Network is a non-standardized local area network with the DATAPOINT Token Bus. It operates at 2.5 Mbps in the standard version (20 Mbps in the new version) with less than 256 machines on coaxial cable (RG-62, 93 Ohm), twisted pair, and optical fiber. Reliable and inexpensive, it is very common in the USA.

ARP Address Resolution Protocol. Protocol used to find the correspondence between IP and Ethernet addresses, defined by RFC 826 and 925. The corresponding Ethernet type field for an ARP frame is 0806.

ASCII American Standard Code for Information Interchange. The code, which has seven bits plus the parity bit, was established to obtain compatibility of services in data exchange. Very common.

ASN.1 Abstract Syntax Notation 1, CCITT recommendation of 1984, standardized by ISO 8824 and 8825 (CCITT X.208 and 209). Specification language which can be used to give a complete and unambiguous description of all types of data or information circulating at the level of the application-level protocols. ASN.1 has also been used to specify application protocols which have now been standardized.

Asynchronous Data transmission mode in which each character or block of characters has its own synchronization (no prior synchronization between the emitter and receiver). In start–stop operation start and stop bits are used to indicate the beginning and end of each character or group of characters transmitted.

ATM Asynchronous Transfer Mode. Fast cell-switching technique which decomposes the input data into fixed-length packets (the cells) multiplexed on the same circuit so that the use of the bandwidth of high-rate channels can be optimized. Technology will be retained for broadband ISDN.

Attenuation Fading of the signal as it travels along the medium, measured in decibels (dB). Increases in importance as the signal frequency and trajectory length increase.

AUI Attachment Unit Interface cable linking the Medium Access Unit (MAU) to the computer NIC. The connections are made using 15 point sockets with a slide latch. The AUI cable is also called the transceiver cable or drop cable.

AWG American Wire Gauge is an American unit for measuring the diameter of a conductor. The conversion formula is of the type: diameter in mm $= A \times \text{coeff}^{\text{AWG}}$, where $A \sim 8.28$ and coeff ~ 0.89.

Backbone Represents the main artery of a network.

Backoff Algorithm used by the Ethernet MAC controller to restart the emission of a frame in the case where a collision has occurred during the previous attempt to emit this frame on the network.

Balun Comes from BALanced–UNbalanced, impedance adaptation element for connecting two different media.

Bandwidth Interval of frequencies dedicated to the channel or data communication system.

Baseband   Transmission of an unmodulated data signal such as that generated by the digital circuit in its original frequency band.

Baud   From Baudot, inventor of the telegraphic code. Unit to quantify the rate of transfer of symbols. Number of symbols (not necessarily bits) transmitted per second.

BBN   Bolt, Beranek, and Newman, Inc. Company responsible for the development of the ARPANET.

BCD   Binary Coded Decimal, four-bit coding scheme for decimal numbers (0–9).

BCS   Bull Cabling System, cabling system offered by the French computer manufacturer Bull, which is based on various types of cable (including Bull A 2 with four pairs) and a specific patching system (BCS 1 and 2).

BERT   Bit Error Ratio Test used to evaluate the quality of a data transmission line, defined by the CCITT.

Big-endian   Order of transmission for bytes or bits in serial mode, beginning with the Most-Significant Bit (MSB) and ending with the Least-Significant Bit (LSB). Similarly, the inverse order (LSB first, MSB last) is called little-endian.

Bit   Abbreviation for BInary digiT. The smallest unit of information in the binary system of notation (0 or 1).

Bit rate   Number of bits transiting per second between corresponding entities via a data network. There exist classes of 'bit rate' which differ according to country. For example, for high rates, we have the levels 1.544, 6.312 and 44.736 Mbps in the USA, 2.048, 8.448, 34.368 and 139.264 Mbps in Europe, and 1.544, 6.132, 32.064 and 97.728 Mbps in Japan.

Bit time   Time taken to emit a bit, that is, 0.1 μs, in the case of Ethernet at 10 Mbps.

BNC   Comes from Bayonet-Neil Concelman, bayonet connector for thin coaxial cable, which is also used for optical fibers (ST connectors).

BootP   Bootstrap Protocol. Protocol based on UDP, used by a node (for example, diskless client) to determine the IP address of its Ethernet controller (function similar to ARP), the address of a server and the name of a file to load into memory and execute. Defined by RFC 951.

Bridge   Device for interconnecting local area networks using identical protocols at the MAC level.

Broadband   Network for which the use of the links is shared between different frequency bands. The data signals are modulated.

Broadcast   Frame emitted by a station to all the other stations of the local area network capable of receiving.

Buffer   Element used in reception or transmission for temporary storage of data units, when the communication between units does not permit constant flow (for example, different rates).

Bus   Topology in which all the stations are connected in parallel on the medium and can simultaneously receive a signal transmitted by the other stations connected to the medium.

Byte   Sequence of successive bits. Generally eight bits (when the term octet is sometimes also used), unless otherwise stated.

Cable One or more electrical or optical conductors placed inside a protective sheath.

CCITT Comité Consultatif International Télégraphique et Téléphonique. International Telegraph and Telephone Consultative Committee, being the body responsible for standardization of the interconnection of telecommunications equipment on the national scale, via its recommendations. Was created in 1956 as part of the ITU, disbanded in 1992.

Channel Logical or physical path permitting data transmission.

Circuit switching Transmission technique which permits the establishment of a temporary physical link between two elements of a network.

CLNS/CLNP Connectionless Network Service/Protocol. Level 3 ISO protocol (IS 8473) which does not require the establishment of a circuit before transmission. It constitutes one of the two options for the network layer, the other being CONS.

CMIS/CMIP Common Management Information Services/Protocol. Level 7 ISO service and protocol for network management and administration. It is associated with a database holding the information obtained by observation of the traffic. Standards ISO 9595 and 9596.

CMOT/CMOL CMIP over TCP/IP and CMIP over LLC correspond to implementations of the CMIP protocol in the DARPA and ISO worlds.

Coaxial Cable consisting of an asymmetric pair: a central conductor (core) and a concentric external conductor (braiding), characterized by its lower attenuation, its bandwidth and its high immunity to interference.

Code Set of rules defining a one-to-one correspondence between the data and its representation by symbols or characters.

Collision Conflict of access, provoked when at least two nodes of the network are simultaneously in an emission state.

Compatibility Ability of two devices to intercommunicate in a meaningful way, that is, to transmit and receive data without software or hardware modifications to either of the two devices.

Conflict Problem which arises when two (or more) data sources simultaneous try to emit data on the same medium. The resulting superposition will result in data loss, if it is not detected. In the worst case, this may lead to damage to the emitter and the receiver if they are not designed to support the voltage and current levels which may result.

Cord Relatively short cable with a connector at at least one of its two ends.

CRC Cyclic Redundancy Check. Field determined using an error detection algorithm, included in the frame before transmission by the emitting station. The receiving station recalculates the CRC and compares it with that which it received. In the case of Ethernet, this sequence of four bytes is also called the Frame Check Sequence (FCS).

Crosstalk (or Xtalk) Measure of the level of perturbation between two pairs of a single cable, where the emitter and the receiver are at the same end (NEXT). NEXT is an abbreviation for Near End Crosstalk. Corresponds to an imperfection in the transmission caused when part of the signal energy passes from one circuit to a neighboring circuit.

Telediaphonic fading is a measure of the level of perturbation between two pairs of a single cable, where the emitter and the receiver are at opposite ends.

CSMA/CA   Carrier Sense Multiple Access with Collision Avoidance. Access method avoiding collisions by means of an acknowledgment procedure prior to emission of the frame.

CSMA/CD   Carrier Sense Multiple Access with Collision Detection is a conflict-managing access protocol in which the machines share the same communication line.

DARPA   Defense Advanced Research Project Agency, previously known as ARPA, is the (US) government agency responsible for research and development for the ARPANET, and subsequently the DARPA Internet.

Data communication   Exchange of data messages between points on communication channels.

Data link   This is the second layer of the Open Systems Interconnection basic reference model which provides the functional and procedural means to establish, maintain and release data link transmissions between network entities. This layer is involved in the establishment of an active link between stations, the control of the synchronization byte, the insertion of the data in frames, error detection and correction, and the regulation of the data stream on the link.

Data transmission   Emission of data at one point for receipt elsewhere. Telecommunications forms the major part of this sector.

DCE   Data Communication Equipment, providing the functions needed to establish, maintain and break a transmission connection (for example, modem). Forwards the data, but does not manage it.

DDN   (Defense Data Network), improperly used to refer to MILNET, ARPANET and the TCP/IP protocols they use. In fact, it refers to MILNET and the associated parts of the Internet which link the American military installations.

DECnet   Protocol suite developed and supported by Digital Equipment Corporation for its DNA architecture. The last version is the ISO-compatible Phase V.

Degradation   Deterioration of the data transmission quality or speed caused by an increasing number of users accessing the system.

DNS   Domain Name System. Protocol of the Internet world defined by RFC 1034–1035. It automatically generates the correspondence between the symbolic name and the IP address of the network machines. The IP addresses are structured in tree-like name spaces managed by the name servers. Thus, DNS allows machines which are not directly on the Internet to have a documented name of this type.

DoD   Department of Defense of the United States of America.

DQDB   Distributed Queue Dual Bus is a MAN derived from QPSX which was standardized by IEEE 802.6. It operates with a double unidirectional bus at 34 Mbps, 45 Mbps (ANSI DS3) or 140 Mbps (CCITT G.703) using an access method with distributed queues and a protocol for dividing the packets into cells similar to SMDS. The two buses are unidirectional and may even be looped. Fair distribution of the accesses depends upon a relatively complex cell reservation procedure.

Driver   Software which manages the exchanges of data between a physical communication port and the programs which use it.

DS   Digital Signal, defines the rates within the hierarchy of carriers in the USA. DS0 = 64 kbps (elementary signal), DS1 = 1544 kbps, DS3 = 44 Mbps.

DTE   Data Terminal Equipment represents the computer and/or the terminal, in contrast to the communication devices. Equipment generating or receiving data.

EBCDIC   Extended Binary Coded Decimal Interchange Code, 8-bit alphanumeric code used by IBM.

EDI   Electronic Data Interchange. Electronic transfer of data and documents between heterogeneous equipment (word processing system, PC, fax, telex) providing services for storage, delayed delivery, multicast, conversion, and processing of message contents.

EGP   Exterior Gateway Protocol. Protocol for communication between gateways (or routers) linking 'autonomous' systems, used to exchange access and routing information. Defined by RFC 888 and 904.

EIA   Electronic Industries Association. American standardization organization specializing in the electrical and functional characteristics of device interfaces. Recently changed its name to the TIA (Telecommunications Industries Association).

Empty slot   Access method in which an empty slot circulates between the machines and can be filled by data under certain conditions.

Emulation   Substitution of the conventions constituting a protocol, used to simulate a different protocol.

ES–IS   End System to Intermediate System. Routing exchange protocol defined by the standard ISO 9542. The End System is a non-router host, while the Intermediate System is a router. The ES always belongs to an area and can re-locate the level 1 IS by capturing the ES–IS packets. It will then use the IS to communicate within its area. This will also enable it to leave its area via communication with other ISs.

Ethernet   Local area baseband network with a bus topology and a CSMA/CD access method, developed jointly by Digital Equipment Corporation (DEC), Intel Corporation and Xerox Corporation (or DIX), standardized by the IEEE under 802.3 10base5, then by the ISO. It uses coaxial cable as the medium (optical fiber and twisted pair were added by the IEEE) at a rate of 10 Mbps, the coding is of Manchester type with LSB first. Implementations at 1 and 100 Mbps have also been defined.

FACTOR   Industrial local area network developed by APTOR.

Fading per unit length   Fading per unit length of the cable in question.

FDDI   Fiber Distributed Data Interface. Fiber optic network with a dual ring topology which uses a delayed token passing method and operates at 100 Mbps. Standardization of the ANSI X3T.5 standard in ISO 9314 is still under way for the SMT (station management) administrative part and other new sublayers.

FOIRL   Fiber Optic Inter Repeater Link. Supplement e of the IEEE 802.3 standard dating from 1987. The characteristics introduced here are explicitly intended to permit the point-to-point interconnection of Ethernet devices (repeater) from different manufacturers over optical fiber. These specifications have been replaced by 10baseFL, which extends their capabilities, but ensures upwards compatibility.

FOMAU   Fiber Optic Medium Attachment Unit, that is, fiber optic transceiver generally with a 15-point socket and two optical connectors (one for emission, one for receipt).

Frame   Group of characters transmitted as a unit according to a predefined format (including, for example, synchronization and/or error control fields). The frame is subject to an encoding procedure prior to emission (physical level).

Frame Relay   New WAN packet-switching technology offering a connection-oriented point-to-point service (CCITT Blue Book I.122). This method, based on the use of permanent virtual circuits, uses an adapted version of the HDLC protocol and involves multiplexing at level 2. It could become the standard for interfacing to WAN packet services.

Front-end processor (FEP)   Peripheral equipment of a central computer, responsible for controlling the communications of the latter.

FTAM   File Transfer Access and Management, ISO standard 8571 developed at level 7 (upper part) of the OSI model for exchanges of files between the nodes of a network and administration. Can be used to establish and break a connection and to select, create, delete, read or write to a file. Similar in its objectives to the DAP protocol of DNA.

FTP   File Transfer Protocol. Standard high-level protocol for file transfer between nodes under TCP/IP. Defined by RFC 959 and the standard MIL-STD 1780.

Full duplex   Denotes a circuit capable of supporting simultaneous transmissions in both directions.

Gateway   A gateway is a specific machine linked to two (or more) networks which routes the packets of one to the other. The term is quite general, but represents, more specifically, the interconnection devices operating on data at level 4 (transport layer) or above.

GOSIP   Government Open Systems Interconnection Profile. Specifications in conformance with OSI imposed by certain governments (USA, EU) for all public purchases.

Half duplex   Denotes a circuit capable of supporting transmissions in both directions, but not simultaneously (which corresponds to alternating communication).

HDLC   High Level Data Link Control is a bit-oriented link-level protocol operating in a bidirectional synchronous mode, standardized by ISO 3309, 4335, 6159 and 6256. CCITT has recently adapted it for its Link Access Protocol (LAP-B) used in X.25 networks.

HELLO   Routing protocol based on measurement of the delay to determine the minimum path. Defined by RFC 891.

Host   Host machine. Entity which receives or emits information on a network but is not responsible for its transfer.

HPFS   High Performance File System for the OS/2 operating system. Microsoft's LAN Manager and IBM's LAN Server are based on this.

Hub   Concentrator located at the heart of a network star topology (Ethernet, Token Ring, ARCnet). For Ethernet, multiport repeater with attachment to twisted pair according to the IEEE 802.3 10baseT standard.

Hyperchannel   High-speed network developed by Network Systems Corporation for the interconnection of large systems. Based on a CSMA/CD access method with priority, with a coaxial cable of the 75 Ohm CATV type as medium. Achieves a speed of 50 Mbps per channel (four channels can be combined per link) and at most 16 ports.

IAB   Internet Activities Board. Coordinating committee (15 researchers) responsible for the architecture, engineering and management of the Internet. The IAB's decisions are public and give rise to RFCs which serve as standards. The IAB is divided into the IETF and the IRTF.

ICMP   Internet Control Message Protocol. Integral part of the IP which manages error and control messages. Defined by RFC 792. Echo Request and Echo Reply packets are used by the command *ping*.

ICS   IBM Cabling System. Cabling system developed by the American computer manufacturer IBM, which is based on hermaphrodite connectors and nine different types of cable, including:
type 1: two shielded twisted pairs, 22 AWG
type 2: two shielded twisted pairs plus four telephone pairs, 22 AWG
type 3: four twisted telephone pairs, 22 or 24 AWG
type 5: two optical fibers (diameters 50/125, 62.5/125 or 100/140 μm)

Idle   State in which a medium or a device is not busy (unoccupied).

IEEE   The Institute of Electrical and Electronic Engineers is a scientific company which publishes magazines of a high technical level together with standards in different areas associated with its activities. These activities cover the description of local area networks (for layers 1 and 2) and, for example, the binary encoding format for floating point numbers on a computer and the standardization of the Pascal programming language.

IEEE 802   Committee created in 1980, which establishes the standards for the interconnection of computer equipment. IEEE standards 802.3, 802.4, and 802.5 describe the physical and link layers (MAC) of ISO's OSI reference model. These different physical media may interface with the IEEE 802.2 standard which describes the upper part of the link layer (LLC). Here is a list of the IEEE 802 working groups and the result of their studies:
DIS = Draft International Standard
PDAD = Proposed Draft Technical Report
IEEE 802 (Standard) Overview and Architecture
IEEE 802.0 Operating Rules Review Group (ORRG)
IEEE 802.1 Glossary, Network Management and Internetworking
The group determines the global relationships between the 802.X. standards.
Supplement B (Standard): LAN/MAN Management, architecture, and protocol for the management of IEEE 802 local area networks.
Supplement C: MAC service provided by all IEEE 802 local area networks
Supplement D (Standard): Medium Access Control Bridges, architecture and

protocol for the interconnection of IEEE 802 local area networks below the MAC layer. Definition of the Spanning Tree algorithm. Taken up by ISO in the standard IS 10038.

Supplement E (Standard): System Load Protocol, services and protocol permitting the loading of core images in a data processing device linked to an IEEE 802 network, using the group addressing concept.

Supplement H (Standard): Bridging for Ethernet V2.0.

Supplement G: Remote MAC bridging

IEEE 802.2 (Standard): Logical Link Control (LLC), type 1: Connectionless, type 2: Connection oriented, type 3: Acknowledged datagram.

IEEE 802.3 (Standard): CSMA/CD Access Method and Physical Layer Specifications (taking over Ethernet from Xerox) 10base5 on coaxial cable, 500 m.

Supplement a: 10base2, on thin coaxial cable RG-58, 185 m

Supplement b: 10broad36, on coaxial cable 75 Ohm, 3.6 km

Supplements c and d: repeater and FOIRL

Supplement e: 1base5, known as StarLAN, on twisted pair, 250 m

Supplement g: method and implementation of conformance tests for AUI cables

Supplement h: relationship between CSMA/CD layers and administrative capabilities

Supplement i, 10baseT on twisted pair, 100 m

Supplement j: 10baseF with stars on optical fiber

Supplement k: specifications of repeaters in baseband

Supplement l: PICS for 10baseT transceivers

Supplements p and q: Managed objects and management layer

Supplement u: 100baseT, or fast Ethernet, at 100 Mbps

IEEE 802.3 10baseF: Supplement j to the IEEE 802.3 standard concerning the use of a medium based on optical fiber (whence F for fiber) instead of coaxial cable. This involves extending the standardization of Ethernet devices on fiber optics previously limited to FOIRL. Topology changes from the bus to the star (as for the twisted pair). Several types of star are included in the standard: active synchronous stars, asynchronous stars (for compatibility with FOIRL), and passive stars.

IEEE 802.3 10baseT: Supplement i to the IEEE 802.3 standard, concerning the use of a medium based on twisted pairs (whence the T, for twisted pair) instead of coaxial cable. This supplement describes the functionality of the hubs (concentrators or stars) and the transceivers attached to them. Note that the topology is no longer that of a bus but that of a star, where all the links between the Ethernet stations and the hub are established as point to point.

IEEE 802.4 (Standard) Token passing bus access method and physical layer specifications (covering MAP)

IEEE 802.5 (Standard) Token passing ring access method and physical layer specifications (covering IBM's Token Ring)

IEEE 802.6 (Standard) Distributed queue dual bus (DQDB) sub-network (metropolitan area network)

IEEE 802.7 (Standard) Broadband LAN (technical advisory and physical layer topics, recommended practises)

IEEE 802.8 Fiber optic technical advisory and physical layer topics
IEEE 802.9 Integrated services LAN (ISLAN or IsoEthenet)
IEEE 802.10 Security and privacy access method and physical layer specifications (standard for interoperable LAN security: SILS)
IEEE 802.11 Wireless access method and physical layer specifications
IEEE 802.12 Demand priority access method (100VG-AnyLAN)
IEEE 802.14 Cable TV set-top box working group

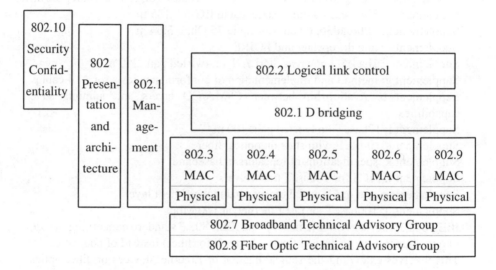

Figure G.2 Relationship between the IEEE 802 standards.

IETF Internet Engineering Task Force, forms part of the IAB. This group of researchers is responsible for proposing and specifying protocols and standards for the Internet network. In addition, it is also responsible for guaranteeing its operation.

Interface Link shared by two adjacent entities. The set of wires linking two adjacent entities corresponds to a physical interface.

Interface protocol Complete set of rules applicable to the communication between one entity and the next. The use of physical wires interlinking two adjacent entities corresponds to their physical interface. The set of logical messages sent between adjacent layers corresponds to their logical interface.

Internet The collection of networks and gateways (including ARPANET, MILNET and NSFnet) which use the TCP/IP protocol suite and operate as a unique and cooperative virtual network (same name space) which serves numerous public research laboratories, universities, and military installations (more than 50 countries, 5000 networks, and 7 million machines). The Internet provides universal connectivity and three levels of network service: unreliable (connectionless routing of packets), reliable (routing in full duplex stream), and application-level services (for example, electronic mail), built on the first two levels.

IP Internet Protocol is a level-3 protocol containing addressing and control information which allows the packets to be routed. Ipv4, the version currently in use, was developed by request of the DoD and defined by RFC 791 and 1009 and the standard MIL-STD-1777.

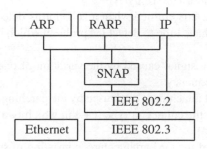

Figure G.3   Three IP encapsulation modes on a CSMA/CD network at 10 Mbps.

The corresponding Ethernet type field is 0800. The numbers of IP networks are assigned by the Internet Assigned Numbers Authority (IANA).

IPX Novell's Internet Packet eXchange protocol is a variation of Xerox's XNS. It is a connectionless datagram protocol (each packet is processed independently). The IPX address is similar to the XNS address, but is represented entirely in hexadecimal.

IRL Inter-Repeater Link. The IRL appears in the ISO 8802-3 standard as a point-to-point link capable of interconnecting two half repeaters for coaxial cable. No details were given, at that level, about the type of medium which may be used.

IRTF The Internet Research Task Force forms part of the IAB and is responsible for research and development relating to new technologies.

IS–IS Intermediate System to Intermediate System is an ANSI routing protocol currently at the stage of Draft Proposal 10589. It defines the exchanges between intermediate systems (routers). Several networks interconnected by routers constitute an area, the lowest level in the routing hierarchy. Several interlinked areas (interlinked by level-2 routers) form routing domains. The concept of routing domain is similar to that of an autonomous system in TCP/IP, and refers to a separately administered region.

ISDN Integrated Services Digital Network represents a CCITT standard covering several areas of telecommunication, including primarily the integration of voice and data.

ISO   The International Organization for Standardization has defined, among other things, the OSI model (Open System Interconnection) which divides the architecture of a telecommunication system into seven layers.

Isochronous   Signal in which the time interval separating any two important times is always a multiple of some unit time interval.

ITU   International Telecommunications Union. This standardization body, which dates from the days of telegraphy (1865), is attached to the UN. It is responsible for supervising the general organization of telecommunications, their general standardization, and the assignment of radio frequencies. CCITT was part of the ITU before it was disbanded in 1992.

Jabber   Abnormally long Ethernet frame, longer than the maximum length imposed by the standard (1518 bytes).

Jam   Sequence of 32 bits emitted when a collision is detected to ensure that the stations concerned have time to detect the problem which has occurred with their frames.

Jitter   Distortion of a signal caused by the variation of one of its characteristics, for example, the frequency.

Jumper cable   Short attachment cord, used by the patching system between patch panels or to change the connector type (case in which two different sockets have to be interconnected).

Layer   Subdivision of the OSI architecture, consisting of subsystems of the same level, responding to requests from the level above using services from the level below.

LAN_Manager   System for sharing the resources of a server (software, disks, printers, streamer, messaging) in the microcomputer world. Very common product developed by Microsoft and 3Com (3+Open) under OS/2.

LAT   Local Area Transport, developed by Digital Equipment Corporation, identified by the Ethernet type field 6004. This protocol cannot be routed, thus it must be bridged.

LLC   Logical Link Control is the upper half of the second layer of the OSI model. It interfaces downwards with the MAC and upwards with the network layer. IEEE 802.2 is the standardized ISO LLC (IS 8802-2).

Local area network (LAN)   Communication network with a teleinformatic purpose, of limited size (building or site, 1 to 20 km), having a potentially high throughput (1 to 20 Mbps) with low transmission delays and error rates. There are two categories: enterprise local area networks and industrial local area networks.

LocalTalk   Elementary local area network developed by Apple, which operates at 230.4 kbps on twisted pair. The topologies are the daisy chain, the bus and the star, and the distances extend to 1200 meters (PhoneNet). Zilog 8530 is a specialized integrated circuit for this technology.

Loopback   Test facility built into communication equipment. The transmission output is connected internally to the receiving input, thereby activating all the circuits, without necessitating real communication with a second similar device. This type of test was integrated in Ethernet V2.0 specifications, with a frame type of 9000.

LU 6.2 Particular type of logic unit (high-level entity of IBM's SNA architecture) permitting symmetrical exchanges between programs.

MAC Media Access Control. Method of obtaining access to a network medium via a station. Forms part of the second layer of the OSI model.

MAN A Metropolitan Area Network has communication capabilities covering geographical areas with a size the order of that of a town (intermediate between the LAN and the WAN).

MAP The Manufacturing Automation Protocol is an industrial local area network which was originally designed (in 1980) by General Motors. Layers 1 and 2 (MAC) are standardized in IEEE 802.4.

MAU The Multiple Access Unit for a Token Ring network is the effective heart of the ring network, to which each machine is linked by two twisted pairs, one for emission and the other for receipt. It is also called the MSAU, for Multistation Access Unit. See under 'transceiver' for an MAU for Ethernet.

Medium Transmission material allowing signals to pass from one data communication device to another.

Message switching Transmission technique which can route a message as a function of the address transported, without necessarily establishing a permanent circuit between the two elements of the network.

MIB Management Information Base. Database for the SNMP management protocol, with a tree-like structure. Thus, it corresponds to the information delivered to the master station by the managed entity.

MIC Medium Interface Connector for Token Ring and FDDI. This denotes the standardized connector with the technology.

MIC Message Integrity Check, or sequence of data associated with the message to control its integrity (one example is the FCS).

Modem Comes from MOdulator–DEModulator and denotes a device capable of emitting and receiving digital data on telephone lines or on leased lines. Depending on the requirements, it may operate in half or full duplex, on two or four wires and at from 300 to 38 400 bps, and more, on leased lines.

Modulation Temporal variation of a physical characteristic (amplitude, frequency, phase) of a signal as a function of the message to be transmitted.

MOP Maintenance Operation Protocol developed by Digital Equipment Corporation, identified by the type fields 6001 and 6002. This protocol cannot be routed and must therefore be bridged.

Multicast Frame emitted by a station to a specific group of stations of the local area network.

Named pipe Virtual communication channels.

NDIS Network Driver Interface Specification developed by Microsoft and 3Com provides a standard driver under DOS or OS/2 for users of the LAN_Manager. NDIS allows several protocol stacks to use the same driver interface, the only limitation being the memory available.

NetBIOS (Network Basic Input Output System) is the standard network session interface for microcomputers, IBM PCs, and compatibles. It enables a client program to find a server process and communicate with it, like named pipes.

NetWare System for sharing the resources of a server (software, disks, printers, streamer, messaging) in the microcomputer world. This product, which is widely spread, was developed by Novell and is based on a proprietary system. The NetWare protocol relies on NFSP (NetWare File Service Protocol, level 6 functionality), NCP (NetWare Core Protocol, level 4), IDP (Internetwork Datagram Protocol) and, finally, on IEEE 802.2 or Ethernet.

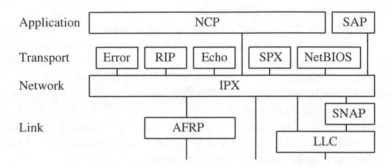

Figure G.4 Protocol architecture used by NetWare.

In Figure G.4, SPX stands for Sequence Packet eXchange. The Ethernet type field corresponding to NetWare frames is 8137.

Network A set of hardware and software elements which permits data transfer locally or over a large distance.

NFS Network File System is a software architecture developed by Sun Microsystems, which is based on IP, and allows one to use shared resources in a transparent manner on a network of stations under Unix (also PCs and Macintoshs). Widely used file and data sharing system defined by RFC 1813.

NIS Network Information Services is a set of services in the Sun environment which propagates information from the master to the recipients. It is used to maintain system files on important networks.

Node Interface unit or station, possessing logic capable of interpreting the network traffic stream passing through it. A node is generally connected to more than one communication network.

NOS Network Operating System denotes the software for bringing together and sharing the overall resources of a set of microcomputers connected to a single network. Such managers include NetWare, LAN_Server, LAN_Manager and Vines.

NSAP Network Service Access Point (ISO 8348/Ad2) is the address corresponding to the point at which the network service is accessible to the level 4 entity of the OSI model. The structure of a conformant NSAP is shown in Figure G.5.

Initial domain part		Domain specific part		
Authority and format identifier	Initial domain identifier	Area	Station ID	Selector
1 byte	Variable	2 bytes	6 bytes	1 byte

Figure G.5   Decomposition of the NSAP into elementary fields.

The selector byte of the NSAP has a similar function to the port number of TCP and UDP.

ODI   Open Data Link Interface represents the driver specifications introduced by Novell in the microcomputer world to allow several protocol stacks (such as TCP/IP or AppleTalk) to use IPX concurrently.

OSI   Open Systems Interconnection reference model defined by ISO standard IS 7498. It establishes an architectural model of data communication for networks with seven layers (from the bottom up):

Physical: electrical, mechanical, and functional characteristics of the medium transporting the binary signals

Link: establishes, maintains and releases a connection between two network entities

Network: responsible for relaying, routing, and sorting the data units of a transmission through several nodes

Transport: responsible for flow and error control, fragmentation, re-assembly, and sequencing of the messages of a communication

Session: responsible for organizing and synchronizing a communication

Presentation: provides the syntax and the structure of the data communicated (code and format)

Application: provides the interfaces which can be used by user applications (semantic processing).

OTDR   Optical Time Domain Reflectometry measures the attenuation at all points of a fiber. It is carried out from one end. The reflectometer emits light pulses and analyzes the signal received (level of reflection and delay) to produce its result in the form of a curve in dB per meter.

PABX   A Private Automatic Branch eXchange is an automatic switch for an establishment's telephone lines, generally called the telephone exchange; it may be public or private.

Packet switching   Transmission technique in which the data is divided into blocks of a controlled size which may use various physical paths in the network during their routing to their destination. Technique standardized by X.25 for WANs.

Patching   Interconnection of lines entering a sub-distributor. Patching is used to modify the physical links by moving jumper cables.

PCM   Pulse Code Modulation.

PDN   Public Data Network refers to public data transmission networks such as X.25 networks provided by national service providers.

PDU   Protocol Data Unit. Data unit exchanged at the level of a protocol, sometimes equivalent to a packet.

Physical   The lowest of the seven layers defined by the ISO Open Systems Interconnection reference model. This layer is responsible for the interface with the medium, the detection and generalization of signals on the medium and the conversion and processing of signals received from the medium and from the link layer.

Ping   Packet InterNet Groper, program which manages the exchange of ICMP Echo request and Echo reply messages, and can be used to test the active and reachable state of a station.

Polling   Method of access by selective calling with centralized control. The central node interrogates each station and, when it judges it necessary, assigns a station the right to emit.

Port   Physical access point on a device, where the signal can be provided, obtained or measured.

Preamble   Series of bits sent by the physical layer at the start of a frame to synchronize the receiving transceiver, consisting of the sequence 1010 (at frequency 5 MHz) for 7 bytes (#55) and ending with the byte 10101011 (#D5).

Prewiring   Cabling infrastructure, implemented before the use to which it will be put has been fully defined. Thus, prewiring is an expression of the wish to put in place a cabling which is potentially capable of meeting the majority of current and future uses.

Protocol   A formal set of rules and conventions governing the format, duration and error control applicable when computers communicate.

PSTN   The Public Switched Telephone Network is the system underlying the telephone service provided by the national carrier. Rates of 14.4 or 28.8 kbps full-duplex can be obtained with V.32bis and V.34 standards, which can also be associated with compression algorithms that can be used to increase this speed further.

PUP   Xerox PARC (Palo Alto Research Center) Universal Packet. Fundamental transfer unit of the protocol developed by Xerox Corp. The corresponding Ethernet type field is 0A00 (formerly 0200).

QPSX   Queued Packet and Synchronous eXchange is the description of a MAN of Australian origin, incorporated in DQDB by the IEEE 802.6 committee.

Recommendation
Standards document relating to telecommunications, published by the CCITT. Recommendation V for analog-network interfaces, X for data networks.

Reflectometer   Measuring device which can be used to check that a transmission line is not mismatched (as a result of a connection error, breaking or crushing of the wires, absence of terminal resistors, and so on). The operation is based on the principle that any mismatch gives rise to reflections.

Repeater Device which propagates the signal from one coaxial cable to another, used to increase the distance and the topology imposed by a single transmission segment (for example, to exceed 500 meters of coaxial cable). For this, it is able to recover the amplitude, shape and frequency of the important data and of collision signals.

RFC Request for Comments. Documents produced by the IAB dealing with the protocols of the TCP/IP suite, characteristics, measurements, and observations of which they describe. These Internet network 'standards' are available from the DDN Network Information Center and via the Internet. They are described by a number, a status, and a state.

RFS Remote File Sharing is another product for distributed file management which is a competitor for NFS promoted by AT&T.

RIP The Routing Information Protocol is used to exchange routing information between machines. It is defined by RFC 1053.

RJ Registered Jack. This is a small modular socket such as RJ9, 11, 12, 45.

RMON Remote Monitoring is based on a standard SNMP MIB which should be enriched by the probe implementing it. Nine groups are available (some are optional), dealing with: statistics, history, alarms, hosts, hosts top N, traffic matrix, filters, packet capture, and events. The new RFC 1271 allows us to standardize the probe work and gain a generic access to all monitoring agents in the network. With all RMON capabilities, a probe can deliver the same service as a fixed network analyzer. A complementary MIB has been defined for Token Ring: RFC 1513.

ROSE Remote Operation Service Element. Set of application level services standardized by ISO 9072 or CCITT X.229. Provides the means of transfer for requests made by CMISE.

Route Denotes the path followed by the network traffic from its source to its destination. This path may cross several gateways and networks.

RouteD Route Daemon is a routing program under Unix using RIP which propagates the routes (paths) between the machines of a local area network.

Router Device interconnecting two networks based on an identical network layer (level 3 of the OSI model), but which are able to use different physical and link levels for each port. The router can also choose between various possible routes for transit.

RPC Remote Procedure Call. Interconnection mode in which procedures are called from different machines on the network. Originally defined by Sun Microsystems, covered by RFC 1831.

RS Recommended Standard of the EIA, for example RS-232, 422, 423, 449.

RS-232C EIA definition of an electrical, functional and mechanical interface for interconnecting terminal and communication equipment. Equivalent to the CCITT Advice V.24 and V.28 and ISO DIS-2110. Exchanges of digital data take place in serial mode, at up to 20 kbps, over distances of 15 m, using unbalanced circuits and DB25 connectors.

RTD/RTT The Round Trip Delay/Time is the usual measure of the communication delay between two access points.

Runt Abnormally short Ethernet frame, which is shorter than the minimum length imposed by the standard for satisfactory operation (64 bytes) and may result from collision on a normal frame or malfunctioning of a device connected to the network.

SAA System Application Architecture represents the set of rules defining a common architecture for communications support and programming for all IBM systems, providing a compatibility independent of the machines and operating systems.

SAP The Service Access Point is the point at which the services of a layer (or sublayer) are provided to the layer immediately above.

SDH Synchronous Digital Hierarchy is the European counterpart of SONET, which defines STS-N (Synchronous Transport Signal at level N) units as multiples of 155.52 Mbps.

SDLC Synchronous Data Link Control is a protocol for a network of IBM computers associated with SNA, the predecessor of HDLC. The protocol provides the control for a single communication line or link, manages a certain number of facilities, and operates in half- or full-duplex mode on private or switched networks.

Server Process executed on a machine which offers access to its resources: peripherals, files or programs. The latter may be distributed or executed on remote machines.

SFD Starting Frame Delimiter ends the synchronization sequence of the Ethernet preamble with two bits set to 1.

Shielding Metallic cladding suppressing electromagnetic and radio interference.

Slot time Defined by the standard IS 8802-3 as a time interval of 512 bit times, considered to be the smallest readable unit on the medium.

SMB Server Message Block. Presentation layer of communications modes of IBM, Microsoft and 3Com adapted to the microcomputer network manager.

SMDS Switched Multimegabit Data Services. MAC-level interface defined by Bell Communication Research (Bellcore) offering connections of the type any-to-any. Based on high-speed technologies (physical level: DS-1, DS-3, SONET or EDH), this service has no theoretical limitations on distance. The SMDS Interface Protocol (SIP) is a subset of the MAC part of DQDB.

SNA System Network Architecture. Layered communication system allowing data transfer in IBM networks (from mainframes down to passive terminals).

SNMP Simple Network Management Protocol. Network management protocol of the TCP/IP world, successor to Simple Gateway Monitoring Protocol (SGMP). Built above UDP/IP, it uses a subset of ASN.1 to encode the MIB data. Defined by RFC 1155 to 1157 and 1158 for the MIB-II. SNMPv1 should be followed by SNMPv2 defined by RFC 1901–1908.

Socket Abstraction provided by BSD Unix which enables a process to access Internet Protocol by opening a connection, specifying the services desired (stream, datagram), association with the destination (bind), and data emission and receipt.

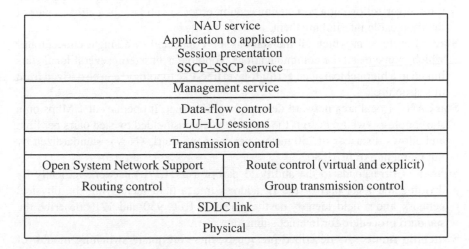

NAU service Application to application Session presentation SSCP–SSCP service	
Management service	
Data-flow control LU–LU sessions	
Transmission control	
Open System Network Support	Route control (virtual and explicit)
Routing control	Group transmission control
SDLC link	
Physical	

Figure G.6   Layered representation of SNA.

SONET   Synchronous Optical Network. Proposed physical-level protocol for broadband synchronous services on optical fiber. SONET is one of the first specifications of a standard for an optical connection interface in the telecommunications world. Moreover, SONET has taken pains to meet future advances by providing for evolutions in speeds. The bit rate OC-M (Optical Carrier at level M) is a multiple of 51.84 Mbps and can go up to 48 Gbps.

ISDN signaling
ATM
SONET

Figure G.7   Example of a stack based on SONET.

Space-division switching   Technique in which a physical path is established between two points, by electromechanical or electronic physical switching.

SQE   The Signal Quality Error is the signal transmitted by the receiver to the NIC when it detects a signal of poor quality on the medium, such as a collision.

SQE test   SQE test or Heart beat is the short signal transmitted to the NIC by the transceiver following a correct emission in order to validate the collision pair of the drop cable interlinking them.

Star   Topology in which all the stations are connected to a single concentrator which manages all the communications. Topologies based on several local stars linked in a hierarchical manner (high-level tree-like topology) can be derived from this structure.

StarLAN   Local area network derived from Ethernet. It operates at 1 Mbps on a star topology (whose heart is the hub) with two unshielded twisted pairs per link, and allows distances of 250 meters per segment. StarLAN was standardized by Supplement e of IEEE 802.3.

Subnet   Corresponds to the ability to partition a TCP/IP network logically by dividing the local part of the IP address into a field identifying the physical network and a field identifying the machine. RFC 950 and 1219 describe the standard procedure for Internet subnetting.

Switching mode   As described previously, there are many switching modes, of which a classification is given in Figure G.8.

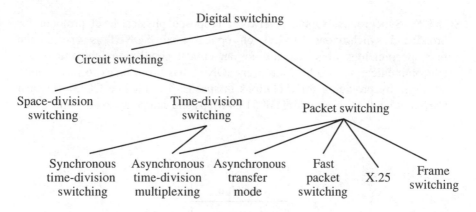

Figure G.8   Classification of the different switching modes.

Synchronous   Data transmission mode for which the clocks of the emitter and receiver are synchronized using a periodic signal.

TCP   Transmission Control Protocol. OSI level-4 protocol. Provides reliable, full-duplex data transmission in stream mode. It is connection oriented and uses the IP protocol. Defined by RFC 793 and the standard MIL-STD 1778.

TDR   Time Domain Reflectometry measures the variation in impedance along a cable, from a cable end. The reflectometer emits electrical pulses and analyzes the signal received (reflection level and delay) to produce its result in the form of a curve.

Telnet   Protocol used to simulate a remote terminal, based on the TCP/IP protocol suite. Defined by RFC 854, 855 and 856 and the standard MIL-STD 1782.

Terminator   Connector with a resistance placed at the end of a cable. By impedance adaptation avoids signal reflections which could create interference.

Test set   Rudimentary portable test device capable of simulating the operation of a station by the emission of Ethernet frames, counting receipts or tracking an echo mode between two sets located in the same network.

Thin cable (RG-58)   Thin Ethernet coaxial cable of the 10base2 type, conforming to the standard IEEE 802.3a (known as Cheapernet), which is less expensive than the thick cable and can only be used to implement segments of a maximum length 185 meters. The connectors are of type BNC.

Time-division switching   Technique in which a path is reconstituted by means of multiplexing, demultiplexing and storage in intermediate buffers.

Token   A token is a frame without a data field which circulates on the network and gives access rights to the medium. If its priority is sufficiently high, a device driver can capture the token and thus acquire the right to emit. There are at least two token-based techniques for sharing the channel: Token Ring (on a ring, circular transmission) and Token Bus (on a bus, linear transmission).

Token Ring   Local area network with a ring topology and a token-based access method, originally developed by IBM and standardized (in part) by IEEE 802.5. It principally uses individually shielded twisted pairs and optical fiber for media, at speeds of 1, 4 or 16 MBps, the encoding is of the Manchester differential type with MSB first.

TOP   Technical Office Protocol is a suite of protocols based on Ethernet at the low levels, whose definition was sponsored by Boeing Computer Services.

Topology   The topology of networks may be centralized or distributed. Centralized (or star) networks have all their nodes connected to a single element. One alternative is a distributed topology, in which each node is connected to all the other nodes. Typical topologies include the bus, the ring, the star, the tree, and the mesh.

Traffic   Measurement of the passage of data (in terms of volume) on a communications medium.

Transceiver   Comes from the beginning of 'transmitter' and the end of 'receiver'. Following IEEE 802.3 the transceiver is referred to as an MAU for Medium Attachment Unit. This component is directly connected to the physical medium (generally coaxial cable) of the local area network system and performs coupling, emission and transmission functions on the transmission medium. This component is connected by the drop cable to the computer interface circuit.

Transport   Fourth layer of the OSI model, responsible for managing routing of the data. Standardized by ISO 8072 (service), 8073 (protocol, mode with connection) and 8602 (protocol, connectionless mode) or CCITT X.224.

UltraNet   Very high speed network (1 Gbps) developed by the company Ultra (acquired by CNT) for connections between large systems and powerful graphics stations. Star topology, medium based on coaxial cables and optical fiber. With the Link Adapter the backbone may extend to 150 meters, links to CRAYs being of the order of 25 m and those to IBM machines of the order of 10 m.

User Datagram Protocol Based on IP, this protocol permits the exchange of datagrams by associating one port number per application in communication. Defined by RFC 768.

UTP Unshielded Twisted Pair. Characteristic of twisted pairs without shielding, such as that provided AT&T's PDS Systimax cabling. There are various qualities of UTP, the most modest being reserved for voice transport, while the best (data grade UTP) are also suitable for high-speed data communications (10 Mbps and above). UTP should be contrasted with STP (Shielded Twisted Pair) such as IBM's ICS type 1 and with FTP.

UUCP Unix to Unix Copy Program. Application program developed in the 1970s for Unix version 7, allowing a Unix time-sharing system to copy files to and from another via a simple line. Based on Usenet. Improperly used to refer to Unix Mail Transfer.

VAN Value Added Network. Public or private network whose capacity is resold to third parties together with various services. The added value may come in various more-or-less complex forms (protocol conversion, invoicing, storage, database access, electronic messaging).

Vines VIrtual NEtwork System for sharing the resources of a server (software, disks, printers, streamer, messaging) in the microcomputer world. Product developed by Banyan, recognized on the international scale for its network management facilities. The corresponding Ethernet type field is 0BAD.

VT Virtual Terminal which can be used to work remotely via a network. ISO level 7 service and protocol (upper part), standardized in ISO 9040 (service) and 9041 (protocol).

V.24 Definition of the exchange circuits between data terminal equipment and data communication equipment (EIA RS-232C).

V.35 CCITT standard for transmission at 48 kbps on primary group circuits in the band 60–180 kHz.

WAN Wide Area Network. Network with communication capabilities covering more extensive geographical areas than those covered by local or metropolitan area networks.

X X Window System Protocol Version 11 (hence the usual name X.11). System of graphics windows defined by RFC 1012 (issued for information, not an Internet standard because the specifications are insufficient to implement the protocol).

XDR eXternal Data Representation. Standard machine-independent data representation system used for external communication, which forms part of NFS. Defined by Sun Microsystems and covered by RFC 1832.

XNS Xerox Network Service. Term used to refer to the internet protocol suite developed by Xerox researchers. Although similar to the DARPA Internet protocols, XNS uses different packet formats. The XNS address has 32 bits for the physical network part (represented in decimal) and 48 bits for the host part (represented in hexadecimal, MAC address). The network and transport layers have been inserted in other architectures (such as NetWare). The corresponding Ethernet type field is 0600.

X.25 Also ISO 8208 (level 3), ISO 7776 (level 2, frame structure and HDLC procedure, LAPB mode), and X.21 (level 1). CCITT recommendation which defines the packet format for data transfer on a public network. Originally designed to link terminals to computers, X.25 provides a reliable stream transmission service which supports remote connections. Widely used in Europe.

X.400 Message Handling System (MHS), CCITT advice 1984, electronic messaging standard for the upper part of OSI layer 7. Its two main components are the Message Transfer System (MTS,) which represents the ability to transport data between different entities using store and forward methods, and the Messaging System (IPMS), which is built above the former and provides personal multimedia communications.

X.500 Standard directory service, CCITT advice dated 1988. It corresponds to the standardization by ISO 9594 of a directory (or distributed database) of people, organizations, and applications. This type of directory holds information such as telephone numbers and network or electronic mail addresses which facilitates communication between individual and processes. X.500 occupies the upper part of OSI layer 7.

Yellow Pages Commercial name for NIS.

Acronyms

AAL   ATM Adaptation Layer
AARP   AppleTalk ARP
AEP   AppleTalk Echo Protocol
AFNOR   Association Française de Normalisation
AFP   AppleTalk Filing Protocol
ANSI   American National Standards Institute
API   Application Programming Interface
APPN   Advanced Peer-to-Peer Networking
ARP   Address Resolution Protocol
ARPA   Advanced Research Projects Agency
ASCII   American Standard Code for Information Interchange
ASP   AppleTalk Session Protocol
ATM   Asynchronous Transfer Mode
ATP   AppleTalk Transaction Protocol
AUI   Attachment Unit Interface
AURP   AppleTalk Update-based Routing Protocol
AWG   American Wire Gauge
B-ISDN   Broadband ISDN
BalUn   Balanced–Unbalanced
BECN   Backward Explicit Congestion Notification
BER   Bit Error Rate
BGP   Border Gateway Protocol
bps   bits per second
BR   Bit Rate
BRI   Basic Rate Interface
BSC   Binary Synchronous Communications
BT   Bit Time
CCITT   Comité Consultatif International Télégraphique et Téléphonique
CLNP/S   ConnectionLess Network Protocol/Service
CMIP/S   Common Management Information Protocol/Service
CMOL/T   CMIP Over LLC/TCP
CMOS   Complementary Metal Oxide Semiconductor
CONP/S   Connection-Oriented Network Protocol/Service
CRC   Cyclic Redundancy Check
CRV   Code Rule Violation
CSMA   Carrier Sense Multiple Access

DA   Destination Address
DAS   Dual Attachment Station
dB   deciBel
DCE   Data Circuit-terminating Equipment
DDCMP   Digital Data Communication Message Protocol
DDN   Defense Data Network
DDP   Datagram Delivery Protocol
DLC   Data Link Control
DLCI   Data Link Connection Identifier
DLS   Data Link Switching
DNA   Digital Network Architecture
DNS   Domain Name System
DoD   Department of Defense
DQDB   Distributed Queue Dual Bus
DRP   DECnet Routing Protocol
DTE   Data Terminal Equipment
DTR   Data Terminal Ready
EDI   Electronic Data Interchange
EIA   Electrical Industries Association
EISA   Extended Industry Standard Architecture
ES   End System
ETSI   European Telecommunication Standards Institute
FCS   Frame Check Sequence
FDDI   Fiber Distributed Data Interface
FDM   Frequency Division Multiplexing
FECN   Forward Explicit Congestion Notification
FFOL   FDDI Follow On LAN
FRAD   Frame Relay Assembler Disassembler
FTAM   File Transfer Access and Management
FTP   File Transfer Protocol
FTP   Foil Twisted Pair
GDMO   Guidelines for the Definition of Managed Objects
GGP   Gateway to Gateway Protocol
GOSIP   Government OSI Protocol
HDLC   High level Data Link Control
HIPPI   High Performance Parallel Interface
HRC   Hybrid Ring Control
HSLAN   High Speed Local Area Network
HSSI   High Speed Serial Interface
I/O   Input/Output
ICMP   Internet Control Message Protocol
IDP   Internetwork Datagram Protocol
IEC   International Electrotechnical Commission
IEEE   Institute of Electrical and Electronics Engineers
IETF   Internet Engineering Task Force

IP   Internet Protocol
IPG   InterPacket Gap
IPX   Internetwork Packet eXchange
IRL   InterRepeater Link
IS   Intermediate System
ISDN   Integrated Services Digital Network
ISO   International Standards Organization
LAN   Local Area Network
LAPB/D   Link Access Protocol Balanced/D channel
LAT   Local Area Transport
LCF   Low Cost Fiber
LLC   Logical Link Control
LME   Layer Management Entity
LMI   Local Management Interface
LSAP   Link Service Access Point
LU   Logical Unit
MAC   Medium Access Control
MAN   Metropolitan Area Network
MAP   Manufacturing Automation Protocol
MAU   Medium Access Unit or Multistation Access Unit
MDI   Medium Dependent Interface
MHS   Message Handling Service
MIB   Management Information Base
MIC   Media Interface Connector
MII   Media Independent Interface
MMF   MultiMode Fiber
MOP   Maintenance Operations Protocol
MSb   Most Significant bit
MSB   Most Significant Byte
MTU   Maximum Transmission Unit
NBP   Name Binding Protocol
NCP   Network Control Program or NetWare Core Protocol
NDIS   Network Driver Interface Specification
NetBIOS   Network Basic Input/Output System
NEXT   Near End CrossTalk
NFS   Network File System
NIC   Network Interface Card
NLSP   NetWare Link State Protocol
NNI   Network-to-Network Interface
NOS   Network Operating System
NRZI   Non Return to Zero Inverted
NSAP   Network Service Access Protocol/Point
NSP   Network Service Protocol
OC   Optical Carrier
OSI   Open Systems Interconnection

OSPF   Open Shortest Path First
PABX   Private Automatic Branch eXchange
PAD   Packet Assembler Disassembler
PBX   Private Branch Exchange
PCM   Pulse Code Modulation
PDN   Public Data Network
PDU   Protocol Data Unit
PEP   Packet Exchange Protocol
PHY   Physical Layer
PICS   Protocol Implementation Conformance Statement
PLS   Physical Layer Signaling
PMA   Physical Medium Attachment
PMD   Physical Medium Dependent
PPP   Point-to-Point Protocol
PRI   Primary Rate Interface
PU   Physical Unit
PVC   Permanent Virtual Circuit
QLLC   Qualified LLC
QOS   Quality of Service
RARP   Reverse ARP
RFC   Request for Comments
RI   Ring Indicator
RIF   Routing Information Field
RII   Routing Information Indicator
RIP   Routing Information Protocol
RJ   Registered Jack
RMON   Remote MONitoring
RPC   Remote Procedure Call
RTMP   Routing Table Maintenance Protocol
SA   Source Address
SABME   Set Asynchronous Balanced Mode Extended
SAP   Service Access Point or Server Advertising Protocol
SAS   Single Attachment Station
SCSI   Small Computer System Interface
SDH   Synchronous Data Hierarchy
SDLC   Synchronous Data Link Control
SGMP   Simple Gateway Management Protocol
SLIP   Serial IP
SMA   Sub Miniature Assembly connector
SMB   Server Message Block
SMDS   Switched Multimegabit Data Services
SMF   Single Mode Fiber
SMI   Structure of Management Information
SMT   Station Management
SMTP   Simple Mail Transfer Protocol

SNA   Systems Network Architecture
SNAP   SubNetwork Access Protocol
SNDCP   SubNetwork Dependent Convergence Protocol
SNICP   SubNetwork Independent Convergence Protocol
SNMP   Simple Network Management Protocol
SONET   Synchronous Optical Network
SPP   Sequenced Packet Protocol
SPX   Sequenced Packet eXchange
SQE   Signal Quality Error
SR   Source Routing
SRB   Source Routing Transparent Bridge
ST   Straight Tip bayonet connector
STP/A   Spanning Tree Protocol/Algorithm or Shielded Twisted Pair
SVC   Switched Virtual Circuit
TAU   Trunk Access Unit
TCP   Transmission Control Procedure
TDM   Time Division Multiplexing
TDR   Time Domain Reflectometry
TFTP   Trivial File Transfer Protocol
THT   Token Holding Timer
TOP   Technical and Office Protocol
TRT   Token Rotation Time
TTRT   Target TRT
UDP   User Datagram Protocol
UNI   User-to-Network Interface
UPS   Uninterruptible Power Supply
UTP   Unshielded Twisted Pair
VICP   VINES Interprocess Communications Protocol
VIP   VINES Internet Protocol
VTAM   Virtual Telecommunications Access Method
WAN   Wide Area Network
WBC   Wide Band Channel
XID   eXchange (Station) Identification
XNS   Xerox Network Systems
YP   Yellow Pages
ZIP   Zone Information Protocol

Index